TIMELINE

A complete text for
Junior Certificate History

Máire de Buitléir
Gráinne Henry
Tim Nyhan
Stephen Tonge

Special advisor
M.E. Collins

The Educational Company of Ireland

First published 2014
The Educational Company of Ireland
Ballymount Road
Walkinstown
Dublin 12
www.edco.ie

The paper used in this book comes from Managed Forests in Northern Europe
For every tree felled, at least one new tree is planted

A member of the Smurfit Kappa Group plc

ISBN 978-1-84536-611-7

Editor: Simon Coury
Design and Layout: Identikit Design Consultants
Indexer: Jane Rogers
Proofreader: Jane Rogers
Cover Design: Identikit Design Consultants
Illustrations: Mike Lacey, Dusan Pavlic, Wes Lowe
Map illustration: Keith Barrett/Design Image, Daghda

Acknowledgements
The publishers wish to thank the following for assistance with photographic material and for permissions to reproduce copyright material.

THE CANTERBURY TALES by Geoffrey Chaucer, translated by Nevill Coghill (Penguin Classics 1951, Fourth Revised Edition, 1977). Copyright 1951 by Nevill Coghill. Copyright © The Estate of Nevill Coghill, 1958, 1960, 1975, 1977; Account of Death of Mussolini (30 April 1945) Copyright Guardian News & Media Ltd 1945; Quote from *The Daily Express* (30 Sept. 1938) © Daily Express/Express Syndication; Extract from Albert Speer's speech (1940) reprinted with permission of Das Bundesarchiv; Letter from Amerigo Vespucci, sourced from *The Oxford Book of Exploration* (*Oxford Books of Prose & Verse*) by Robin Hanbury-Tenison (Oxford University Press, USA, 2010); Quotation courtesy of Gill & Macmillan publication of *Dublin Tenement Life* by Kevin C. Kearns. Alamy; andrewjonesfoto.com; AKG Images; The Art Archive / Private Collection / Gianni Dagli Orti; Bridgeman Art Library; The British Library; Corbis; Getty Images; Independent Newspapers Ltd; *The Irish Times*; istockphoto; Military Archives, Defence Forces Ireland; The National Archives; National Library of Ireland; Cold War cartoon by Leslie Gilbert Illingworth: Kennedy and Khrushchev, Daily Mail 29/10/1962, supplied by Llyfrgell Genedlaethol Cymru / National Library of Wales and reproduced by permission of Llyfrgell Genedlaethol Cymru / National Library of Wales and Solo Syndication; National Museum of Ireland; Battle of Kinsale from *Pacata Hibernia*, courtesy of Neptune Gallery; Mary Evans Picture Library; RTÉ Stills Library; Science Photo Library; Shutterstock.com: Elzbieta Sekowska / Shutterstock.com; Francesco Dazzi / Shutterstock.com; ganblade / Shutterstock.com; Henner Damke / Shutterstock.com; Iryna1 / Shutterstock.com; Marcio Jose Bastos Silva / Shutterstock.com; Rodrigo Garrido / Shutterstock.com; Semmick Photo / Shutterstock.com; silky / Shutterstock.com; meunierd / Shutterstock.com; vadim kozlovsky / Shutterstock.com; Vlad G / Shutterstock.com; Stradbally Hall © Sotheby's / akg-images; Topfoto; *The Castro/Libau/Aud* courtesy of T. Burke; Waterford County Museum

Contents

PART 1

Contents

PART 2

Contents

PART 3

Foreword

Timeline 2nd Edition is a fully updated edition of the bestselling Junior Cert History title first published in 2008. *Timeline 2nd Edition* covers the Junior Certificate level History course in a comprehensive way and includes all of the options in Third Year.

It is written in clear, **concise** and **simple language** and has been tested in line with the SMOG readability scale.

Timeline 2nd Edition includes a number of high-quality **primary sources** that seek to challenge and inspire students and encourage an enquiry-based approach to history.

The **historical photographs** are carefully chosen and contain informative captions. Diagrams and illustrations are also clearly labelled.

This new edition includes new **features**:

A list of **key learning objectives** at the start of each chapter, in the form of **questions** designed to **focus** the student's thinking (and the teacher's approach). The learning objectives are reinforced by **key headings** within that chapter.

A list of **key terms** appears at the end of each chapter which can be used to provide a **literacy focus** or in order to revise/review the main **vocabulary** and **concepts** specific to that chapter. **Explanations** are also given for the difficult concepts in each chapter. Interesting anecdotes are included in the *Did you know?* boxes throughout the book and important terms are explained.

Each section includes a number of **People in History** questions, sample answers and **spider-diagrams** which function as plans for answering this question on the exam. These will prompt and enable students to draw on the key information in the section and to summarise key elements as they independently plan and execute answers to the People in History exam questions. Exam questions have been fully updated and different **styles** of **exam questions** are included in each section of the book to allow students to practise the skills of the historian. Different levels of questioning are employed to challenge students of all abilities.

A wide range of digital resources is available with this book. **Teacher handouts** (containing key terms, useful website links, sample questions and answers) as well as **interactive presentations** for each section (with timelines, videos, photos, quizzes and much more) and **three WebQuests** (web-based learning activities) are available for teachers at ***www.edcodigital.ie***. Students can also test their knowledge by completing multiple-choice quizzes at ***www.edcoexamcentre.ie/timeline2***.

Finally, information on what every student needs to know from each section in order to answer questions in the Junior Certificate Exam are included in the useful **Student Exam Guide** located at the back of the book for handy reference.

Enjoy!

TIMELINE

PART 1

Section 1

The Work of Historians and Archaeologists

Chapter 1

What Does a Historian Do?

Key Learning Objectives

- **What is history?**
- **What is a source?**
- **How do historians use sources?**
- **How do historians put events in order?**

What is history?

History is the study of the past and the story of human activity. This story goes right up to today. Events that happened before you came into class are now part of history.

History is not just about battles and the lives of kings and queens. When we study history we look not only at famous people but at the everyday lives of ordinary people as well. For example, historians are interested in finding out about:

- The types of houses in which people lived
- The jobs they did
- How they spent their leisure time
- The sports they played

What is the difference between history and prehistory?

There is an important difference between the time when people didn't use writing and the time when written documents were made.

- The **prehistoric period** is before writing was used. For example, the Stone Age was in the prehistoric period. We rely on **archaeology** for our evidence in this period.
- The **historic period** is when people used writing. For example, we know a lot about the lives of monks in Early Christian Ireland because they wrote books.

Term

Archaeology
The study of the remains left by our ancestors.

What is a source?

> ***Term***
>
> **Sources**
> Evidence, for example documents and pictures, used by historians to find out what happened in the past.

Evidence that helps historians to build up a picture of the past is called a **source**. This can be something written, or a picture or object which has survived from the past. In the next chapter, we will look at how objects from the past are found and examined – this is the job of **archaeologists**.

In this chapter, we will examine both written sources and other types of source.

Historians are a bit like detectives. They try to piece together the story of what happened from the evidence available. The sources are like clues for a detective. Sometimes, the evidence is very good and so the story is very accurate. It is easy to solve the crime!

At other times, historians have to work very hard to find out exactly what happened. The crime may even remain unsolved! Let's look at how historians work.

Newspaper headlines about September 11, 2001, when terrorists attacked the World Trade Center in New York. This dramatic event is closely studied by historians

What is the difference between a primary and a secondary source?

Sources are divided into two main types: **primary sources** and **secondary sources**.

1 Primary sources

Primary sources come directly from the past. For example, if a historian was going to write a history of your class, your copy books or school reports could be examined.

Here is a selection of primary sources that historians use:

Source	Description of primary sources
Interviews	Also called **oral sources**, these could include an interview with an old woman describing how life has changed in the last 50 years
Diaries	A record that a person keeps of day-to-day events. Diaries give us an idea of how people lived. They can also comment on important events that were happening at the time
Letters, emails	In the past, people used to send letters to friends and family. Now they often send emails. Both are very useful sources

Source	Description of primary sources
Speeches	Usually given by important people, e.g. in the Dáil. Sometimes they can be listened to on a CD or a computer
Government records	Include laws passed by the Dáil and government reports. Probably the most important is the calculation of the population held every 5 years. This is called a **census**
Autobiography	An account of a person's life written by the actual person
Photographs, posters, paintings	Visual records of the past. Before the invention of the camera we relied on paintings and drawings
Newspapers, magazines	Reports on important political, social and sporting events
Artefacts	Objects found by archaeologists (examined in the next chapter)

Did you know?

Before the invention of the printing press, all books and documents were written by hand. They are called **manuscripts.**

2 Secondary sources

Secondary sources are evidence that comes from a later date. They are based on primary sources, but they are written or made after the event. This book is a secondary source as it was written long after most of the events that it describes. Here are some other examples:

Source	Description of secondary sources
Biography	The story of a person's life written by another person
Movies	Some films tell the story of real people and historical events, e.g. *Michael Collins*
TV or radio documentary	An investigation into a particular event, person or period of history, e.g. programmes on the History Channel
Internet	A popular way to find out about history and to research events
History books	Most authors of history books lived after the events that they write about

Movies such as *Michael Collins* can be an entertaining way to learn about events in the past, but they may not be very accurate

How do historians use sources?

First, historians have to find sources of information about the event they want to study. They could interview people involved in the event. They could visit a place where written sources are stored. These include archives, libraries and museums.

When examining a source to gather evidence about the past, historians follow a number of steps:

- First, they will read or look at the source carefully.
- They will then ask themselves **where** was the source created, **when** was it made, **why** was it made and by **whom**.
- They will look at how close the author of the source was to the event being described. Historians call this the **time and place rule**. An eyewitness account is more important than an account of the same event written by someone who was not there.
- They will then judge whether the source can be trusted. No piece of evidence is taken at face value!
- Historians will look at as many sources as possible and then compare what they have found. This is to make sure that the story of the past is as accurate as possible. This is called **cross-checking**.

The National Library of Ireland contains many important documents about Irish history

… trust their sources?

…en deciding if they can trust a …ging its **reliability**:

… views of the author have to …

…story sites on the Internet …

… it really is can be a …

…mes false information) … the source makes one side … ars, reports of battles usually …

…bing an event that happened fifty years … ails. A person describing an event he/she did not … of the facts.

… have to be able to separate fact from opinion. They have to … when they read diaries, newspapers, speeches and letters.

…ortant to remember that primary sources are no more reliable than secondary …urces. In some cases, secondary sources such as a TV documentary can be more accurate as they are based on a large number of primary sources.

How do historians put events in order?

When historians find out information about the past, it is important to get the events in the right order. They usually use dates to do this. This makes it easier for people to follow the story of what happened.

Measuring time

There are a number of ways historians measure time:

- If the event they are interested in occurred over a short period of time, historians will use months, days or even hours!
- They can say the event happened before or after the birth of Christ. The letters BC (Before Christ) or AD (Anno Domini – the year of the Lord) placed next to a date tell us this.

  Example: Christopher Columbus first reached America in AD 1492 – this means he reached America 1,492 years after the birth of Christ.

What can historians learn about transport in Belfast from this picture of Minehead Square, Belfast, 1907?

- They use **centuries** to place events in a wider context. A century lasts 100 years. The twenty-first century started in 2001 and will end in 2100.
- If events happened over a very long period or a very long time ago, historians may use a **millennium** – this is a period of 1,000 years
- Historians can use **timelines** to show the order in which events happened. Here is a short timeline of events in Irish history between 1919 and 1923:

TIMELINE Ireland 1919–23

1919	War of Independence started
1920	Northern Ireland created
1921	Treaty between Ireland and Britain
1922	Start of the civil war
1923	Civil war ended

- When studying the lives of famous people it is useful to know the year they were born and the year they died. The important events in their lives can be placed in between these two events.
- In some cases historians don't use dates at all but organise events by using some feature of the period of history. This is often done when historians have few or no written sources. The following timeline is based on the main materials used to make tools and weapons.

TIMELINE Stone Age, Bronze Age, Iron Age

Stone Age	Stone was the main material used for tools and weapons
Bronze Age	Bronze – a metal made of copper and tin – was used for tools and weapons
Iron Age	Iron weapons and tools were used

Do you understand these key terms?

archaeology
source
prehistory
history
primary source
secondary source
manuscript
time and place rule
cross-checking
reliability
bias
propaganda
century
millennium
timeline

Research topic

Find out five important events that happened in the history of two of the following countries in the twentieth century:

- United States of America
- United Kingdom
- Germany
- Russia

QUESTIONS

1. Where would a historian visit to find sources to use?
2. Giving examples, show clearly the difference between a primary and a secondary source.
3. Why is time and place so important when looking at a source?
4. What is bias in a source?
5. Why is it important to cross-check sources?
6. What do the letters AD and BC stand for?
7. 'All sources are very reliable.' Do you agree? Give four reasons to support your answer.
8. Draw up a timeline of the main events in your life. Start with the year you were born and finish with this year. Make sure to get the events in the right order.
9. If you were asked to write a history of your local area, list five sources that you would use. Explain how each source would help you.

SOURCE QUESTION

› Study the section from the Census of Ireland, 1911 below. Write down five pieces of information that you learned from it.

Number.	NAME AND SURNAME. No Persons ABSENT on the Night of Sunday, April 2nd, to be entered here; EXCEPT those (not enumerated elsewhere) who may be out at WORK or TRAVELLING, &c., during that Night, and who RETURN HOME ON MONDAY, APRIL 3RD. Subject to the above instruction, the Name of the Head of the Family should be written first; then the names of his Wife, Children, and other Relatives; then those of Visitors, Boarders, Servants, &c. Christian Name. 1.	Surname. 2.	RELATION to Head of Family. State whether "Head of Family," or "Wife," "Son," "Daughter," or other Relative; "Visitor," "Boarder," "Servant," &c. 3.	RELIGIOUS PROFESSION. State here the particular Religion, or Religious Denomination, to which each person belongs. [Members of Protestant Denominations are requested not to describe themselves by the vague term "Protestant," but to enter the name of the Particular Church, Denomination, or Body to which they belong.] 4.	EDUCATION. State here whether he or she can "Read and Write," can "Read" only, or "Cannot Read." 5.	AGE (last Birthday) and SEX. Insert Age opposite each name:—the Ages of Males in column 6, and the Ages of Females in column 7. For Infants under one year state the age in months, as "under 1 month," "1 month," "2 months," &c. Ages of Males. 6.	Ages of Females. 7.	RANK, PROFESSION, OR OCCUPATION. State the particular Rank, Profession, Trade, or other Employment of each person. Children or young persons attending a School, or receiving regular instruction at home, should be returned as *Scholars*. [No entry should be made in the case of wives, daughters, or other female relatives solely engaged in domestic duties at home.] Before filling this column you are requested to read the instructions on the other side. 8.
1	Edward	Byrne	Head of Family	Roman Catholic	Read and Write	51		Butcher
2	Annie Maria	Byrne	Wife	Roman Catholic	Read and Write		43	—
3	Lily	Byrne	Daughter	Roman Catholic	Read and Write		21	—
4	Edward	Byrne	Son	Roman Catholic	Read and Write	18		Butcher
5	James	Byrne	Son	Roman Catholic	Read and Write	16		Butcher
6	Herbert	Byrne	Son	Roman Catholic	Read and Write	14		Scholar
7	Alfred	Byrne	Son	Roman Catholic	Read and Write	12		Scholar
8	Joseph	Byrne	Son	Roman Catholic	Read and Write	8		Scholar
9	Una	Byrne	Daughter	Roman Catholic	—	[illegible]	6	Scholar
10	Kevin	Byrne	Son	Roman Catholic	—	4		Infant
11	Sheila	Byrne	Daughter	Roman Catholic	—	[illegible]	2	Infant
12	Bernard	Plunkett	Apprentice	Roman Catholic	Read and Write	21		Butcher

Chapter 2

What Does an Archaeologist Do?

Key Learning Objectives

- What is archaeology?
- How do archaeologists excavate a site?
- How do archaeologists decide how old an object is?
- What can archaeologists learn from a skeleton?

What is archaeology?

Archaeology is **the study of what has been left behind by people from the past**. Archaeologists dig up the ground to find clues left by our ancestors. These may be bones or objects that people have made. The man-made objects they find are called **artefacts**. These include jewellery, pottery, tools, weapons and buildings.

Term

Artefacts
Objects made by humans, e.g. coins, tools and pottery.

Archaeology is not about hunting for treasure. An old rubbish tip can often tell an archaeologist more about what life was like for our ancestors than a find of gold or silver.

Archaeologists work with historians to build up a better picture of what life was like for people long ago. In your local area there is probably an old church, cemetery or castle. This is evidence that people have lived there in the past. Archaeologists investigate this evidence by looking for remains left in the ground.

How do objects end up in the ground?

Objects end up in the ground for many reasons:

- Some are lost.
- Some are buried for safekeeping.
- In pre-Christian times bodies were buried with objects that it was believed they would need in the afterlife.
- Over time abandoned buildings will be covered by soil.
- In cities old buildings will be knocked down and new buildings built over them.

How well are objects preserved in the ground?

In most cases living things will decay when buried in the soil. That is why archaeologists usually find bones rather than bodies. However, this is not always the case. Objects found in very wet or very hot conditions are sometimes well preserved. Look at some examples in the box below:

The Tutankhamen tomb in Egypt was probably the most important find in history. It was discovered in 1922

Type	Example	Find
Very wet conditions	bogs	Well-preserved human bodies known as **bog bodies** have been found in Ireland
Very hot conditions	deserts	The bodies or **mummies** of ancient Egyptian rulers called pharaohs have been found in the desert

How are sites chosen to be excavated?

- Some sites are chosen because there is reason to believe that objects might be found. There might be an old document showing that a building once existed on the site. This is called **research archaeology**.
- Archaeologists often dig on a site before a road or a new building is built. They want to make sure that no objects or evidence from the past are lost. This is called **rescue archaeology**.
- Many finds are discovered by accident, e.g. a JCB digs up a human skull or a farmer ploughing a field comes across a sword. Archaeologists are then called in to investigate.

Did you know?

The word *archaeology* comes from two ancient Greek words meaning *the study of ancient things.*

How do archaeologists excavate a site?

In recent years, there have been many new roads built in Ireland. This has led to the discovery of a large number of archaeological sites. Archaeologists **excavate** these sites. Let's see how they do this:

Term

Excavate
When archaeologists dig in the ground looking for remains from the past.

1 Preparation

A **survey** of the site is carried out. This will help the archaeologists decide where to start digging.

- Archaeologists might carry out a **geophysical survey**. This is like an X-ray, using a machine to look at the soil underneath the surface. It can tell them how much the earth has been disturbed by human activity.
- They will dig **test trenches** so that they can get some idea of the amount of remains they can expect to find.

Term

Survey
A study carried out on a site before archaeologists start digging.

- **Aerial photographs** are taken. These show the size of the site and can show features that may be missed on the ground.
- A detailed **plan** is then made. The site is divided into numbered squares, one metre by one metre, that the archaeologist will study.

Sometimes archaeologists can discover sites from the air that may not be visible from the ground

2 The dig

The excavation or **dig** then begins. The topsoil is removed, often with a JCB. Spades and pickaxes are also used. Once the topsoil is cleared the archaeologist can begin to look for remains from the past.

While working on a site, archaeologists will use a large number of tools:

- Layers of earth are scraped away using a **trowel**.
- A **hand-pick** is used to loosen soil.
- When an object is discovered, archaeologists have to be careful not to damage it. They will use **brushes** and even toothbrushes to make sure that this doesn't happen.
- As some objects are very small, the soil is often put through a **sieve** to make sure that nothing is missed.
- Once an object has been uncovered, a **photograph** will be taken of it.

Did you know?

Large numbers of gold and silver objects are often found together. They were buried for safekeeping and their owners didn't come back for them. Archaeologists call this type of find a **hoard**.

Even if no objects are found, the soil itself can tell an archaeologist a lot about the past:

- Wooden poles used for building houses leave dark round patches called **post-holes**.
- A square dark patch suggests a fireplace.
- A layer of darker soil may mean that the site was destroyed by fire.

Archaeologists make careful records of what they have found. All objects are cleaned, bagged and labelled to show where they were found in the site. Computers are often used to help to record the information.

How do archaeologists decide how old an object is?

One of the biggest problems archaeologists face is to date artefacts that they have found. If they are lucky they might find a coin beside a sword. Coins usually have dates on them and this helps the archaeologists to find out how old the sword is. Pollen from plants found at the site can help to date objects. The design of an object or the decoration on it can also tell the age of an item, e.g. a piece of pottery.

Some other important methods of dating include **stratigraphy**, **carbon dating** and **dendrochronology**.

- Objects can be dated by the depth at which they are found. As a rule, the deeper an object is found, the older it is. This is called **stratigraphy**.
- **Carbon** or **radiocarbon dating** is a scientific method used to find the age of an object that was once alive. All living objects, including humans, plants and animals, contain **carbon 14**. When they die the amount of carbon 14 begins to decline – the older an object, the less carbon 14 is present.
- **Dendrochronology** is used to date wooden objects such as parts of buildings or ships. Each year a tree grows a new ring. The number of rings inside the trunk tells you the age of a tree. By studying the pattern of these rings archaeologists can estimate the age of a wooden object.

Artefacts on display in a museum

The **artefacts** are then removed from the site and stored in a university or a museum. Some will go on display to the public.

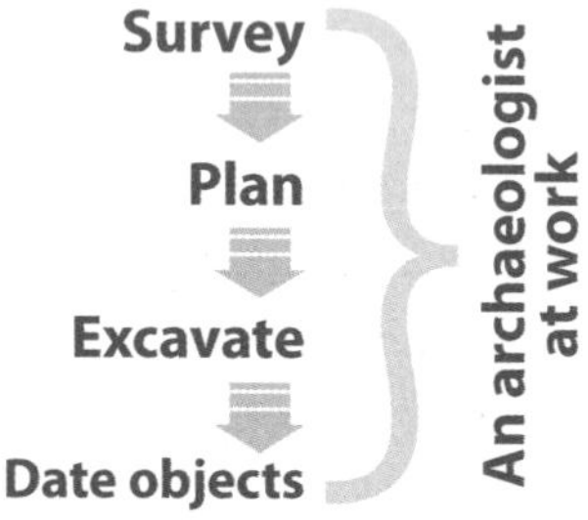

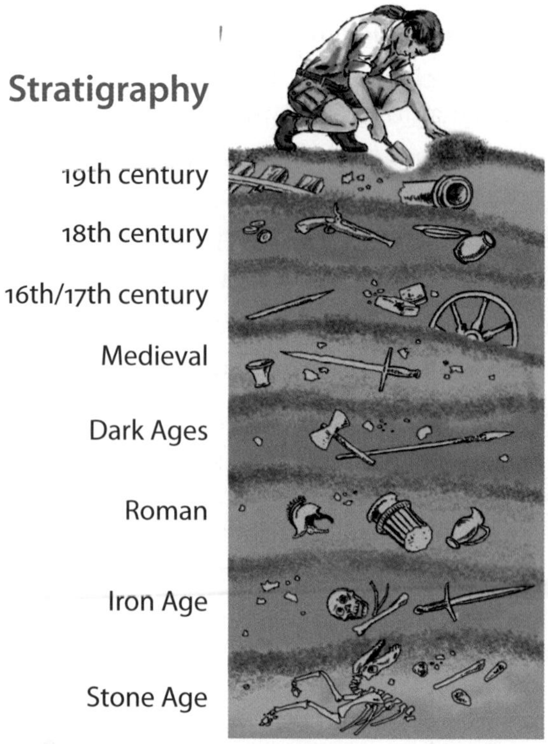

When digging in a big city like London an archaeologist could find the layers shown above. As you can see, the deeper the object is found, the older it is

What can archaeologists learn from a skeleton?

Archaeologists will use clues provided by the bones to piece together a picture of the person's life.

1 Was it a man or a woman? This can be told by the pelvis and skull.
2 The height can be estimated by the length of the thigh, i.e. the femur bone.
3 The age at death can be told by the teeth.
4 There may be evidence of a wound that can help with cause of death, e.g. a hole in the skull.
5 If there are goods such as pottery found with the body, the person was probably not a Christian.
6 If the skull is well preserved, it may be possible to reconstruct the face.
7 Scientific analysis of the bones can tell archaeologists what type of diet the person had.

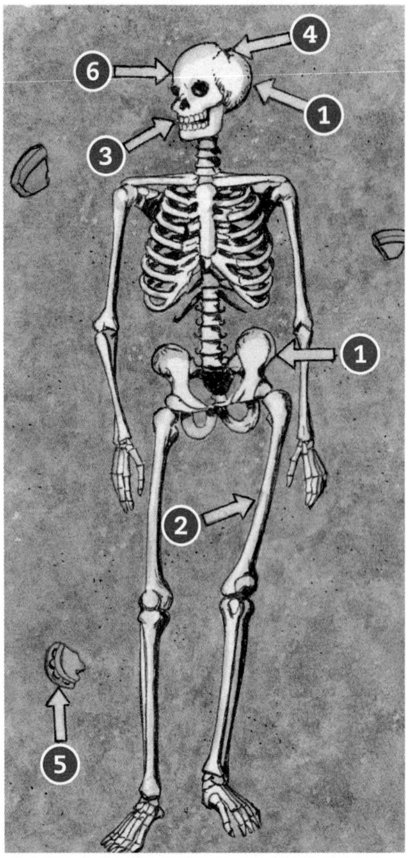

DNA testing

In recent years archaeologists have used **DNA testing** to find out more about skeletons.

DNA is present in the cells of our bodies. It is passed from generation to generation. DNA samples taken from bones can be matched with the DNA of living relatives to identify the body. In 2013 a skeleton found in England was identified as King Richard III (killed in 1485) through DNA testing of living relatives.

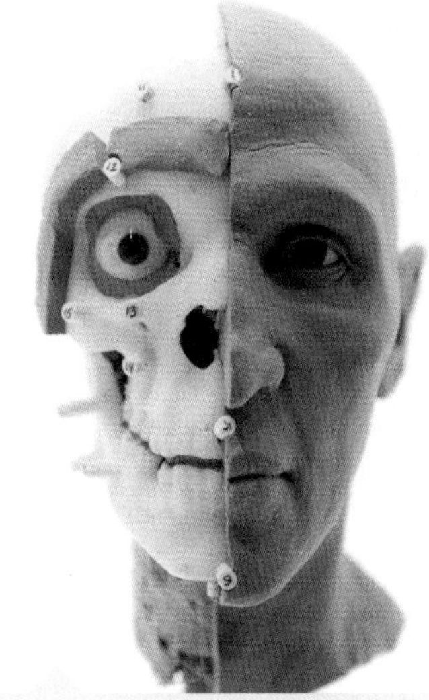

Archaeologists were able to reconstruct what this person looked like from the skull that they found

An archaeologist digging up a skeleton on a site. What tools can you see in the picture?

Do you understand these key terms?

artefact	**excavate**	**trowel**	**post-hole**
bog body	**survey**	**hand-pick**	**stratigraphy**
mummy	**test trench**	**brush**	**carbon dating**
research archaeology	**aerial photograph**	**sieve**	**dendochronology**
rescue archaeology	**dig**	**hoard**	**DNA testing**

QUESTIONS

1. Give two reasons why objects end up in the ground.
2. In what conditions are objects such as bodies well preserved?
3. Name two ways in which sites are chosen to be excavated.
4. 'Archaeologists survey a site before they dig.' Explain what this statement means.
5. Name three tools that archaeologists use during an excavation.
6. Why are archaeologists careful with objects that are found?
7. Briefly explain two methods of dating used by an archaeologist.
8. Give three pieces of information that an archaeologist can learn from a skeleton.
9. What happens to objects after they have been found by archaeologists?
10. 'A coin found with the date 50 BC on it is of no use to archaeologists.' Do you agree? Give one reason to support your answer.
11. Make a list of ten items that you would bury today in a time capsule to be opened in 100 years. Explain how each object that you choose would tell somebody in the future about life today.

People in History

Write about an archaeologist at work.

Use the plan below as a guide.

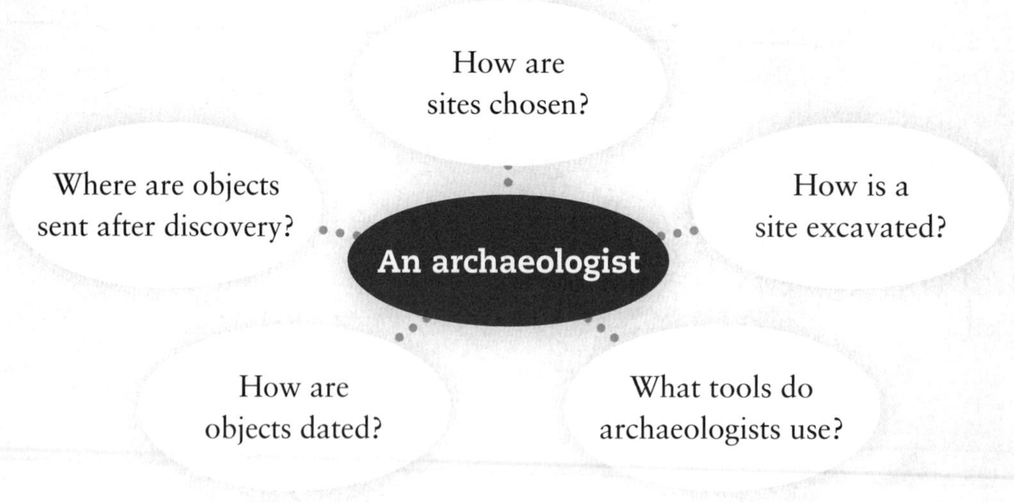
How are sites chosen?
Where are objects sent after discovery?
An archaeologist
How is a site excavated?
How are objects dated?
What tools do archaeologists use?

Hint

Make sure to include and explain words such as *artefact*, *rescue archaeology*, *survey*, *post-hole*, *stratigraphy*, *dendrochronology* and *carbon dating*.

TIMELINE

PART 1

Section 2

Early Ireland

Chapter 1

Our Roots in Ancient Civilisation

Key Learning Objectives

- Who were the Mesolithic people?
- How do we know about them?
- What do we know about them?

Who were the Mesolithic People?

Archaeologists believe that the first people who settled in Ireland arrived about 9,000 years ago. Before these first settlers arrived most of Ireland was covered in a thick sheet of ice. At that time, Ireland was not an island but was joined to Britain and the continent of Europe.

In 7000 BC the Irish Sea was much narrower than it is today. The journey by sea between the north-east of Ireland and Scotland would have been short. The country was covered in thick forests, with lots of rivers and lakes. Animals such as red deer, wild boar, wolves and foxes lived in the forests, and there were plenty of fish in the rivers and lakes.

Archaeologists have named these people **Mesolithic** or **Middle Stone Age** people. All their tools and weapons were made from stone and they lived by hunting, and gathering food such as berries, fruit and nuts.

Term

Mesolithic
A period when hunter-gatherers used simple stone tools.

How do we know about them?

These early settlers left us no written records. Archaeologists, however, have found evidence of their lives at Mount Sandel, near Coleraine, Co. Derry. Excavations at this site began in the 1970s. It is one of the oldest sites from Mesolithic times in Ireland, and has been very well studied. Carbon dating shows that people lived at this site from about 7000 BC to 6500 BC.

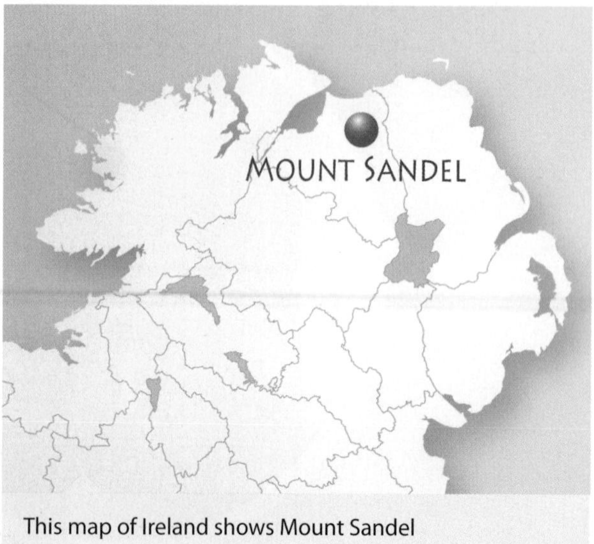

This map of Ireland shows Mount Sandel

What do we know about them?

What tools and weapons did they use?

During excavations at Mount Sandel lots of stone tools and small pieces of broken flint were found. **Flint** is a very hard rock that splits into sharp pieces when it is broken. Mesolithic people would have used big pieces of flint to make spears and axe-heads for hunting and fishing. The small pieces would have been used as knives and scrapers to skin animals and cut up meat.

Flint is not found everywhere in Ireland, but along the north-east coast there is plenty of it. This may be the reason why people settled in Mount Sandel.

Flint tools and weapons similar to those found at Mount Sandel

How did they make their homes?

At Mount Sandel archaeologists found signs of Mesolithic huts. They discovered a circle of **post-holes**. There is evidence that fires were lit in the centre of the circle, probably for cooking and heat. The post-holes tell us that wooden branches were placed here. These branches were then bent to make the shape of an upside-down bowl, or a dome. Animal skins or sods of earth were probably then put on top to cover the branches, making a tent-like home.

How did they find their food?

The people who lived at Mount Sandel were **hunter-gatherers**. The men hunted and fished in the rivers and lakes. The women and children gathered berries, fruit and nuts. We know that these people had a varied diet because archaeologists found:

Term

Hunter-gatherers
People who get food by hunting animals and gathering nuts and berries.

- Fish shells and fish bones
- Bones of deer, duck and wild pig
- Hazelnut shells

Food was cooked over an open fire

The Mesolithic people hunted wild boar

Do you understand these key terms?

Mesolithic **flint** **hunter-gatherer**

QUESTIONS

1 What does Mesolithic mean?
2 Where have archaeologists found evidence of Mesolithic people in Ireland?
3 When did Mesolithic people live in Ireland?
4 What does the term 'hunter-gatherer' mean?
5 What evidence do we have that Mesolithic people ate a variety of different foods?
6 Write an account of the lives of Mesolithic people in Ireland, using dates and references to housing, food and tools.

Chapter 2

The Neolithic Period: 4000 BC to 2000 BC

Stone axes and hammers from the Neolithic period

Key Learning Objectives

- Who were the Neolithic people?
- What was life like in Neolithic Ireland?
  - Tools and weapons
  - Houses
  - Skills
- What can we learn from megalithic tombs?

By studying **pollen samples**, archaeologists can see that important changes were beginning to take place around 4000 BC.

- They found that there was less pollen from trees and more pollen from grass.
- They found pollen from wheat and barley – crops that had to be planted from seed.
- They found bones of cattle, sheep and goats dating back to this time.

All this evidence shows that a major shift in the way people lived was starting to take place. It proves that people were starting to **farm**.

Before 4000 BC	After 4000 BC
The country was covered in forests	Trees were cut down to make way for grasslands and pastures
Only wild plants grew	Crops were planted by the people
Animals were found only in the wild and were hunted	People began to raise animals like sheep and cattle

Who were the Neolithic people?

Archaeologists believe that around 4000 BC new people came to settle in Ireland. They were **farmers**. Since tools and weapons were still made from stone at this time we are still in the **Stone Age**. However, there is a marked change in the way people lived and worked. Archaeologists call it the **New Stone Age** or the **Neolithic** period.

Term

Neolithic
Period when people farmed and used better stone tools.

Who were the first farmers?

Farming began in **Mesopotamia** (modern Iran and Iraq) around 8000 BC. Some people started to collect and sow seeds and to tame wild animals. Gradually, they relied less on hunting and gathering to feed themselves and their families. Farming provided them with a regular supply of food. Since they had to care for crops and animals, people became more settled. They started to build more permanent places to live.

The skills of farming spread very slowly across Europe. The first farmers who came to Ireland probably came from Britain.

Life in Neolithic Ireland

What tools and weapons did they use?

The Neolithic farmers developed better stone tools and weapons than those made by the Mesolithic people. As well as using flint the Neolithic people used porcellanite, a tougher and heavier stone. It made very good axe-heads, which were used to cut down trees to clear the forests for farming.

Archaeologists have found several quarries where the early Irish farmers got stone to make tools. There were very good supplies of porcellanite in **Antrim** and **Rathlin Island.** Axe-heads and other porcellanite tools have been found all over Ireland and Britain, many of them made from stone quarried in Antrim. This tells us that Neolithic people travelled and traded.

A Neolithic grinding stone

How did they make their homes?

Excavations at **Lough Gur** in Co. Limerick give us a very good insight into how the first Irish farmers lived. Archaeologists found traces of Neolithic farmhouses there.

- The houses were made from wood, and were either rectangular or round in shape.
- The frame of the house was made by putting thick planks of wood in the ground to form a frame.
- The walls were then made by weaving branches in and out through the planks, like a huge basket.
- Mud and straw were plastered onto the woven walls to cover the cracks and keep out draughts.
- This method of building walls is called **wattle and daub.**
- Once the walls were made, a roof of thatched reeds was put on top of them.

Inside the house there was only one room. On the floor, in the centre of the room, there was a space for a big open fire. As there was no window or chimney, smoke from the fire had to escape through the thatched roof. These houses must have been very dark and smoky.

Life in a Neolithic farm. Can you say what the men and women are doing?

What skills did they have?

Clothes

With the development of farming, wool from sheep was available for making clothes. People discovered how to spin and weave cloth. Dyes were made from berries and plants. We know that Neolithic people wore jewellery, because necklaces, made from bone, and stone pendants were found at Lough Gur.

During the Neolithic period people learnt how to weave cloth

Pottery

Neolithic farmers discovered how to make pottery from clay. They were the first people to learn this skill. To make a bowl, they took a lump of wet clay and moulded it into the shape of a pot with their fists. They left the pots to dry and then baked them in a fire. Some pots were decorated with patterns by pressing sticks or even fingernails into the wet clay before baking. Examples of Neolithic pottery have been found all over Ireland.

Quern stone

Farming

Neolithic farmers built stone walls to make fences around their fields. We know this because archaeologists have found stone walls buried under a bog at the **Céide Fields** in Co. Mayo. They discovered that these walls stretched for several kilometres across the hillside. Archaeologists have been able to work out that people lived at this site between 4000 BC and 3000 BC.

By building walls around their fields, farmers could keep their sheep and cattle safe from attacks by wild animals. They could also stop them from wandering off. Cattle provided them with milk and meat, and sheep gave them wool and meat.

As well as keeping animals, the first farmers grew crops. They probably ploughed some of the fields near their houses and planted wheat, oats and barley. A **quern stone** would have been used to grind grain into flour for bread.

Neolithic farming ended at the Céide Fields around 3000 BC. Nobody knows why this happened. But the bog that grew over the fields has preserved the evidence of how these early farmers lived and worked.

Prehistoric field walls at the Céide Fields. The modern interpretative centre is in the background

Archaeological sources

Neolithic people, like the Mesolithic people who came before them, have left us no written records. We get all our information about them from archaeological sources. We know what they might have looked like from bones and teeth preserved in bogs and studied in labs.

We know that the average height for a man was 1.7 metres, and for a woman was 1.6 metres. The evidence found at the Céide Fields tells us that they were well organised and skilful. However, most of our information comes from the tombs they left behind.

QUESTIONS

1 When and where did farming first begin?
2 What changes do archaeologists notice in Ireland around 4000 BC and how do they explain them?
3 Where in Ireland have archaeologists found evidence of Neolithic farmers?
4 What is a quern stone?
5 List two new skills Neolithic people brought to Ireland.

What can we learn from megalithic tombs?

Most ancient people didn't see death as the end to life. They believed that the spirit left the body and moved on to live somewhere else. The Neolithic farmers in Ireland believed in an afterlife. We know this because they went to great trouble to build very sophisticated tombs for their dead. Archaeologists call them **megalithic tombs** because they were made from large stones or **megaliths** (*mega*=large, *lith*=stone). The tombs tell us a lot about the Neolithic people and their beliefs.

There are over 2,000 megalithic tombs in Ireland. They were built over 5,000 years ago. The fact that they have survived all these years shows us how skilled the Neolithic people were, bearing in mind that they only had stone tools to work with.

Archaeologists divide megalithic tombs into three types: **court cairns, dolmens** and **passage tombs.**

Court cairn at Creevykeel, Co. Sligo

Court cairns

Court cairns are sometimes called **court tombs**, and are found mainly in the northern half of the country. They are the earliest type of megalithic tomb. They get their name from an open area – a **court** – at the entrance to the tomb. This may have been used for religious ceremonies before a burial took place. The tomb is made of upright stones covered over with earth and stones. The word **cairn** means a mound of stones. From the outside that is exactly what it looks like. However, inside the cairn there is a passage leading to a chamber in the centre. Pottery bowls containing cremated (burnt) human remains have been found in some chambers. Objects such as stone axes and pottery for use in the afterlife have also been found.

Term

Dolmen
A tomb made of upright stones.

Term

Capstone
A large, flat stone that lies on top of a dolmen.

Dolmens or portal tombs

Dolmens look like huge stone tables. To make a dolmen two or three large stones are put standing upright. Another very large stone, called a **capstone**, is placed on top. Some capstones weigh over 100 tonnes. Archaeologists think that the large stones were brought to the site on rollers made from logs. The capstone was put in position using wooden levers and ramps made from mounds of clay.

Archaeologists found the remains of twenty-two people at the Poulnabrone dolmen in the Burren, Co. Clare. Dolmens can be found all over Ireland.

Poulnabrone dolmen, Co. Clare

Passage tombs

The most impressive megalithic tombs are the **passage tombs**. They are similar to court cairns but much bigger. From the outside, the passage tombs look like a hill or circular mound of earth. Inside, there is a long passage leading to a chamber. Archaeologists have found the remains of cremated human bodies in the chambers. The passage tombs vary in size. There are over 200 of them in Ireland. The most famous one is at Newgrange, Co. Meath.

The passage tomb at Knowth, Co. Meath

Newgrange

Archaeologists began excavating (digging) at Newgrange in the 1960s. It is one of a number of passage tombs built on a bend on the River Boyne. Later, excavations were carried out at nearby Knowth and Dowth. By carbon dating artefacts (objects) found at Newgrange, archaeologists discovered that it was built between 2675 BC and 2485 BC. This means that it is older than Stonehenge in Britain and the pyramids in Egypt.

The exterior of Newgrange, Co. Meath

The passage at Newgrange is over 19 metres long and the chamber is 6 metres high. Leading off the central chamber there are three smaller chambers. The walls of the passage are made from standing stones. Some of these were brought from Wicklow, over 60 kilometres away. The sheer size of the tomb leads archaeologists to believe that it could have taken 400 men over 16 years to build it.

Other amazing discoveries were made during excavations at Newgrange, including the following: **artwork**, the **corbelled roof** and the **roof box**.

The interior passage leading to the main chamber at Newgrange

Artwork

Many of the stones along the passage and in the chamber are decorated with spiral, circle and diamond patterns. The most dramatic decoration is on the huge stone at the entrance to the tomb.

Corbelled roof

The roof is an extension of the walls. Each layer of the wall is placed slightly inside the one below, overlapping until they meet at a single stone in the centre, making a cone effect. This is called a **corbelled roof**. After 4,500 years there are no leaks in the roof at Newgrange.

The roof box

The roof box at Newgrange allows the sun to enter the tomb. In the foreground is the large decorated stone

Over the entrance to Newgrange there is a square stone opening. Archaeologists working on the dig there were puzzled by this. They could not decide what it was for. Then one archaeologist noticed that it faced south-east. He had heard local legends that the sun shone into the tomb on certain days, so he decided to do an experiment. On 21 December, he went into the chamber at sunrise. To his amazement light began to creep up through the passage and into the chamber. This dramatic event lasted for 17 minutes at dawn and then the light faded. He realised that the roof box was there to allow a shaft of sunlight to shine through the passage and light up the chamber. The people who built the tomb must have planned this very carefully. They must have studied the movements of the sun. This spectacular event only happens once a year, at the **winter solstice** (the shortest day of the year).

Why was Newgrange built?

We don't know why Newgrange was built. The remains of burnt human bones have been found in the chamber, so **it was used as a tomb**. However, because so few remains were found there, archaeologists think that only important people or leaders of the community were buried there. Maybe the people who built it believed in a sun god. Could Newgrange have been built as a temple to honour their gods? Perhaps the human remains found there were offerings sacrificed to their gods. It is also possible that the Neolithic farmers used it as a **calendar** to tell them when it was the shortest day of the year.

The passage tomb is now restored with the help of archaeological evidence found during the excavations. It tells us important facts about the Neolithic people who built it:

- They were skilful builders.
- They understood the movements of the sun and astronomy.
- They were very artistic.
- They believed in an afterlife.
- They had great respect for their dead.

Do you understand these key terms?

pollen sample	**wattle and daub**	**megalithic tomb**	**passage tomb**
Neolithic	**quern stone**	**court cairn**	**capstone**
porcellanite	**megalith**	**dolmen**	**corbelled roof**

QUESTIONS

1 How do we know that Neolithic people in Ireland believed in an afterlife?
2 What does 'megalithic' mean?
3 List three types of megalithic tomb found in Ireland.
4 Draw a dolmen and list two places in Ireland where one can be found.
5 Write a paragraph on Newgrange.

EXAM QUESTIONS

1 In the picture below, what do you call the stone marked X?

2 Why did Stone Age farmers build structures like this?
3 Give two reasons why that period was called the Stone Age. (HL)
4 Write about the life of a farmer living in Ireland around 2500 BC.

Chapter 3

The Bronze Age in Ireland

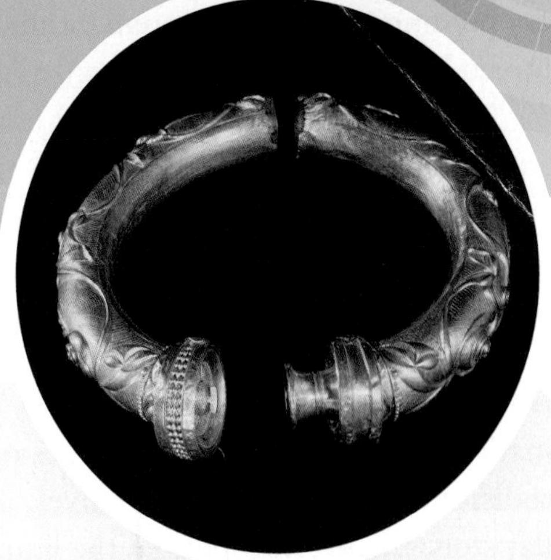

Key Learning Objectives

- What was the Bronze Age?
- What skills did Bronze Age people have?
- What was life like in Bronze Age Ireland?
- What monuments did they leave?

What was the Bronze Age?

The Stone Age lasted for thousands of years. Then around 2500 BC, in the Middle East, people learnt how to get copper from rocks. They used this metal to make tools and weapons. But copper is a very soft metal and tools broke easily. Gradually, people discovered that by adding tin to copper they made a much harder metal – **bronze.**

Over time, the skill of making metal spread across Europe. Archaeologists call this time the **Bronze Age.**

Who were the Beaker People?

Pottery dating from around 2000 BC has been found in sites around Europe. It is very different from the type made by Neolithic people, which suggests it was made by new settlers. Because the pots they made are shaped like a drinking beaker, archaeologists call these settlers the **Beaker People.**

Beaker People used metal. We know this because copper and bronze tools have been found in the same sites where beaker pottery has been excavated. Archaeologists think that it was the Beaker People who brought the Bronze Age to Ireland, around 2000 BC.

Bronze Age copper mining and smelting

1 Fires were lit close to a rock with copper in it.

2 When it got very hot, cold water was thrown on it. This cracked the rock and exposed the copper.

3 Pieces of rock containing copper were dug out of the rock face.

4 Stone hammers were used to break up the pieces of rock.

5 The rocks containing copper were put into a big fire to melt the copper to liquid and separate it from the stone.

6 The liquid copper was mixed with tin and poured into stone moulds to make tools and weapons.

What skills did Bronze Age people have?

Archaeologists have found several copper mines that date from the Bronze Age in Ireland. The most important one is at **Mount Gabriel** in Co. Cork. Here evidence of extensive copper mining has been found. Study the pictures on page 27 and explain how copper was mined by people during the Bronze Age.

Huge fires were needed to first crack the rock (**mining**) and then to separate the copper from the rock (**smelting**). There was not much tin available in Ireland so it was probably brought in from Cornwall, in England, to mix with the copper to make bronze.

Tool-making

Term

Smith
A person who made metal objects.

The skilled people who made objects from metal were called **smiths**. They made moulds by carving the shapes of tools, such as axe-heads and knives, into flat stones. Then they poured the liquid metal into the moulds and left them to set. This was called **casting**. When the castings were ready the smiths removed them from the moulds. They now had metal tools which were stronger and sharper than stone tools.

Archaeologists believe that smiths moved around the country, and may have buried their tools for safekeeping. This explains why Bronze Age axes, knives and other tools have been found in large numbers (**hoards**) in the ground all over the country.

Bronze Age tools. Can you guess what they were used for?

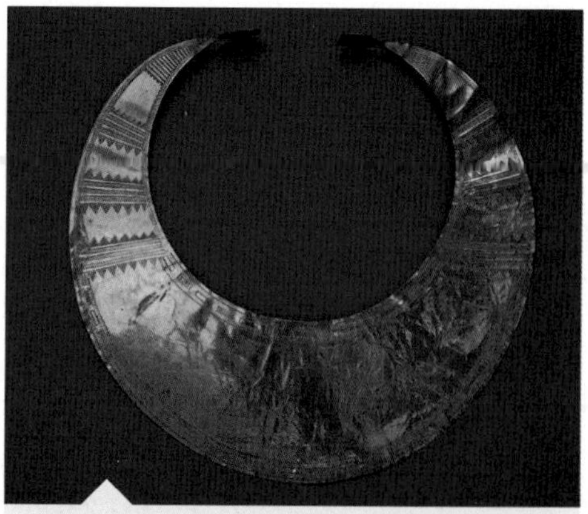

A lunula from the Broighter Hoard

Bronze Age jewellery

Bronze Age smiths also made jewellery. Earrings, bracelets, necklaces and other ornaments dating from this time have been excavated around the country. Some of the pieces are made from copper and bronze, but many of them are **gold**. The gold came from the Wicklow and Sperrin Mountains. It was probably collected from streams rather than by mining.

The best examples of Bronze Age jewellery are the **lunulae** and **torcs**. Gold collars and dress fasteners were also found.

One of the most famous Bronze Age hoards discovered in Ireland was the **Broighter Hoard**. It was found in 1896 in Co. Derry by a farmer while he was ploughing his field. Included in this hoard are gold collars, torcs and a miniature gold boat with tiny oars. The Broighter Hoard can be seen, along with other Bronze Age artefacts, in the National Museum in Dublin.

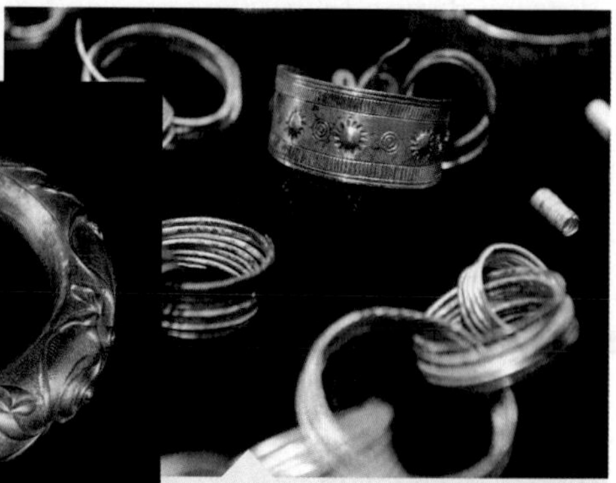

Bronze Age jewellery

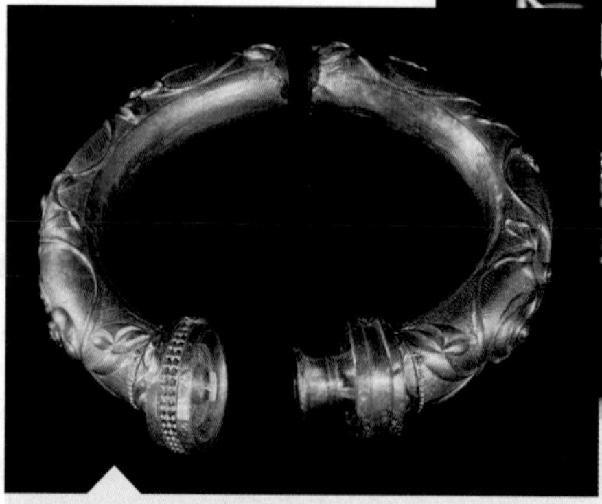

A torc from the Broighter Hoard. Torcs and lunulae were worn around the neck

Life in Bronze Age Ireland

How did they farm?

The changeover from the Stone Age to the Bronze Age was gradual. For a while people continued to use stone tools and weapons, as well as metal ones. They still farmed the same crops and kept the same animals as before. However, there was one big difference. For the first time in Ireland **horses** were used. Archaeologists have found bones of horses dating from this time.

What did they eat?

Bronze Age people ate much the same food as the Neolithic people – meat and bread.

However, they cooked in a different way. They dug pits near rivers. They lined the pit with wood and filled it with river water. Beside the pit they lit a fire and heated stones in it. When the stones were red hot they put them into the pit, making the water boil. Then they wrapped joints of meat in straw and put them in the water to cook.

The Celts would later call this Bronze Age cooker a **fulacht fiadh** (or *fia*) meaning 'deer roast'. The fulacht fiadh may have been used all year round or just in summer time. A reconstructed fulacht fiadh can be seen at the National Heritage Park in Wexford.

A fulacht fiadh. How, do you think, were the hot stones moved from the fire to the cooking pit?

What sort of homes did they have?

Bronze Age huts have been excavated in Counties Tipperary and Cork. Like Neolithic homes, these huts were thatched and made from wattle and daub. Only one hut had a place for a fire. Can you guess why? The huts were surrounded by wooden fences or stone walls, probably for protection.

A reconstruction of a Bronze Age hut

What monuments did they leave?

Bronze Age people buried their dead in **cist graves** and **wedge tombs**.

A cist is a pit in the ground, lined with stone slabs. Some contained cremated remains, others had bodies buried in a crouched position.

Often pots, personal artefacts or practical tools were buried with the body. This tells us that Bronze Age people believed in life after death.

Wedge tombs were built with large, flat stones. The front of the tomb is wider and higher than the back, like a wedge, hence its name.

Bodies were cremated and the ashes were put into pottery containers in wedge tombs. They are the most common type of Bronze Age tomb found in Ireland.

A cist tomb lined with stone slabs

A wedge tomb, Co. Clare

Stone circles

Stone circles dating from the Bronze Age have been found. These are tall upright stones arranged in circles or rows. Some of them have human remains buried within them. All of them are built to line up with the movements of the sun. This suggests that they may have had some religious meaning, or perhaps were used as calendars. Can you explain why archaeologists might come to this conclusion, from the evidence in the picture here?

The Drombeg stone circle, Co. Cork

Do you understand these key terms?

bronze	**mining**	**lunula**	**cist grave**
Bronze Age	**smelting**	**torc**	**wedge tomb**
smith	**casting**	**fulacht fiadh**	**stone circle**

QUESTIONS

1. What important new discovery was made in the Middle East around 2500 BC?
2. Where was copper found in Ireland?
3. Explain how copper was mined.
4. What two metals are used to make bronze?
5. What is a fulacht fiadh? Make a drawing to show how it looked.
6. What do we know about burial and religious customs during the Bronze Age?
7. Draw a stone circle and describe what might have happened there.
8. What is a lunala? Where can one be seen today? What does Bronze Age jewellery tell us about this period in history?
9. Put the following periods in chronological order (i.e. order of time):
   - Bronze Age
   - Ice Age
   - Neolithic times
   - Mesolithic times

Chapter 4

The Iron Age and the Celts

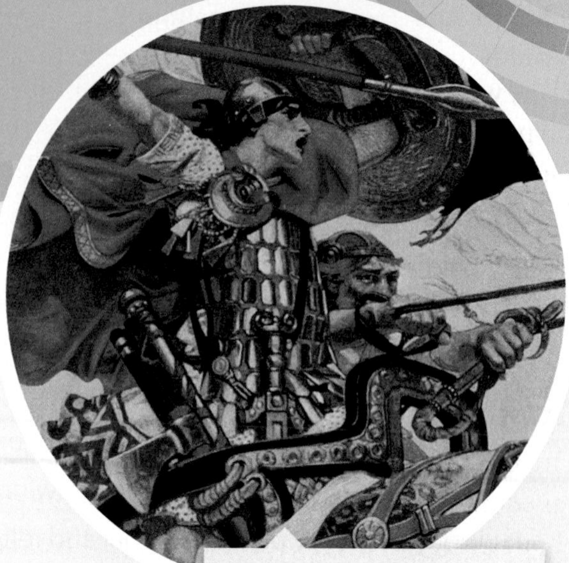

Cú Chulainn rides his chariot into battle

Key Learning Objectives

- What was the Iron Age?
- How do we know about the Celts?
- How was Celtic society organised?
- Where did the Celts live?
- What was life like in Celtic Ireland?

What was the Iron Age?

The Iron Age began around 1400 BC. A new metal – **iron** – was discovered. People gradually started using iron until this metal replaced bronze in tools and weapons. The Iron Age began in Ireland around 500 BC when the **Celts** arrived.

The Celts were a farming and warlike people who came from central Europe. They became a powerful group, taking over many parts of Europe. Their power was based on their skills in the use of iron.

Celtic jewellery and metal art

How do we know about the Celts?

We know more about the Celts than about any of the earlier settlers who came to Ireland. Our main sources of information about them come from:

- Archaeological evidence found in Europe, Britain and Ireland
- Ancient Greek and Roman writers
- Written records of the early Christian monks in Ireland

Archaeological evidence

Archaeologists have discovered Celtic sites all over Europe. The most famous ones are at **Hallstatt** in Austria and **La Tène** in Switzerland.

Hallstatt was a salt-mining area. Excavations show that the Celts lived there between 700 BC and 500 BC. Salt, like peat, preserves objects. Many artefacts were found at this site. They included iron tools and weapons, jewellery, pottery, items of clothing and human remains. The earliest Celts are known as the **Hallstatt Celts.**

Later, Celts lived at La Tène. A large hoard of iron tools, weapons and ornaments was found there in the nineteenth century. The ornaments are decorated with spirals, circles and curved patterns. This style is different from that found at Hallstatt. Archaeologists think that these Celts lived after 500 BC. They have given their name to **La Tène art**, which can be found all over Europe, including Ireland.

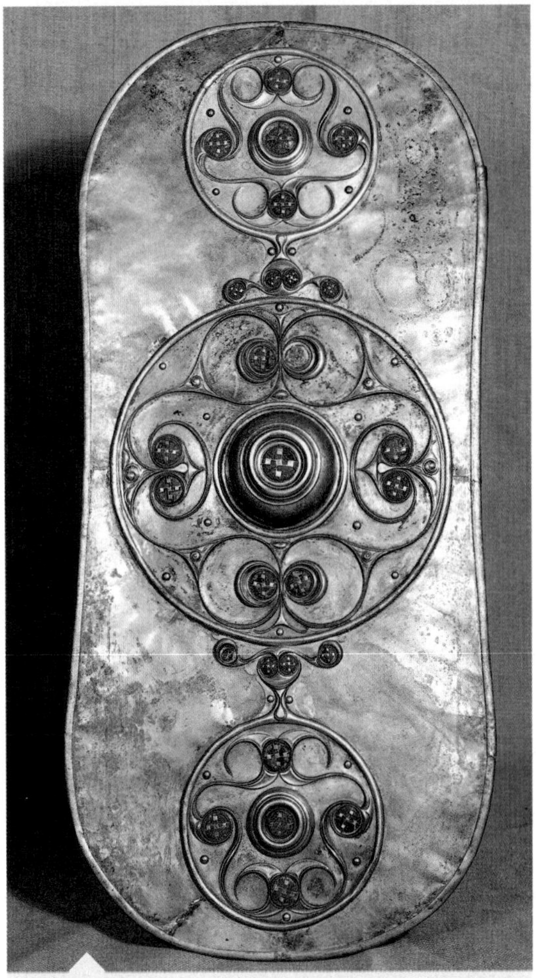

This Celtic shield was found in the River Thames in London. Can you say why it is an example of La Tène art?

Greek and Roman writers

The Greeks called the Celts *Keltoi* and the Romans called them *Gauls*. Written primary source evidence about the Celts comes from Greek and Roman writers. For example, Plato, the great Greek philosopher, wrote that they were a warlike people who drank too much wine. Many Roman writers use the word *excessive* (too much) to describe their appearance and dress, as well as their attitudes to religion and war.

The Greeks and Romans regarded people outside their own culture as inferior and uncivilised. Their accounts of the Celts may be biased, but they still give us valuable information about the Celts.

Irish sources

A pot from about 200 BC decorated in Celtic style

Christianity came to Ireland in the fifth century. With it came the skill of writing. The Celts soon became Christians. They learned how to read and write and copied down the laws they used to govern their society. These laws are called **Brehon laws.** Historians are able to use these records to help them to understand how Celtic society worked.

The Celts had an oral tradition of storytelling. Monks in the eighth century wrote down these stories and legends. The most famous legend was the ***Táin Bó Cuailgne.*** It tells of a fight between the men of Connacht and the men of Ulster over a bull. The hero of the story is the warrior Cú Chulainn. These stories provide us with useful information about life in Celtic Ireland.

The monks also kept records of the main events that happened in Ireland each year. These are called **annals** and some of them give us valuable information about pre-Christian times in Ireland.

QUESTIONS

1 Name the new settlers who came to Ireland around 500 BC. Where did they come from?
2 What new metal did they bring to Ireland?
3 List three sources of information that we have about them.
4 What did Greek and Roman sources say about the Celts? Are they reliable sources?

How was Celtic society organised?

Term

Tuath
The land and the people ruled by the king.

Rí
A Celtic king.

Derbhfine
The Celtic royal family.

The tuath

Celtic Ireland was divided up into several small kingdoms. The people and the land they lived on were called the **tuath**. There were over 150 tuatha in the country and each one was ruled by a **rí** or king. He belonged to the **derbhfine** (royal family). When he died a new king was chosen from the derbhfine. The rí's job was to lead and protect his tuath.

The warriors

After the rí and the derbhfine, the most important group of people in the tuath were the **warriors**. They were the nobles and they owned land and cattle. Their main role was to defend the tuath. War and fighting played a big part in the lives of the Celts. We know this from archaeological evidence and from the myths and legends. Written sources confirm this view. One Roman writer says: 'the whole nation is mad for war'.

Did you know?

Julius Caesar in his book *De Bello Gallico* tells us about fierce battles between the Romans and Celts in Gaul and Britain. He mentions that the Celts used chariots and preferred single combat in battle.

The Aos Dána

The learned and skilled people were next in importance to the warriors. They were called the **Aos Dána** and were highly respected. They included:

- **Judges** (Brehons) who trained for a long time to become experts in the Celtic laws (Brehon laws). Their job was to help the rí make judgements and rule justly.
- **Druids** (priests) who organised religious ceremonies and offered sacrifices to the gods. Their training took up to twenty years.
- **Doctors** who knew about herbal remedies and how to treat diseases. They, too, had to train for many years before they could work at their job.
- **Filí** (poets) who wrote praise poems about the rí and the heroic deeds of warriors. They also wrote long poems about the history and customs of the tuath.
- **Bards** and musicians who entertained the rí and the warriors with recitations and music.
- **Craftspeople** who were skilled as carpenters, goldsmiths, blacksmiths and stone masons.

Gold torcs like these were worn as jewellery by the most important Celts, such as the warriors and the Aos Dána

Farmers and slaves

The **farmers** were the biggest group in the tuath. They rented land from the warriors, grew crops and looked after the animals. The noble classes looked down on them, but the whole tuath depended on them to supply food.

The lowest class in Celtic society were the **slaves**. Most of them were prisoners captured in wars with neighbouring tuaths or from abroad. They were owned by their masters and had to work for them for free.

Did you know?

Archaeologists have found chains that they believe were used to keep slaves from running away.

Women in Celtic society

Noble women held an important position in Celtic society. Under Brehon law they could own property. The famous queen **Maedbh** of Connacht was a powerful ruler in Ireland. **Boudicca** was a Celtic warrior queen in Britain who led a revolt against the Romans. In the old sagas, we learn that Cú Chulainn was trained to be a warrior by two women, Aoife and Scatha.

Noble men could have more than one wife and divorce was common. However, most women did not belong to the noble classes, and had little power or influence. They spent their time cooking, spinning, weaving and taking care of children.

QUESTIONS

1 What was a tuath and who ruled over it?
2 What do we know about Celtic warriors?
3 Who were the Aos Dána? List three types of people who belonged to it and say what job each of them did.
4 What was the role of women in Celtic society?

Where did the Celts live?

Celtic settlements

Archaeologists have found four main types of Celtic settlement in Ireland:

- Raths, sometimes called ringforts or cashels
- Crannógs
- Hillforts
- Promontory forts

What are raths?

Raths were forts enclosed by circular ditches or mounds of earth. The fort was usually built of timber, but in places where wood was scarce stone was used. Stone raths are called **cashels**. Archaeologists are able to spot these using aerial photographs. Over 40,000 of them have been found in Ireland.

Archaeologists think several families lived inside the rath. They excavated a rath at Deer Park, Co. Antrim. Old houses were discovered, which were round, with wattle and daub walls.

During the day, animals would graze in nearby fields and were brought inside the walls of the rath at night. Underground passages called **souterrains** have been found under many raths. They might have been used for storing food or as hiding places when the rath was under attack.

Iron Age rath outside Newtonstewart, Co. Tyrone

What are crannógs?

Crannógs were man-made islands in lakes. The name comes from the Irish word for tree, *crann*. A circle of wooden stakes was put into the bed of the lake. Then layers of stones, mud and twigs were put into the circle to build a mound higher than the water level. A wooden fence was put around the mound and houses were built inside the fence. The houses were similar to those found in raths.

Some crannógs were linked to the mainland by a wooden bridge. Others had secret stepping stones or boats hidden along the shore to take the people who lived in the crannógs across the water.

Archaeologists have found evidence of over 1,200 crannógs. They have found many bronze and iron tools, as well as items of clothing and the bones of cattle, sheep, pigs and goats.

A reconstruction of a crannóg

Did you know?

Some crannógs were built after the Iron Age and were still lived in until the sixteenth century.

What are hillforts?

Hillforts were like raths but much bigger and built on a hill. Over fifty of them have been found in Ireland. Archaeologists think that they were used for important events such as religious festivals or markets.

The old Celtic legends tell us that hillforts were the headquarters of important Celtic kings. They refer to hillforts at **Emain Macha** (Co. Armagh) and **Tara** (Co. Meath).

The hillfort at Emain Macha, Co. Armagh

What are promontory forts?

Promontory forts were built on clifftops. They are found mainly on the west and south coasts of Ireland. The best example is **Dún Aengus** on Inis Mór in the Aran Islands. Excavations have been going on at Dún Aengus for many years. The inner enclosure has a rectangular platform like a table or altar facing west out into the sea. Archaeologists think that the site was used for religious purposes.

Dún Aengus on Inis Mór in the Aran Islands

QUESTIONS

1 List the different kinds of places where the Celts lived.
2 How were crannógs built?
3 Where can we find examples of hillforts?

Life in Celtic Ireland

Farming played an important part in the lives of most Celts. Cattle, sheep and pigs were kept. They were killed for meat and their skins were used to make clothes. Cattle were particularly important to the Celts. Under Brehon laws, wealth was measured in cattle.

The animals were slaughtered in autumn and preserved in salt for winter. Extra food was obtained by hunting when meat was scarce. The Celts cooked meat on spits or in huge pots (cauldrons) over open fires.

Did you know?

Fines were common punishments for crimes. These were paid for in cattle. Fifty cows were as important as one person.

Crops such as wheat, barley and oats were grown. Barley was used to make a drink like ale. Porridge was made from oats, and wheat was ground into flour using a **rotary quern stone**. The flour was then used to make bread.

A rotary quern stone used to grind corn

Did you know?

Under Brehon law, the width of a **bóthar** (road) had to be wide enough to allow two cows to pass in opposite directions.

Fashion and jewellery

The Celts cared about their appearance. Their clothes were made from linen and wool. Rich men wore a knee-length linen tunic called a **léine** which was tied at the waist by a **crois**.

Women wore ankle-length linen tunics. In winter, both men and women wore woollen cloaks (**brats**) pinned at the shoulder with a gold or silver brooch. Rich people's clothes were dyed in bright colours and richly embroidered. Men and women wore make-up made from herbs and berries. They also wore earrings, gold torcs, collars and bracelets.

Poor men wore wool trousers and women wore a long, plain wool tunic. Legends tell us that the Celts were tall and good looking. The Roman Strabo writes that their hair was fair, but that they dyed it to make it even lighter: 'they often wash it with lime-wash'.

Did you know?

The Celts made a blue dye from a plant called **woad**.

Religion and burial customs

The Celts believed in many gods. Here are some of them:

- **An Dagda** was the chief god and also the god of the after-life.
- **Lugh** was the god of war. The festival of **Lughnasa** was held in August in his honour.
- **Brigid** was the main goddess.
- **Boann**, the river goddess, gave her name to the River Boyne.

The Celts worshipped in woods and beside streams, where they felt closer to the gods. The oak tree was sacred to them.

Religion played an important part in their lives because their priests – the druids – were held in high esteem. Julius Caesar wrote about the Celtic druids and how respected they were by the Celts. They wore white linen tunics when they performed religious ceremonies. They offered sacrifices to the gods. These were usually animals, but sometimes human sacrifices were also offered.

The Celts had many religious holidays or festivals. The most important were: Samhain, Imbolc, Bealtaine and Lughnasa. Can you recognise any of the months in Irish from these festivals?

The Celts cremated (burnt) their dead and buried the ashes in the ground. Archaeologists have found personal belongings buried with the human remains. This shows us that the Celts believed in an afterlife.

The druids were like priests. They wore white robes. We think this is what they may have looked like

Ogham stones

The graves are often marked by standing stones. Some of the stones have a form of writing on them called **ogham**. Lines were carved on the edge of the standing stone. It is thought that the lines spell the name of the person buried in the grave. Ogham is the earliest form of writing in Ireland.

During the fifth century, the Celts in Ireland became Christians. The druids lost their power. However, many pagan traditions continued to exist alongside Christianity. The Christian Church in many ways adapted to the customs of the Celts.

The Aghascrebagh ogham stone in Co. Tyrone. Can you see the ogham writing? It is read from bottom to top. There are about 400 ogham stones in Ireland

Do you understand these key terms?

Iron Age	**cashel**
Brehon law	**souterrain**
annals	**crannóg**
tuath	**hillfort**
rí	**promontory fort**
derbhfine	**rotary quern stone**
Aos Dána	**léine**
druid	**crois**
filí	**brat**
bard	**woad**
rath	**ogham**

QUESTIONS

1 What is a rotary quern stone used for? Draw one in your copy book.

2 Why were cattle so important to the Celts?

3 Describe how the Celts dressed.

4 What did the Celts eat and how did they cook their food?

5 Why were druids so important in Celtic society?

6 Name two important Celtic festivals.

7 What is ogham? Where can it be found?

8 Name two types of dwelling place from Celtic Ireland.

9 Write an account of the following:

- religion in Celtic Ireland
- warriors in Celtic Ireland.

People in History

Write about a farmer in Ireland in either the Stone Age, the Bronze Age or the Iron Age.

Sample Answer

A farmer in the Iron Age

Cormac lives with his family in the province of Connacht in Ireland. They are Celts. It is the year 400 BC.

They live in a rath, with two other families. There is a circular ditch around their rath. Their houses are round. The walls are made of wattle and daub, like a basket with mud plastered in between the gaps to keep out the wind and cold. The roofs are thatched with straw. There is a souterrain under the rath. They use it to store food, but last year when their rath was attacked they were able to hide in there. Cormac wears woollen trousers and a linen léine. They eat porridge, bread and meat. The best food is always kept for the rí and his warriors.

Cormac's family and their neighbours are all farmers. They rent their land from one of the rí's warriors, who is a rich nobleman. They have to work very hard to make sure the rí, the warriors and the Aos Dána have plenty of food. They grow wheat, barley and oats. In the summer Cormac helps his father and brothers to look after the crops. In the autumn they pick the ripe grains. His mother uses a rotary quern stone to grind the seeds into flour.

They keep cattle, sheep and pigs. The animals graze in fields during the day. At night, they bring them into the rath to keep them safe from thieves and from wild animals. Cattle are very important; a man's wealth is measured by the number of cattle he has. The warriors own most of the cattle, but Cormac's family keep a few cows in case they get into trouble with the Brehons and have to pay a fine. They only kill them for food on special occasions. His father often goes hunting for meat.

When someone dies in the tuath they cremate the remains and bury the ashes in the ground. The druids organise the funeral ceremony. In the grave they put weapons and some personal belongings, which the dead person may need in the afterlife.

Chapter 5
Early Christian Ireland

St Patrick in a thirteenth-century manuscript

Key Learning Objectives

- How did Christianity come to Ireland?
- What were the early Christian monasteries in Ireland?
- What was life like in a Celtic monastery?
- What was the Golden Age and why did it end?

How did Christianity come to Ireland?

At the time that Christ lived the Romans ruled most of Europe. In AD 43 they conquered Britain. After AD 312 Christianity began to spread rapidly throughout the lands ruled by Rome. The Romans never ruled Ireland. Some historians believe that there were some Christians living in Ireland before AD 430. These were probably traders from Roman Britain who had settled on the east coast of Leinster.

There is evidence that a bishop called **Palladius** visited Irish Christians in AD 431.

Who was St Patrick?

As a young boy Patrick lived in Roman Britain and his family were Christians. Historians think he came to Ireland between AD 430 and 490. He was captured by Irish raiders and sold as a slave to a farmer in Co. Antrim. After six years he escaped from Ireland. Later, he became a priest and returned as a missionary to convert the Irish people to Christianity. We know this because he wrote two books:

- *The Confession*. This is an account of his life in Ireland and explains why he came to preach Christianity to the Irish.
- *A Letter to the Soldiers of King Coroticus*. Coroticus was a king in Britain. His soldiers raided Ireland and kidnapped people to sell as slaves. Patrick wrote this book asking them to stop the raids.

In *The Confession* Patrick tells us he 'baptised thousands' and 'ordained clerics everywhere'. We know that the druids and some of the ríthe (kings) didn't accept the new religion, because Patrick wrote that he 'lived in daily expectation of murder, treachery or captivity'.

Even after Ireland became Christian, people still lived much as they had done for hundreds of years. The tuath was still ruled by a rí. However, the power of the druids ended. Christian priests and bishops gradually replaced them.

After he died, Patrick became a hero. Many legends were told about him and passed on through the generations. Some of the stories were like the ones the Celts told about their gods. The legends associate him with different parts of the country, but he probably worked only in Co. Down and Co. Armagh.

What were the early Christian monasteries in Ireland?

Term

Monastery
A place where people who had devoted their lives to God lived.

During the third century, some Christians believed they could get closer to God by devoting their lives to prayer in remote places. Some of them lived alone. Others went with small groups of people who shared their wish to dedicate their lives to God. They became known as **monks** (men) and **nuns** (women). Monks lived in **monasteries** and nuns lived in **convents**.

Celtic monasteries

Inis Mór

The first Irish monastery was set up around AD 490 by St Enda on Inis Mór, one of the remote Aran Islands. As well as being a centre for prayer, Enda's monastery became a place of learning. Other holy men travelled there to study the Bible and become monks. Later, they went on to set up their own monasteries in other parts of Ireland and abroad.

Beehive huts on Sceilig Mhichíl. We have no written records from the monks who lived there

Sceilig Mhichíl

Sceilig Mhichíl is a rock in the Atlantic Ocean, off the coast of Kerry. Monks brought soil from the mainland so that they could make a garden to grow vegetables there. The remains of six small stone huts where the monks once lived can still be seen on Sceilig Mhichíl.

Clonmacnoise

Not all of the early Celtic monasteries were built in remote places. Many of them were built near rivers which made them easy to get to. Clonmacnoise, set up by St Ciarán in AD 545, is on the Shannon. It grew to be the largest Celtic monastery in Ireland. People came from all over Europe to study there. Many kings are buried at this site.

The round tower at Clonmacnoise dates from the twelfth century

St Brigid

Some women set up convents in Ireland at this time. There are many stories about Brigid of Kildare. As with St Patrick, much of what we know about Brigid is mixed in with myths and legends. We know very little about her from historical sources.

What did a Celtic monastery look like?

The buildings in the earliest monasteries were made from timber and have not survived. However, using sources written by the monks and archaeological evidence we know what the Celtic monasteries looked like.

A Celtic monastery

Celtic monasteries looked like ringforts. They were surrounded by a stone wall or banks of piled-up earth. Inside, there were several buildings:

1 The church was where the monks went to pray.
2 A round tower was used as a belltower to call the monks to religious services, and as a look-out post and hiding place for the monks and their valuables when the Vikings attacked the monasteries.
3 The scriptorium was where manuscripts were copied.
4 The refectory was where the monks had their meals.
5 The cells were where the monks lived, in single huts (beehives).
6 Monks who died were buried in a graveyard beside the church, inside the walls of the monastery.

What was life like in a Celtic monastery?

Monasteries were busy places with lots of people living and working there. The monks believed that work brought them closer to God. Each monk had a role to play in the life of the monastery:

- **Farmers** worked on the land to provide food for the monks who lived in the monastery.
- **Cooks** prepared the food for the other monks.
- Skilled **craftsmen** spent their time making beautiful works of art.

The monks have left us with rich sources of art in the form of manuscripts, metalwork and stonework.

Did you know?

Examples of round towers can be seen today in Glendalough, Swords, Clonmacnoise and Clondalkin.

Did you know?

Glendalough was set up by St Kevin during the sixth century.

The monastery at Glendalough, Co. Wicklow. In the foreground is St Kevin's Church

Manuscripts

The monks introduced reading and writing to Ireland. Since printing had not yet been invented, books had to be copied by hand. These books are called **manuscripts**. The monks copied down the Bible, and many of the old Celtic legends.

The manuscripts were made by **scribes**, who worked in a **scriptorium**. The scribes wrote on **vellum** (calf skin) or on **parchment** (sheep skin). For pens they used **quills** (goose or swan feathers) dipped in ink made from plants and powdered rocks. Many of the manuscripts were beautifully illustrated (decorated).

Some illustrations were made from gold leaf. Many manuscripts still survive today. These are the most famous:

- **The Cathach of St Columba** is the oldest Irish manuscript. It dates from the sixth century.
- **The Book of Durrow** is a copy of the four gospels. It is the oldest decorated manuscript.
- **The Book of Kells** is also a copy of the four gospels. Historians think it was written by Irish monks in Iona, Scotland.

Did you know?

Cathach got its name from the old Irish word for battle. The O'Donnell clan took it into battle with them as a good luck charm.

The Book of Kells is the most famous Irish manuscript and dates from around AD 800

The Book of Durrow is beautifully decorated and dates from the seventh century

Metalwork

The monks made beautiful objects in gold and silver, and decorated them with precious stones. The designs are Celtic, similar to La Tène art. Many examples survive today. The most famous are:

- The Ardagh Chalice
- The Derrynaflan Chalice
- The Cross of Cong
- The Tara Brooch

The Ardagh Chalice. The raised metal decoration is known as filigree

Stonework

Between the eighth and eleventh centuries the monks made stone high crosses. At this time few people could read or write. The monks wanted to teach them about Christianity. They carved scenes from the Bible on huge stone crosses and used these to tell people stories from the Bible. Examples can be seen at Clonmacnoise and Monasterboice (St Muireadach's Cross).

Muiredach's Cross, Monasterboice, Co. Louth. The monks carved scenes from the Bible on stone crosses. Why do you think they did this?

What was the Golden Age?

At this time, Europe was going through a period known as the **Dark Ages**, a time after the fall of the Roman Empire when tribes were at war all over the Continent. Art and learning were kept alive by the Celtic monks, and Ireland became known as 'the island of saints and scholars'.

Irish monks went abroad to found monasteries and spread Christianity. St Colmcille set up a monastery in Iona, Scotland. Monks from Iona preached to the Scots and English. St Columbanus set up monasteries at Bobbio in Italy and at Luxeuil in France. The Irish monks are still remembered today in parts of France, Italy and Germany.

By AD 800 the Irish monasteries had become famous all over Europe. Many students came to study at them. The period is known as the **Golden Age** in Irish learning.

How did it end?

However, stories about the rich treasures kept in monasteries had spread and they became targets for attack. Raiders from Scandinavia, called **Vikings**, began arriving in search of treasures. In AD 795 they attacked a monastery on Lambay Island. Over the next few centuries many other monasteries were attacked. Treasures from Irish monasteries have been discovered by archaeologists in Denmark and Sweden. The arrival of the Vikings ended the Golden Age of Irish monasteries.

Do you understand these key terms?

monk	**round tower**	**beehive huts**	**quill**
nun	**scriptorium**	**scribe**	**Dark Ages**
monastery	**refectory**	**vellum**	**Golden Age**
convent	**cell**	**parchment**	**Vikings**

QUESTIONS

1 How do we know that there were Christians in Ireland before St Patrick?
2 What sources do we have about St Patrick?
3 Did the coming of Christianity bring many changes to Ireland? Explain your answer.
4 Mention two important functions of the round tower in the early Christian monastery.
5 Who set up the first Celtic monastery and where was it?
6 Name three Celtic monasteries.
7 What is the oldest manuscript called? Name two other famous manuscripts.
8 What did the monks write on and where did they get the materials they used to produce a manuscript?
9 What other works of art did the monks produce in the monasteries?
10 Why did the Irish monks travel to Europe?
11 What happened when the Vikings came to Ireland?

Research topic

Find out more about the Vikings in Ireland.

1 If there was a Viking settlement in your area, write a local history project on the topic.
2 Do a project on Viking Dublin, Waterford or Limerick.
3 Do a project on the Battle of Clontarf, 1014.
4 Write an account of the excavations at Wood Quay, Dublin.

People in History

Write an account of the life of a monk in a Celtic monastery.

Use the plan below as a guide.

A monk in a Celtic monastery

- Why did he become a monk?
- Where in Ireland is the monastery he lives in?
- What is daily life like in the monastery?
- What are the main buildings in the monastery?
- What work do the monks do in the monastery?

Hint

Be sure to give a time context, i.e. a date between AD 490 and AD 850. Do not refer to Viking attacks unless your date is after AD 795.

TIMELINE

PART 1

Section 3

Ancient Rome

Chapter 1

Who Were the Romans?

Key Learning Objectives

- **What was the Roman Empire?**
- **How do we know about the Romans?**
- **What happened at Pompeii and Herculaneum?**

What was the Roman Empire?

Rome started out as a group of small villages around 750 BC. The people who lived there were called **Latins**. Gradually, the villages came together to form the **city of Rome**.

Two thousand years ago, Rome was the most important city in Europe. About one million people lived there. It controlled Italy and all the land around the Mediterranean Sea. We call this area the **Roman Empire**.

> ***Term***
>
> **Empire**
> An empire is where one country controls several other lands.

- By AD 120, as you can see from this map, this empire included much of Western Europe and stretched from the Middle East across North Africa.
- It had a population of 50 million, and included people of many different races, religions and languages.
- Its power lasted over 1,000 years until about AD 500.

In this section, we look at the lives of the people who lived in Rome and its empire.

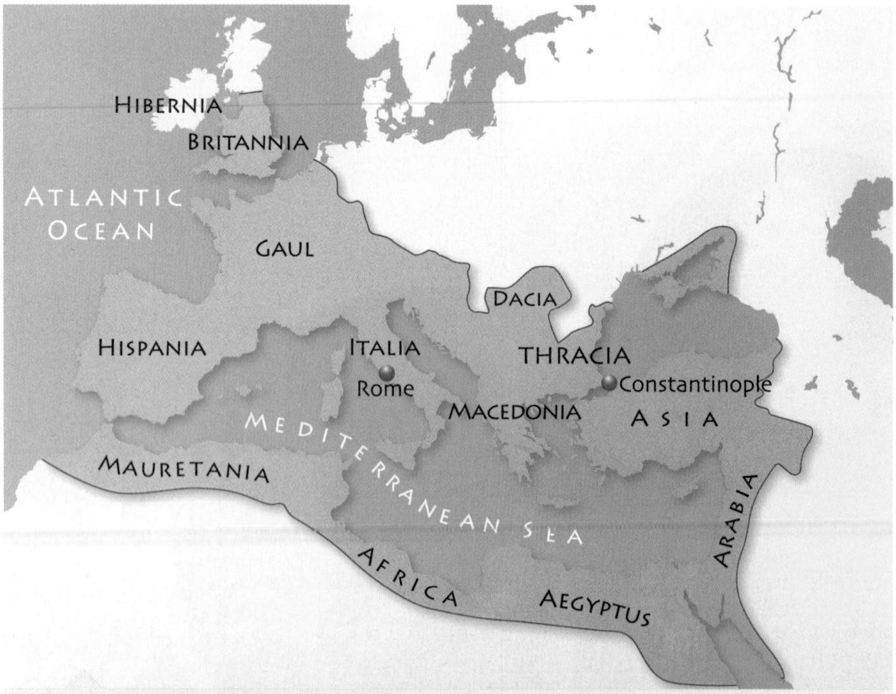

A map of the Roman Empire in AD 120. The areas conquered by Rome were called provinces. Many of these provinces later became countries. Can you name any of them?

How do we know about the Romans?

One of the most important ways of learning about the Romans is to look at what they have left behind.

- Archaeologists have **excavated** (dug up) many places where the Romans lived. There are many ruins of Roman buildings, and they have found Roman artefacts including coins, statues and paintings.
- The Romans wrote many stories, histories, plays and other books, so it is easy for us to find out how they thought and felt. They wrote in **Latin** and for centuries people all over Europe learned Latin. Even today, it is taught in some schools.

Did you know?

Even ordinary Romans could write. In Pompeii we can still read the messages people wrote on the walls 2,000 years ago.

Here are four primary sources from Ancient Rome. What can we learn about the Roman Empire from each of these sources?

A Roman carving

The ruins of the Forum

We were in thick darkness
and a heavy shower of ashes
rained down on us...
You could hear the shrieks of
women, the screams of children
and the shouts of men.

Pliny the Younger, a Roman writer, wrote this description of the eruption of Vesuvius that destroyed Pompeii and Herculaneum. You can read more about it on the next page

A Roman coin showing the face of the Emperor Nero

Term

Forum
The main public space in the centre of Rome. It was originally a marketplace.

What happened at Pompeii and Herculaneum?

Two famous Roman towns that have been excavated are **Pompeii** and **Herculaneum**. They were wealthy cities, south of Rome. They were built on the side of **Mount Vesuvius**, a volcano that had been quiet for 800 years. On a sunny August day in AD 79, it suddenly erupted. Tonnes of ash spurted up into the sky.

Most people survived the first day but on the second day Vesuvius erupted again and red-hot rock, gas and ash poured from the volcano. Travelling at 100 kilometres an hour, much faster than people could run, the rocks and ashes quickly covered Pompeii and Herculaneum. Thousands of people died horribly.

For 1,500 years the two cities lay undisturbed beneath the ash and lava. In the late 1700s archaeologists discovered the two Roman cities, almost exactly as they had been on that terrible day. People lay where they fell when the ashes covered them. Archaeologists were able to make casts of the bodies. Houses with their furniture and beautiful wall paintings were just as they had been when their owners died. Meals lay uneaten on tables.

Did you know?

Many Romans kept guard dogs. You can still see signs in Pompeii that say *cave canem* (beware of the dog).

The remains of Pompeii with Vesuvius in the background. What material are most buildings made from?

Do you understand these key terms?

empire
Latin
Forum

QUESTIONS

1. How big was the Roman Empire and what was its population?
2. Give five examples of primary sources from which we can find out about the Romans.
3. Write the story of what happened in Pompeii and Herculaneum in AD 79.
4. Why are Pompeii and Herculaneum so important for us now?
5. Look at the pictures on the previous page. Write down five things these sources tell you about Ancient Rome.

Chapter 2

Ruling the Roman Empire

Key Learning Objectives

- How was Roman society organised?
- How did the Romans control their empire?
- How did Rome become an empire?

How was Roman society organised?

Rome was ruled at first by kings, but soon the Romans set up a new type of government called a **republic**. This meant that Roman citizens could choose their own government. They elected people to the **Senate**.

Term
Senate
The name for the Roman government.

Roman citizens

There were two types of Roman citizen: patricians and plebeians. The **patricians** were rich landowners and the **plebeians** were ordinary workers and farmers.

Both groups were meant to have equal rights. They were expected to fight in the army when needed and both elected the Senate which ran Rome. In reality, most plebeians were poor and had no time for politics. The patricians had all the power. Also, not every Roman was a citizen. Women and slaves were not allowed to be citizens, so this excluded more than two-thirds of the population.

Term
Patricians
Rich Romans were called patricians.

Term
Plebeians
Poor Romans were called plebeians.

Patricians were wealthy landowners

Most plebeians were poor workers and small farmers

Did you know?
The word 'republic' comes from two Latin words, *res publica*, which mean 'a matter for the people'.

Slaves

About one-third of the people living in Rome were slaves. Some slaves were criminals, but most were foreigners whom Roman soldiers had taken prisoner when they conquered a country. As the Roman Empire got bigger, more and more slaves were brought to Rome to do all the hard work.

- Slaves belonged to their masters and had no rights.
- They had to work for no pay.
- They had to do as their masters said.
- They worked in houses, on farms and building sites and down mines.
- They fought as gladiators and raced chariots.
- Some slaves were educated, so they worked as teachers and doctors.

Sometimes a master freed a slave who had served him well. Freed slaves lived like ordinary Romans but they could never become Roman citizens.

Did you know?

Sometimes the slaves rebelled. The most successful slave revolt was led by **Spartacus**, who had trained as a gladiator. The Roman army crucified over 6,000 slaves who had taken part in this revolt.

How did the Romans control their empire?

The army

The real rulers of the Roman Empire were the soldiers. The Roman army held the empire together and remained unbeaten for centuries. Soldiers had excellent discipline and training. They were trained to march more than 30 kilometres a day. They were also well paid and allowed to sell any prisoners they captured as slaves.

The army was divided into **legions**. Each legion had about 5,000 soldiers and there were thirty legions in the whole empire.

The soldiers had to serve for **twenty years**. They had to be Roman citizens, which meant that most were volunteers. Many were the sons of soldiers. They were very proud of their legion and so they fought very hard in battle.

After every victory the Roman army would return to Rome and parade through the city, led by their generals. To the sound of trumpets they would show off their captives and their loot. In this picture they are marching through a **triumphal arch** built specially for a parade like this

They could also serve in a back up-army called the **auxilia.** These army units were made up of conquered armies and friendly tribes. The soldiers served for twenty-five years and, at the end of their service, they became citizens of Rome.

The provinces

The Romans also controlled their Empire by dividing it into **provinces.** You can see some of these on the map on page 48. The provinces were run by **governors,** who paid huge taxes and sent grain to Rome. Sea routes and **good roads** meant that there was good communication and trade between Rome and the provinces. Britain became a Roman province in about AD 40. In Britain, about 10,000 kilometres of road were built in 100 years.

A Roman soldier

1 Helmet
2 Woollen tunic
3 Body armour
4 Belt showing position in the army
5 Shield with a special design for each legion
6 Javelin
7 Dagger used in hand-to-hand combat
8 Short sword
9 Marching sandals with metal grips

Julius Caesar (100 BC–44 BC)

How did Rome become an empire?

The Romans loved their army generals and sometimes they became very powerful. One of these was **Julius Caesar**, who lived around 50 BC. He felt there was too much infighting in the Senate. He was also generous to poor people. He brought in fair taxes and he sold land cheap to help the unemployed. He became so popular that he was able to rule Rome without the Senate.

Caesar was eventually killed by members of the Senate, as they were envious of his power. His adopted son became the first emperor of Rome in 27 BC. This meant that he did away with the Senate and ruled alone. He was called **Emperor Augustus** and after that the Roman Empire was always ruled by an emperor.

Did you know?

Caesar died in the Senate. He was stabbed twenty-three times.

If Roman soldiers were attacked they protected themselves with their shields. This was called the testudo (tortoise). Here you can see a modern reconstruction of what it would have looked like

Do you understand these key terms?

republic	**patricians**	**legion**	**province**
Senate	**plebeians**	**auxilia**	**governor**

QUESTIONS

1. When was the city of Rome founded?
2. Who ruled Rome at first? What replaced them?
3. Who could vote in the Senate?
4. Roman citizens were divided into two classes. What were they?
5. Who could not be a Roman citizen?
6. What was a slave? How did a person become a slave?
7. Why was the Roman army so important?
8. How was the Roman army divided?
9. Who could become a member of a Roman legion?
10. Give two reasons why they fought so hard.
11. What was the auxilia?
12. Give two reasons why roads were so important in building up the Roman Empire.
13. How did Julius Caesar come to rule Rome?

Chapter 3

Life in the Roman Empire

Key Learning Objectives

- What was life like in the Roman Empire?
- What sort of entertainment did the Romans enjoy?
- What happened to the Roman empire?
- How have the Romans influenced our lives?

What was life like in the Roman Empire?

The Roman streets were lined with houses, blocks of flats, shops and workshops. People threw their rubbish onto the streets, so these were filthy. Stepping stones were often placed on the street so that people could avoid getting their feet dirty.

Stepping stones on a Roman street

Where did the patricians live?

A rich (patrician) Roman family would live in a big country house called a **villa**. In the town their house was called a **domus**. Archaeologists think a domus looked like the picture here:

A Roman domus

1. Atrium
2. Walled garden (peristyle)
3. Impluvium (shallow pool)
4. Slaves' quarters
5. Front rooms sometimes opened onto the street and were used as shops

- The domus was surrounded by a high wall. There were very few windows on the street side for protection.
- Inside the front door was a hall, open to the sky, called an **atrium**. The atrium had marble columns and bronze statues of gods or of the owner. There were pools, fountains and flowers.
- Other rooms opened off the atrium. There were bedrooms, a dining room, reception rooms, as well as kitchens, storerooms and places for the slaves to live.
- There was very little furniture – just chairs, couches and beds. The floors had colourful **mosaics** and there were bright paintings (**murals**) on the walls. At night, light came from oil lamps, which burned olive oil.

The interior of a Roman domus. At the top is the shrine to Lares – the household gods

Term

Mosaics
Pictures and designs made from tiny pieces of glass or tiles.

A mosaic from Pompeii

Where did the plebeians live?

Plebeian families lived in blocks of flats called **insulae**.

Term

Insulae
Roman blocks of flats where plebeians lived.

- They were usually four or five storeys high, with shops at street level.
- They were cheaply built of wood, so fires were common.
- The flats were small. The whole family – parents, grandparents and children – were crammed into one or two rooms.
- We think that people only used their flats for sleeping. It would have been too dangerous to have fires for cooking, so the plebeians probably ate at the food shops called **thermopolia**, which lined the streets.
- The higher up you lived in the flats the cheaper the rent.
- Piped water was only supplied to the ground floor, so you had to carry buckets of water and everything else you wanted up many flights of stairs.
- There were no indoor toilets. People went to the public toilets or used pots. They threw the contents of these pots, along with other rubbish, out of the window onto the streets!

Public toilets were great places to go for a gossip and the latest news

How was the Roman family organised?

The **father** was the head of the Roman family. He had power over everyone in the family from his wife to the slaves. Men often beat their wives and children. They could sell them into slavery and, when a baby was born, the father decided whether it lived or died.

Blocks of flats in Rome were called insulae

Children were expected to obey their parents in all things. The father arranged the marriages of all his children.

Roman women could not become citizens or vote in elections. But they could inherit property and we know some were successful in business. Among the plebeians, women ran shops and worked in trades and crafts. They were especially good at weaving, silverwork and making perfumes.

Women could become priestesses, hairdressers, midwives and even gladiators. There were some female doctors but most were men.

Roman women. What do you think they are doing?

Did you know?

Most Romans preferred to have sons. In the fourth century, the Senate had to pass a law forbidding people from leaving newborn baby girls out to die.

QUESTIONS

1 Was Rome a clean or dirty city? Give a reason for your answer.
2 Describe a patrician's home and draw a diagram of it.
3 What were insulae?
4 Give two advantages of living in an insula and two disadvantages.
5 Why were there so many fires in Rome?
6 'The father was the head of the Roman family.' Give two reasons why you would agree or disagree with this statement.
7 'Roman women had no power.' True or false? Give a reason for your answer.

How were Romans educated?

Education was important to the Romans. Most children from poor families did not go to school, but many still learned to read and write.

Boys from rich families might be taught by an educated slave. Others went to school. The school day started at dawn. The boys sat on backless benches. They studied reading, writing and arithmetic.

At 12 or 13 years of age the boys went to schools where they learned about Greek and Latin writers, and discussed their ideas. They practised **oratory**, which is the art of public speaking. This was to help them later if they were elected to the Senate.

Did you know?

Roman books were handwritten. We still call handwritten books manuscripts, from the Latin words for hand (*manu*) and write (*scripto*).

The Romans used numerals, which are different from our numbers. Do you know them?

Roman numerals

I	=	1	VI	=	6	XI	=	11	XC	=	90	DC	=	600
II	=	2	VII	=	7	XV	=	15	C	=	100	CM	=	900
III	=	3	VIII	=	8	XX	=	20	CXL	=	140	M	=	1,000
IV	=	4	IX	=	9	XL	=	40	CC	=	200	MM	=	2,000
V	=	5	X	=	10	L	=	50	D	=	500			

Example: 2014 = MM (2,000) + X (10) + IV (4) = MMXIV

Write out the year of your birth in Roman numerals.
Can you see any problems in using these numbers?

Did you know?

Paper was too expensive to waste, so students practised writing on boards covered with wax, which could be smoothed over after each use.

Girls married young, usually in their early teens. Some rich girls had tutors at home who taught them about Greek literature and how to play an instrument. Mothers taught daughters how to manage a household and to spin, weave and sew.

What did they eat?

The Romans didn't eat much during the day. For breakfast they had bread dipped in wine, with olives, cheese or raisins. For lunch they had cold food such as bread, salad, fruit and nuts. Wine, often mixed with water, was the usual drink.

The main meal (the **cena**) was in the evening. It often lasted several hours.

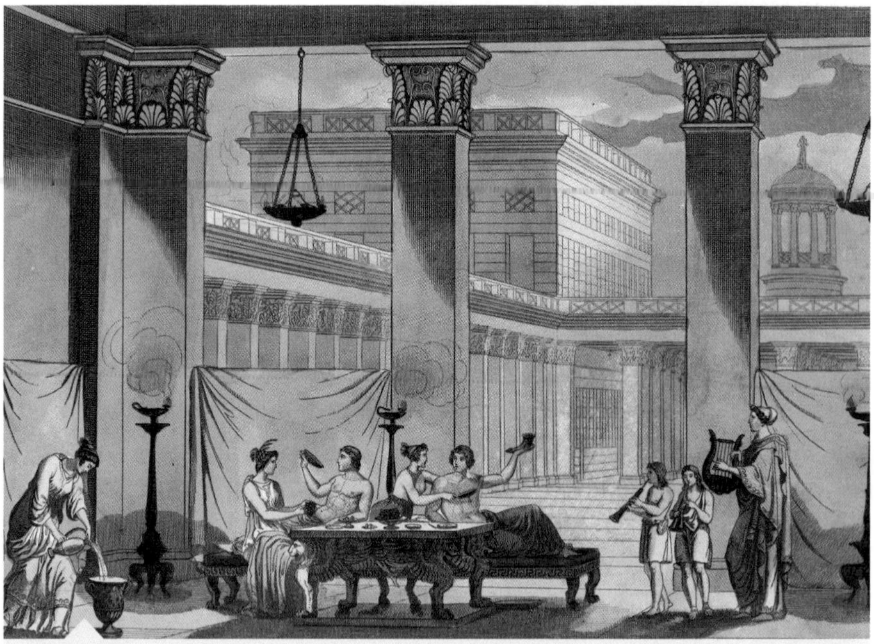

Romans often had entertainment at their evening meal. What kinds of musical instrument can you see?

A **patrician dinner** would have three courses.

- For **starters** there were savoury dishes such as oysters, mussels and raw or cooked vegetables.
- **Main courses** were usually roast or boiled meat, covered in rich, spicy sauces. Romans used rich sauces to cover up the taste of food that was not very fresh.
- For **dessert**, Romans ate pastries, nuts and fruit such as figs and grapes. Honey was used to sweeten the food.

Did you know?

The Romans had spoons and knives, but there were no forks.

Guests lay on couches, propping themselves up on their left arm. They used their right hand to stretch for food. They ate with their fingers and between courses slaves came around with water and towels so that the guests could wash their hands.

Poor Romans ate bread, porridge, beans, lentils and maybe a little meat. Most Romans depended on handouts of bread from the government to survive. This was called **dole**.

Did you know?

In his eleventh year of power Emperor Augustus gave free grain to at least 250,000 people.

How did they dress?

The official dress of a Roman citizen was the **toga**. It was like a sheet draped in graceful folds around the body.

Togas were cold and uncomfortable so most of the time men wore a **knee-length tunic**. It was like a long T-shirt, tied around the waist. The tunic was made of cool linen in summer and warm wool in winter.

Roman men wore togas

Roman women wore stolas

Women wore long tunics belted at the waist. After a girl married, which could be as young as twelve, she wore a long woollen tunic called a **stola**. Rich women used plenty of make-up and often dyed their hair red. They wore a lot of jewellery – rings, earrings, bracelets and necklaces. Both men and women wore leather sandals in the house and shoes outside.

What arts and crafts were they good at?

Ancient Romans were skilled craftspeople. Potters made thousands of red clay pots that were used as containers. They also carved beautiful designs on vases.

Making **mosaics** was another important craft. The maker placed coloured tiles or stones in wet mortar to create a design or picture, usually on the floor. You can see a picture of one on page 56.

Romans learnt the art of **glass-blowing**, which meant they could shape glass to make things like bottles and drinking glasses. Artists designed **murals** or wall paintings.

Engineers used arches and domes in their buildings. This made it possible to build **vaulted (arched) ceilings** without crossbeams. Look at the picture on the next page. Can you see the vault effect in the baths at Caracalla?

A Roman vase. What material was used to make this vase?

QUESTIONS

1 How were most girls educated in Ancient Rome? Explain your answer.
2 Name four subjects that rich boys learned when they went to school.
3 What did most Romans have for breakfast?
4 Describe the dinner of a wealthy Roman.
5 What was dole?
6 How did men and women dress in Rome most of the time?
7 What was a stola?
8 Are the following statements true or false? If false, write in the correct answer.
- Oratory is a way of speaking.
- Patricians were poor Romans.
- Women and slaves could be Roman citizens.
- Slaves could never win their freedom.
- Roman men wore togas all the time.

9 What was mosaic-making?
10 Name two types of craftspeople in Rome, and say what they did.

A painting of what the baths at Caracalla in Rome would have looked like

What gods did they believe in?

The Romans believed in many gods and saw them as a kind of a family. Here are some of them:

- The father of the gods was **Jupiter** and all the other gods feared him. His temple was the most important in the Forum.
- **Venus** was the goddess of love.
- **Mars** was the god of war.

Romans prayed to different gods, depending on what they wanted. For example, a soldier going into battle might pray to Mars for his own safety and to Venus if he wanted success in love. Gods had their own temples. Many were in the Forum.

The **Pantheon** was a temple to all the gods in Ancient Rome.

The Pantheon is one of the best preserved of ancient Roman buildings. The portico (porch) at the front has columns and a triangular pediment which are typical of Roman architecture

Household gods: the Lares

Every family, both rich and poor, had a shrine at home to its household gods. They were called the **Lares**. Romans thought they were the spirits of their ancestors who watched over them. The family prayed to them each day.

The Lares were household gods

Did you know?

Romans often wrote prayers on clay tablets and left them at the temple. Thousands of these tablets survive and they tell us a lot about the worries of ordinary Romans.

A new religion

Romans were tolerant of foreign gods. As long as people obeyed the emperor and did not cause trouble the Romans didn't mind what gods they followed. But everyone was expected to worship Roman gods alongside their own. The emperors saw this as the best way to keep the empire united.

Christianity was started after AD 30 by the followers of Jesus. The problem for the Romans was that Christians were taught that there was only one god and they refused to give offerings to the Roman gods. The Romans saw this as **treason**. Christians were tortured and hundreds executed. But the new religion became more and more popular. Eventually, in AD 337, the Emperor **Constantine** became a Christian and Christianity was made the official religion of the empire.

Term

Treason
Betraying your country.

Emperor Constantine

How did they bury the dead?

Term

Catacombs
Underground graveyards where the dead were buried.

When a person died, the family put coins on their eyes to pay their fare to the next world. People believed the dead person's spirit was rowed across a mystical river called the **Styx** to the next world.

The funeral of an important man was held in the **Forum**. The body was carried from his home, accompanied by musicians, dancers and professional mourners who wailed and cried. Members of the family followed, riding in chariots. It was forbidden to cremate or bury a person in the city, so the remains were placed **outside the city walls.**

Bodies were cremated and the ashes were placed in **urns** (jars). With the coming of Christianity, many were buried in the underground cemeteries, the **catacombs**, which lined the roads into Rome.

The dead were buried in the catacombs

QUESTIONS

1 Name three Roman gods and say what each of them looked after.
2 How do we know what ordinary people prayed for?
3 What were Lares?
4 Were the Romans tolerant of other religions? Give a reason for your answer.
5 Why did Roman emperors think that everyone should worship Roman gods?
6 What new religion started around AD 30 in the Roman Empire? Why did the Romans not like it?
7 Why did Romans put coins on the eyes of their dead?
8 Describe a rich person's funeral in Rome.

What sort of entertainment did the Romans enjoy?

Great wealth flowed from the Roman Empire into the city of Rome. This meant that entertainment was cheap, so even plebeians could afford many luxuries.

Roman baths

The Romans loved bathing, so there were **public baths** in every Roman city. Pompeii had three and there were said to be 900 in Rome. They were cheap and children were allowed in free.

Men and women bathed separately. In big baths there was a men's area and a women's area. In small ones, they went at different times.

Most Romans went to the baths every day, not just to bathe but to exercise, meet friends, and perhaps shop or read in the library.

Did you know?

Some Roman baths had room for up to 3,000 people.

Visiting the Roman baths

When you went to the baths:

1 A slave would first **massage** you with olive oil.
2 Then, if you wished, you could go to the **exercise yards** and do weightlifting or wrestling.
3 After that you had a choice. You could relax and chat with your friends in the warm room, or you could go to the hot room called the **caldarium**. It had a tub of very hot water in which you could sit.
4 Finally, there was also a cold room called a **frigidarium** with a refreshingly cool pool.

Chariot racing in the Circus Maximus

Chariot races were held in the **Circus Maximus**. This was a great racetrack on the edge of Rome. It had room for 250,000 people.

Usually four teams competed in the race. They were called after colours: the Reds, the Greens, the Whites and the Blues. The fans wore the colours of their team and there was heavy betting on each race.

Four horses, running abreast, pulled the chariots. At breakneck speed, they raced seven times around the track (about eight kilometres). Crashes were common and drivers and horses were often killed.

A chariot race in the Circus Maximus. Which teams can you see here?

Gladiator contests in the Colosseum

Romans also loved to watch fights between **gladiators**. The fights were held in the Colosseum, which was near the Forum. Its ruins are still there today and you can see below what archaeologists think it looked like.

The Colosseum held nearly 50,000 people and shows could go on for weeks. Sometimes a great awning (shade) would be drawn across to protect the audience from the hot sun. There were special seats for the patricians and important people like the emperor.

Term

Gladiators
Slaves who fought each other or animals for the entertainment of the crowd.

Gladiator contests were held in the Colosseum in Rome. This picture of what it would have looked like gives you an idea of the huge scale of the building

Did you know?

The games organisers sometimes flooded the centre of the Colosseum with water and staged mock naval battles.

Gladiators were usually slaves. They belonged to the men who managed the fights. Each man had his team of fighters.

The gladiators wore armour and had to fight each other. Sometimes both men had swords. Usually one man had a sword, while the other had a net and a forked spear called a **trident**. He would try to entangle his opponent in the net and kill him with the trident.

Successful gladiators were often adored by their fans, a little like football players today. If they lived, they could win their freedom and retire as wealthy men.

To make the contests more interesting, gladiators were made to fight blindfolded or against wild animals. This picture show a *retiarius* with his net and trident

Did you know?

The Emperor Trajan held games that went on for 123 days. During that time 11,000 animals were killed. On one day alone 3,000 men died.

QUESTIONS

1 How often did Romans visit the baths?
2 Describe a Roman bath.
3 Name the two favourite sports of the Romans.
4 Describe a chariot race.
5 How do we know that gladiators were popular? Give two reasons for your answer.
6 Which of the Roman entertainments would you have liked best? Give a reason for your answer.
7 Are the following statements true or false? If false, write the correct answer.
- The Romans worshipped one god.
- Mars was the father of the gods.
- Chariot racing took place in the Circus Maximus.
- It was expensive to go to the baths in Rome.

What happened to the Roman Empire?

Around the edges of the Roman Empire, especially in the area we now call Germany, there were many warlike tribes. They included the Vandals, the Goths, the Saxons and the Franks. The Romans called them **barbarians** because they could not write and did not live in cities.

Did you know?

From the Angles we get the modern name England, i.e. the land of the Angles.

Rome is defeated

Around AD 400, German tribes poured into the Roman Empire, looking for land. In AD 410, they reached Rome itself and took many of its treasures.

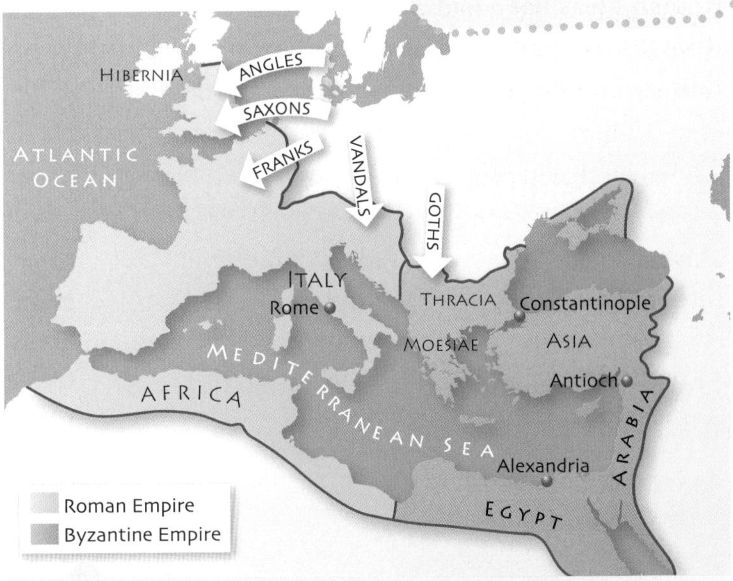

From AD 330 Rome was ruled from Constantinople

After that, new 'barbarian' kingdoms appeared. They took over different parts of Europe. The area the Romans called **Gaul** became the kingdom of the **Franks** (France). In England, two barbarian tribes, the **Angles** and the **Saxons**, replaced the Romans and the Celts.

The barbarians were not as organised as the Romans and gradually the great buildings, the roads, the temples and the aqueducts of imperial Rome fell into ruins. However, the Roman Empire was not dead. It remained strong in the east and became known as the **Byzantine Empire**. Later, many of the old Roman ideas came back to Europe from the east. This was called the Renaissance, and we will read about it in Section 5.

How have the Romans influenced our lives?

The Roman Empire still influences us today:

- The alphabet we use is the **Roman alphabet** and the way we form our letters is the same as the Romans.
- Italian, French, Romanian, Spanish and Portuguese are modern versions of the **Roman language, Latin.**
- We use a version of the **Roman calendar**, with all months having 30 or 31 days, except February which has 28, or 29 in a leap year. This idea was developed by Julius Caesar.
- We have also kept the **Roman names for the months.** Which emperors do you think the months of July and August were called after?
- In science, all plants, animals and insects are known officially by their **Latin names.**
- **Over 30 per cent of the words we use in English come from Latin.** You have read some of them in this section. Three examples are: villa (a house); circus (a round area); senate (an elected body). Can you find two more?

Look at this inscription. Can you read what it says?

Laws

The Romans had a well-developed system of laws. Today, Roman law still forms the basis of law in many European countries. For example, the way the courts are run and the names of officials such as **barristers** come from Roman law.

Engineering

Roman ideas have had a great influence on engineering and styles of building. The Romans used a system of under-floor heating in their homes. Warm air rose from burning furnaces in the cellar. The Romans had the first apartment blocks and shopping centres.

Do you understand these key terms?

villa	**mural**	**toga**	**urn**
domus	**insulae**	**stola**	**caldarium**
atrium	**oratory**	**Lares**	**frigidarium**
peristyle	**cena**	**treason**	**gladiator**
mosaic	**dole**	**catacombs**	**barbarians**

QUESTIONS

1 When and how did the Roman Empire come to an end?
2 Where do the names 'France' and 'England' come from?
3 Can you name any modern countries that were part of the Byzantine Empire?
4 List four ways in which the Romans still influence us today.
5 Name four sources from which we get information about life in Ancient Rome.
6 Can you match up the following?

Plebeian	A place where gladiators fought
Caldarium	Male clothing
Goths	Bread
Colosseum	A hot tub
Toga	A tribe from Northern Europe
Dole	A poor Roman

EXAM QUESTIONS

1 Name two achievements of a named ancient civilisation outside of Ireland. (HL)
2 Explain how information about this civilisation was discovered. (HL)
3 Write an account of two of the following aspects of the named ancient civilisation:
(a) burial customs and religion
(b) food and clothing
(c) arts, crafts and work. (HL)

PART 1

People in History

Write about a slave in Ancient Rome.

A slave in Ancient Rome

I am a slave and I live in Rome around AD 100. The Roman Empire is very powerful and I was brought here as a prisoner when the Romans took over my homeland, Gaul. I don't get paid for the work I do but I am lucky. I am a house slave and the work is not too hard. Because I am educated, I help to teach the master's sons. Other slaves have to work in the vineyards or down the mines.

Home

I live in the slaves' quarters in my master's domus. It is a beautiful house with lovely statues and mosaics on the floor. When you enter the house, there is an entrance hall called an atrium. It has a fountain and is open to the sky.

> *Exam tip*
>
> You could draw a diagram of a domus with labels, for extra marks.

Family life

My relatives live in one of the many blocks of flats that you find around Rome. These are called insulae. They live on the fifth floor and have to carry their water up the stairs from the fountains below. They cannot cook in their homes because the flats are made of wood and it would be too dangerous to have a fire in the room. They eat in one of the fast-food shops out on the street.

Food

I get well fed in the domus. For breakfast I have bread dipped in olive oil or with cheese. For lunch I have salad and for dinner I have porridge, beans, lentils and a little meat. My master has huge banquets that go on for hours.

Religion and burial customs

The Romans believe in many gods. Jupiter is head of the family of gods and Venus is the god of love. The Lares are the household gods. When I die I am sure they will put coins on my eyes to pay for my passage over the River Styx to the next world. Recently, I have become a Christian so I don't believe in any of this. But I keep my mouth shut. The Romans don't like Christians and I don't really want to be thrown to the lions!

Entertainment

When I am free I go to the baths or to the Circus Maximus for the chariot racing. I love the baths. You get to meet everyone and you can do wrestling as well. I support the Red Chariot team but I don't like the gladiator fights. Last week there were 120 killed in the Colosseum. It got a bit too much for me.

> *Exam tip*
>
> You could gain extra marks by drawing a diagram of the baths, with labels.

TIMELINE

PART 1

Section 4

The Middle Ages

Chapter 1

Life in the Middle Ages

Key Learning Objectives

- What were the Middle Ages?
- What was the feudal system?
- What was a manor?
- How was it farmed?
- What was life like in a medieval village?
- How were law and order kept?

What were the Middle Ages?

The time from about AD 500 to about 1500 is called the **Middle Ages** or the **medieval period**. It is the time between the end of the Roman Empire and what we call modern times. When the Roman Empire broke up in the fifth century there was no central government and no single currency. Roads and towns fell into ruins. Bandits and outlaws attacked people, so travel and trade became very difficult. People looked to local lords to protect them and the lords became very powerful. Gradually they set up the feudal system.

What was the feudal system?

The feudal system was how society was organised in the Middle Ages. This is how it worked.

Term

Feudal system
This is how land was owned and society was organised in the Middle Ages.

1 The king owned all the land. But he could not control or farm it all himself so he gave some to his followers. He kept about a quarter of the land for his own use. This was called a **demesne**.

2 The king's followers were called his **vassals**. Some vassals were lords with titles such as earl or count. Others were bishops or abbots.

3 The lords gave some of their land to their **knights** in return for their loyalty. Knights were soldiers who rode into battle on horseback and fought for their lords.

4 **Peasants** farmed the land. They had to pay heavy taxes and rents to the lords and the king. There were two types of peasants: **serfs** and **freemen**.

Most peasants were **serfs.** They belonged to the lord and farmed his land. They got their own small piece of land to farm, and in return they had to work for free on the lord's private land. They could not leave the manor or get married without his permission. They also paid taxes to him and to the priest. Some serfs had as much as 30 acres to farm. These were called **villeins.**

Some peasants were **freemen.** They did not have to give free labour to the lord but paid him rent. They could travel and marry as they pleased. But they still had to pay their taxes to the lord and the priest.

Did you know?

The land a king ruled was called a **kingdom**. The word **county** used to mean the land that a count got from the king.

Term

Peasant
A person who worked on the land.

Serf
A person who belonged to the lord and farmed his land.

Freeman
A man who paid rent and tax to the lord but could travel as he pleased.

Life in a medieval village

Most people lived in the countryside during the Middle Ages. They lived in small villages and farms owned by the local lord or knight. These were called **manors.**

Term

Manor
The land and everything on it owned by the lord.

What was a manor?

The picture opposite shows a medieval manor village. There were usually twenty to thirty houses in a village. The peasants farmed the land around the village, which was divided into three big fields and a commons.

A medieval manor village

1 The manor house is where the lord lived. It was usually at the edge of the village. Only rich and powerful nobles lived in a castle.

2 A serf's house.

3 A serf's one-acre strip of land. Every serf had strips of land in each of the three big fields.

4 In the centre of the village is the church. The priest lived in a house beside it. He said Mass for the peasants on Sunday, baptised and buried them. They paid him by giving him one-tenth of their crops. This was called the **tithe**.

5 The **commons** is where all the peasants' animals grazed together.

6 The forge is where the blacksmith worked making nails, knives, axes and horseshoes.

7 The water mill is where the miller ground the peasants' wheat into flour.

8 The river is where the peasants washed their clothes and got their drinking water.

9 The alehouse is where poor people drank beer. Only taverns could sell wine and this was more expensive.

10 The forest is where the peasants got the wood to build their houses.

11 The bailiff's house. He looked after the lord's accounts and kept law and order on the estate.

How was it farmed?

The peasants farmed using a method called the **open-field system.** This is how it worked:

- The land of the manor was divided into two parts.
- One part was a big meadow called the **commons.** All the animals belonging to the peasants grazed on the commons.
- The other part was where the crops grew. It was divided into three huge open fields. Each field was then divided into long **strips.** Every peasant family had some strips in each of the three fields.

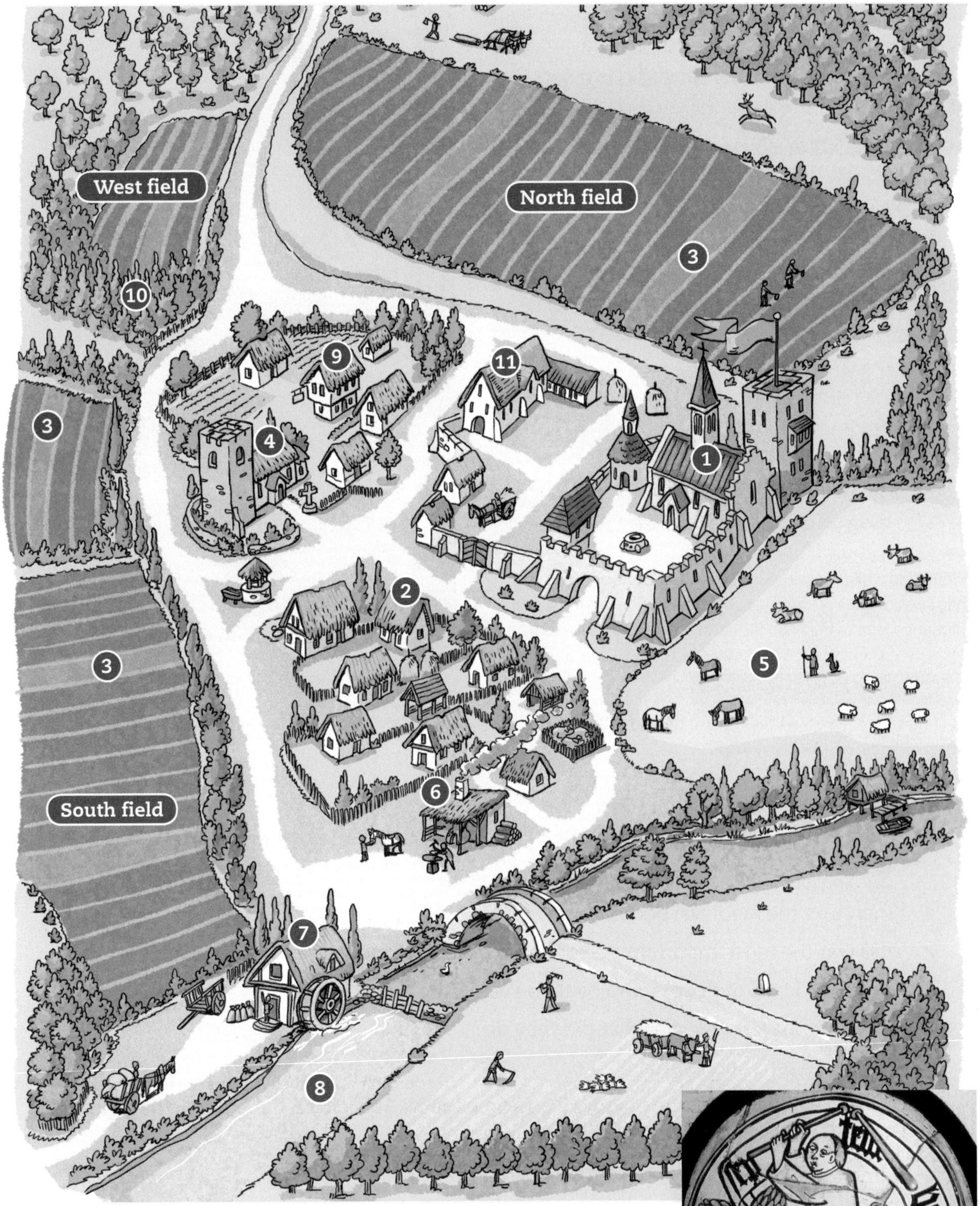

› Each year one of the three open fields was left **fallow**, with nothing growing. This meant that the soil was rested, and would be fertile again the next year.

This was called rotating the crops or **crop rotation.** You can see how it worked in one field in the table here.

South field	
Year 1	Oats, rye or barley
Year 2	Fallow
Year 3	Wheat

A peasant using a **flail** to separate grains from their husks. A flail was two sticks tied together

Ploughing with four oxen, sowing seed, and harrowing. A harrow was a heavy frame with iron teeth. You dragged it over ploughed land to break up the earth before sowing seeds

Cutting hay. The men have **scythes** and the women have **pitchforks**

Term

Ox
A type of cattle used for heavy work.

QUESTIONS

1 When was 'the medieval period'?
2 Who was the most important person in a medieval kingdom?
3 Name two kinds of people who could be vassals of the king.
4 Who were the knights and what did they do?
5 What were serfs and freemen?
6 Look at the drawing of the manor village on page 71. Apart from the church, the houses were all made of wood. Can you guess why?
7 Name three buildings you see in the village.
8 What was the tithe? Why did the peasants pay it?
9 In a medieval village who worked in the forge? What did he make there?
10 Why did the peasants have to have land in each of the three fields?
11 Explain, with a drawing, how the open-field system worked. Give two reasons why this was not a very efficient method of farming.
12 The pictures above are from medieval calendars. Are they a primary or a secondary source? Write down three pieces of information they give us about the Middle Ages.

What was life like in a medieval village?

Did you know?

Even the dung on a manor farm belonged to the lord.

The houses of the peasants

A peasant's house usually had one room. Families would have cooked and slept in the same room. Children would have slept in a loft if the house was big enough. Peasants built their own houses using a method called **wattle and daub** (see page 20). The roof was thatched with straw. In winter, they brought their animals into the house for safety and warmth.

Look at this picture of a peasant's house and describe what you see

Clothes

Peasants made their own clothes. They were made of linen or wool. They dyed them with berries or mosses. The women wore long dresses with a bonnet or headscarf. The men wore tunics with a belt around the waist.

Did you know?

Peasants bathed when they could in rivers, lakes and hot springs. Most of the time they were dirty. Lice crawled in their hair, and their bodies were covered in fleas and bugs they picked up from sleeping on straw.

Peasant dress. It was not thought proper for a married woman to go out with her head uncovered

Food

Peasants rarely ate meat. On the right is a typical peasant menu.

Pastimes

Peasants didn't work on Sundays and holy days, which could add up to ninety days a year! Some of their pastimes are still popular today, such as noughts and crosses, draughts, wrestling and carol singing. Another game was called 'hoodsman blind'. What do you think we call this now?

Breakfast at dawn
Lump of dark bread, ale

Lunch at 11am
Dark bread, cheese and ale or cider

Main meal at 5pm
Pottage (vegetable soup with oatmeal), bread, cheese and ale or cider

Ale (weak beer) was safer to drink than water, which was usually dirty. Can you list two things missing from this menu which most of us would have every day? Do you know why they are not there?

Music and singing were popular pastimes. Do you recognise any of the instruments?

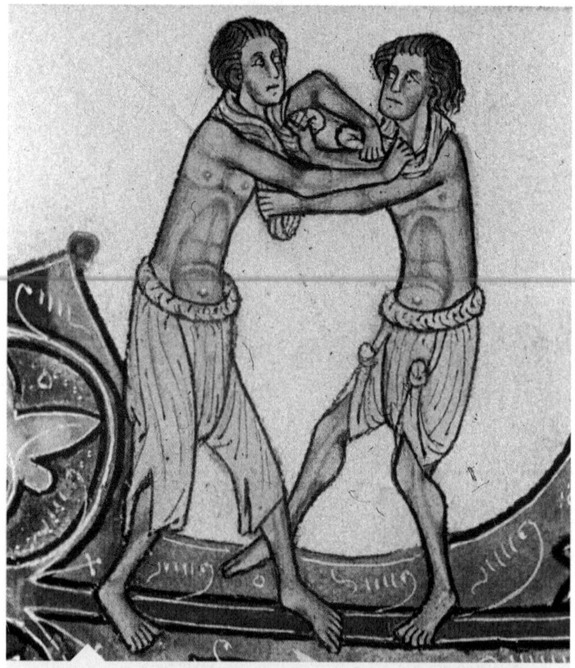

A picture of two men wrestling, from a medieval manuscript

How were law and order kept?

The lord appointed a **bailiff** to oversee the village for him. The bailiff made sure the peasants paid rents and taxes. He also looked after law and order.

Sometimes peasants stole from the lord's orchards or poached deer in his forest. Others got drunk or started fights. And serfs were often caught running away. If a serf could remain free for a year and a day he could become a **freeman**. The bailiff brought those accused of a crime to the manor house, where the lord decided their punishment.

- The most common punishment for small crimes was a **fine**.
- Another punishment was to put people in the **stocks**. Their legs and sometimes hands were locked between planks of wood. Passers-by spat at them or threw things at them.
- A **pillory** was like the stocks, but it held the head and hands.
- A thief could have his hand cut off.
- A **ducking stool** was used to punish women who made trouble. They were tied to a chair and lowered into the water, again and again.
- Really serious criminals like murderers or traitors were **hanged**.

Did you know?

Sometimes a person hunted by the bailiff ran into a church or monastery. The bailiff could not arrest him there. That was called **sanctuary**.

- Another crime that was harshly punished was **witchcraft**. Witches could be hanged, and sometimes **burned to death**.
- People were not put in prison. The local castle had **dungeons**, but these were only used for soldiers who were captured in a war.

Women suspected of being witches were sometimes burned alive at the stake. Witch-burning went on into the sixteenth century or later. This is a picture of a German burning in 1555

Do you understand these key terms?

Middle Ages	**knight**	**county**	**open-field system**
medieval	**peasant**	**manor**	**stocks**
feudal system	**serf**	**tithe**	**ducking stool**
demesne	**villein**	**commons**	**sanctuary**
vassal	**freeman**	**bailiff**	

QUESTIONS

1 What were the peasants' clothes made of? Describe the clothes they wore.
2 List three types of entertainment common in the Middle Ages.
3 What did the bailiff do in the village?
4 Name three types of crime and three types of punishment in the medieval village.
5 What was sanctuary?

SOURCE QUESTION

> *The Miller was a chap of sixteen stone*
> *A great stout fellow big in brawn and bone.*
> *He did well out of them, for he would go*
> *And win the ram at any wrestling show…*
> *He could heave any door off hinge and post,*
> *Or take a run and break it with his head.*

› The text on the right comes from *The Canterbury Tales* by Geoffery Chaucer. Read it and answer the questions that follow.

(a) What does this poem tell you about how people in the Middle Ages spent their free time?

(b) Many surnames come from the Middle Ages. What common surname do you see in this poem? Where does the name come from?

People in History

Write about the life of a serf in a medieval village.

Use the plan below as a guide.

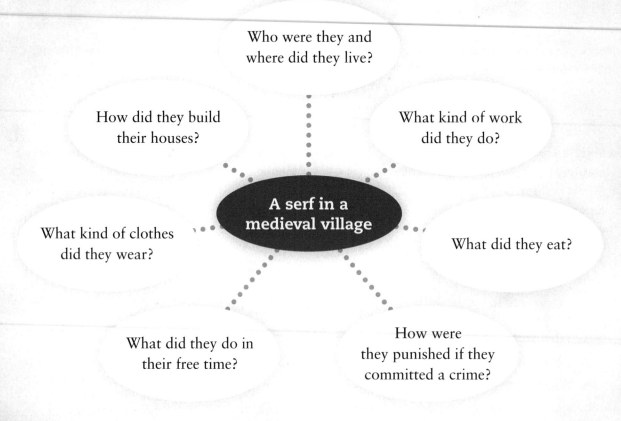

A serf in a medieval village

- Who were they and where did they live?
- What kind of work did they do?
- What did they eat?
- How were they punished if they committed a crime?
- What did they do in their free time?
- What kind of clothes did they wear?
- How did they build their houses?

Chapter 2

Life in a Medieval Castle

Key Learning Objectives

- How were castles built?
- What was a siege?
- What was it like to live in a medieval castle:
  - for the lord?
  - for the lady?
  - for the knights and other soldiers?

How were castles built?

As soon as a lord got land from his king, he built a castle on it. He needed it to defend himself and his people from enemies.

The first castles were called **motte and bailey** castles. They were made of wood and very simple to build. The drawing on the right shows you what one looked like.

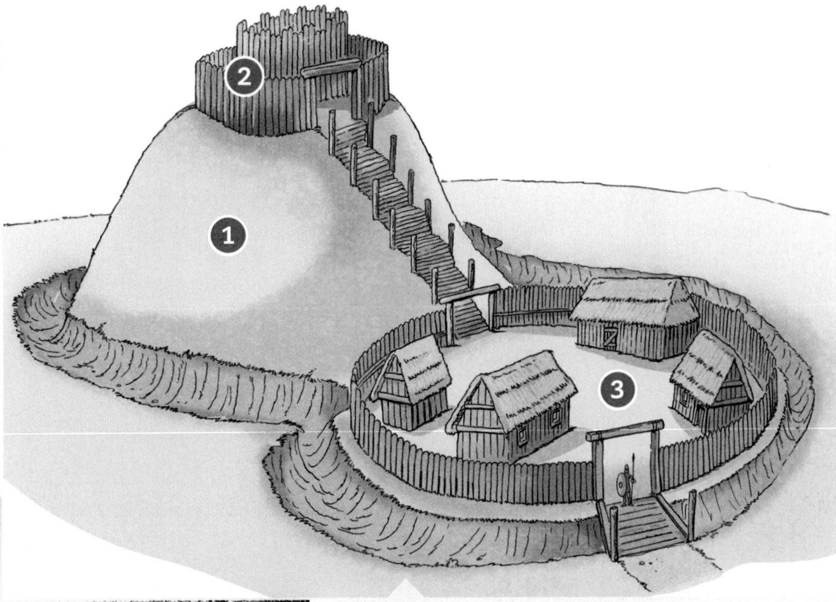

Motte and bailey castle

1. The lord got his peasants to build a small hill. This was a **motte**.
2. On top of the motte they built a wooden **fort**. From this lookout post, the lord's soldiers could see an enemy approaching.
3. Below the motte was a big enclosure. This was called the **bailey**. Most of the time, the lord and his soldiers lived in the bailey, but if an enemy attacked, they went up into the motte.

Can you see where the motte and bailey were in this picture? Why do you think the wooden fort here was replaced by a stone castle?

Stone castles

When a lord had control of the local countryside he replaced the motte and bailey castles with stone castles. The picture below shows a medieval stone castle.

A stone castle

1 The **keep** was the main building in the castle. This was where the lord and lady, their family and some soldiers lived. The windows were narrow slits. That made it difficult for the enemy to fire their arrows into the castle.

2 The **battlements** were at the top of the keep. All day long, soldiers kept guard on the battlements, watching for an enemy.

3 **Curtain walls** were the outer walls of the castle.

4 **Turrets** were strong towers along the walls.

5 The **drawbridge** was raised at night or if an enemy approached.

6 The **portcullis** was an iron grille that could be lowered in front of the castle gate.

7 The **ramparts** ran along the top of all the walls. They were wide enough for soldiers to walk along.

8 The **moat** was a ditch around the castle walls filled with water. Often it was part of a nearby river or stream.

9 In front of the keep was an open space called a **courtyard** or **bailey** (in Ireland it was also called a **bawn**).

10 The **latrines** were the toilets of the castle. They were usually in the corner of one of the towers in the keep.

Much of the life of the castle went on in the courtyard. It contained:

- The **stables**, where the knights' horses were kept
- **Pigeon houses**, as pigeons were used for food and to carry messages
- The **kitchens**, where food was prepared. It was safer to have the kitchen here than in the castle where it could cause a fire
- The **forge**, where the blacksmith worked. He made shoes for the horses and weapons for the soldiers
- The **well**, which was vital for fresh water

What was a siege?

When an enemy approached a castle, local people rushed inside the walls for safety. They often brought their animals with them. The castles were strong and at this time there was no gunpowder which could blast the walls. Often the enemy surrounded the castle and stopped anyone going in or out. This was called laying a **siege**. A castle could hold out for several months under siege, but gradually weapons were invented that could help take over a castle.

A siege at a castle

1 Attackers used a **battering ram** to pound the gate.

2 They used giant **catapults** to hurl huge boulders or fireballs over the walls.

3 A machine like a giant crossbow called a **ballista** was also used to fire large arrows.

4 **Siege towers** were like enclosed ladders; they were used to get near and scale the walls.

5 Sometimes the attackers dug **tunnels** under the walls, hoping they would collapse.

6 **Siege ladders** were used to try and climb the walls.

Trim castle in Co. Meath. Can you identify the labelled parts?

In the 1400s, gunpowder and the cannon were invented. They made it much easier to capture castles and after that castles were no longer used in war.

QUESTIONS

1 What was the first kind of castle? How was it built?

2 Explain each of the following:
   (a) Keep
   (b) Battlements
   (c) Drawbridge
   (d) Portcullis
   (e) Ramparts

3 List three activities you might have seen in a castle courtyard.

4 Why was a well vital for a castle?

5 Describe three ways an enemy might try to capture a castle. Which was the best, do you think?

6 Why were castles no longer used after the 1400s?

Did you know?

Castles were usually built near rivers or the sea, or on high ground. Why do you think this was?

What was it like to live in a medieval castle?

The lord of the castle

The most important person in a castle was the lord, who lived there with his family. The castle and all the land around it belonged to him. But if the lord betrayed the king he would lose it all.

The keep

The lord and his family lived in the **keep**. This picture shows the different parts of it.

Term

Keep
A large square tower lived in by the lord's family.

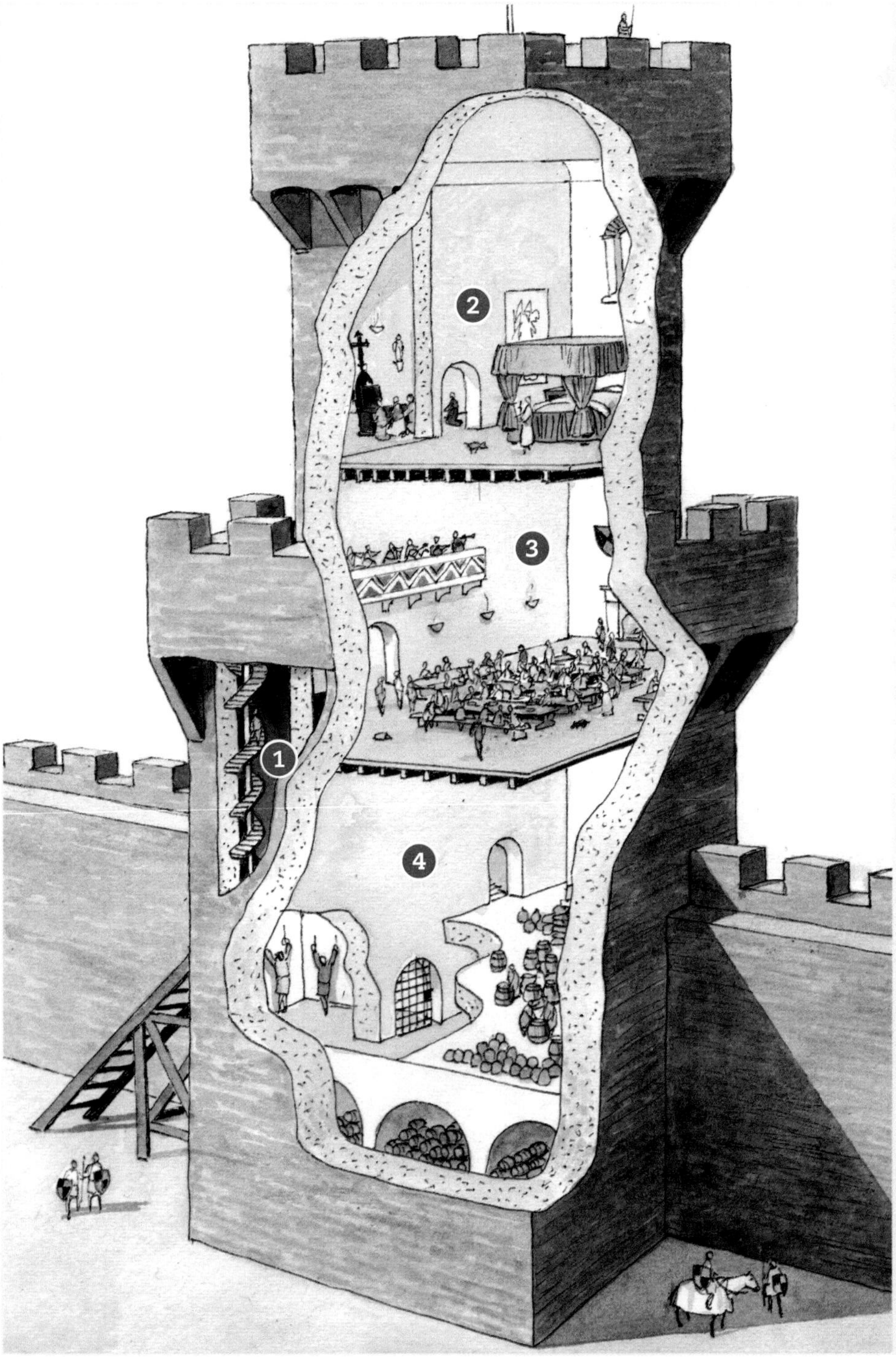

Inside the keep

1 The **stairs** were narrow. Castles had spiral staircases which circled to the right. Since most people hold their sword or spear in their right hand, that made it easier to fight going down the stairs than up.

2 On the **top floor** were the lord's private apartments, the **solar** and the chapel.

3 On the **middle floor** were the great hall and the minstrels' gallery.

4 On the **lower floor** there were storerooms for food and drink. There were also **dungeons** where soldiers captured in war were kept.

Term

Solar
The room which the lady of the castle used for work such as embroidery.

Rooms in the castle

On the top floor were the lord's private rooms. It was cold there because the windows had no glass, only shutters. They hung **tapestries** (carpets with pictures) on the walls and curtains around the beds to keep warm. Beside the bedroom was the **chapel**. Their priest said Mass there every morning.

The **great hall** took up the entire next floor. This is where everyone ate. Big fires at each end of the hall provided heating. Here the lord gave orders to his soldiers and collected rents and taxes from the peasants. Criminals were brought there to be tried.

Education

Up to the 1300s, most lords could barely read or write. They had no need to, because they kept a priest to do that for them. He also acted as schoolmaster to the lord's sons until they were seven years old. Good manners and fighting skills were thought of as more important than reading or writing.

Did you know?

When schools became common they were mostly for boys. They began at 5am and didn't finish until 6pm!

Food

Rich people ate a lot of meat. In the castle there were usually two meals a day. Dinner was at noon and supper was at about 4pm. But the amount of food they ate could be enormous. One meal might include duck, rabbit, hare, pork, boar, lamb and birds.

At a feast, important people sat at the top tables in the dining hall. The food was served on wooden plates or on big slices of bread called **trenchers**. They cut meat with their knives and ate with their fingers. They drank wine or ale.

Did you know?

In 1465, an English bishop invited 2,500 people to be his guests for a few days. Between them they ate 1,000 sheep, 4,000 pigeons and 2,000 pigs.

Clothes

Rich men wore long tunics. Shoes were made of leather and were pointed. The long toes were stuffed with horsehair. Women wore long dresses. It was fashionable for them to trail on the floor. They were usually made of wool, but Crusaders coming back from the Holy Land also brought silk. The headdress was called a **wimple**.

Entertainment

A favourite pastime for rich people was **hawking**. This was where a hawk was trained to sit on a person's hand and hunt songbirds, ducks and small animals. **Tournaments** were also popular. Knights acted out mock battles. They could fight in teams (**melées**). Or one knight could fight against another

Term

Hawking
Hunting with trained birds of prey (hawks).

Tournament
An event where knights fought mock battles with each other.

Hawking was a popular pastime

(**jousting**). Blunt swords and lances were used, but there were still many deaths. At night people often listened to **minstrels** singing and watched **jesters** doing tricks.

Jousting

The lady of the castle

In medieval times, the main role of a woman was to marry and have children. A noblewoman did not marry for love. Her parents arranged her marriage like a business contract. They would give her a **dowry**. It could be money, cattle or household utensils. In return, her husband would agree to support her for the rest of her life.

Term

Dowry
Money or goods that a woman's family gave to her husband when they got married.

Like their husbands, most noblewomen could not read or write, but they learned spinning and weaving, needlework, music and embroidery so that they could make beautiful tapestries. They also learned how to run a large household and how to use herbs to cure illnesses. When the lord was away his wife had to look after and defend the castle.

A noblewoman weaving. What are the other women doing?

QUESTIONS

1 Where did the lord and his family live?
2 What would you find in each of the following: (a) solar and (b) dungeon?
3 How was the lord of a castle educated?
4 What kind of food did rich people eat?
5 List three entertainments enjoyed by the people of the castle.
6 What was the main duty of a medieval noblewoman?
7 Explain how marriages were arranged.
8 List four things the lady of a castle had to see to.

The lord's soldiers

There were three kinds of soldier in the castle:

- **Foot soldiers** carried swords, daggers and shields.
- **Archers** used bows and arrows. Some had longbows and some crossbows, which were more powerful.
- **Knights** were the most important soldiers in a medieval army. They wore armour and rode horses.

The Bayeux Tapestry tells the story of how William, Duke of Normandy, became King of England in 1066. It is kept in the Bayeux museum in France. What kind of weapons can you see in this picture? Why, do you think, did the Normans win this battle?

The knight

In battle, each knight carried a lance, a sword, a mace and a battle-axe. You can see some of their weapons in the pictures. Only the sons of lords could afford to be knights because their horses and armour were so expensive.

A knight dressed for battle

1 Helmet
2 Lance
3 Visor to protect the eyes
4 Sword
5 Shield
6 Mace

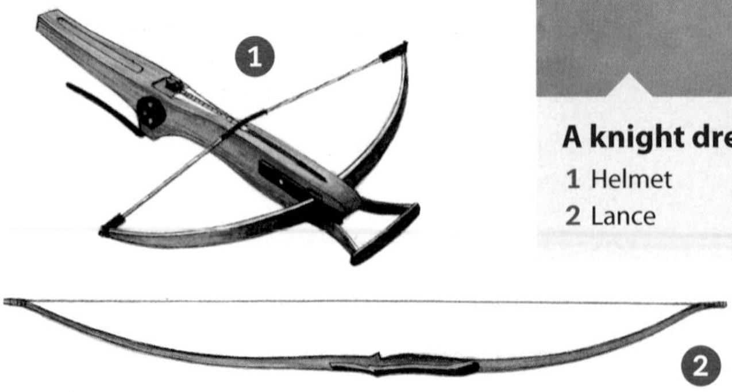

Weapons used by archers

1 Crossbow
2 Longbow

How did a boy become a knight?

It took thirteen years of training for a boy to become a knight. There were three stages:

- **The page:** When a lord's son was seven years old, his father sent him to another castle to be a page. He learned how to ride a horse and use a sword. He also learned to sing, dance and have good manners. He served the lady of the castle at table and helped the lord to dress.
- **The squire:** When the boy was fourteen years old, he became a squire. He learned to fight on horseback. If there was a war he went with his lord. He carried his lord's weapons and helped him with his armour and his horse.
- **The knight:** When the squire was twenty-one years old, he became a knight. The ceremony at which that happened was called **dubbing**. The squire spent the previous night praying in the church. In the morning, he knelt before his lord who put on his armour, piece by piece. The squire then swore to uphold the code of **chivalry**. That was a promise to be loyal to God, to protect women and children, and never to run away in a battle. Then his lord touched him on the shoulder with his sword and said 'Arise, Sir Knight'.

Did you know?

So many knights were killed in tournaments that the Church banned them. Until 1300 knights who died in them were refused a Christian burial.

Term

Chivalry
A code of honour that said that a knight should be brave, love God and protect women and children.

Do you understand these key terms?

motte	**ramparts**	**dungeon**	**jousting**
bailey	**moat**	**tapestry**	**dowry**
keep	**siege**	**trencher**	**archer**
battlements	**battering ram**	**wimple**	**page**
curtain walls	**catapult**	**hawking**	**squire**
turret	**ballista**	**tournament**	**dubbing**
drawbridge	**siege tower**	**melée**	**chivalry**
portcullis	**solar**		

QUESTIONS

1. Name the three kinds of soldier you would have found in a castle and list the weapons each of them carried.
2. What is the Bayeux Tapestry? Where is it kept?
3. What was a squire?
4. What was dubbing?
5. What was a tournament? Explain the two types of mock battles fought by knights.

People in History

1 **Write about the lord in a medieval castle.**

Sample Answer

The lord's story

Castle

The lord lived in the keep with his family. When times became more peaceful he lived in a manor house. The castle had three storeys. Food and weapons were stored in the basement. On the ground floor, there was the great hall. The lord entertained here and tried criminals. The upper floor was the family's private quarters.

Manor farm

The lord owned one or many farms called by manors.

Hints

Draw a diagram of a manor farm here and label it.

Employees

The lord had many people to help him run his estates. He had a bailiff to help collect rents and stop crime on the estate. His serfs belonged to him and had to work for him. His freemen paid him rent, but could move away if they wished.

Food

The lord ate mainly meat and some pottage (vegetable soup with porridge). He had two meals a day, at about 12pm and 4pm, in the great hall. He liked to drink wine or ale.

Education

Most lords could barely read or write. Boys were educated at home by a priest. It was more important for a lord to learn to have good manners and to be able to fight. He trained for thirteen years to be a knight. He was first a page and then a squire before being dubbed a knight. He swore to follow the code of chivalry. He had to be brave, love God and protect women and children.

Pastimes

The lord spent a lot of his time at war, but when he was free he liked to fish and go hawking. This was where a hawk was trained to sit on the lord's hand and hunt other birds. He also liked to take part in tournaments (mock fights) and listen to court jesters and minstrels in the evening.

2 **Write about a knight in medieval times. Use these headings: armour and weapons; training; chivalry; food; dress; pastimes.**

Chapter 3

Life in a Medieval Town

Key Learning Objectives

- **What was it like to live in a medieval town?**
- **Who lived in the town?**
- **How did a boy become a master craftsman?**

What was it like to live in a medieval town?

Medieval towns grew up around many big castles or on rivers. Most towns had fewer than 1,000 people.

Arriving in a medieval town

When you came near a town the first thing you could see were the huge **high walls**. You could only enter the town through one of the **gates**. Strangers were stopped and asked their business. Anyone who wanted to sell goods in the town had to pay a **toll**. At sunset the gates were closed and not opened again until dawn.

Term

Toll
A tax that traders had to pay at the town's gates.

Inside the town

Look at the picture on the following page and you will see some of the important buildings and places in a medieval town.

Only the main street was paved with stones or wooden planks. It was often called **High Street**. Other streets were narrow lanes. They were not paved so they usually became very muddy in winter.

Every town had its **parish church**. It was made of stone and towered above the other buildings.

Did you know?

The names of the gates still survive in modern place names. For example, in Dublin, St James' Gate, where Guinness is made, is the site of a medieval gate.

Houses

Most other buildings in a medieval town were made of wood. Rich merchants had their houses on the High Street. These had three storeys, each storey leaning out over the one below, which must have made the street dark. Some streets were so narrow that two people could shake hands with each other out of the windows of the third storey! Some houses had a long back garden where the family grew vegetables and kept pigs, hens or even a cow. Craftspeople lived over their shops. As you moved away from the centre, the houses became smaller and the people poorer.

Did you know?

Only churches and important buildings like the town hall were made of stone. Ordinary houses usually had wooden walls.

A medieval town

1 High walls
2 Gates
3 High Street
4 Parish church
5 Rich merchant's house
6 Market square, where markets were held
7 Fair green

Fairs

The highlight of the year was the annual fair. It could last up to three weeks and was held on the **fair green** outside the town walls. Merchants came from all over the world. They sold silk and spices from Asia, brightly dyed woollen cloth from Italy and furs from Russia. Craftspeople bought things they needed for their work. Acrobats, musicians and jugglers entertained the crowds.

tr
sam
have st
after trade
Fishmonger

Curfew

Because the houses were made of wood, there were strict rules about fire safety. At sunset, church bells rang out to mark the arrival of the **curfew**. That meant that all fires in the town had to be put out. The word curfew means 'cover the fire'.

Term

Curfew
The time when all fires had to be out in the town.

A narrow street in the centre of Shrewsbury, England. Originally the lane was not paved, but just a mud track. What does this picture tell us about a medieval town?

Dirt

Towns were very dirty. There were no sewers. An open drain ran down the middle of the street. People threw everything into it, including the contents of their chamber pots. People walking by had to be careful that they didn't get something nasty on their heads!

Disease

People seldom washed and they all had fleas. Many suffered from skin diseases. A common one was **leprosy**. Sores broke out all over a person's body. Lepers were not allowed to mix with others. They had to live in a special place, usually outside the town walls. This is how Leopardstown, near Dublin, got its name.

Did you know?

People of the same ... ade liked to live in the ... area, so you often ... reets named ... s, such as ... Street.

PART 1

The Black Death. People did not realise that the disease could be passed on so easily. They often left dead bodies in the street to be picked up by carts

QUESTIONS

1 Name two kinds of places where towns grew up in the Middle Ages.
2 What was a toll?
3 Where in a medieval town would you find the homes of rich merchants?
4 What was a curfew? Why was it imposed on medieval towns?
5 Why were diseases common in medieval towns? What disease appeared in 1347?
6 What caused the Black Death?
7 Which buildings in a medieval town were made of stone?
8 Why were fairs so popular? Give two reasons.

Who lived in the town?

A charter from the king

A **charter** was a legal document in which the king agreed to let a town run its own affairs. Under the charter, the citizens could elect a council or **corporation** to run their town. They could also hold fairs. In return, the town would pay the king or local lord a tax.

Citizens and slaves

In a medieval town, everyone had their place. People mixed with their own kind. The rulers of the town were the members of the **guilds**. They were the citizens who could vote for the corporation. But most townspeople were not citizens. They were 'unfree'. Up to AD 1000, it was even common for people to be sold as slaves.

Term

Charter
A legal document granted by the king that allowed people to run their own towns.

Guild
An organisation that every craftsperson had to belong to. Each guild controlled its own craft.

Craftspeople

The **craftspeople** made the things that people needed. Even the smallest town had over thirty different craftspeople. Some of them are listed in the box. Many of the first surnames came from the names of crafts that people did. For example, Robert the smith became known as Robert Smith.

Term

Craftsperson
A person who has learned a craft.

What kind of craft work are these people doing?

A medieval town had lots of different craftspeople:

- Shoemakers
- Weavers (made cloth)
- Tailors (made clothes)
- Carpenters
- Blacksmiths
- Coopers (made barrels)
- Bakers
- Butchers
- Millers (made flour)
- Fishmongers
- Masons (builders who used stone)
- Tanners (made leather)
- Chandlers (made candles)
- Apothecaries (pharmacists)

How many surnames can you find in this list?

Guilds

Every craftsperson who worked in a town had to belong to a guild. There was a bakers' guild, a carpenters' guild and so on. Each guild regulated its trade. For example, the guild set examinations to make sure the craftspeople were good at their trade. It set standards of work and decent wages. It looked after old or sick members and paid for their funerals. We know there were many craftswomen. However, many women were only allowed to become members of a guild if their husbands had died and they wanted to carry on his trade.

How did a boy become a master craftsman?

A boy who wanted to practise a craft went through three stages:

- The **apprentice**: At twelve, he became an apprentice. For seven years he lived in the house of a master craftsman to learn the trade. While there, he worked without pay.
- The **journeyman**: After seven years the apprentice became a journeyman. Now he was paid for his work. He could leave his old master and travel around, looking for better wages. We know that skilled masons travelled all over Europe, building churches.

A meeting of the guild of fish-sellers in Venice, Italy, in the fourteenth century

- The **master:** To become a master craftsman a journeyman had to produce a **'masterpiece'**. Then he could have his own workshop and sell his goods in the town. A carpenter might make a table or a tailor a coat. Along with the masterpiece, the man had to give a large payment to the guild. Most journeymen could not afford this, so they never got to be masters.

Do you understand these key terms?

fair green	**Black Death**	**craftsperson**	**journeyman**
toll	**plague**	**guild**	**master**
curfew	**charter**	**apprentice**	**masterpiece**
leprosy	**corporation**		

QUESTIONS

1. What was a charter and who granted it?
2. What was the name of the group of people who ran a medieval town?
3. Who were the citizens in a town?
4. How many different types of crafts and trades were carried out in even small towns?
5. What was a guild and what did it do?
6. How did a boy become a master in a guild?
7. What trades do you think were carried on in Cook Street and Winetavern Street in Dublin?

People in History

Write an account of the life of a craftsman in a medieval town.

Use the plan below as a guide.

Hint

You can use the material in Chapter 1 to write about pastimes.

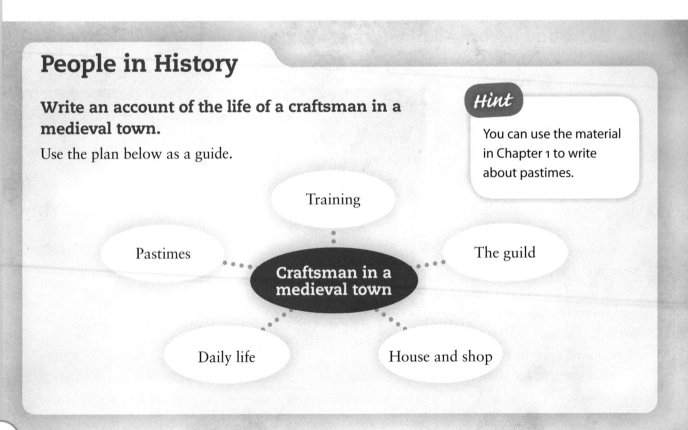

Craftsman in a medieval town

- Training
- The guild
- House and shop
- Daily life
- Pastimes

Chapter 4

Religion in the Middle Ages

Key Learning Objectives

- How was the Church in Europe organised?
- What were Romanesque churches?
- What were Gothic churches?
- What was it like to be a monk in a medieval monastery?
- What were friars?

In the Middle Ages, most of Europe was Christian. People could not imagine a world without God. Even rulers believed they would go to hell if they did not obey the Church's teachings.

How was the Church in Europe organised?

The leader of the Church in western Europe was the **pope**, who lived in Rome. At local level, the Church was divided into **parishes** and **dioceses**. The parish priest ran the parish and the bishop ran the diocese.

Usually the manor farm was also a parish and the local priest baptised, married and buried everyone in the parish. Often the priest was the only person in a parish who could read or write. So he helped people with legal documents and advised them on all kinds of problems. Bishops were rich and owned a lot of land. In each diocese, the bishop built a big church called a **cathedral**. Many churches were very impressive in the Middle Ages. They were meant to help people think of heaven.

What were Romanesque churches?

Around AD 1000 Christians began to build big stone churches. The first stone churches were built in a style called **Romanesque**. The picture on the next page shows Clonfert Cathedral, Co. Galway. It is a typical Romanesque-style church. The round arches and decorations over the doors tell you that this is a Romanesque church.

A Romanesque church was dark and gloomy inside. The roof was held up with heavy round columns and thick walls. That meant that all windows had to be small, so little light got in.

Clonfert Cathedral, Co. Galway. How do you know that this is a Romanesque church?

Did you know?

This is what you will see in a Romanesque church:

- Round arches
- Thick, round columns
- Dark interiors

The interior of a Romanesque church

What were Gothic churches?

Later, a new style of architecture became popular. It was called the **Gothic** style. Gothic cathedrals usually have spires and towers. The arches over the windows and doors are pointed. There are often stone statues carved into the doorways.

There are arches on the outside to support the weight of the roof. These are called **flying buttresses**. Can you see them in the picture below?

This meant that inside the church the walls could be held up by slim columns. These churches also had big windows with beautiful stained glass. When the sun shone through the glass, the whole church glowed with light and colour.

Did you know?

This is what you will see in a Gothic church:

- Spires
- Pointed arches
- Slim columns and stained glass windows
- Flying buttresses
- Stone statues over doors and windows

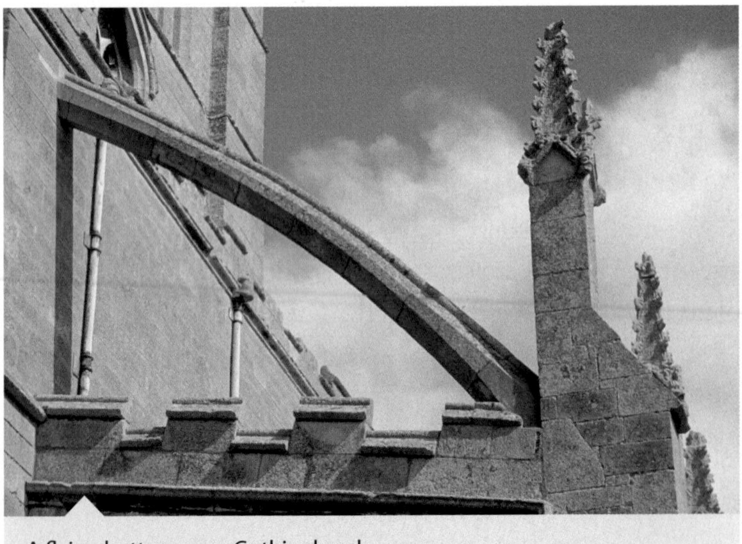

A flying buttress on a Gothic church

'Rose' patterns in the stained glass windows were popular

QUESTIONS

1 What did a parish priest do in the Middle Ages?

2 Explain the words 'diocese' and 'cathedral'.

3 Which style of church developed in Europe around AD 1000? List three of its main features.

4 Name the other style of medieval church building. List four of its features.

SOURCE QUESTION

› Look at the picture and answer the following questions.

(a) In which style is this church built?

(b) List two features which support your answer.

Monasteries

Many people liked to get away from the crowd and pray. They set up communities of men or women which were called **monasteries** and **convents**. The men were called monks and the women nuns. They followed strict rules. They had to pray regularly, fast and obey the abbot or the abbess who was the head of the monastery (or **abbey**, as it was sometimes called). There were different orders of monks and nuns such as **Benedictines, Cistercians** and **Poor Clares**.

Monasteries were used as inns and hospitals, and poor people often went there for help. Boys and sometimes girls were educated in monasteries. Part of a monk's job was to read and copy books by hand in a special room called the **scriptorium**.

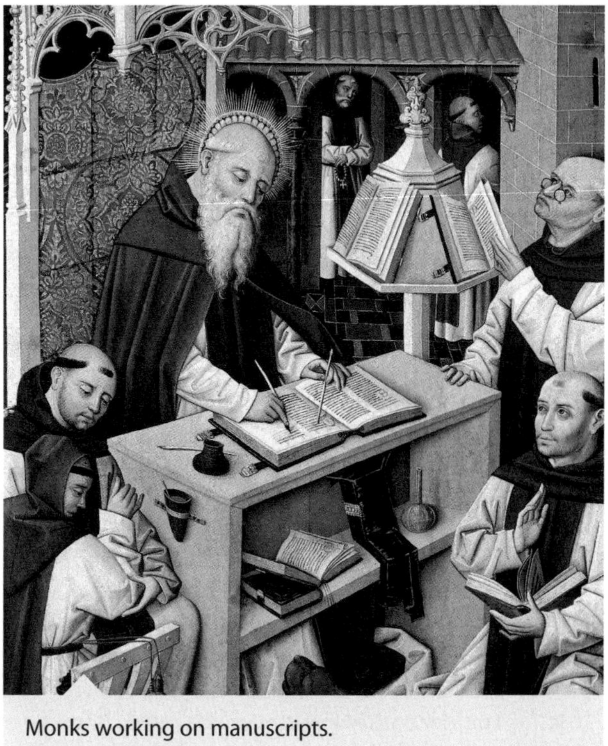

Monks working on manuscripts. What was a manuscript?

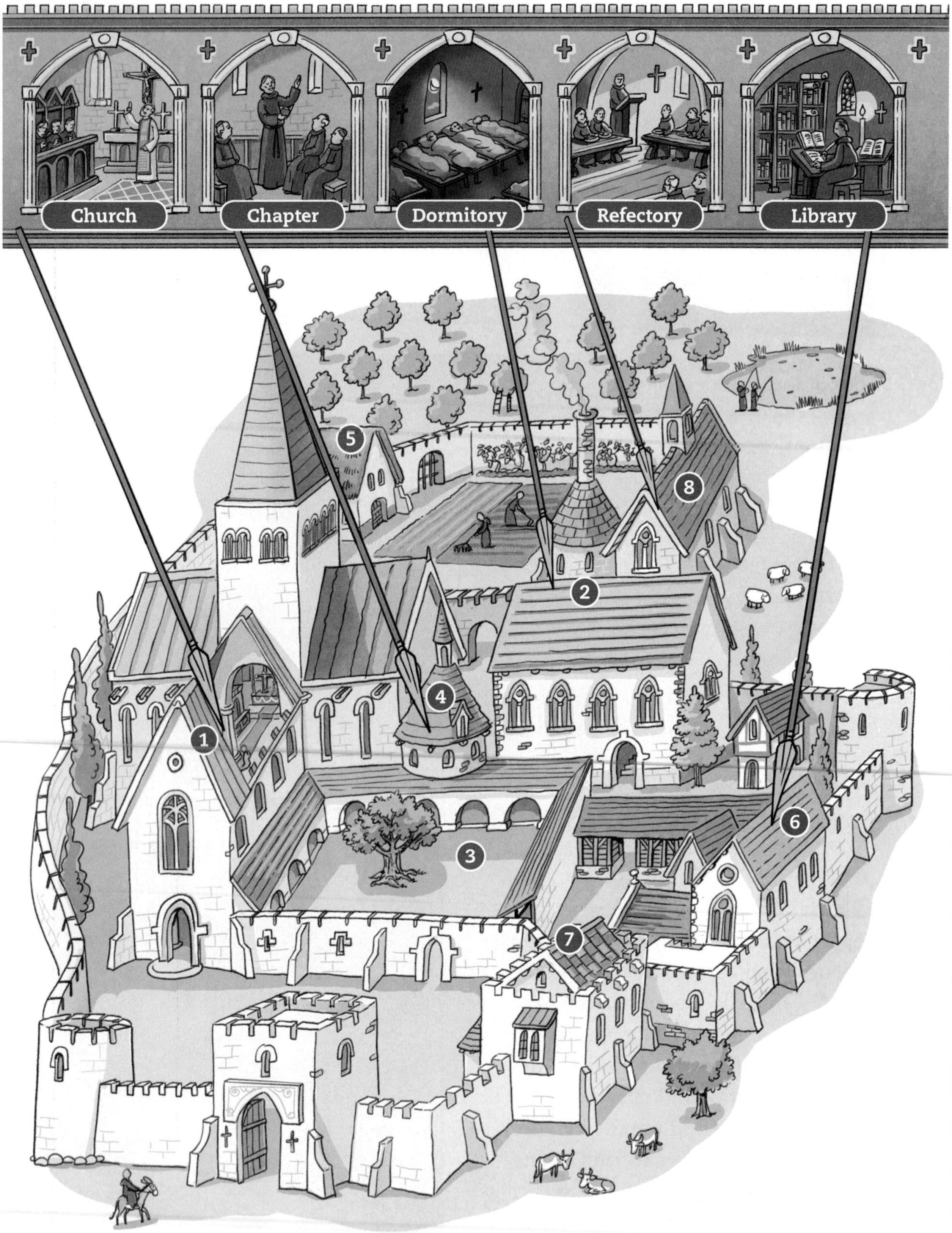

A medieval monastery

1 The **church** where the monks prayed seven times every day.
2 The **dormitory** where the monks slept.
3 The **cloisters** where the monks walked and prayed.
4 The **chapter house** where the monks met to discuss the business of the monastery and elect the abbot.
5 The **infirmary** where the sick were nursed.
6 The **library** where monks studied. It might include a **scriptorium** where they copied manuscripts.
7 The **guest house** where the monks gave food to poor people and travellers.
8 The **refectory** where the monks ate their meals.

A cloister. Is the architecture Gothic or Romanesque?

Term

Cloister
A square in the centre of the monastery surrounded by covered walkways where monks would walk and pray.

What was it like to be a monk in a medieval monastery?

Becoming a monk

- When a boy joined a monastery he was called a **novice**. He had to learn the rules and see if the life suited him. If the abbot thought the novice would make a good monk, he let him take **solemn vows**.
- These were promises of **poverty** (he must not own anything), **chastity** (he must not marry) and **obedience** (he must do what the abbot told him).
- Then his hair was cut in a **tonsure**. This was a bald patch in the middle of his head. It showed that a man was a monk.

A monk's tonsure. What is the monk writing with?

Daily life in a medieval monastery

The Rule of St Benedict, which most monasteries followed, laid down a strict timetable for the monks.

3am	Day begins. The monks get out of bed to sing **matins** (morning prayers) in the church
4–6am	Return to bed for a brief sleep
6am	Silent prayer
7am	Breakfast, like all meals, was eaten in strict silence
8–9.30am	Work in the fields or in the library
10am	High Mass in the church
11am–2pm	Work again
2pm	Dinner was the main meal of the day
2.30pm	Reading
3–5pm	Work
5pm	**Vespers** (evening prayers)
6pm	Supper
8pm	**Compline** (night prayer) and retire to bed

As you can see, the monk's day was divided between prayer, work and study. Every monastery grew its own food, made its own furniture and provided for itself. Each monk had his own special job:

- The **abbot** was head of the monastery and was elected by the monks.
- When he was away on business his place was taken by the **prior**.
- The **almoner** looked after the poor when they visited.
- The **infirmarian** looked after the sick and kept a record of the herbs used in the monastery.
- The **librarian** looked after the library.
- The **hosteller** looked after travellers.

What were friars?

If people needed the help of monks or nuns, they had to go to them. But around 1200, a different kind of monk appeared. They were called **friars.** Friars travelled from place to place, working with the poor. One group of friars was called the **Franciscans** after its founder, St Francis of Assisi. Other groups were called **Dominicans** and **Augustinians**.

Ross Errilly friary, Co. Galway. A place where friars lived was called a friary. Most friaries were in towns. Why do you think this was?

Do you understand these key terms?

parish	**dormitory**	**solemn vows**	**prior**
diocese	**cloisters**	**matins**	**almoner**
cathedral	**chapter house**	**vespers**	**infirmarian**
Romanesque	**infirmary**	**compline**	**hosteller**
Gothic	**novice**	**abbot**	**friar**

QUESTIONS

1. Name the man whose rules most medieval monks followed.
2. In a medieval monastery, say what each of the following was for: (a) cloister, (b) library, (c) dormitory and (d) chapter house.
3. Describe how a boy became a monk.
4. In a monk's day, what were (a) matins, (b) vespers and (c) compline?
5. What did (a) the abbot, (b) the prior and (c) the almoner do?
6. Who were the friars and how were they different from the monks?
7. Name two groups of friars.

People in History

Write about the life of a monk in a medieval monastery.

Use the plan below as a guide.

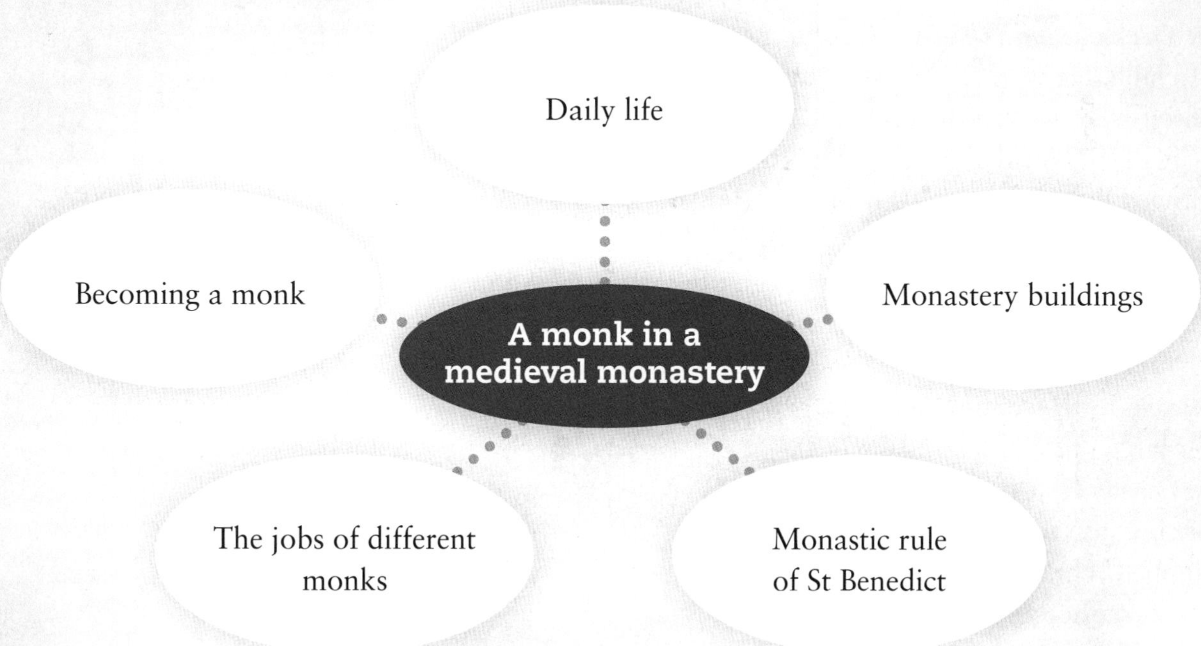

Tip

Remember, it is a good idea to draw diagrams and pictures in your answer. This will gain you a lot of marks.

Chapter 5

How the Normans Changed Ireland

Key Learning Objectives

- Who were the Normans?
- How did they come to Ireland?
- What changes did the Normans bring?

Who were the Normans?

The **Normans** brought the **feudal system** to Ireland in the 1200s. They were descended from Vikings and settled in Normandy, in France. After 1066 they ruled England.

How did they come to Ireland?

The Gaelic king of Leinster, Dermot MacMurrough, invited the Normans to Ireland. He wanted their help to defeat the other Gaelic kings and make himself High King of Ireland.

In 1169, Norman lords arrived in Wexford. The king of England, Henry II, followed three years later. He had an army of 4,000 soldiers and 500 knights. The Gaelic lords swore loyalty to Henry. They hoped he would protect them from the Norman lords who were beginning to plunder and capture lands in Ireland. Henry declared that he was the Lord of Ireland.

After Henry left, the Norman lords went on taking over large parts of Ireland. They easily beat the Gaelic Irish because they were better equipped. The Normans had knights on horses with heavy armour, lances and swords. They had archers who showered the Gaelic armies with thousands of arrows.

You can see the areas the Normans conquered on the map opposite.

A section from the Bayeux Tapestry showing a Norman sailing fleet on their way to England

What changes did the Normans bring?

1 Norman castles and manors

When the Normans conquered an area, they built a **motte and bailey castle** (see page 77). Later, Norman lords built stone castles like the one at Carrickfergus on the next page. They usually built them on high places or near rivers. Four of the biggest Norman castles are Dublin, Limerick, Trim and Carrickfergus.

In the 1400s and 1500s, the Normans and the Gaelic Irish built smaller castles. They are called **tower houses** and you can see one in the picture below. In all, the Normans built over 2,000 castles in Ireland.

Near their castles, the Normans set up manor farms. They encouraged peasants to come to Ireland from England and Wales and to farm the land like they did at home.

Do you know any place in Ireland with the word 'manor' in its name?

A tower house

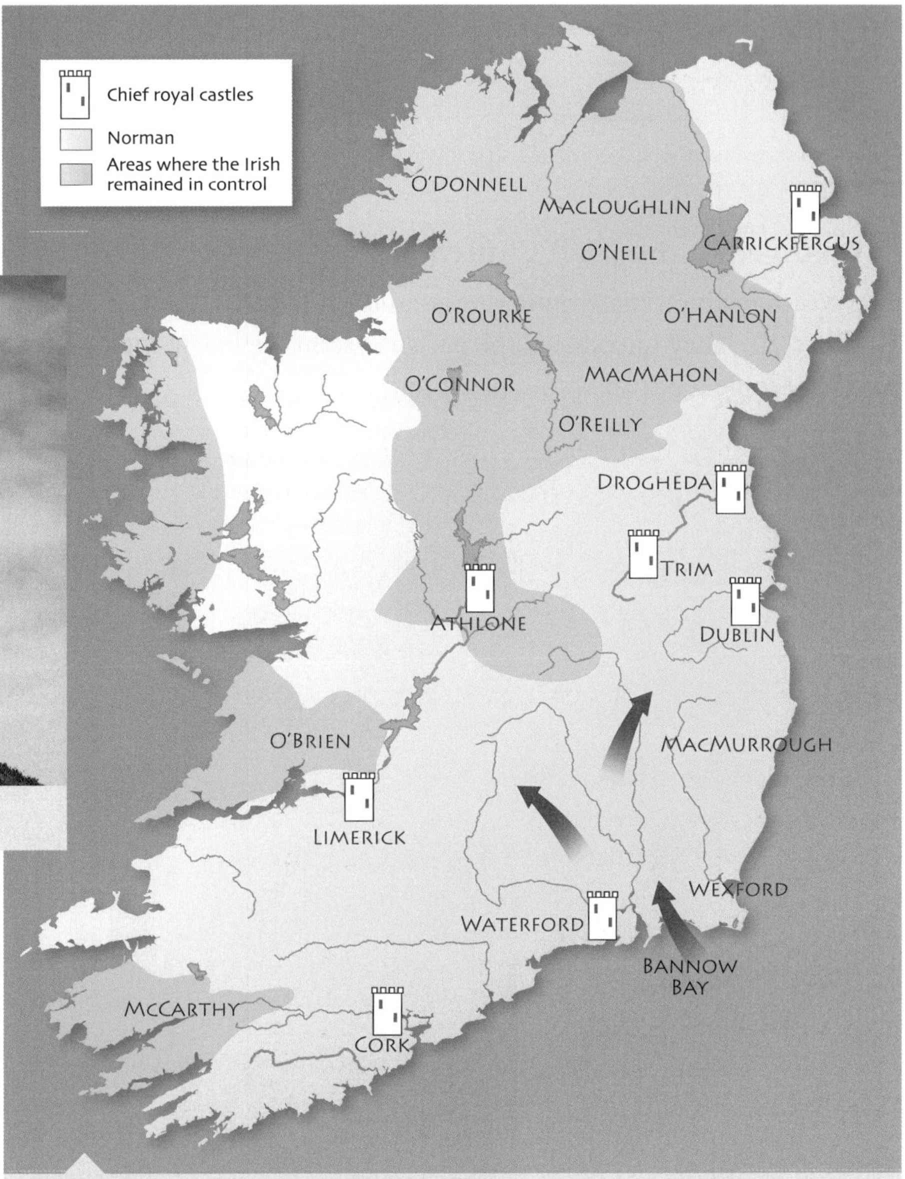

Look at the route of the Normans through Ireland in the twelfth century. Where did they conquer first? Why was this?

Carrickfergus Castle. What part of Ireland is this in? Why did the Normans need to build a strong castle here?

2 Changes in the Irish Church

The Normans built many monasteries and cathedrals. Most of them were in the **Gothic** style. They introduced the **parish system** we know today. Each manor farm would become a parish with a priest and a church.

Dunbrody Abbey in Co. Wexford. What style of architecture can you see here?

3 New Irish towns

When the Normans arrived in Ireland they found very few towns. The Vikings who had come to Ireland in the 800s had built Dublin, Waterford, Wexford and Limerick, but most Gaelic people lived in scattered farms.

The Normans thought towns were important because people could trade in them. Norman lords set up many towns. You can see them on the map here.

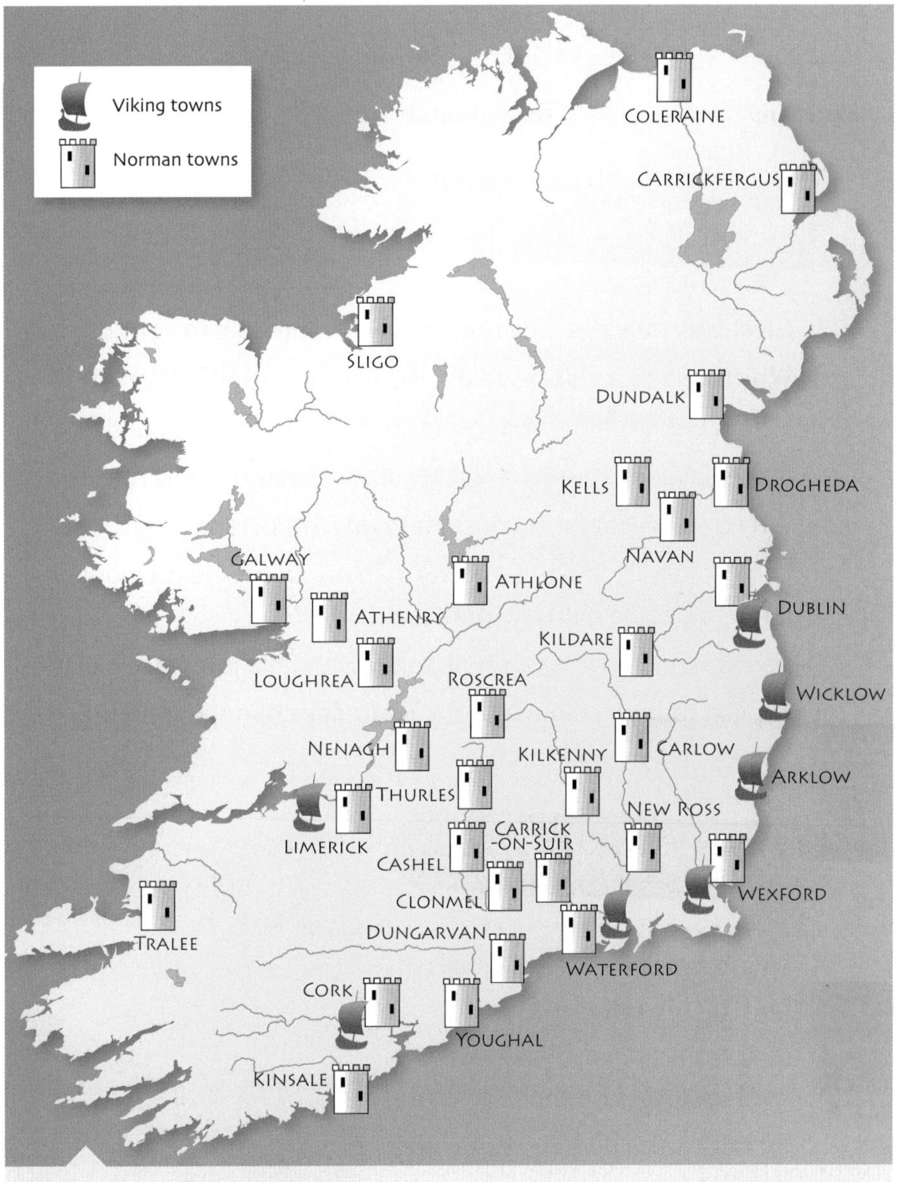

This map shows Viking towns and Norman towns

4 Norman ancestors and names

The Normans brought in farmers, craftsmen and merchants from England, Wales and France. New **surnames** appeared. These people are the ancestors of many people in Ireland today.

5 New language

When the Normans arrived, everyone in Ireland spoke Gaelic. The Normans and the settlers that followed them were the first people to use a form of English here.

6 Parliaments

The Normans set up the first **parliament** in Ireland.

7 Law

The Gaelic Irish had their own system of laws, called the Brehon laws. Under it, all land belonging to a family was divided among the sons of the family. Under Norman law, the eldest son inherited his father's entire land.

8 Farming

The main activity of Gaelic farmers was tending herds of cattle. The Normans brought new methods of farming. They tilled the land and grew wheat, oats, barley and vegetables.

> **Did you know?**
>
> **Fitz** was the Norman word for 'son of'. So, all names beginning with Fitz meant 'son of'. This is a list of some Norman names in Ireland: Barry, Bermingham, Burke, Cleary, Fitzgerald, Fleming, Nugent, Power, Prendergast, Plunkett, Roche, Smith, Taylor, Walsh.

Do you understand these key terms?

Normans **tower house** **parish system** **parliament**

QUESTIONS

1 Give three reasons why the Normans were able to conquer Ireland.
2 Which two types of castle did the Normans build? Name one castle they built.
3 What changes did the Normans make to the Irish Church?
4 Is the Bayeux Tapestry a reliable source? Why or why not?
5 Why did the Normans consider towns important?
6 Look at the list of names of Norman origin on the previous page. Can you think of five famous people with any of these names?
7 Can you find any names here to do with (a) a job or (b) a place?
8 Explain four ways in which the Normans changed Ireland.

SOURCE QUESTION

› This is a picture of a small hill built by the Normans.

(a) In your opinion, what was built on top of this hill?

(b) Why is the building not there any more?

EXAM QUESTIONS

1 In the medieval monastery what was the role of the abbot?
2 Explain two of the following terms related to the knight in the Middle Ages:
› page › dubbing › chivalry › jousting.
3 Give two reasons why the annual fair was popular during medieval times.
4 Write an account of two of the following:
(a) Duties of the lady of the castle
(b) Training of the medieval craftsman
(c) Life of a serf on a medieval manor. (HL)

PART 1

Section 5

The Renaissance

Chapter 1

What Was the Renaissance?

Key Learning Objectives

- What was the Renaissance?
- Why did the Renaissance start in Italy?
- Why were patrons important?
- Who were the great patrons and what did they do?

What was the Renaissance?

The **Renaissance** started about 1400. People began to change the way they looked at the world around them. They questioned the old ideas of the Middle Ages and they took a new interest in the achievements of the Ancient Greeks and Romans. The Renaissance lasted over 200 years. Many historians believe that it marks the beginning of the modern world.

Term

Renaissance
A time when people began to take a new interest in the world of Ancient Greece and Rome.

Did you know?

The word Renaissance means **'rebirth'**. Historians call this age the Renaissance because it was almost as if the Greeks and Romans had come back to life.

Humanism

This renewed interest in ancient learning was known as **humanism**. The same word has been used to describe the Renaissance way of looking at the world. Humanism puts human beings at the centre of everything. Medieval people thought that life here on earth mattered less than life in heaven after a person died. People in the Renaissance were interested in all aspects of life on earth. They studied and painted the natural world, and especially human beings who were part of it.

Sandro Botticelli's *La Primavera* (Spring). How would you know that this is a Renaissance painting?

Why did the Renaissance start in Italy?

1 The old Roman Empire in Italy

Italy had been the centre of the old Roman Empire. In every town in Italy there were ruins of old Roman buildings. These reminded the Italians of the achievements of their ancestors. The Italian language was based on Latin, the language of the Romans. It was easy for Italians to read books by Roman writers.

2 The influence of Greek scholars

In 1453, the Turks conquered the Greek city of Constantinople. **Greek scholars** escaped to Italy. They brought many Greek manuscripts with them. This made many Italians interested in Greek ideas as well.

3 Wealthy Italian merchants

Italian merchants were rich. They brought silks and spices from Asia and sold them to the rest of Europe. This trade made them immensely wealthy. As a result, they had money to spend on grand buildings and beautiful pictures and statues.

4 The influence of new ideas

Trade brought Italian merchants into contact with people such as the Arabs and the Chinese, who had much more advanced civilisations than Europeans. These merchants brought home many ideas from their travels and became more critical of the old ways of doing things in Europe.

5 Independent city-states

In the rest of Europe, kings and nobles ruled over the people. But Italy had no overall king. It was divided into **city-states** and each city had its own ruler. The citizens were very independent and were open to new ideas.

Here are the most important cities. Can you find them on the map?

- The pope ruled **Rome**.
- The Medicis, a wealthy banking family, ruled **Florence**.
- The Sforza, a military family, ruled **Milan**.
- In **Venice**, the richest families elected a council to run their city.

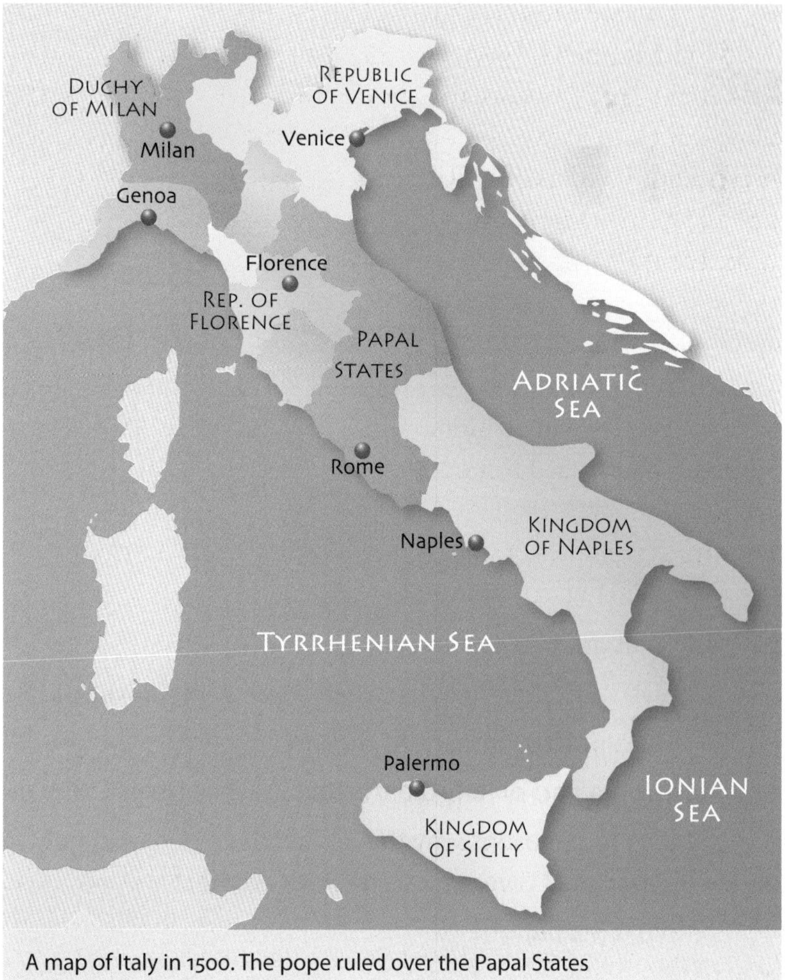

A map of Italy in 1500. The pope ruled over the Papal States

Why were patrons important?

A **patron** is a person who commissions an artist to produce a work of art. In Italy, at the time of the Renaissance, many people and cities had enough money to become patrons.

Florence was the richest city in Italy in 1400. The people there made their money from the wool trade and from banking. Florentines were very proud of their city. Because they were so rich, they could afford to pay for the best architects, painters and sculptors to make it beautiful.

This is where the Renaissance started.

Term

Patron
A person who pays an artist to produce a work of art.

Florence in the 1500s. How can you tell from this picture that Florence was a wealthy city? Give two reasons for your answer.

Did you know?

Merchants from Florence travelled around Europe buying high quality wool. In florence local people wove it into colourful cloth. The merchants then sold the cloth to kings and nobles at a huge profit.

QUESTIONS

1 What does 'Renaissance' mean?
2 Give two differences between the way medieval and Renaissance people thought.
3 Explain what 'humanism' means.
4 In what part of Italy did the Renaissance begin? Why did it start there?
5 Give four reasons why the Renaissance began in Italy. Which do you consider the most important? Give reasons for your answer.
6 What is a patron?

Special Study: Cosimo de Medici (1389–1464)

The richest bankers in Florence were the **Medicis**. Cosimo de Medici was the head of the family in the middle of the fifteenth century (1400s). He was a businessman who made a great fortune. He was also a great Renaissance patron.

Cosimo de Medici was a great Renaissance patron

Cosimo and literature

Cosimo admired the writings of Greek and Roman scholars.

- He sent agents around Europe to search monastery libraries for old, forgotten manuscripts. If they found any, they were to copy them and carry the copies back to Florence.
- He built a library to house his manuscripts. It became the largest library in Europe. It was also the first public library because it was open to everyone.
- He also set up an academy where scholars could study manuscripts. He called it the **Platonic Academy** after the Greek writer Plato.

Cosimo and the arts

Cosimo was a great patron of the arts.

- Cosimo invited artists and inventors to stay in his home and paid them to work for him.
- He also paid for many public buildings. For example, he paid a famous architect, **Brunelleschi**, to build a parish church in Florence in the new Renaissance style.

Cosimo – ruler of Florence

At this time, Florence was a **republic**. That means the people elected the government. But Cosimo used his money to make sure his friends were elected to the government. That made him the real ruler of Florence.

- He ruled the city for thirty years.
- He made alliances with other cities. These alliances kept the peace between the different states of Italy and allowed trade to flourish.
- Under his rule, Florence became the cultural capital of Europe.

The Basilica (large church) of San Lorenzo in Florence, designed by Brunelleschi. In what ways does the architecture copy the ideas of the Romans?

Lorenzo the Magnificent (1444–1492)

Cosimo's grandson, Lorenzo, took over when he was only twenty years old. He was a great sportsman, who also wrote poetry and was a patron of the arts. Because of this he was called 'Lorenzo the Magnificent'. Among the artists he supported were Michelangelo and Leonardo da Vinci, whom we will study in detail in the next chapter.

Popes as patrons

Soon after Lorenzo died, the king of France invaded Italy. This started a war that lasted for many years. Florence was heavily involved and its wealth was reduced. After that the popes became the main patrons in Italy. Two popes who were patrons were **Julius II** and **Leo X**. As we will see, they employed artists to build great churches and to make them beautiful with pictures and statues.

Pope Julius II was also a patron of the arts. Portrait painting became very popular in the Renaissance

Do you understand these key terms?

Renaissance **humanism** **city-state** **patron**

QUESTIONS

1 List four ways in which Cosimo de Medici acted as a patron of the arts.
2 How did Cosimo rule Florence?
3 How did Lorenzo de Medici get his nickname, 'Lorenzo the Magnificent'?
4 Why did Florence's wealth decline after Lorenzo's death?
5 When Florence became poorer, who became the main patrons of the arts in Italy?
6 Name one Renaissance patron and write an account of his activities.

Chapter 2
Renaissance Painting

Madonna and Child by Raphael

Key Learning Objectives

- **How did painting change in the Renaissance?**
- **Who were the great artists and what did they do?**
  - **Leonardo da Vinci**
  - **Raphael**
  - **Pieter Bruegel**

How did painting change in the Renaissance?

Artists began to make pictures more lifelike during the Renaissance. You can see the difference between medieval and Renaissance painting if you look at these two pictures.

Picture A was painted by a medieval artist and picture B was painted during the Renaissance. Both show the Virgin Mary with Jesus but in very different ways. List four ways in which the paintings are different from each other. Look at the colours, the details in the pictures and the Virgin Mary.

A *Rucellai Madonna* by Duccio di Buoninsegna. This painting is an icon. It was used as an altarpiece in a cathedral in Florence

New developments in painting

Renaissance artists developed new ways of making paintings look more real.

- **Anatomy** (study of the body): Some artists cut up dead bodies to find out where the bones were and how the muscles worked. This made their paintings of bodies more accurate.
- **Perspective:** Artists began to paint people and objects at the back of the picture smaller than those at the front. This is called perspective. It gives the illusion of depth and space in the painting. Can you see this in picture B?

Term

Icon
A painting of a religious subject made as an object of worship or prayer.

Anatomy
The study of the human body.

Perspective
Adding depth to a picture.

B *Madonna of the Meadow* by Giovanni Bellini

- **Portraits** of people became popular for the first time. The *Mona Lisa* (see opposite) is an example of a portrait.
- **Sfumato:** Artists began to use a new technique called *sfumato*. They used tiny brush strokes to blend areas into each other. This meant that there were no hard outlines. They used it to paint very realistic shadows and skin tones.
- **Oil paint:** Medieval painters mixed their colours with egg white. It dried quickly so they had little time to get the effects they wanted. Renaissance artists began to mix their paints using **linseed oil.** Oil paints dried more slowly and gave artists time to work in more detail.
- **Canvas:** Medieval artists painted on wooden boards, while Renaissance artists started to use **canvas** to paint on. The paint dries more slowly on canvas, so it is less likely to crack.
- **Frescos:** Many Renaissance paintings were frescos. A fresco is a painting done directly onto wet plaster. Frescos were used to decorate the walls and ceilings of churches and houses.

Did you know?

The word ***sfumato*** comes from the Italian word meaning 'smoke'. This refers to the slightly hazy effect that *sfumato* achieves.

A fresco by Masaccio painted about 1427 in a church in Florence, Italy

Term

Fresco
A picture painted straight onto a wall or ceiling. The paint is applied to wet plaster.

Term

Canvas
Cloth from which sails are made. It makes a good surface for painting when stretched tight.

QUESTIONS

1. List two ways in which a Renaissance painting was different from a medieval painting.
2. Explain each of the following: perspective; *sfumato*; portrait.
3. What did early Renaissance painters first use to mix their paints? What did they later use? Why was that better?
4. What was a painting on a wall called? Where else did Renaissance artists paint pictures?
5. Look again at the two pictures on the previous page. Give three reasons why picture B is more realistic.

Special Study: famous Renaissance painters

Leonardo da Vinci (1452–1519)

Leonardo da Vinci was one of the greatest geniuses of the Renaissance. He was a marvellous painter and inventor.

Leonardo was born in 1452 in Vinci, near Florence. That is where he got his name. Leonardo's father wanted him to become a lawyer, but Leonardo was interested in painting. At fifteen years of age he was apprenticed to **Verrocchio**, a leading Florentine artist, and learned to paint. It soon became clear that Leonardo was better than his master.

Leonardo's paintings

After Florence became involved in war, Leonardo moved to Milan. There he painted ***The Last Supper*** on the wall of a convent church. It was a fresco, but Leonardo tried out a new recipe for making the paint. It did not work. Soon after the picture was done, the paint began to peel away. You can see this in the painting.

Leonardo was the first artist to use *sfumato*. You can see it in his most famous picture, the ***Mona Lisa***. People have argued for a long time about the expression on her face. Is it one of sadness or happiness? What do you think?

He also painted ***The Virgin of the Rocks***, which shows his love of nature.

The *Mona Lisa* by Leonardo da Vinci. The scenery in the background is typical of a Renaissance painting

The Virgin of the Rocks. This painting shows the Virgin Mary with baby Jesus, John the Baptist and an angel. The angel is meant to show da Vinci's ideal woman. Would you agree she is beautiful?

The Last Supper by Leonardo da Vinci. Can you see the perspective in this painting?

Leonardo's notebooks

When Leonardo wrote in his notebooks he used **mirror writing** (from right to left). For that reason no one read his notes until many years after his death. Today, we have over 5,000 pages of his notebooks. They contain diagrams of machines as well as notes on botany, geology and engineering.

Leonardo the inventor

In Milan, Leonardo worked for the **Duke of Milan**. He invented several weapons of war for the duke such as a **tank** and a **cannon**. His notebooks were full of new ideas including designs for a **helicopter**, a **submarine** and a **parachute**. But Sforza was not interested in these and would not give any funding for them.

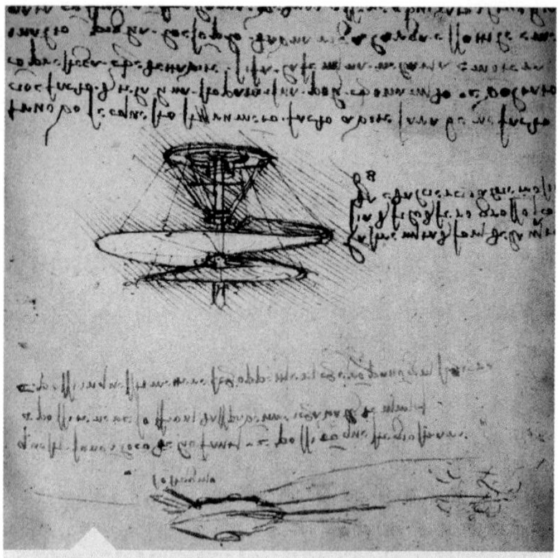

Leonardo's helicopter. The picture above is from Leonardo's notebooks

Leonardo and people

If he saw an interesting face on the street, he would draw it in his notebook. Sometimes he followed the person home so that he could finish the drawing. He **dissected** (cut up) more than thirty bodies of men and women in order to study the human form more closely.

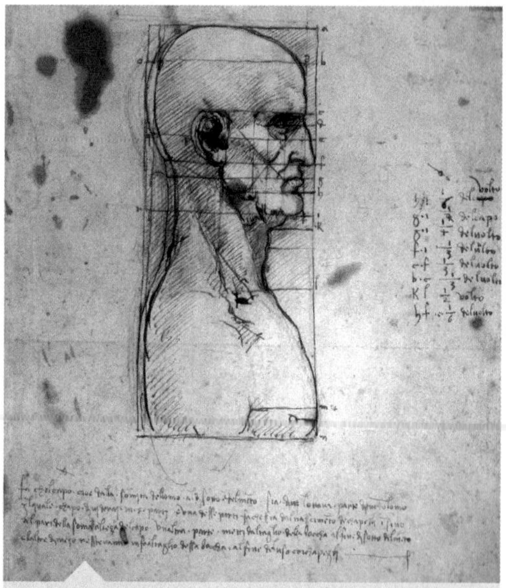

Leonardo's sketch of the head proportions (from Vitruvius' *The 10 Books on Architecture*) What do you think the straight lines around the head are for?

Leonardo and nature

Leonardo had a great interest in nature, plants and animals. He made great discoveries. He worked out how rocks were formed and how to tell the age of a tree by counting the rings.

Leonardo's last years

When a French army captured Milan, Leonardo had to leave. He went to Florence and Rome, but younger artists such as Michelangelo and Raphael were more popular than he was. The king of France invited Leonardo to France to work for him. He died there three years later.

A portrait of Leonardo da Vinci

Leonardo's sketch of rushes

Raphael (1483–1520)

Another Italian painter was **Raphael Sanzio.** As a young man, he went to Florence where he studied the paintings of Leonardo. He learned how to use *sfumato* and studied anatomy. Raphael became famous for his paintings of the **Madonna** (Mary, the mother of Jesus). You can see a detail of one of them at the top of page 111. The paintings were modelled on real women that Raphael knew.

The Marriage of the Virgin by Raphael. What Renaissance artistic techniques does this picture clearly show? How else would we know it was a Renaissance painting?

QUESTIONS

1 Where did Leonardo come from?
2 Name one of Leonardo's paintings and describe it.
3 Name two of the techniques Leonardo used in his pictures.
4 Name one other Italian Renaissance painter. Say who his patron was and name one of his pictures.
5 Name two of Leonardo's discoveries.
6 What was strange about Leonardo's notebooks?
7 Look at Leonardo's *Virgin of the Rocks*. Give four reasons why you can tell it's a Renaissance painting.

People in History

Write about an artist who worked in Italy during the Renaissance.

Look at the chapter and use the plan below as a guide.

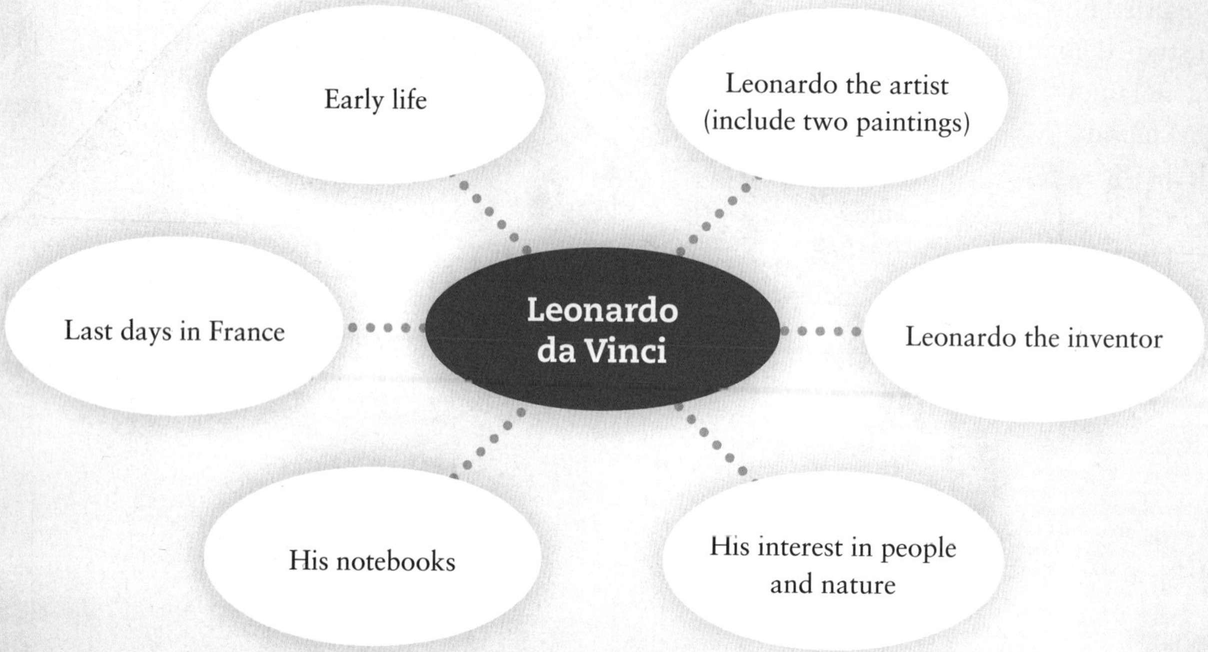

Renaissance artists outside Italy

Artists came from all over Europe to see the new art that had started in Italy. Some Italian artists, such as Leonardo da Vinci, were also asked to go and work for patrons in other parts of Europe. In this way, the ideas of the Renaissance spread. One famous Renaissance painter who was not from Italy was the Dutch artist **Pieter Bruegel.**

The Hay Harvest by Pieter Bruegel. How can you tell that this is a Renaissance painting?

Pieter Bruegel (c.1525–69)

Pieter Bruegel was born in the village of Brueghel in the Netherlands, around 1525. No one knows much about his early life, because Bruegel's father was a poor peasant (farmer) and there are few records left about him.

The Fight between Carnival and Lent by Pieter Bruegel. On the left is the inn, which represents the carnival and pleasure. On the right is the church, which represents Lent and religion

We know Bruegel was apprenticed to the painter Pieter Coecke van Aelst and he later married his master's daughter. He spent some time in France and Italy and in 1551 he was accepted into the **painters' guild** in Antwerp as a master painter.

Bruegel is famous for his paintings of **scenery and nature.** Look at the painting *The Hay Harvest* opposite. Bruegel was the first European painter to paint landscapes for their own sake rather than as a backdrop to something else. He also painted wonderful winter landscapes. Most of his paintings of the countryside tell a story or have a moral message.

Bruegel painted **ordinary people.** This was rare at that time because most artists painted portraits of rich people who could give them money. His paintings tell us a lot about the everyday life and manners of poorer people and this makes his paintings interesting for us. His painting *The Fight between Carnival and Lent* is set in the market square of a town and shows both the festive and religious sides of people's lives.

The people in Bruegel's pictures often appear to be ugly and stupid. Bruegel lived at a time when there were a lot of wars over religion. People did awful things to each other and Bruegel didn't have much faith in human nature.

Some art historians believe that Bruegel was sorry for the peasants because they were so poor and uneducated. He wanted to show in his paintings that they didn't have much chance in life. What do you think?

About forty-five of Bruegel's paintings survive, but many others were lost. Bruegel also did a lot of drawings and engravings. He was only forty-four when he died. His sons Pieter and Jan also became famous painters.

What does the picture *The Peasant Wedding* tell you about people in Belgium at that time?

Do you understand these key terms?

anatomy	**sfumato**	**canvas**	**mirror writing**
perspective	**oil paint**	**fresco**	**Madonna**

QUESTIONS

1 How did the ideas of the Renaissance spread outside Italy? Mention two ways.
2 Name a famous Renaissance artist from outside Italy and name two of his works.
3 Where was Pieter Bruegel born?
4 Name two of Bruegel's paintings.
5 Give two reasons why Bruegel's paintings are so famous.
6 How did peasant people appear in Bruegel's paintings?
7 Look at Bruegel's paintings *The Hay Harvest* and *The Peasant Wedding*. Explain two ways in which they are the same as Italian Renaissance paintings and two ways in which they differ.

Chapter 3

Renaissance Sculpture and Architecture

Key Learning Objectives

- **How did sculpture change in the Renaissance?**
- **Who was the greatest sculptor and what did he do?**
  - **Michelangelo Buonarroti**
- **How did architecture change in the Renaissance?**

How did sculpture change in the Renaissance?

In the Middle Ages, sculptors carved statues that were part of buildings, usually churches. The statues were not lifelike.

Old Greek and Roman statues stood alone and were skilfully carved to show the human body as it really was. Renaissance sculptors copied them and made realistic figures. Unlike medieval statues, theirs were often **nude**. When they carved a statue they tried to show the bones and muscles. To do this, they often cut up (dissected) dead bodies to see how they were made.

Donatello was one of the first sculptors to do this. He lived in Florence. Below is his **bronze** statue of David.

Term

Sculptor
An artist who makes statues or other sculptures, using stone, metal or wood.

Did you know?

Renaissance sculpture is lifelike and not part of a building.

Statue of *David* by Donatello. What material is it made from?

Statues carved on a Gothic church

Special Study: a sculptor

Michelangelo Buonarroti (1475–1564)

The greatest sculptor of the Renaissance was **Michelangelo Buonarroti.** He was born near Florence. When he was 13 years old his father apprenticed him to a sculptor. Soon afterwards Michelangelo made a copy of an old Roman statue. **Lorenzo de Medici** saw it and was amazed at its beauty. He invited Michelangelo to join the school for sculptors that he had in his palace.

Portrait of Michelangelo

Michelangelo's Pietà

After Lorenzo's death, Michelangelo went to Rome. There he made a statue called the ***Pietà***, which means 'sorrow'. It shows Mary holding her son Jesus after his death on the cross. This *Pietà* is made of white marble. It is the only statue Michelangelo ever signed.

Term

Pietà
Mary holding Jesus in her arms.

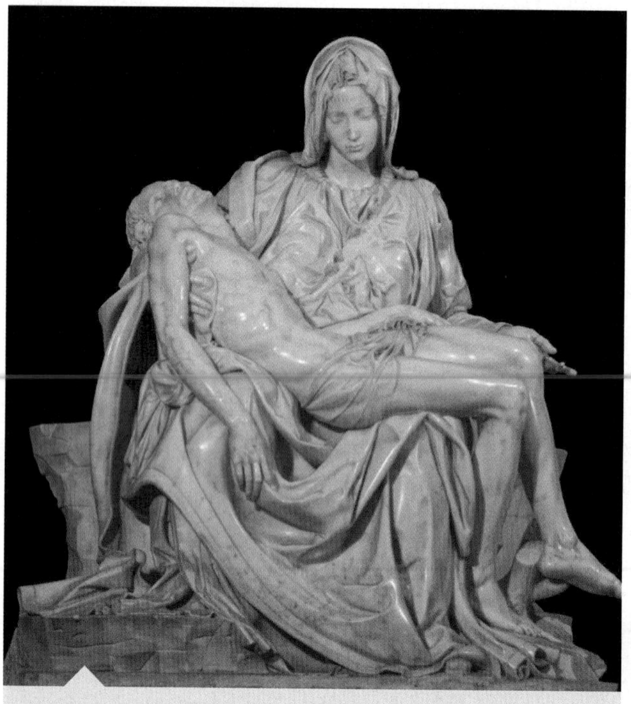

The *Pietà* by Michelangelo. Can you see the folds in the material?

David by Michelangelo. Today a copy of this statue still stands in the central square of Florence. The original is kept in a museum for safety

Michelangelo's David

At this time, there was a war between Florence and France. Although France was more powerful, the Florentines won. To celebrate, the town council held a competition. Both Leonardo da Vinci and Michelangelo entered work, but Michelangelo won the contract. Florence's victory reminded Michelangelo of the Bible story of the boy David defeating the giant Goliath. He found a block of white marble and carved a huge statue of David. It is five metres high. Look at the statue. Notice how you can see every vein and muscle.

Michelangelo in Rome

Pope Julius II then hired Michelangelo to go to Rome and paint **frescos** on the ceiling of the **Sistine Chapel** in the Vatican.

Michelangelo preferred sculpture to painting, but he didn't dare refuse the pope. For four years he worked on the frescos. In them, he told the story of the **creation** of the world from the Bible. He began with God creating Adam, and ended with Noah and the flood.

He became so involved in his painting that he often forgot to sleep or eat. He dismissed assistant after assistant. Only an old servant and Pope Julius were allowed to watch him work. When he finished, the whole ceiling was covered with over 300 figures. The figures are life-size and done in beautiful colours. It is one of the greatest masterpieces of all time.

Later, when Michelangelo was an old man, he painted a huge fresco called *The Last Judgement* on one of the walls of the Sistine Chapel.

Part of the ceiling in the Sistine Chapel. The area highlighted is the section called *The Creation of Adam*. You can see it more clearly in the close-up below

Michelangelo, poet and architect

Michelangelo was a fine poet. He wrote over 300 love poems. Most were **sonnets**. His poems are some of the best ever written in Italian.

Term

Sonnet
A poem of fourteen lines, with rhymes.

He was also a great architect. Before his death he designed the great dome of **St Peter's Basilica**. He also finished the rest of the building. You can see it on the next page. Michelangelo designed many other buildings such as the **Laurentian Library** in Florence.

Michelangelo was almost 90 years old when he died. He never married and he said his statues and paintings were his children.

St Peter's Basilica. What Roman influences can you see in this architecture?

QUESTIONS

1 What is a sculpture? What is the name of the person who does this work?
2 Give two features of medieval sculpture.
3 Name three features of Renaissance sculpture.
4 Who was the most famous Renaissance sculptor?
5 What is a pietà?
6 Name two of Michelangelo's patrons.
7 Look at Donatello's statue of *David* on page 119 and Michelangelo's statue of *David* on page 120.
   (a) What are the two statues made of?
   (b) How could you tell these statues were made in the Renaissance period? Give two reasons for your answer.

How did architecture change in the Renaissance?

Renaissance architects turned away from the medieval Gothic style and brought in new ways of building that were based on the ideas of the Greeks and the Romans. You can see in the table below the differences between Renaissance architecture and Gothic architecture, which was used mainly in churches.

How do we know that this is an example of Gothic architecture?

Gothic style	Renaissance style
Spires	Domes
Less symmetry	More symmetry
Pointed arches	Round arches
Flying buttresses	Pediments and columns

Developments in architecture

The dome

The first famous architect of the Renaissance was **Filippo Brunelleschi** (1377–1446). He went to Rome and studied the old Roman buildings, especially the **Pantheon** (see page 60), and worked out how to build a dome. He built the dome on the cathedral in Florence. It took sixteen years to complete but the dome became part of the typical architecture of the Renaissance.

Symmetry

All Renaissance buildings followed an exact **symmetrical plan**. In houses there had to be the same number of windows each side of the door. In churches you had the same number of arches each side of the aisle.

The cathedral in Florence showing Brunelleschi's dome

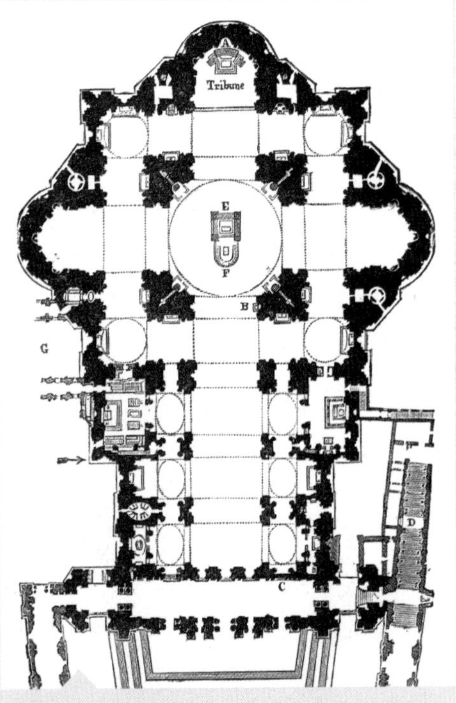

Raphael's unused plan for St Peter's basilica. Can you see how important symmetry is?

Round arches

Arches became hugely popular and architects used them to support and decorate buildings. Look at this picture of the **Palazzo Rucellai** designed by the architect **Alberti.** How many arches can you count?

Palazzo Rucellai

Pediments and columns

Pediments and **columns** in the Roman style became fashionable again. Look at the house below designed by the architect **Andrea Palladio** (1508–80). He designed 150 houses for wealthy Italians. His style became known as **Palladian,** and houses and important buildings were built all over the world in this style.

Term

Pediment
Structure in architecture, usually triangular, that is supported by columns.

A Palladian house. What Roman influences can you see in this building?

Do you understand these key terms?

sculptor	**dome**
nude	**symmetry**
pietà	**pediment**
sonnet	**columns**

QUESTIONS

1. List three features of a Renaissance building. Where did the ideas for them come from?
2. Name two Italian architects and say why they are famous.
3. Look at the Palladian house above. Give three reasons why we know it's a Renaissance-style building.

EXAM QUESTION

› Describe the main changes in architecture that took place during the Renaissance. (HL)

Chapter 4

The Invention of Printing

Key Learning Objectives

- **Who invented printing?**
- **How was a book printed?**
- **How did printing change the world?**
- **Who was William Shakespeare and what did he do?**

Manuscripts

A **manuscript** is a book written by hand. Ever since writing was invented, books had been written by hand. It was a very slow process.

Books were rare and expensive. Only rich people like the Medicis or the popes could afford to own more than one or two. Most people were illiterate. They did not know how to read or write. But all that changed when printing was introduced to Europe during the Renaissance.

Who invented printing?

The Chinese invented printing. They carved pictures in wood or metal and pressed them on to paper. But it was **Johannes Gutenberg** in Europe who invented a printing press which used **moveable type.** This is where you can use small metal letters over and over to make new words. It was much quicker and cheaper to produce a book this way.

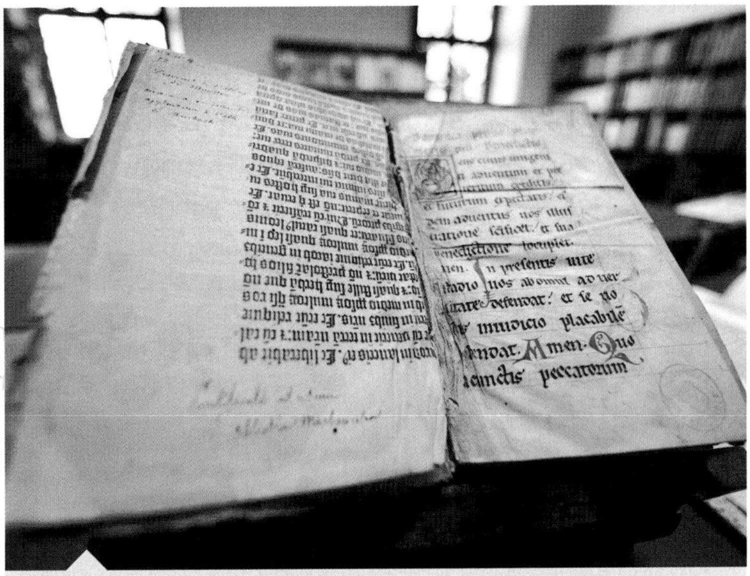

Gutenberg's printed Bible on display. What language is it written in?

Gutenberg was a goldsmith from Mainz in Germany. He produced the first printed book in Europe, which was a copy of the Bible. You can see how he did it on the next page.

The Bible had 1,300 pages and only forty-seven copies of it still exist. It is one of the most valuable books in the world.

How was a book printed?

1 The metal letters are put into boxes.

2 The letters are made into words and set out in pages.

3 Ink is spread onto each page.

4 The inked page is put face down on the paper and a large screw presses down hard on the page.

5 The sheets are hung out to dry.

6 The pages are bound into books.

The spread of printing

After Gutenberg, other people began to use moveable type to make printed books. In 1476, an English printer called **William Caxton** set up business in London. He printed over a hundred books. One of the first books he printed was *The Canterbury Tales* by Chaucer (see page 76). By 1500, there were over a thousand printers working in Europe and over one million printed books had appeared.

How did printing change the world?

The invention of printing is one of the most important events in human history. It changed the world in many ways.

- Because books were easily available, more people learned to read and write.
- Books became much cheaper, so more people could afford to own them.
- New ideas spread more easily because people could write books about them.
- It became harder for kings or popes to stop a new idea that they disliked, because people could make many copies of a book about it. We will see later how this helped the Reformation to develop.

A new literature

New ways of writing now became popular.

- In the Middle Ages, most manuscripts were in Latin. Now people wanted to read books written in their own languages like Spanish, Irish or English. Writers began to write in the everyday language of the people. This is called **vernacular literature.**
- They began to write more about everyday human problems and less about religious themes.
- New styles of literature such as **plays** and **novels** became popular.

Term

Vernacular literature
Literature written in the everyday language of the people and not in Greek or Latin.

Cervantes

A Spanish writer, **Miguel de Cervantes**, wrote a novel in 1605. It was called *Don Quixote* and it was a funny story about the travels of an idealistic knight and his world-weary servant. It was one of the first books to tell the story of ordinary people like shepherds and innkeepers. Another famous writer who wrote in English was **William Shakespeare**.

William Shakespeare

Special Study: a Renaissance writer

William Shakespeare (1564–1616)

Shakespeare was born in Stratford-upon-Avon in England. When he was eighteen years old he married Anne Hathaway and soon after that he moved to London.

He became an actor and then began writing plays. Queen Elizabeth I loved drama, so plays were very popular.

The Globe

Shakespeare became one of the owners of a theatre company, which became known as the **King's Men**. They built their own theatre on the banks of the River Thames. It was called **the Globe**.

Look at the reconstruction of it in the picture on the right. It could hold 3,000 people. At that time, there was no lighting, so plays were put on during the day and in the open air. Most people stood and watched.

We know that Shakespeare acted in his own plays and was called 'Will' by his friends.

This is what we think the Globe Theatre was like. Poor people stood in front of the open air stage. Rich people had seats in the balcony

A kingdom for a stage, princes to act.
And monarchs to behold the swelling scene.
(from *Henry V*)

What were his plays about?

Shakespeare's plays included **histories** such as *Henry V* and *Richard III*. He also wrote **comedies** such as *Twelfth Night* and *As You Like It*, and **tragedies** such as *Hamlet* and *Romeo and Juliet*. Like many Renaissance writers, he based some of his plots on stories from Ancient Greece or Rome.

His characters were often kings and queens and nobles, but there were always ordinary people in them as well. He wrote about everyday problems and the common mistakes people make in their relationships with others. His plays are still popular today because he wrote about human emotions such as love and jealousy.

Did you know?

Only men could become actors so the younger boys had to act the women's roles.

Poems

Shakespeare also wrote over 150 **sonnets**. They were mostly about love. Some were to a mysterious 'dark lady'. No one is sure who she was.

Do you understand these key terms?

moveable type **comedy** **tragedy** **novel**
vernacular literature **play**

QUESTIONS

1 What is a manuscript? Why were books so expensive?
2 Who first used moveable type in Europe? Explain how it works.
3 Name the first printed book in Europe.
4 Name the first English printer and one of the books he produced.
5 List three ways in which printing changed the world.
6 List two ways in which literature in the Renaissance was different from literature during the Middle Ages.
7 What is meant by 'vernacular literature'? Name two writers who wrote vernacular literature.

Chapter 5

Science during the Renaissance

Key Learning Objectives

- What were the new ideas in science during the Renaissance:
  - in medicine?
  - in astronomy?
- Who was Galileo?

Did you know?

The most common cure for any illness at this time was blood-letting. Doctors cut a person's arm to make it bleed. They believed the 'bad' blood was being let out.

What were the new ideas in science during the Renaissance?

During the Renaissance there were many new scientific ideas. These included new discoveries in **medicine** and in **astronomy**.

Medicine

Medieval medicine

During the Middle Ages people knew a lot about **herbal medicine,** but doctors did not understand how the human body worked.

They based their ideas on the writings of an Ancient Greek doctor called **Galen**. But Galen had never dissected the human body and many of his ideas were wrong.

The Church was against the cutting up of bodies and in 1300 the pope banned it. That made it more difficult for doctors to find out about the organs of the human body and how they worked.

Two Renaissance doctors – **Vesalius** and **Harvey** – showed that some of the old ideas were wrong.

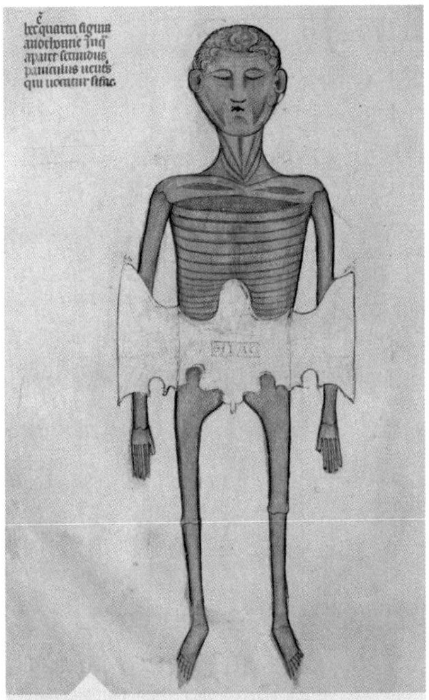

This picture shows what medieval people thought the human skeleton looked like. What faults can you see in this skeleton?

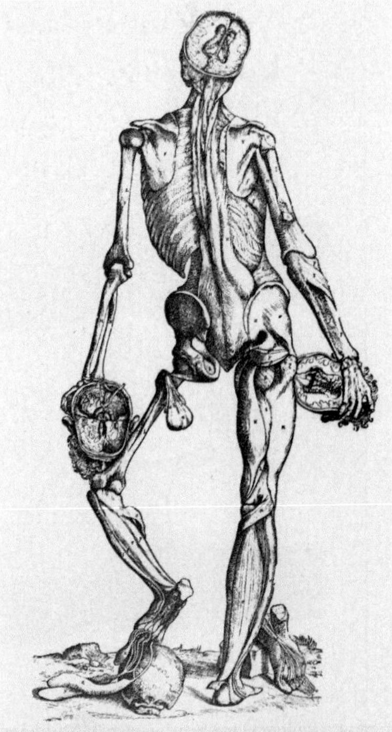

Vesalius' drawing of a skeleton. List three differences between this skeleton and the medieval sketch

Vesalius, the father of anatomy

Andreas Vesalius (1514–64) made great breakthroughs in anatomy. He was born in Brussels and became professor of **anatomy** at Padua University, in Italy, when he was only twenty-three years old. He held public dissections at the university and huge crowds of students came to see them. He even stole bodies from graveyards in order to dissect them! His book *On the Fabric of the Human Body* has 270 drawings of every part of the human body. His wonderful sketches are still used today.

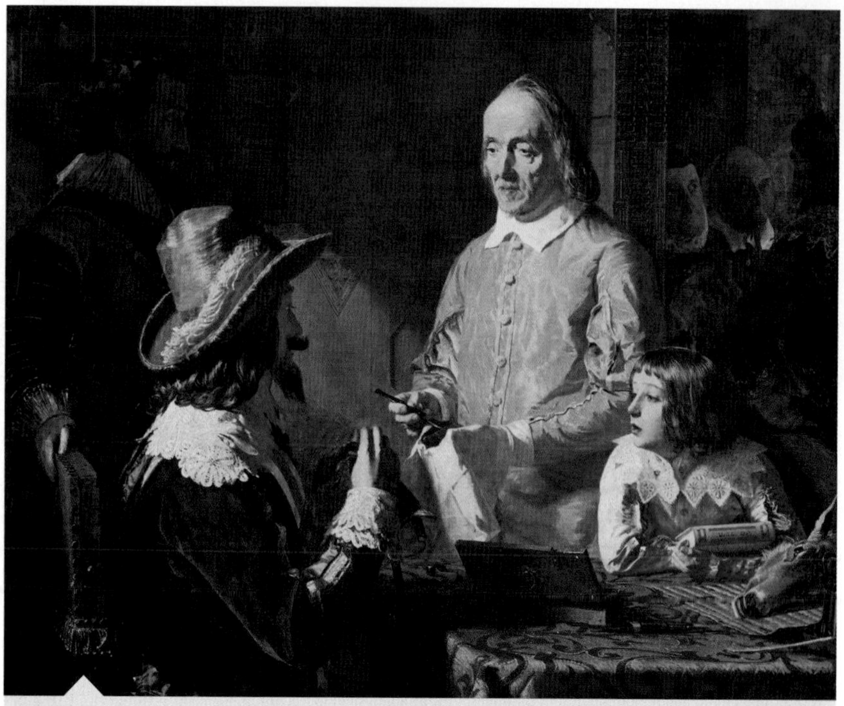

William Harvey demonstrating his theory of the circulation of the blood to King Charles I of England. Why would Harvey demonstrate this to the king?

William Harvey

Galen wrote that blood was burnt up in the body and remade in the liver. But William Harvey (1578–1657), an English doctor, showed that the heart pumped it around the body. He developed theories on the **circulation of blood.**

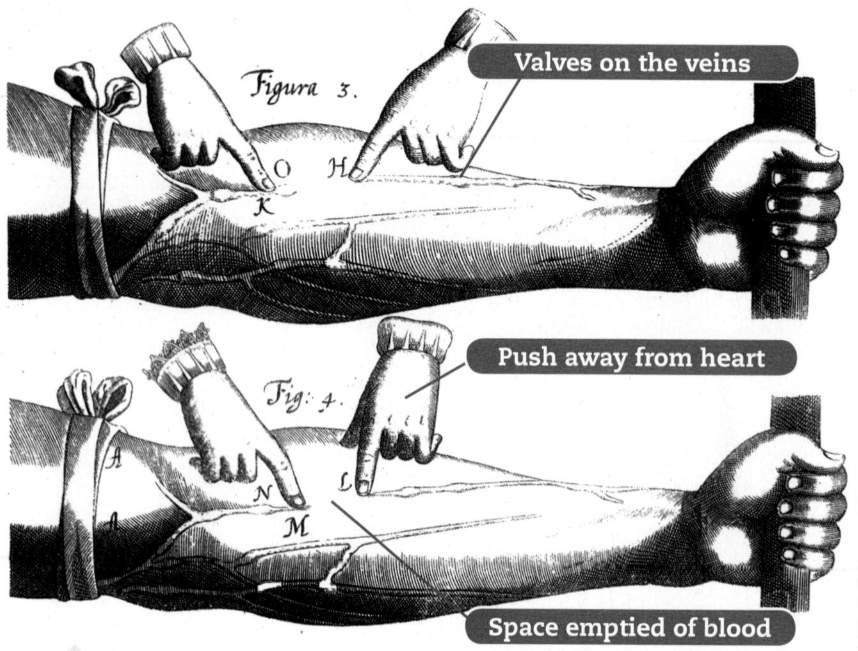

William Harvey's experiment on blood circulation

Did you know?

If you bandage your arm you can see the valves in your veins. Then if you push with your finger away from the heart the space between the two valves O and H will empty of blood. This proves that the blood is going only one way around the body.

Astronomy

Term

Astronomy
The study of the universe including the sun, moon, stars and planets.

Does the sun move?

In the Middle Ages, people believed that the earth was at the centre of the universe and that the sun, moon and stars moved around it. The Bible and the Church supported this theory. Every day people saw the sun rise in the east, move across the sky and set in the west. The moon and planets also moved across the sky. So people believed they moved around the earth, which stood still.

But these ideas were questioned by two Renaissance astronomers – **Copernicus** and **Galileo.**

Nicholas Copernicus

Nicholas Copernicus

Nicholas Copernicus (1473–1543) was a Polish priest. Every day he watched the movements of the sun, moon and stars. Using mathematics, he worked out that **the earth revolved around the sun,** and not the other way around.

However, there were no telescopes then so he could not prove that it was true. It was a hundred years later before another scientist proved it. His name was Galileo.

Copernicus' theory. Can you see the sun in the centre of the planets?

Special Study: a Renaissance scientist

Galileo Galilei (1564–1642)

Galileo Galilei was a famous astronomer

Galileo was born in Pisa in Italy. He had a great interest in **mathematics** and he believed that all the laws of nature could be proved by calculation and experiment.

The law of falling bodies

Galileo is said to have dropped two balls of different weight from the Leaning Tower of Pisa. This was to prove that all solid objects fall at the same speed whatever their weight. He called this **the law of falling bodies**. Up to then, people had thought that heavier objects would fall faster than light ones.

Galileo's telescope

A Dutchman, **Hans Lippershey**, invented the telescope in 1608, but Galileo designed and built a much more powerful version of it. Galileo's telescope could magnify something thirty-two times. He was the first person to use the telescope to study the skies.

Term

Magnify
To make things look bigger.

Galileo's theories

Galileo was able to see things no human being had ever seen before. He discovered spots on the sun and mountains on the moon. He saw that Jupiter had four moons moving around it. He realised that Copernicus was right. The earth could not be the centre of the universe. The sun was the centre of the solar system and the earth moved around it.

Catholic Church bans Galileo's findings

When the Catholic Church heard Galileo's theories, they banned his books. The Church believed that the earth had to be the centre of the universe, because the earth was created by God. It is where Christ was born.

When Galileo published a book called the *Dialogue*, containing his findings, the pope summoned him to Rome where he was put on trial. Galileo was afraid that he was going to be burnt at the stake and he finally agreed to say he was wrong. He was not allowed to write about astronomy after this, but his ideas still lived on.

Galileo built over 100 telescopes. This is a modern picture of him showing one to Church leaders. What is the book on the left, do you think?

Galileo is tried by the Catholic Church

Did you know?

There is a legend that after his trial, Galileo muttered (about the earth), 'And yet it moves.' However, we don't know if the story is true.

Advances made in learning during the Renaissance

Printing	Invention of moveable type (Gutenberg); books no longer copied by hand
Literature	Writers using vernacular languages, not Latin. Shakespeare (English) and Cervantes (Spanish) writing plays and novels about human problems like love
Medicine	Better knowledge of skeleton (Vesalius); circulation of the blood (Harvey)
Science	Importance of experimenting; telescope invented; proving that the earth goes around the sun (Copernicus, Galileo)

Do you understand these key terms?

anatomy **astronomy** **telescope** **magnify**
circulation of the blood **law of falling bodies**

QUESTIONS

1 Why was it almost impossible for medical experts to dissect bodies in the Middle Ages?
2 Why is Vesalius called 'the father of anatomy'?
3 What did William Harvey discover?
4 Who was Copernicus?
5 What was Copernicus' theory about the sun and the earth?
6 What was Galileo's theory of 'the law of falling bodies'?
7 Which invention did Galileo develop? What did this help to prove?
8 Who were against Galileo's theories? Explain why.

Chapter 6

The Impact of the Renaissance

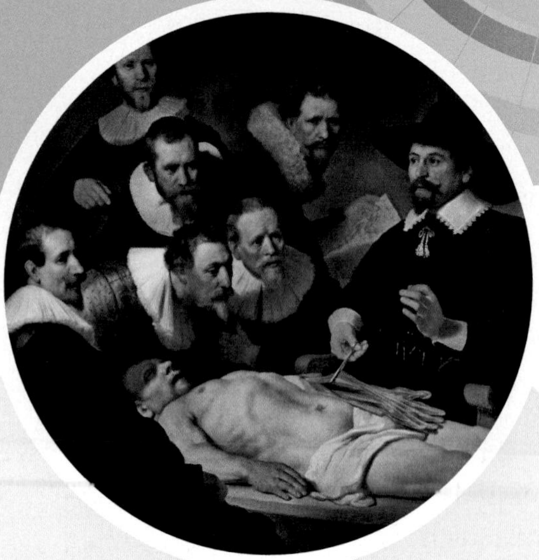

Key Learning Objectives

- **Where are all the women?**
- **Who were the famous Renaissance women?**
- **What was the importance of the Renaissance?**

Where are all the women?

Not everyone benefited equally from the progress made during the Renaissance. If you look back over the last few chapters on Renaissance art, architecture, literature and science, you will notice that all the famous names during the Renaissance were men. Why is this?

At that time, people believed that a woman's role was to be a good housekeeper and a good mother. Therefore, when sons began to learn Latin and go to school most daughters stayed at home and learned household skills. Women were not allowed to attend universities and most didn't even learn to read and write.

Did you know?

Up to the Middle Ages most healers were women. But during the Renaissance women were not allowed to attend lectures and demonstrations in anatomy and new medical learning. By the late 1600s, even midwives who helped women during childbirth were mainly men!

What do you notice about the students at this university lecture?

The natural order is that women should serve men, for it is just that the lesser serve the greater.

(Church leader, 1140)

What does this statement tell you about attitudes to women in the Middle Ages?

Famous Renaissance women

Some women overcame these problems and became famous. Most of them came from wealthy families and they were often related to male scholars.

Female painters

Two famous Renaissance painters were women. **Artemisia Gentileschi** (1593–*c.*1653) was Italian and she drew women in most of her works. It was difficult for female artists to draw men as they were forbidden to study the male nude.

Judith Leyster (1609–60) was Dutch. She painted domestic scenes and **still lifes.** Until the twentieth century, people thought Judith Leyster's pictures were painted by a man.

> *Term*
> **Still life**
> A painting of objects such as flowers or fruit.

Boy Playing the Flute by Judith Leyster

Female scholars

A German-Dutch woman, **Anna Maria van Schurman** (1607–78), became a famous scholar. She was so brilliant at school that she got special permission to attend lectures at the University of Utrecht in Holland. Even then she had to stand behind a curtain! She knew fourteen languages such as Hebrew, Arabic, Latin and Greek, and she wrote an Ethiopian grammar.

Anna Maria van Schurman

Judith and the Maidservant with the Head of Holofernes by Artemisia Gentileschi. This painting is based on a story from the Bible

What was the importance of the Renaissance?

The Renaissance changed the way people in Europe did things and the way they thought about the world. Here are a few changes that came about because of it.

New skills and discoveries	Invention of printing	Confidence grew	People questioned the Church
› Art: perspective, *sfumato* › Medicine: anatomy, blood circulation › Science: the earth moves around the sun, telescope	› Made books more available and cheaper › Encouraged more people to read and write › Ideas spread more quickly	› People began to think for themselves › They challenged old ideas on geography and the human body	› People challenged the power of the Church › This led to the Reformation

QUESTIONS

1 In Renaissance times, why did people think there was no need to educate women?
2 Give two reasons why there were so few women artists or scientists in the Renaissance.
3 Name one female scholar and one female artist of the Renaissance.
4 Write an account of two of the following aspects of the Renaissance:
(a) Literature (b) Science/Medicine (c) Architecture (d) Printing

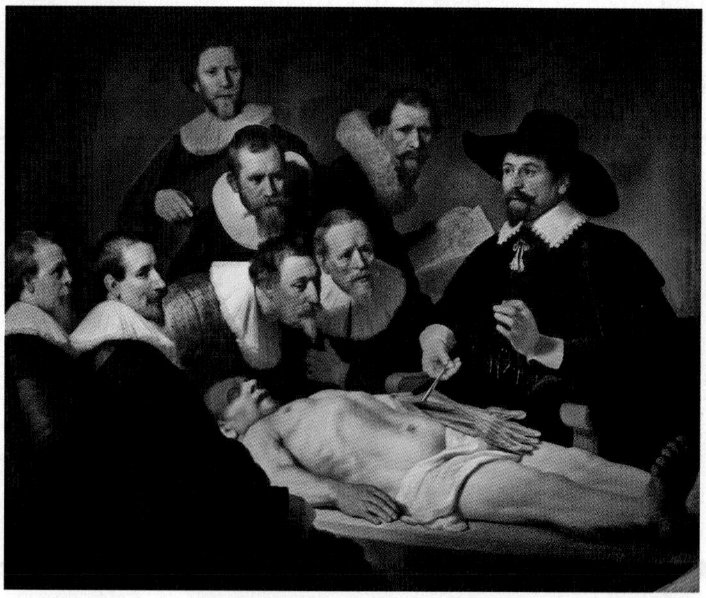

EXAM QUESTIONS

Look at the picture of an oil painting by Rembrandt called *The Anatomy Lesson* and answer the questions below. (HL)

1 Why were examinations of dead bodies such as that shown here not very common before the Renaissance?
2 Why did Renaissance artists such as Michelangelo and Leonardo da Vinci study anatomy?
3 Name two Renaissance discoveries that increased scientific knowledge.
4 Give two reasons why you know this is a Renaissance painting.

TIMELINE

PART 2

Section 6

The Age of Exploration

Chapter 1

Why Did the Age of Exploration Begin?

Key Learning Objectives

- **What were the main reasons for the Age of Exploration?**
- **What were the main improvements in shipbuilding and navigation?**
- **What was life like on board a ship?**

What were the main reasons for the Age of Exploration?

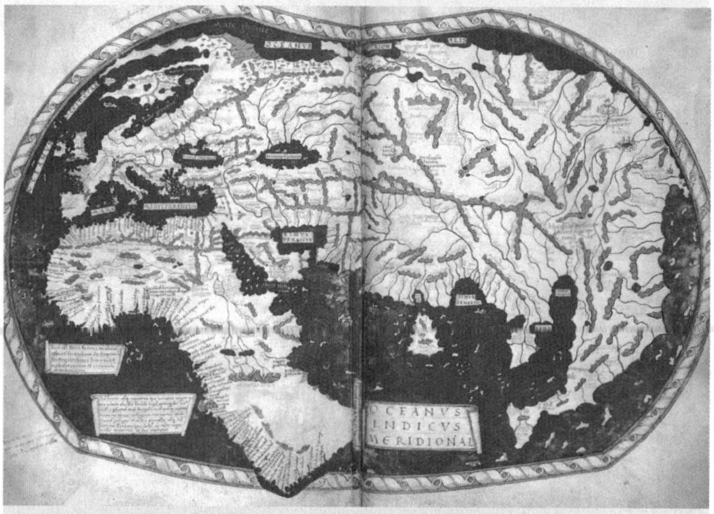

Mapmakers in the 1400s thought the world was like this

Look at the two maps here. What are the main differences between them? The first map shows what Europeans knew of the world before the Age of Exploration. For example, much of Africa and all of America are missing. In this section, we will learn about some of the most important discoveries that were made during the fifteenth and sixteenth centuries. These changed the way we see the world.

We must first understand the reasons why the Age of Exploration began around 1400.

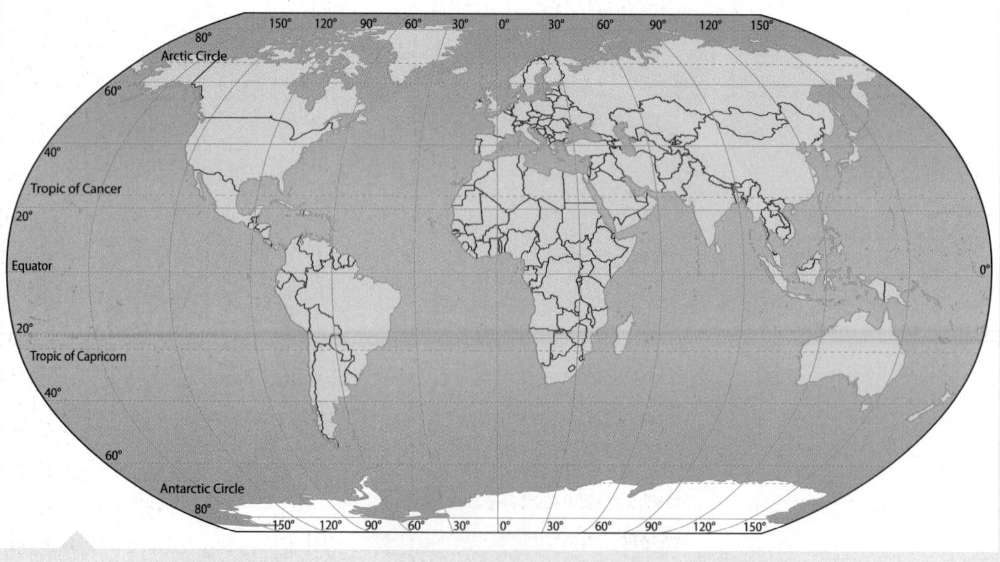

A map of the world today. What differences can you see between the two maps?

1 The demand for spices

The key reason for the Age of Exploration was the need to find a new route to Asia. This was in order to gain control of the **spice trade.** Spices came from Asia and there was great demand for them in Europe. They were worth a lot of money!

The spice trade was a difficult business:

- Spices were transported **overland** on a long and dangerous route that was controlled by Muslim rulers.
- When they reached the Mediterranean, merchants from Genoa and Venice bought them.
- They brought them to Europe where they were sold for a great profit.
- The **taxes** charged by the Muslim rulers were high.
- Often the Muslims were at **war** with the Christians in Europe and this cut off the trade.

Because of these difficulties, rulers and merchants in Western Europe began to look for a new route to the East. The capture of the Christian city of **Constantinople** in 1453 was a major factor in pushing the Europeans to find a new sea route to Asia.

The main spices were:

Cinnamon that came from China

Nutmeg and **cloves** from the Spice Islands (or the Moluccas)

Pepper that was grown only in India

Let's look at why there was great demand for spices in Europe.

What were spices used for?

When you go home today, you may get some food from the fridge. However, a person living in 1400 did not have a fridge to **preserve food.** Spices were used to do this. They also **added flavour** to food. When meat was stored for too long it went off and pepper was used to hide the taste.

Spices were also used to **cure disease.** It was believed that nutmeg helped cure chesty coughs and even the plague! Cloves relieved earache and toothache. Women put cloves in a locket around their neck to keep their breath fresh. Pepper helped with the common cold.

A modern spice market in India

PART 2

2 The support of rulers throughout Europe

Explorers needed the permission and financial support of kings and queens before they set sail. Why were rulers prepared to support the voyages of discovery?

- The most important reason was **to gain control of the spice trade from the East** – this would bring great wealth.
- Many rulers were interested in **gold and precious jewels** that, they believed, would be found in undiscovered lands.
- They saw their chance to conquer the land that was discovered and **build an empire.** It would make their country powerful.
- The **spreading of Christianity** was another reason, as rulers saw these voyages as a great opportunity to win converts. This was a very important motive, especially for the Spanish.

Term

Mapmaking
The making of maps is also called **cartography**.

3 The Renaissance

As we saw in the last section, the Renaissance was a time of new learning. There was a great interest in finding out more about the world. One area where this interest was shown was in **mapmaking.**

Around 1400, the work of the Greek geographer **Ptolemy** was rediscovered. Mapmakers used his work to make more accurate maps. His work inspired many who wanted to find out how big the world really was.

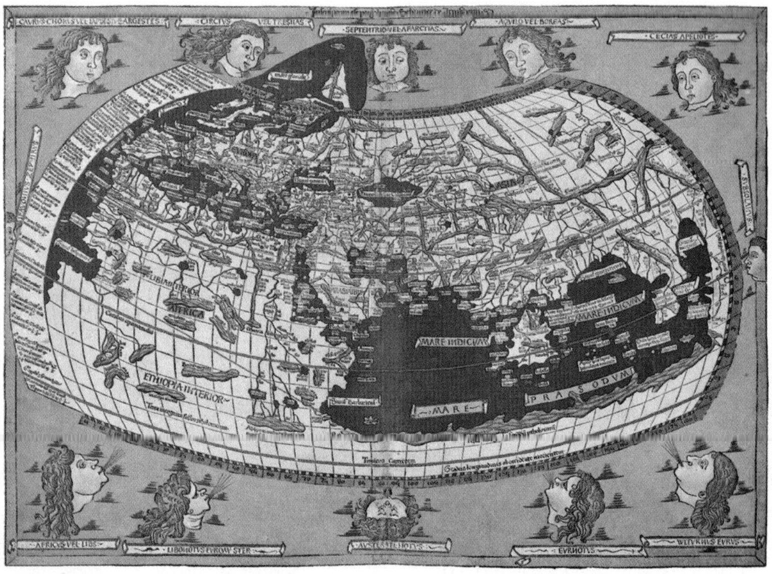

Ptolemy's map inspired great interest in discovering more about the world

4 Myths and legends

Both rulers and explorers were influenced by myths and legends. Here are some of the most famous:

- The Portuguese were searching for **Prester John** – a Christian king in Africa.
- Explorers believed in stories of great wealth – gold and silver – that existed in Africa and America. In South America many were looking for **El Dorado** – a fabulously wealthy city with a leader covered in gold dust.
- Some explorers were looking for the **Fountain of Youth** – if anyone drank from the fountain they would not grow old.

Explorers hoped to gain fame and wealth by making important discoveries.

5 Shipbuilding and navigation

The Age of Exploration would not have been possible without improvements in ships and navigational instruments. These made it possible for ships to sail on long voyages and have a chance of returning.

The main parts of a ship

1 Main mast
2 Foremast
3 Bow of ship
4 Rudder for steering
5 Captain's cabin
6 Cook
7 Anchor
8 Guns

What were the main improvements in shipbuilding and navigation?

> **Did you know?**
>
> North of the equator sailors usually relied on the North Star for navigation. South of the equator they used the sun.

Ships

The boats that were used in early voyages of exploration had square sails. They were slow and difficult to steer, especially into the wind. They were not suited to exploring close to the coast where the water was shallow.

Around 1400, the Portuguese invented a new type of ship called a **caravel**.

- These ships were **small, fast and easy to steer.**
- They used **triangular 'lateen' sails** that allowed the ship to sail into the wind. These were copied from Arab ships.
- They used strong **clinker-built hulls** to protect the ships in storms.
- The **decks were watertight** to stop water getting into the ship during bad weather.
- They were ideal for exploring as they could sail close to the coast and up rivers.

Later, larger ships called **carracks** or **naos** were used. They had both square and lateen sails. They were bigger than caravels and this meant they could carry more cargo, especially precious spices.

Navigation

When going on a voyage it is important that you have some idea about where you are going – this is called **navigation**. To do this effectively, sailors need to be able to do the following:

- Calculate the ship's **position**
- Find out what **direction** the ship is going
- Work out what **speed** the ship is travelling at

Traditionally, sailors had relied on observing the sun or stars, wind speed and current. A number of new instruments made it easier for sailors to navigate their ships. Let's look at how sailors used these instruments to navigate their ships.

An astrolabe measured latitude

Position

Sailors used an **astrolabe** to find the ship's position north or south of the equator. This is called **latitude.** The astrolabe measured the angle of the sun or the North Star. It was hard to use in heavy seas, so often sailors went ashore to get a better reading. It was first used at sea by the Portuguese in the fifteenth century.

Quadrants and **cross-staffs** were also used to measure latitude. Developed around 1500, cross-staffs were not affected by stormy seas. However, using both instruments involved looking directly at the sun and this could affect the eyesight of sailors.

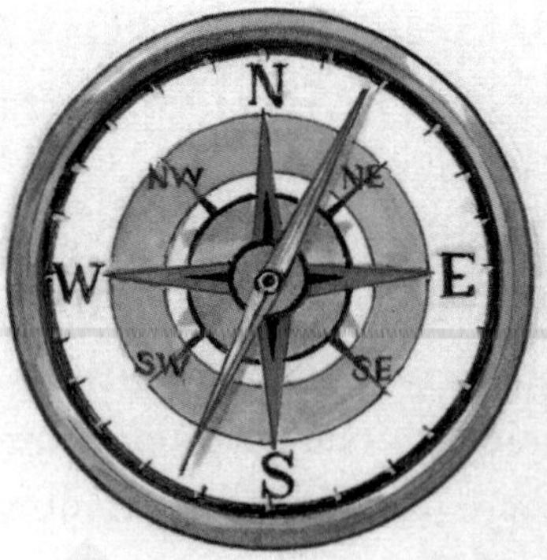

A compass measured direction

Direction

Most ships were equipped with a **compass.** Originally invented by the Chinese, the compass was much improved by the start of the fifteenth century. A magnetic needle pointed to magnetic north. The compass was kept in a case on deck. This meant it could be used in a storm. At night a lamp was used to read the compass.

Speed

The **log and line** was developed to measure speed. A sailor threw a piece of wood (**log**) into the sea from the back of the boat. This was attached to a reel of knotted rope (**line**). The amount of rope that was pulled by the wood in one minute was then measured. Sailors would then be able to calculate the ship's speed.

Time was measured using a sand **hourglass.**

Log and line in action

Did you know?

Today the speed of a ship is still measured in knots.

What was life like on board a ship?

No matter what the reason for the voyage, life at sea was tough. Let's find out more about what it was like to go to sea in the fifteenth and sixteenth centuries.

The **captain** was in charge of the ship. He was helped by the **first mate.** At mealtimes sailors ate with their fingers. Biscuits called **hardtack** were commonly eaten. The biscuits often became infested with small black beetles that the sailors tapped out before they ate them. Other foods sailors ate included cheese, onions, dried beans, and fresh or salted fish.

The absence of fresh fruit or vegetables could lead to a deadly disease called **scurvy.** This disease was the biggest killer of sailors during long voyages. Another problem was keeping the water fresh. It was stored in barrels, but it went bad when the ship was at sea for a long time. Fresh water was often the first item a crew looked for when they landed. Infected water on a voyage was very dangerous as it could spread a disease called **dysentery.**

Did you know?

Scurvy was caused by a lack of vitamin C, which is found in fresh fruit and vegetables. It caused gums to bleed and teeth to fall out. If left untreated, it would lead to a sailor's death. The cure was very simple: eat fresh fruit. But it was not until the late 1700s that this was discovered.

What were the main dangers crews faced?

During the Age of Exploration, life at sea was very dangerous. Many sailors were afraid of sea monsters or of falling off the edge of the world. These fears were imaginary, but other were very real.

- As we have seen, **disease** was a big killer. Captains often carried twice the men they needed because they knew so many would die of illnesses.
- **Storms** could lead to shipwreck and drowning.
- Sailors were often attacked by **hostile natives.**
- Crews could also suffer from **thirst and hunger** when they ran out of food and water.

Oil painting of a storm at sea

PART 2

In the next two chapters, we will examine the countries that led the Age of Exploration: Portugal and Spain.

- The Portuguese sought to reach Asia by sailing down the coast of Africa.
- The Spanish tried to reach the East by sailing westwards but stumbled on a new continent, America, instead.

The causes of the Age of Exploration

- The search for a new route to the East
- Wealth and new empires
- The desire to spread Christianity
- Improvements in ships and navigation
- Myths and legends

Do you understand these key terms?

spice trade	**carrack**	**latitude**	**log and line**
mapmaking	**nao**	**quadrant**	**hardtack**
caravel	**navigation**	**cross-staffs**	**scurvy**
lateen sails	**astrolabe**	**compass**	**dysentry**

QUESTIONS

1. Why did countries in Western Europe look for new routes to the East?
2. Name three spices that were popular in Europe.
3. For what purposes were spices used?
4. Give two reasons why rulers were prepared to sponsor voyages of exploration.
5. What was a caravel?
6. Name an instrument of navigation and explain what it was used for.
7. How did the Renaissance influence the Age of Exploration?
8. Mention two myths or legends that led to voyages of discovery.
9. Write a paragraph on two of the following topics:
   - Improvements in shipbuilding
   - How ships navigated at sea
   - Life for sailors on board a ship
   - The main dangers that crew faced
10. Write an account explaining why the spice trade was a major cause of the Age of Exploration.

Research topic

Find out the main navigational instruments that are used on ships today. Make two lists: one showing the instruments around 1500, the other showing the instruments today.

Chapter 2

Explorers from Portugal

Key Learning Objectives

- **Who were the main Portuguese explorers and what did they do?**
- **What was the impact of the Portuguese voyages?**

It was **Portugal** that began the Age of Exploration. The main aim of Portuguese rulers was to find a sea route to Asia and the Spice Islands. Portuguese explorers sailed down the coast of Africa looking for a passage to the East.

Prince Henry the Navigator. His role was similar to that of a patron during the Renaissance: he paid for the voyages

Who were the main Portuguese explorers and what did they do?

Prince Henry the Navigator (1394–1460)

Henry the Navigator was a prince who started the Portuguese exploration. He was the third son of King John I. In 1415, he helped conquer the town of Ceuta, a Muslim stronghold in Morocco. There he learned about the riches of Africa. He hoped that Portugal could gain some of these treasures, especially gold.

A very religious man, Henry also wanted to spread Christianity. He believed a legend about a Christian king in Africa called **Prester John**. He hoped to join with him to defeat Portugal's Muslim enemies. Although he did not actually sail himself, Prince Henry paid for ships to explore down the coast of Africa. He set up a school for exploration at **Sagres** on the southern tip of Portugal. Here, he brought together mapmakers, navigators, sailors and shipbuilders. They helped to develop the caravel that you read about in the last chapter. Year after year ships left the nearby port of Lagos to journey down the coast of Africa.

On these voyages, the sailors mapped the coastline on maps called **portolan charts**. The islands of **Madeira** and the **Azores** were discovered. After a number of failed attempts, an expedition sailed around **Cape Bojador** in 1434. Henry's voyages opened up trade links with African rulers, and gold and slaves began arriving in Portugal. By the time of his death in 1460, over 2,400 kilometres of the African coastline had been mapped.

Term

Portolan charts
Maps made of the coastline on voyages of discovery.

PART 2

Bartholomew Diaz (1450–1500)

After the death of Prince Henry, the Portuguese continued to send ships down the African coast. In 1487, an experienced sailor, **Bartholomew Diaz**, led an expedition of three ships down the coast of Africa. He hoped to sail around the tip of Africa and reach Asia. In January 1488 he was caught in a violent storm and lost sight of land for thirteen days. When the storm ended, he realised he had rounded the tip of Africa.

Bartholomew Diaz was the first European to enter the Indian Ocean. He wanted to sail on to Asia, but because there was a shortage of food his crew forced him to return to Portugal. As a result of the weather he had experienced, Diaz called the tip of Africa the **Cape of Storms**. The king of Portugal, John II, realised the importance of Diaz's discovery. He wanted sailors to round the Cape again so he renamed it the **Cape of Good Hope**.

Bartholomew Diaz. In this modern picture he is shown holding an astrolabe

Vasco da Gama (1460–1524)

In 1497, **Vasco da Gama** left Lisbon with three ships to try and sail to the East. On his voyage he used the maps drawn by Diaz. To gain helpful winds and avoid the dangerous coast of Africa, he sailed into the Atlantic. He was out of sight of land for three months. He rounded the Cape of Good Hope and on Christmas Day he landed on the coast of Africa. He named it **Natal** (after the Portuguese word for Christmas).

Vasco da Gama made one of the greatest discoveries in history – the route to the East

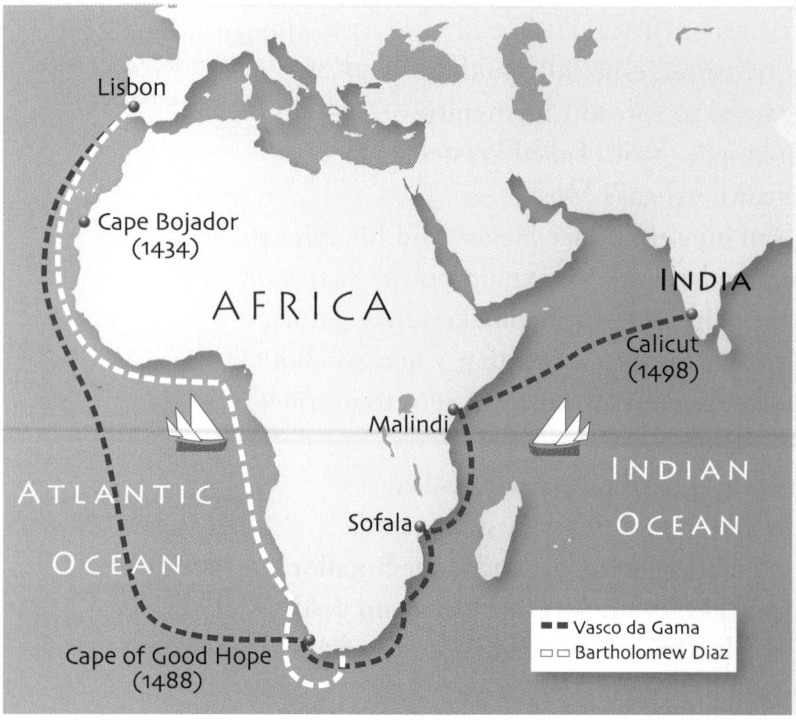

The Portuguese voyages down the coast of Africa showing Cape Bojador (1434), the Cape of Good Hope (1488) and da Gama's voyage to India (1498)

Vasco da Gama sailed up the east coast of Africa where a local ruler agreed to help him cross the Indian Ocean. In May 1498, with the help of an Arab pilot (or guide), he reached the rich city of **Calicut** in India. This was a major trading port where spices from the East could be bought. Da Gama loaded his ships with spices such as cinnamon and pepper.

Unfortunately for da Gama, the return journey across the Indian Ocean took three months. Many of his crew died of scurvy before they reached the safety of the African coast. In 1499, da Gama returned to Portugal. The spices that he had brought back paid for the voyage many times over.

Did you know?

Portuguese maps were the best in Europe. Other countries sent spies to try and steal them!

Controlling the spice trade

Da Gama's achievement was very important. He had discovered a sea route to the East and the fabulous wealth of the Spice Islands. Despite the length of the voyage and the loss of men, he became a hero and was now a wealthy man. The Portuguese were determined to control this new route to the East.

In 1500, **Pedro Cabral** set sail for India with thirteen ships. His expedition was blown off course and as a result he discovered **Brazil**.

When Cabral reached Calicut he established trading links with the local ruler. Later Portuguese expeditions, including one led by da Gama, fought with the Muslim rulers who controlled the spice trade. They seized Goa in India and captured the main port in the Spice Islands. Forts were built to protect their conquests. Da Gama died in India in 1524.

What was the impact of the Portuguese voyages?

- Portugal's explorers had discovered the sea route to the East.
- Their expeditions had greatly improved the knowledge of the coast of Africa.
- They established trade links with African rulers and brought gold and slaves back to Europe.
- They built up a large empire in Asia and in Brazil in South America.
- They broke the Muslim control of the spice trade and this helped to reduce the price of spices in Europe. Spices became more affordable for ordinary people.

A summary of Portuguese exploration

Prince Henry the Navigator
Sponsored voyages of exploration down the coast of Africa

Bartholomew Diaz
Rounded the Cape of Good Hope

Vasco da Gama
Discovered the sea route to the East

Do you understand this key term?

portolan charts

QUESTIONS

1 Give two reasons why Prince Henry sponsored voyages of exploration.
2 What was set up at Sagres by Prince Henry?
3 Name two achievements made by voyages sponsored by Prince Henry.
4 Write a brief account of the voyage of Bartholomew Diaz.
5 What port did Vasco da Gama reach in 1498? Describe his return voyage.
6 How was Brazil discovered?
7 How did Portugal establish control of the route to the East?
8 Write a paragraph on two of the following:
- The importance of Prince Henry the Navigator
- The voyage of Vasco da Gama
- The impact of the Portuguese discoveries

9 What were the achievements of the Portuguese voyages of exploration?

EXAM QUESTION

- What was the contribution of Portugal to the Age of Exploration?

Chapter 3

The Discoveries of Spain

Key Learning Objectives

- **What happened on the voyage of Christopher Columbus?**
- **What was the impact of Columbus' voyage?**
- **What happened on the voyage of Ferdinand Magellan?**

Special Study: the voyage of Christopher Columbus (1451–1506)

The Italian **Christopher Columbus** is probably the most famous explorer in history. His voyages led to the discovery of a vast new continent later known as America.

He was born in the large port of **Genoa** in 1451 and sailed on many voyages to Atlantic countries – including Ireland. He became a wealthy man.

Christopher Columbus

Why did Columbus set sail?

Columbus studied old maps and decided that the world was round. He thought if he sailed west from Europe he could reach Asia and the Spice Islands. At the time, this area was called the **East Indies** so he called his proposal **The Enterprise of the Indies.** Columbus had got the distances involved completely wrong and didn't know that an undiscovered continent stood in his way.

Why did Spain support his voyage?

Columbus needed to get a ruler to agree to his proposed voyage. He explained his idea to the king of Portugal, but the king refused to pay for the journey. The Portuguese were more interested in searching for a route to Asia by going down the coast of Africa.

Columbus moved to Spain and put his proposal to **King Ferdinand and Queen Isabella.** After a long delay they agreed to finance his voyage. They hoped that this voyage might beat Portugal in the race to control the wealth of the East. They also wanted to spread Christianity.

PART 2

What were the main events of the voyage?

Columbus set sail from the port of **Palos** on 3 August 1492 with three ships: the *Nina*, the *Pinta* and the *Santa Maria*. Columbus travelled on the *Santa Maria*. In total there were about ninety men on the three ships. At first they sailed to the **Canary Islands** where they took on supplies and carried out repairs to the ships.

On 6 September, Columbus left the Canaries on his very risky voyage. Ships rarely went out of sight of land unless they knew where they were going. Columbus was now planning to sail out into the open ocean. As the weeks went by some of the men began to think that they would never see Spain again.

Then on the morning of 12 October land was sighted by a lookout on the *Pinta*. Columbus went ashore and claimed the land for Spain. He named the island **San Salvador**.

Because he thought he had reached Asia, he named the native people **Indians**. He continued on his voyage looking for a passage to the East. He reached **Cuba** by the end of the month. He thought Cuba was Japan!

From Cuba he sailed to the island of **Hispaniola** (present day Haiti and the Dominican Republic). There, on Christmas day, the *Santa Maria* hit a rock and had to be abandoned. Columbus decided to return home on the *Nina*. He survived terrible storms and reached Portugal in March 1493. Soon after he returned to Spain.

Did you know?

The three ships were about 20 metres in length and weighed between 60 and 100 tonnes. A modern ferry can weigh up to 20,000 tonnes.

Did you know?

Even today historians are not sure on which island Columbus first landed. Most believe it was Watling Island in the Bahamas.

A modern copy of the *Santa Maria*

Did you know?

Columbus was the first sailor who kept a detailed record or **log** of his voyage. This is a very important source of information for historians about the voyage.

Term

Log
A record of the voyage kept by the captain.

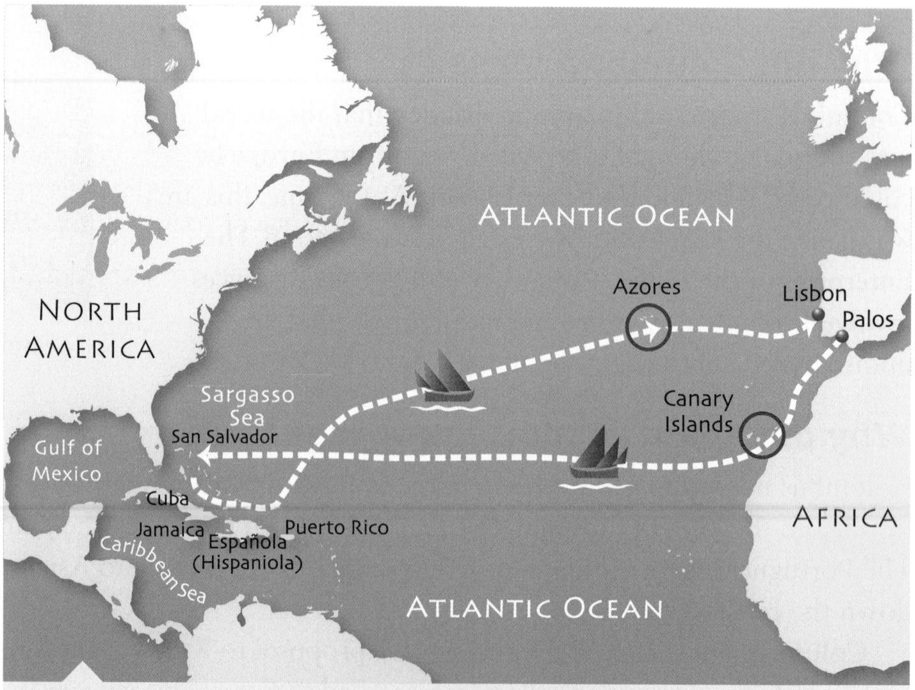

This map follows Columbus' first voyage, showing Palos, the Canary Islands, the Bahamas, Cuba and Hispaniola

What was the impact of Columbus' voyage?

News of Columbus' discovery spread rapidly throughout Europe. He received a hero's welcome in Spain. He brought some kidnapped Indians with him and a little gold. Ferdinand and Isabella were delighted at the prospect of great riches in the lands Columbus had discovered. They wanted to conquer this land for Spain. They agreed to a second voyage.

Columbus urged them to protect the new discoveries. So in 1494, at the **Treaty of Tordesillas**, Portugal and Spain agreed to divide the unknown world between them. Any land discovered to the west of a line drawn in the Atlantic Ocean went to Spain and land to the east went to Portugal.

In all, Columbus sailed on three more voyages. He explored Central and South America, but he never reached North America. He discovered Puerto Rico, Trinidad, Jamaica, Panama and the mouth of the Orinoco River.

However, no matter how hard he searched for the passage to the East, Columbus never reached China. He returned to Spain for a final time in 1504. He became very ill and in 1506 he died at Valladolid.

Though he still believed that he had found a new route to Asia, many people began to realise that he had in fact discovered a **New World**. This inspired many later explorers to sail westwards.

Term

New World
The name given at the time to the land discovered by Columbus – present-day North and South America (the Americas).

Did you know?

On his return to Spain Columbus brought back items that had not been seen in Europe before. These included pineapples, turkeys, tobacco and a hammock for sleeping.

Did you know?

Inspired by Columbus' discoveries, the Italian **Amerigo Vespucci** led voyages to what he called the 'New World'. His accounts of his voyages were widely read. The new lands were called after him: America.

PART 2

QUESTIONS

1. What was 'The Enterprise of the Indies'?
2. Why did Portugal reject Columbus' idea?
3. Give two reasons why Ferdinand and Isabella of Spain approved his voyage.
4. Name the three ships on Columbus' voyage. On which one did Columbus travel?
5. Why were many sailors worried on the voyage?
6. Why did he call the natives 'Indians'?
7. What welcome did Columbus receive in Spain? Explain your answer.
8. Name some of the places discovered on Columbus' later voyages.

Special Study: the voyage of Ferdinand Magellan (1480–1521)

Why did Magellan set sail?

As you can see on the map, the **Treaty of Tordesillas** had divided the newly discovered world between Portugal and Spain. The main issue for both countries was the location of the Spice Islands – were they in the Spanish or Portuguese half? In 1519, a voyage set sail from Seville in Spain to prove that they were in the Spanish half of the world. It was led by **Ferdinand Magellan**.

Born in 1480, Magellan was an experienced Portuguese sailor. He had quarrelled with his king and had offered his services to Spain. He persuaded the young Spanish king, Charles (we will read more about him in Section 7, The Reformation), that he could reach the Spice Islands by sailing west. He wanted to sail down the coast of America, cross the ocean and claim the islands for Spain. However, like Columbus, he had completely miscalculated the size of the ocean he planned to cross.

Ferdinand Magellan

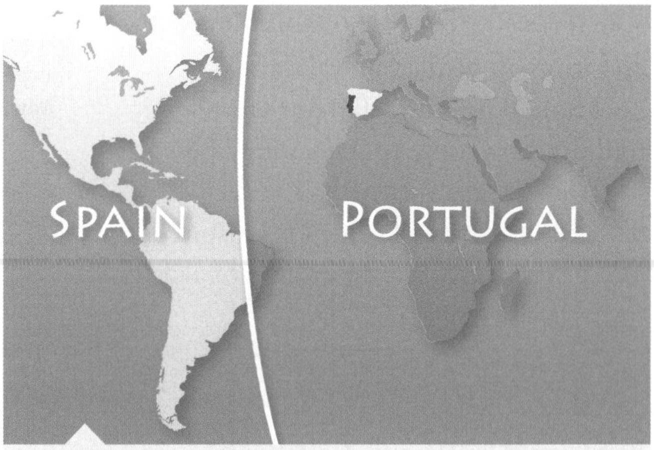

The Treaty of Tordesillas divided the undiscovered world between Spain and Portugal

What were the main events of the voyage?

Magellan set sail from Seville in August 1519 with five ships: the *Trinidad*, the *Concepcion*, the *San Antonio*, the *Santiago* and the *Victoria* (Magellan's ship). In total, there was a crew of 270 men.

They sailed down the coast of South America looking for the passage that would lead to the Spice Islands. They spent the winter months at **Port St Julian**. The Spanish captains did not like being commanded by a Portuguese and they revolted. Magellan crushed the attempted **mutiny**. Soon after, one of his ships, the *Santiago*, was wrecked in a storm, although the crew made it safely back to Port St Julian.

Term

Mutiny
When the crew disobeys the captain and takes over the ship.

Did you know?

As Magellan did not survive his voyage we rely on two sources for information about his journey:

1. The account of the Italian **Antonio Pigafetta** who was a member of the crew.
2. The interviews conducted by the king's secretary, **Maximilianus Transylvanus**, with the survivors of the voyage.

The expedition sailed further down the coast of South America. Eventually Magellan found a passage through the **straits** that are named after him today (Magellan Straits). One of the ships, the *San Antonio*, deserted and returned to Spain. The straits had been very stormy, with rough seas, and Magellan was so pleased to reach a calm ocean that he called it the **Pacific** (peaceful).

The Pacific Ocean was much bigger than Magellan expected. Magellan's crew ran out of food and started to die from scurvy. More than 100 men died.

Magellan eventually reached a group of islands that later became known as the **Philippines**. He got involved in a tribal war and, on 26 April 1521, he was killed in a battle. His remaining crew sailed on to the Spice Islands.

On September 1522, the *Trinidad*, captained by **Sebastian del Cano**, with eighteen survivors on board, reached Spain. They were all that remained of the 270 men who had left three years earlier. Their achievement was very important. They were the first to **circumnavigate** (or sail around) the world. This proved beyond any doubt that the world was round.

In the next chapter, we will look at the dramatic consequences of the discoveries that you have read about.

Term

Straits
A narrow passage between two land masses.

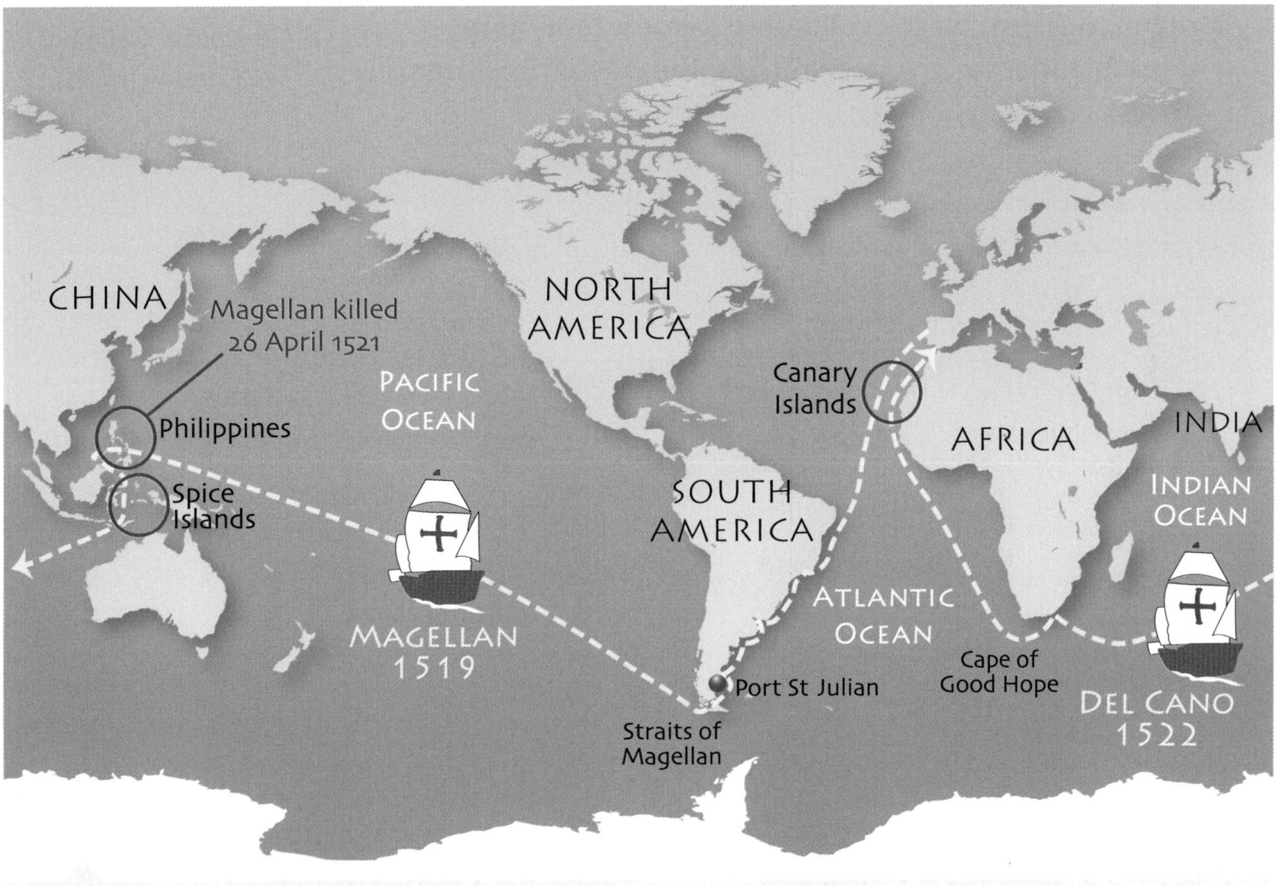

This map shows the voyage of Magellan

Do you understand these key terms?

log	**mutiny**	**Pacific**
New World	**straits**	**circumnavigate**

QUESTIONS

1 What was agreed at the Treaty of Tordesillas?
2 Why did Magellan set sail from Spain?
3 Name three ships that were part of his fleet.
4 Who rose in mutiny against Magellan?
5 What difficulties did Magellan face in the Pacific?
6 How did Magellan die in the Philippines?
7 Who commanded the ship that returned to Spain?
8 What was the significance of the voyage?

PART 2

People in History

Write an account on the following person in history: a named leader on a voyage during the Age of Exploration.
Use the plan below as a guide.

Hint
You should choose either Christopher Columbus or Ferdinand Magellan

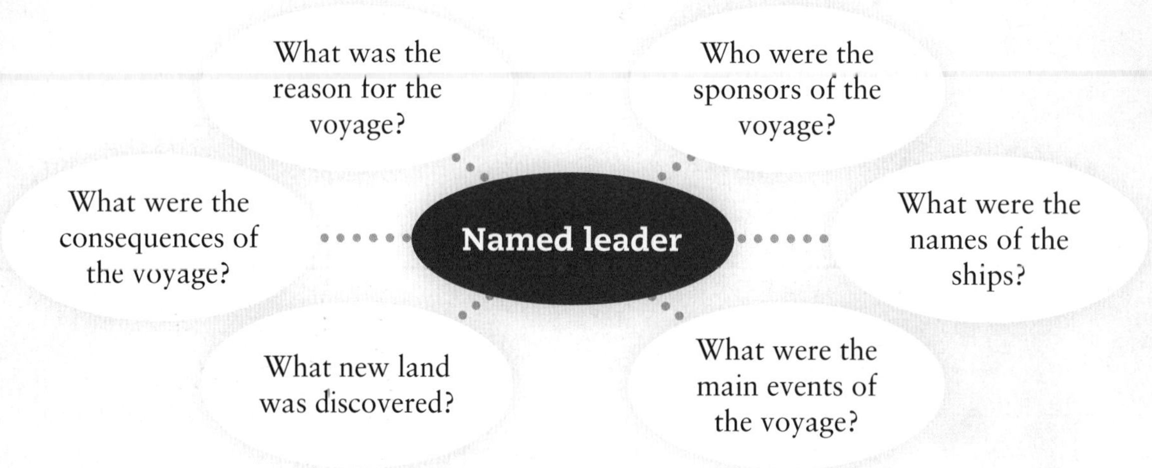
What was the reason for the voyage?
Who were the sponsors of the voyage?
What were the consequences of the voyage?
Named leader
What were the names of the ships?
What new land was discovered?
What were the main events of the voyage?

Chapter 4

The Consequences of the Age of Exploration

Key Learning Objectives

› **What were the consequences of the Age of Exploration?**

What were the consequences of the Age of Exploration?

The discoveries of the explorers had a major impact on both Europeans and the natives of the lands that were found. In this chapter we will look at some important consequences:

1 The creation of empires in the discovered lands
2 New goods exchanged between Europe and the New World
3 Changes in the European view of the world
4 The impact on the natives
5 The growth of the slave trade
6 Conflicts between European powers

Cortes was the brave but ruthless conqueror of the Aztec people. He became a rich and powerful man as a result of his success

1 The creation of empires in the discovered lands

When a land was discovered European countries sent soldiers to conquer it. As we saw in Chapter 2, the Portuguese gained a large empire in Asia as a result of the discoveries of her explorers.

However, it was in the New World that some of the most dramatic conquests were made. There, explorers built a large empire for Spain. These men were called the **conquistadores** or the conquerors. The most famous were **Hernando Cortes** and **Francisco Pizarro.**

Cortes and the Aztecs

In 1519, Hernando Cortes (1485–1547) set out from Cuba with a force of 600 men. He wanted to explore Mexico and win an empire for Spain. When he landed, he learned from the native people about the **Aztec Empire.** He travelled to their capital, **Tenochtitlan.**

The Aztec ruler **Montezuma** welcomed the Spanish, but Cortes took him hostage. The Aztecs then rose up after Spanish troops killed many Aztecs at a religious ceremony. Montezuma was killed and Cortes was forced to flee.

The next year Cortes returned with a large force made up of Spaniards and native Indian allies. As the Aztecs were cruel rulers many Indians were willing to help the Spaniards.

After a three-month siege the Spaniards captured the city. Tenochtitlan was destroyed and Cortes built Mexico City on its ruins. After the fall of Tenochtitlan, the rest of the Aztec Empire was quickly captured. Cortes sent the gold and treasure back to Spain.

Montezuma, as painted by a sixteenth-century European artist

Pizarro and the Incas

After the victory of Cortes over the Aztecs, the explorer Francisco Pizarro was given permission to conquer the **Inca Empire** in South America. In 1531, he set sail with 180 men to conquer an empire of 12 million people!

His small force met the Inca emperor, **Atahualpa**, at Cajamarca in 1532. They were vastly outnumbered by the Inca warriors, but Pizarro launched a surprise attack and captured Atahualpa. Over 10,000 Inca soldiers were killed for the loss of five Spaniards.

Atahualpa offered to fill a room full of gold and silver if he was released. Pizarro agreed and the Incas brought the precious metals. The gold and silver was melted down and sent back to Spain. Pizarro had Atahualpa killed anyway. It was too dangerous to keep him alive in case he led a rebellion against Spanish rule.

Pizarro soon captured the Inca capital, **Cuzco**. He founded the city of Lima, which became the capital of the new Spanish **colony**, Peru.

Term

Colony
A country that is controlled by another more powerful country.

The funeral of Atahualpa. This picture was painted in the nineteenth century, and imagines the scene

PART 2

The Spanish Empire in the New World

The Spanish set up the **Council of the Indies** to run the new lands that had been conquered for Spain. Spain's colonies in the New World became known as the **Spanish Main.**

The wealth from Spain's new empire made it Europe's most powerful country. Every year a treasure fleet sailed for Spain loaded with gold, silver and spices.

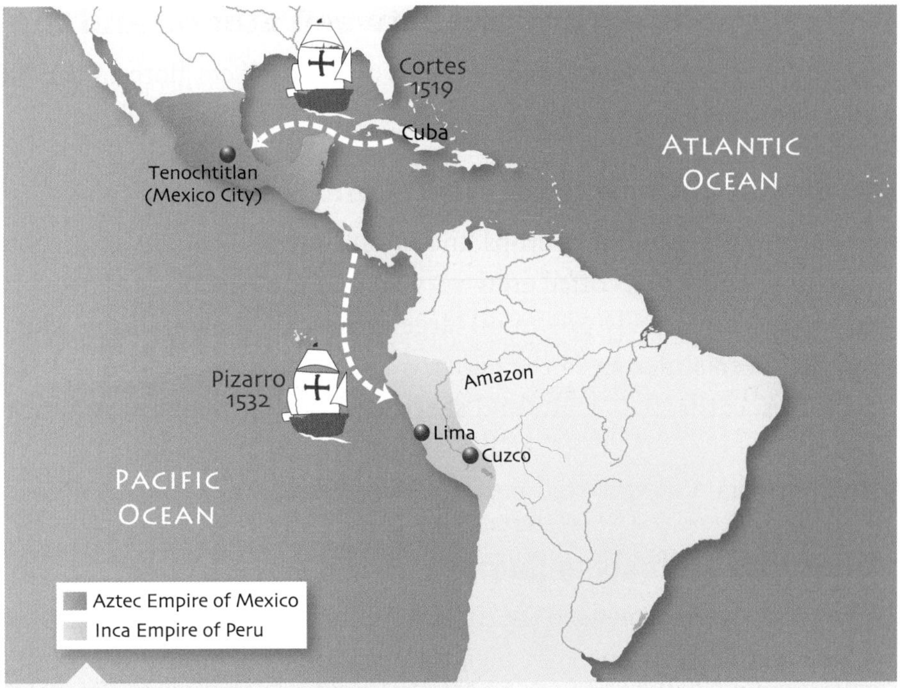

This map shows the Aztec and Inca Empires

Other European powers

Other European powers also built up large empires as a result of discoveries and conquest.

- The English settled on the east coast of North America. (We will read more about their colonies in North America on page 215.)
- The French controlled Canada and the Mississippi river valley.
- The Dutch won the Spice Islands from the Portuguese.

The traditional trading ports with the East, Venice and Genoa, went into decline. They were replaced by the Atlantic ports of Seville, Antwerp, Amsterdam and Rotterdam.

Did you know?

Gold and silver mines were discovered in Peru. By 1560 the gold shipped back from Peru had doubled the amount of the metal in Europe.

QUESTIONS

1 Who were the conquistadores?
2 Why did Cortes set out for Mexico?
3 Why did the Aztecs revolt against the Spanish?
4 Why were other Indians prepared to help the Spaniards against the Aztecs?
5 Describe how Pizarro treated the Inca ruler, Atahualpa.
6 Give one major consequence for Spain of the conquest of the Inca Empire.
7 Name two other countries that developed empires as a result of the Age of Exploration.

2 New goods exchanged between Europe and the New World

The discoveries saw new foods, animals and crops sent both to the New World and to Europe.

Goods and animals to the New World

The Europeans found that crops known in Europe such as wheat, cotton, sugar cane and, later, coffee grew very well in the Americas. Cotton, coffee and sugar were usually grown on large farms called **plantations**. The land used had been stolen from the native owners.

Horses, cattle, pigs, goats and sheep were also brought to America. Columbus introduced them on his second voyage (1493–96). Tea grown in Asia was imported into the New World.

Term

Plantation
Large farm where slaves grew crops such as sugar and tobacco.

Did you know?

Chocolate was originally taken as a drink by the Indians. When sugar was added it became a very popular drink in Europe. Chocolate bars date from the 1840s.

Goods and animals to Europe

New goods were brought back to Europe for the first time. These included: chocolate (cocoa beans), turkeys, tobacco, pineapples, corn, vanilla, chilli peppers and potatoes.

The wider availability of spices and crops grown in the New World revolutionised the diet and lifestyle of many Europeans:

- Sugar grown in the New World was added to coffee and **coffee houses** sprang up throughout Europe in the seventeenth and eighteenth centuries.
- Smoking **tobacco** became a popular pastime.
- The **potato** soon became the main part of the diet of people in Ireland.

3 Changes in the European view of the world

Look at the map. It was drawn around 1570. As you can see from the map, people now had a much better picture of how the world looked. During voyages, maps were made of coastlines and land that was explored. This meant that maps became more accurate as more and more discoveries were made. These new maps made navigation easier for later voyages.

A map of the Americas *c.*1570. How accurate is it?

Major discoveries

Here are some of the major discoveries that helped to change the European view of the world:

- The coastline of Africa was known and the tip of the continent was reached.
- A new sea route was found to the East and the Spice Islands.
- The world was much larger than was previously thought.
- A new continent called America existed.
- A vast ocean called the Pacific separated Asia and America.
- It had been proved beyond doubt that the world was round.

Did you know?

One result of Spanish rule in Central and South America is that most of the region speaks Spanish today.

4 The impact on the natives

The arrival of the Europeans was not good news for the native Indians.

They lost their land and were forced to work for their new European masters. The settlers treated them little better than slaves. Many priests and monks, who worked among the Indians, tried to defend them against poor treatment, but they could do little to help them.

Engraving of Bartolomé de las Casas, a Spanish colonist and priest, who defended the rights of native Indians in the early sixteenth century

Diseases

However, the most dramatic impact on the natives was the arrival of new diseases. When the native Indians came into contact with Europeans they also came into contact with European diseases such as smallpox, the flu, measles, typhoid and the bubonic plague. The Indians had no immunity to them and as a result millions died. The native population of the Caribbean that Columbus first encountered was wiped out by European diseases.

Smallpox was deadly. The native population in Mexico fell from about 30 million in 1519 to 3 million in 1568 as a result of smallpox.

Did you know?

Smallpox is a bit like chickenpox but far more serious.

5 The slave trade

Conditions aboard slave ships were very bad. Many slaves died on the voyage

One terrible consequence of the European discoveries was the growth of the **slave trade**. The Portuguese began the slave trade with Africa in 1441. In the New World there was a great demand for workers to mine the gold and silver. Slaves were also needed to work on the plantations.

At first, the native Indians were used. However, as we have seen, millions died of disease and a new source of labour was needed. The Spanish and the Portuguese were the first to introduce African slaves into the New World. They shipped Africans to their colonies in America and the Caribbean. The English, the French and the Dutch also transported slaves.

This dreadful trade in human beings lasted for over 300 years. It made great fortunes for European merchants. But it brought terrible misery. It is estimated that over 10 million Africans were forcibly moved to the New World, while 4 to 6 million died on the crossing.

The slave trade was abolished in the British Empire in 1807. Most countries in South America ended it in the 1820s. In the USA, it was not abolished until 1865.

Did you know?

Often traders gave rum to the African rulers in exchange for slaves. The slaves were sold in the New World and sugar was bought. This sugar was used to make the rum that was then sold to the Africans.

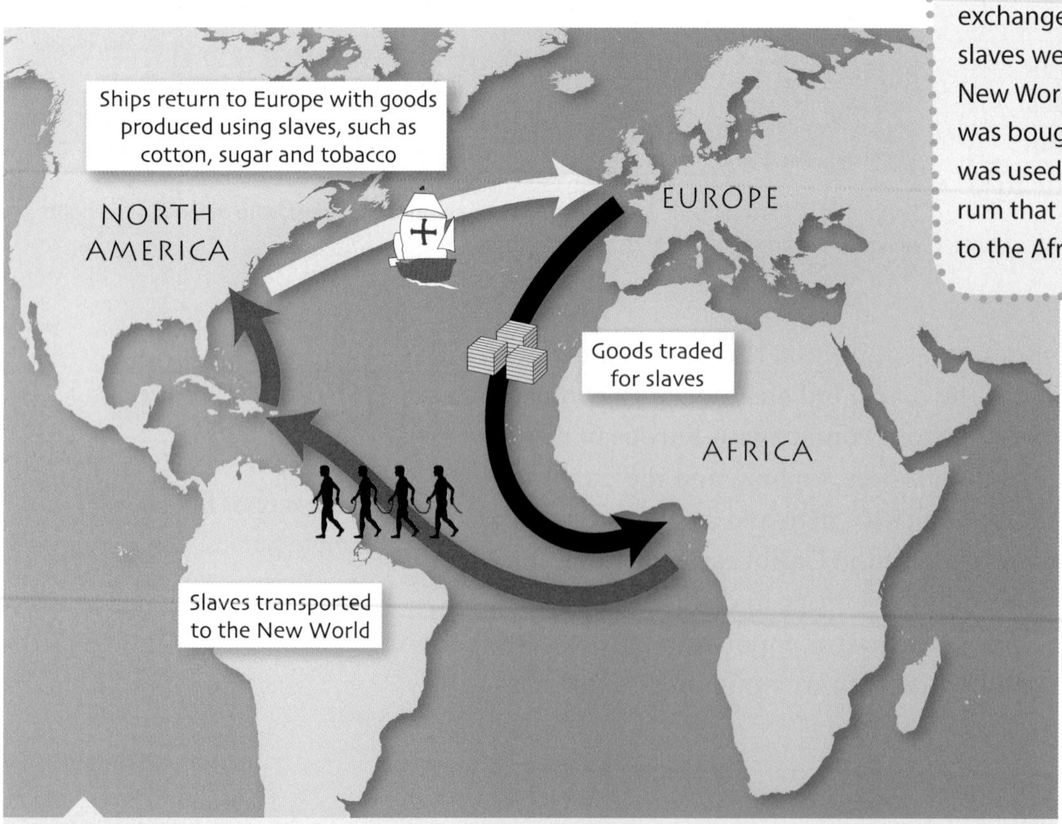
Ships return to Europe with goods produced using slaves, such as cotton, sugar and tobacco
NORTH AMERICA
EUROPE
Goods traded for slaves
AFRICA
Slaves transported to the New World

The slave trade

PART 2

6 Conflicts between European powers

With the great wealth and land available as a result of exploration, rivalry and wars were bound to develop between countries.

- Spain and Portugal were the first to come into dispute over their discoveries. The **Treaty of Tordesillas** divided the unknown world between them.
- Other countries such as England and France did not recognise the Treaty of Tordesillas. They wanted some of the wealth of the New World for themselves.
- The English attacked Spanish colonies. The ships bringing gold and silver back to Spain were particular targets.
- The Dutch conquered many Portuguese colonies, including some of the Spice Islands.
- Wars later broke out between the Dutch and the English over colonies.
- The French and the English were rivals in America, the Caribbean and India.

Did you know?

As a result of one of these wars the Dutch swapped New Amsterdam (New York) for a tiny spice island.

French and British ships fighting off the coast of America

Do you understand these key terms?

conquistador	**Inca**	**plantation**	**slave trade**
Aztec	**colony**	**smallpox**	

QUESTIONS

1 List four goods introduced from Europe into America and four goods introduced into Europe from America.

2 In the Americas, what were plantations?

3 Explain why the quality of maps improved as a result of the Age of Exploration.

4 How would you describe the treatment of the native Indians by the Europeans? Give evidence to support your answer.

5 What impact did smallpox have on the native Indians?

6 Why did the Spanish and the Portuguese introduce slavery into the New World?

7 Why did countries become rivals over land that was discovered? Give two examples of this rivalry.

8 Study the map and answer the questions that follow.

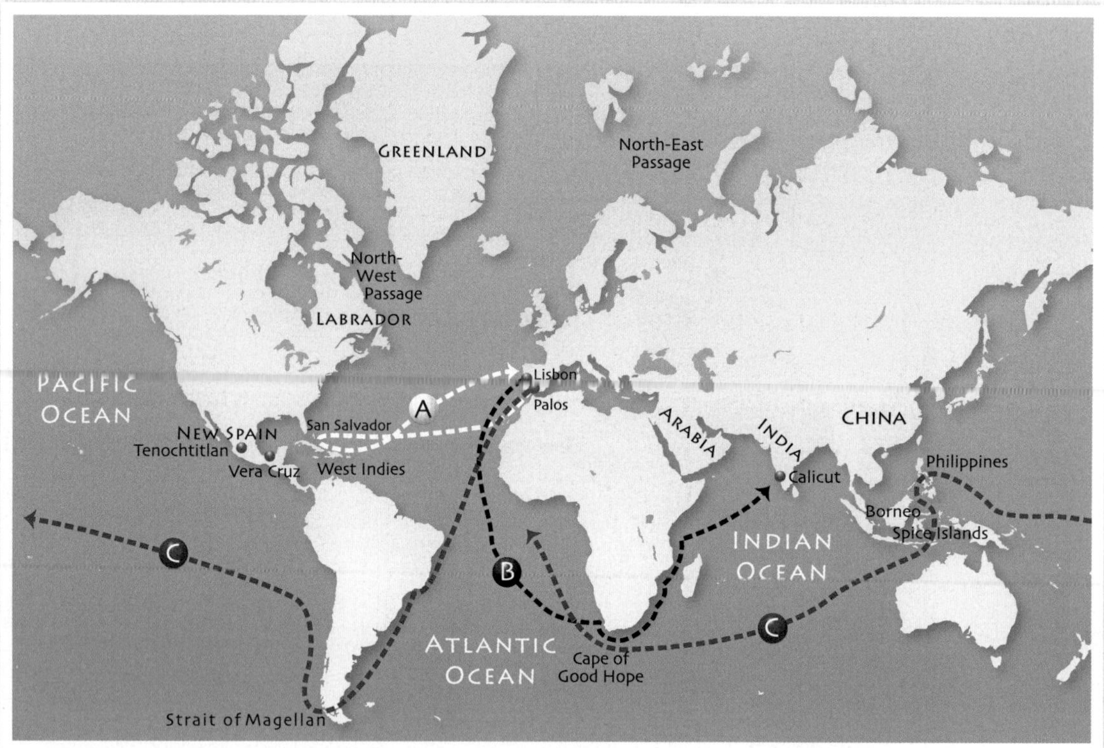

(a) Identify the three voyages marked A, B and C.

(b) Briefly explain the importance of each of the voyages.

9 Write an account of two of the following:

- The conquest of the Incas or the Aztecs
- The new goods introduced to Europe and the New World
- The slave trade
- How the voyages of discovery changed European knowledge of the world

EXAM QUESTION

› Letter from Amerigo Vespucci to his patron, Lorenzo de Medici (1500).

We were absent thirteen months on this voyage, exposing ourselves to terrible dangers, and discovering a very large part of Asia, and a great many islands, most of them inhabited.

According to the calculations I have several times made with the compass, we sailed about five thousand leagues.... We discovered immense regions, saw a vast number of people, all naked, and speaking various languages. On the land we saw many wild animals, various kinds of birds, and an infinite number of trees, all aromatic.

We brought home pearls in their growing state, and gold in the grain. We brought two stones, one of emerald, the other of amethyst, which was very hard, at least half a span long and three fingers thick. The sovereigns esteem them most highly, and have preserved them among their jewels.... We brought many other stones which appeared beautiful to us, but of all these we did not bring a large quantity, as we were continually busy in our navigation, and did not stay long in any one place.

When we arrived in Cadiz, we sold many slaves. Finding two hundred remaining to us... thirty-two having died at sea.... However, we are satisfied with having saved our lives, and thank God that during the whole voyage, out of fifty-seven Christian men, which was our number, only two had died, having been killed by the Indians.

The Oxford Book of Exploration, page 327

(a) How far did Vespucci and his crew sail?
(b) Mention two things they discovered.
(c) Name two things they brought back.
(d) Why did so many slaves die on the voyage?
(e) Why did rich patrons like de Medici sponsor voyages such as this? (HL)

TIMELINE

PART 2

Section 7

The Reformation

Chapter 1

Why Did the Reformation Happen?

Key Learning Objectives

- **What was the structure of the Catholic Church around 1500?**
- **What were the main problems in the Church?**
- **What was the influence of the Renaissance?**

This section of the course examines the religious changes that occurred in Europe in the sixteenth century. This period of history is called the **Reformation**.

Many people were unhappy with the Catholic Church and wanted to reform or change it. This led to a division among Christians and gave us a new word – **Protestant**. In later chapters, we will look at some of the people who played an important role in this period, including Martin Luther, John Calvin and Henry VIII.

Term

Reformation
Period of religious change that led to a division among Christians.

Protestants
Christians who broke away from the Catholic Church.

What was the structure of the Catholic Church?

Before we examine the causes of the Reformation we need to look at the structure of the Catholic Church around 1500. At that time, nearly all of the people in Western Europe were members of the Catholic Church. The Catholic Church was far more powerful than it is today and it had greater control over the lives of the people. Let's see how the Church was organised:

- The head of the Church was the **pope**, who lived in Rome. He was also the ruler of central Italy and played an important role in Italian politics.
- He was elected by **cardinals**, who helped the pope run the Church.
- Every country was divided into **dioceses** ruled over by a **bishop**.
- In each diocese there were a number of **parishes**. Each parish had at least one priest.
- The people who lived in the parish paid a **tithe** or tax to the Church. This money was used to pay the priest.
- There were also **monasteries** and **convents** where monks and nuns lived. The monasteries helped to look after the sick and the poor. Special monks called **friars** (e.g. Franciscans, Augustinians) lived and worked in towns where they preached to the people.

What were the main problems in the Church?

Around 1500, religion was a huge part of most people's lives. It was very important for people to find out what happened to them when they died. They wanted to win **salvation** – a reward that meant they would go to heaven. The Catholic Church taught that you could win salvation by a mixture of **faith** and **good works** (actions). However, there were problems with the Church that caused many people to lose confidence in its teachings.

1 The Renaissance popes

The problems started at the top. At that time many popes were not very holy men. Some were more interested in art or politics than in religion. They are called the **Renaissance popes** by historians.

- **Pope Sixtus IV** (1471–84) supported art and science. He was involved in a plot to have the ruler of Florence, Lorenzo de Medici, murdered during Mass!
- **Pope Julius II** (1503–13) and his successor **Pope Leo X** (1513–21) sponsored artists such as Leonardo da Vinci and Michelangelo. They were also involved in wars in Italy.
- The worst of these popes was **Alexander VI** (1492–1503). He lived a very unholy life. He had mistresses and made his son a cardinal!

Julius II was nicknamed 'the warrior pope'

2 The wealth of the Church

Most bishops were from wealthy, noble families. Some helped kings to run their countries. Many built great palaces for themselves to show their power and wealth. Some bishops forgot that their main job was to look after the religious needs of the members of the Church. For example, **Cardinal Wolsey** was the chief advisor to King Henry VIII of England. He built one of the biggest palaces in England, Hampton Court, as his home. We will find out more about him in Chapter 4.

A church was usually the largest building in every town in Europe

The Church was also an important landowner. Many rich people left large sums of money to monasteries to pray for their souls after they died. Some monasteries became very rich and owned huge amounts of land. The **abbots**, who ran the monasteries, did not always make sure that monks led holy lives.

PART 2

3 The abuses in the Church

As a result of this bad leadership, a number of serious abuses had developed in the Church.

The main abuses were as follows:

Abuses in the Church

Nepotism	Appointing a relative to an important position in the Church, e.g. bishop or cardinal. Sixtus IV appointed his six nephews as cardinals, including the future Pope Julius II
Simony	The buying and selling of Church positions. It was widely believed that Alexander VI paid money to some cardinals to be elected pope
Pluralism	Holding more than one position in the Church, e.g. bishop of two dioceses. As people paid a tax to the Church this could bring in a lot of money!
Absenteeism	Bishops or priests not living in their dioceses or parishes. This abuse was closely associated with pluralism. Some bishops rarely visited their dioceses, as they were too busy acting as advisors to their kings. In England, Cardinal Wolsey only visited his diocese shortly before he died

Poorly educated priests

While bishops and abbots were usually well-educated, the same could not be said for ordinary priests. Some had very little knowledge of the Bible. They could not even understand or speak Latin – the language that was used during Mass.

Indulgences

A further abuse was the selling of **indulgences**. According to the Church, an indulgence shortened the time that people spent being punished in **purgatory** after they died. It could be given to a person who prayed or gave time or money to a good cause. In the Middle Ages, the Church started selling these indulgences to make money. We will read more about indulgences in the next chapter.

Term

Purgatory
According to the Catholic Church, the place where a person was punished for their sins and purified before going to heaven.

Indulgences
The Church said that indulgences reduced the time a person spent in purgatory.

What was the influence of the Renaissance?

In Section 5, we looked at the Renaissance. It was a time when people questioned accepted ideas. As a result, many people also began to doubt both the power and the teachings of the Catholic Church. They argued for reform of the Church.

Writers known as **humanists** were very critical of the wealth of the Church. They felt people should read the Bible themselves and not just accept what they were told by priests and bishops. In England, **Sir Thomas More** was one of the humanist critics of the Church. However, it was his friend, **Erasmus of Rotterdam**, who was the most famous critic.

- Erasmus wrote a book called *In Praise of Folly* (folly means foolishness) which poked fun at the lives of leading churchmen.
- He translated the New Testament into Greek. This showed that the version of the Bible used by the Church contained mistakes.

The newly invented printing press meant that many people read the work of Erasmus, and his advice was sought by important people. It was said at the time that 'Erasmus laid the egg and Luther hatched it'.

In the next chapter we will read about **Martin Luther**. He was the man who started the Reformation.

Erasmus of Rotterdam (1466–1536)

Causes of the Reformation

- The behaviour of popes and bishops
- The wealth and power of the Church
- Abuses: simony, nepotism, pluralism and absenteeism
- Poorly educated priests
- The sale of indulgences
- Renaissance: questioning of accepted beliefs

Do you understand these key terms?

Reformation	**faith**	**simony**	**indulgences**
Protestant	**good works**	**pluralism**	**purgatory**
salvation	**nepotism**	**absenteeism**	**humanists**

QUESTIONS

1 What was the role of the pope around 1500?

2 What was the job of the friars?

3 Give two examples to show that some popes did not live holy lives.

4 Explain why the Church was very wealthy.

5 What were the following abuses in the Church: simony; nepotism; absenteeism; pluralism?

6 How did the Renaissance help to cause the Reformation?

7 Explain why Erasmus was such an important writer.

8 Write a paragraph on two of the following:
- The Renaissance popes
- The power and wealth of the Catholic Church
- The influence of the Renaissance

9 Do you agree with the following statement?

'By 1500 the Church badly needed a lot of reform.'

Give four reasons to support your answer.

Chapter 2

Martin Luther

Key Learning Objectives

- **Who was Martin Luther and what did he do?**
- **Why and how did Luther split from Rome?**
- **What were Luther's main beliefs?**
- **How did Luther's ideas spread?**

Special Study: Martin Luther (1483–1546)

In 1517, a German monk called Martin Luther attacked the sale of indulgences by the Catholic Church. This event was to trigger off the Reformation. Let's look at what happened.

Early life

Martin Luther was born at Eisleben in Saxony in 1483. He came from a large family and his father was a rich copper-miner. Following his father's wishes, he went to university at Erfurt to study law. In 1505, after being caught in a thunderstorm, he decided to become a monk. This decision angered his father, but Martin Luther joined the Augustinians and started studying **theology** at Erfurt University.

Term

Theology
The study of religion.

Luther questions the Church's teachings

In 1512, Luther became Professor of Theology at the University of Wittenberg. This university had recently been founded by the ruler of Saxony, **Frederick the Wise**. Although Luther led a very holy life, he was unhappy as a monk. He believed that he was a terrible sinner. He read the Bible closely and became convinced that the Church's teaching on how to get to heaven (win salvation) was wrong.

The Catholic Church taught that a mixture of faith and good works was needed to get to heaven. Luther believed that a person was saved by faith alone. His idea became known as **Justification by Faith Alone**.

Did you know?

We know that Luther came from a wealthy background because he went to university. Only a few people would have been able to afford to go to university.

Why and how did Luther split from Rome?

The issue that saw Luther publicly disagree with the Church was the **sale of indulgences.** Pope Leo X had ordered their sale to pay for the rebuilding of St Peter's Basilica in Rome. The Dominican friar **John Tetzel** sold indulgences in the area around Wittenberg. Luther was unhappy to see people from Wittenberg buying them. He felt that it encouraged people to think they could buy their way into heaven.

In 1517, as a protest against the sale of indulgences, he sent a letter to his bishop, **Albrecht of Brandenburg,** hoping that the he would act against it. He included a list called the ***95 Theses*** or arguments against it. On 31 October 1517, he was said to have nailed the *95 Theses* to the door of the Castle Church in Wittenberg. He then started to write pamphlets (small books) explaining his beliefs.

What was the reaction of the pope?

Term

Heretic
Someone who disagreed in public with the Church's religious teachings.

Pope Leo X ordered that Luther's actions be investigated. Luther was told to go to Rome. However, he was saved by his ruler, Frederick the Wise, who made sure that Luther stayed in Germany. Frederick was very powerful and was proud that a professor at his new university had become so famous.

In 1520, Pope Leo X wrote a **papal bull** (letter) condemning Luther. It was called *Exsurge Domine* (Arise O Lord!). It gave Luther sixty days to recant (take back) his teachings. If he refused, he would be condemned as a **heretic** and **excommunicated** (thrown out of the Church). Some of Luther's pamphlets were burned by the Church and in revenge Luther publicly burned the papal bull and other Catholic books.

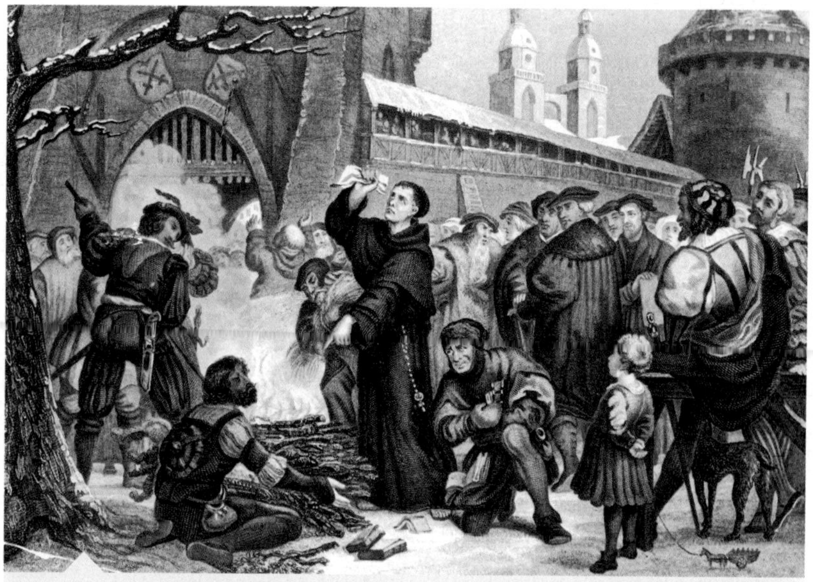
Luther burns the papal bull. Do you think the artist approved of what Luther did?

QUESTIONS

1. How do we know that Luther was a good student?
2. In 1505, what major decision did Luther make about his future?
3. Was Luther happy as a monk? Explain your answer.
4. Explain Luther's idea of 'Justification by Faith Alone'.
5. What caused Luther to publicly criticise the Church?
6. What was the name of Luther's bishop?
7. Who was the pope at the time? Who was the ruler of Saxony?
8. What did the pope order Luther to do in 1520? How did Luther react?

What happened at the Diet of Worms?

The pope asked the new Holy Roman Emperor, **Charles V**, to deal with Luther. Charles had been elected emperor in 1519. One of his jobs was to defend the Catholic Church. He was alarmed at Luther's ideas and wanted to stop them spreading. However, one of the seven electors who chose the emperor was **Frederick the Wise**. Charles had to proceed very carefully. Frederick put pressure on Charles V to allow Luther to attend a meeting of German princes at the town of Worms. This meeting was known as a **Diet**. He agreed, as he did not want to annoy Frederick.

Charles V painted by the artist Titian

Luther was promised a safe conduct to attend the **Diet of Worms**. In April 1521, he set out. He was greeted as a hero in all of the towns he travelled through.

At the Diet, Luther refused to take back his teachings. He was condemned as an outlaw by the **Edict of Worms**. This meant that he could be killed and the person responsible would not be arrested. Charles V kept his word, though, and he allowed Luther to return to Saxony.

Term

Edict
A law passed by an emperor.

Luther at the Diet of Worms. His bravery in defending his beliefs has served as an inspiration to Protestants ever since. This is a picture from the nineteenth century

Luther at Wartburg

Frederick the Wise now came to Luther's rescue. He had Luther kidnapped and hidden in a remote castle at **Wartburg**. He did this to take Luther out of the limelight until matters calmed down. While at the castle Luther translated the New Testament into German. This took only eleven weeks. For Luther it was very important that ordinary people could read the Bible in their own language. A few years later, he translated the Old Testament as well.

By 1522, it was safe for Luther to go back to Wittenberg, where he took charge of the religious changes that were happening there.

Martin Luther translating the bible at Wartburg Castle

What were Luther's main beliefs?

Luther did not see himself setting up a new Church but reforming the Church back to the way God had intended. The table below compares Luther's beliefs with those of the Catholic Church:

Term

Sacrament
A very important Christian ritual.

Teaching	Luther	Catholic Church
What was the source of beliefs?	Bible source of all teachings	Bible and traditions
How did a person get to heaven?	Faith in God (Justification by Faith Alone)	Faith and good works needed
Who was the head of the Church?	The prince in each state	The pope
What was the main weekly religious event?	Communion service in German	Mass said in Latin
How many sacraments were there?	Two sacraments: baptism and the Eucharist	Seven sacraments
Was Christ present at the Eucharist?	Both the bread and wine and body and blood present at communion	Bread and wine changed totally into the body and blood of Christ
How important were priests?	All Christians were equal and should read the Bible for themselves – the priesthood of all believers	Priests were a special group who were trained to properly understand what the Bible meant
Could priests marry?	Allowed to marry	Not allowed to marry

How did Luther's ideas spread?

Luther's ideas spread quickly around Germany, with the help of the newly invented printing press. He became a popular hero as he stood up to the might of the Catholic Church.

Did you know?

The ruler of Germany was called the **Holy Roman Emperor** (see the map). However, Germany was divided into many states and the rulers of these states jealously guarded their power. The most powerful states were ruled by **electors**, who chose the emperor.

This map shows the extent of the Holy Roman Empire and the spread of Luther's ideas

More and more Germans left the Catholic Church and became followers of Luther (**Lutherans**). At first, his ideas proved popular in towns throughout Germany. When a town became Protestant, the Mass was replaced by a service in the German language. From 1525 onwards some of the rulers of the German states also started adopting his ideas. Most of the states of Northern Germany, including Saxony, left the Catholic Church. Soon **Denmark, Sweden** and **Norway** followed.

Term

Lutheran
A follower of Martin Luther.

In 1529, when Charles V tried to ban Luther's ideas, a number of princes protested and Luther's followers became known as **Protestants**. This term was soon used to describe any group of Christians that broke away from the Catholic Church.

Attempts to find a compromise solution failed and war soon broke out between the Protestant states and the emperor. The war ended with the **Peace of Augsburg** in 1555. This agreement established the principle that the ruler of a state decided the religion of his people.

Luther's later life

In 1525, Luther married a former nun, **Catherine von Bora**. Their marriage was happy and they had six children. He continued to write pamphlets and preach. He also wrote a number of hymns including the famous 'A Mighty Fortress is Our God'. He was not a rich man and rented rooms in his house to students to make some money.

When he grew older his health was poor and he became very bad-tempered. In 1546, he died of a heart attack at his birthplace of Eisleben.

The religious revolution he had started became known as the **Reformation**.

Did you know?

We rely on the paintings of the artist Lucas Cranach the Elder for many of the images from this period. He was a follower of Luther and was the best man at Luther's wedding.

Luther and his wife, Catherine von Bora, painted by Lucas Cranach (1472–1553)

TIMELINE Martin Luther

1483	Luther was born at Eisleben in Saxony
1505	He became an Augustinian monk
1512	He was appointed a professor at the University of Wittenberg
1517	He began his protest with his *95 Theses* against the sale of indulgences
1518–20	Luther's ideas spread with the help of the printing press
1520	Pope Leo X condemned Luther's teaching – Luther burned the papal letter
1521	Luther attended the Diet of Worms where he was condemned by the Edict of Worms
1522	He translated the *New Testament* into German. Returned to Wittenberg
1525	Throughout Germany princes started converting to his ideas He married Catherine von Bora
1534	He published the complete Bible in German
1546	Luther died at his birthplace of Eisleben

Do you understand these key terms?

theology **papal bull** **excommunicate** **Holy Roman Emperor**
Justification by Faith **heretic** **edict** **elector**
95 Theses **Diet** **sacrament** **Lutheran**

QUESTIONS

1 Who was the Holy Roman Emperor? Why did he have to be careful in his treatment of Luther?
2 Describe what happened at the Diet of Worms.
3 How did Frederick the Wise come to Luther's rescue?
4 Give two reasons why Luther's translation of the Bible into German was important.
5 Explain the origin of the term Protestant.
6 Give two reasons why Luther succeeded as a reformer.
7 Show how two of Luther's teachings differ from those of the Catholic Church.
8 Describe briefly Luther's life after 1525.
9 Write an account of two of following topics:
   (a) Why Luther led a protest against the Church
   (b) The Diet of Worms
   (c) The spread of Luther's ideas
   (d) The main beliefs of Martin Luther
10 Why, do you think, was Luther a hero to many Germans in the sixteenth century?

SOURCE QUESTION

› Study the following parts (A–C) of the letter sent by Martin Luther to his bishop Albrecht of Brandenburg protesting at the sale of indulgences on October 31 1517. Answer the questions that follow.

Part A

To the Most Reverend Father in Christ and Most Illustrious Lord, Albrecht of Magdeburg and Mainz, Archbishop and Primate of the Church, Margrave of Brandenburg, etc., his own lord and pastor in Christ, worthy of reverence and fear, and most gracious.

Part B

Papal indulgences for the building of St Peter's are being distributed under your most distinguished name. I do not bring accusation against the preachers so much as ... I grieve over the wholly false impressions which the people have conceived from them; the unhappy souls believe that if they have purchased letters of indulgence they are sure of their salvation; again, that so soon as they cast their contributions into the money-box, souls fly out of purgatory.

Part C

But what can I do, good Bishop and Most Illustrious Prince, except pray your Most Reverend Fatherhood by the Lord Jesus Christ that you would agree to look [on this matter] with the eye of fatherly care, and do away entirely with that thesis and impose upon the preachers of pardons [indulgences] another form of preaching;

May the Lord Jesus have your Most Reverend Fatherhood eternally in His keeping. Amen.

From Wittenberg on the Vigil of All Saints, 1517.

(a) According to Part A name three titles by which Luther addresses his bishop, Albrecht of Brandenburg.

(b) According to Part B what are the papal indulgences for?

(c) From Part B what 'wholly false impressions' does Luther claim the people have taken from the preachers?

(d) According to Part C what does Luther ask his bishop to do?

(e) Looking at the three parts of the letter would you agree with the view that Luther is very respectful towards Albrecht of Brandenburg? Give three pieces of evidence from the sources to support your answer.

Chapter 3

John Calvin and Geneva

John Calvin was the most famous reformer after Martin Luther

Key Learning Objectives

- **Who was John Calvin and what did he do?**
- **What were Calvin's main beliefs?**
- **How did he put his beliefs into effect?**
- **How did Calvin's ideas spread?**

Special Study: John Calvin (1509–1564)

After Luther, the Frenchman **John Calvin** was probably the most famous and most influential reformer. He was born in Noyon in northern France in 1509. His father was a lawyer who worked for the Church. When he was fourteen years old Calvin went to study at the University in Paris. While at university he converted to Luther's teachings.

In 1534, **King Francis I** started persecuting Protestants. It was now dangerous to be a Protestant in France. Calvin left the country and went to the city of Basle in Switzerland. The city was Protestant and here Calvin was safe.

What were Calvin's main beliefs?

While in Basle, Calvin wrote a book that made him famous. It was called the *Institutes of the Christian Religion*. This book contained his main beliefs:

- Like Luther, he said the Bible was the source of all teachings.
- He believed that there should be **no pope or bishops**.
- He thought that there were only two **sacraments** – baptism and the Eucharist.
- He agreed with Luther that services should be in the language of the people, e.g. French rather than Latin.
- However, Calvin differed with Luther on some issues. He believed that God had chosen those who were going to heaven before they were born. This was called **predestination.** Those chosen he called the **elect**.
- Unlike Luther, Calvin argued that there was no presence of Christ at communion.

How did he put his beliefs into effect?

In 1536, Calvin visited **Geneva.** The Reformation had recently spread to this French-speaking city and Calvin was persuaded to stay to help Geneva become Protestant. However, his ideas proved unpopular and he left Geneva.

He then lived in Strasbourg for three years. In 1541, he was invited back to Geneva. He took control of the city, which had a population of about 13,000. Now he was able to put his religious ideas into effect.

As we have seen, there were no bishops in Calvin's church. There were four types of minister who looked after the members of his Church:

1. **Pastors** preached the word of God and administered the sacraments of baptism and the Eucharist.
2. **Doctors** were responsible for doctrine (church teachings). Calvin said he was a doctor.
3. **Elders** looked after the daily life of the community and made sure people lived good lives. They also chose the ministers.
4. **Deacons** cared for the poor and the sick. They did the work that had traditionally been done by monks and nuns.

Geneva became known as the **'City of God'**. The Church that Calvin founded became known as the **Reformed** or **Presbyterian Church** after the Greek word for elder: *presbyteros*.

In Geneva, churches were now very bare, with no statues or crucifixes. On Sunday, the main part of the religious service was the sermon. This was given from a **pulpit**. There were also strict rules governing the everyday lives of the citizens. People were expected to live good and holy lives. Dancing, gambling and plays were forbidden. Sunday was a day of rest when no work was permitted. People who disobeyed these rules could be fined, imprisoned or in some cases sentenced to death.

Term

Pulpit
A raised platform from which the pastor gave a sermon.

As you might imagine, Calvin's ideas were not popular with everyone! However, he believed he was doing God's work. He did not like to be criticised and he had some opponents executed.

Interior of a Catholic church. What differences do you notice?

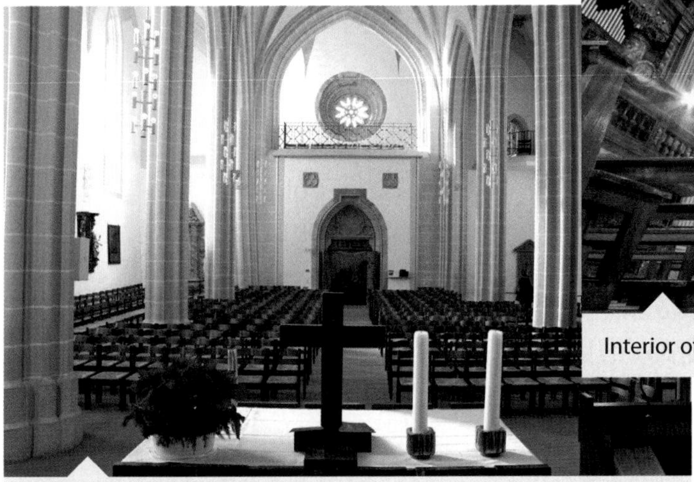

Interior of a Protestant church

PART 2

How did Calvin's ideas spread?

Despite the strict rules Geneva was an inspiration for Protestants from all over Europe. Many saw it as the Protestant Rome. Many young men travelled there to learn more about Calvin's ideas and to hear him preach. Calvin founded the **Academy of Geneva** to train them in the beliefs of his church. They then returned to their home countries, spreading his views.

Most of the missionaries went to France where his followers were known as **Huguenots.** Calvin's ideas were also popular in the Netherlands, England and Hungary. In England his followers were known as **Puritans.** In other countries they were called **Calvinists.**

Some Lutheran states in Germany also adopted his ideas. If an area became Protestant after 1550 it generally followed Calvin's ideas.

One country in which Calvin's religious ideas proved very popular was Scotland. They were brought there by **John Knox.** As we will read in the next section, in the seventeenth century King James I ordered the plantation of Ulster. Many of the settlers came from Scotland. They brought their religious ideas with them. To this day their descendants live in Ulster.

Calvin's health had always been poor and in 1564 he died in Geneva.

This map shows Switzerland and some of the cities that became Protestant during the Reformation

Did you know?

At his request, Calvin was buried in an unmarked grave.

Do you understand these key terms?

Eucharist	**pastor**	**deacon**	**Huguenot**
predestination	**doctor**	**Presbyterian**	**Puritan**
elect	**elder**	**pulpit**	**Calvinist**

QUESTIONS

1. Why did Calvin leave France?
2. What book did Calvin write in Basle? Why was this book important?
3. Why did Calvin visit Geneva?
4. How did Calvin turn Geneva into the 'City of God'?
5. Why was the Academy of Geneva important?
6. From the following list identify the countries to which Calvin's ideas spread: Spain; France; Italy; Netherlands; England.
7. Who brought Calvin's ideas to Scotland?
8. How did Calvin's ideas come to Ireland?

EXAM QUESTION

- Write an account of Calvin's church in Geneva. (HL)

People in History

Write an account of a named religious reformer at the time of the Reformation.

Use the plan below as a guide:

Hint

You should choose either Martin Luther or John Calvin.

Reformer

- What were the main events in his early life?
- What were his reasons for leaving the Church?
- What were his main beliefs?
- How did his beliefs spread?
- What were the consequences of his reforms?

Chapter 4

Religious Change in England

Henry VIII (1491–1547) was very well-educated, and was interested in religion and Renaissance ideas. However, he could be very cruel when dealing with opponents – real or imagined!

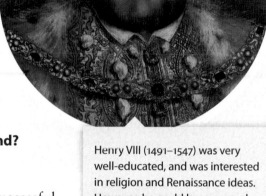

Key Learning Objectives

- **Why did Henry VIII break with Rome?**
- **What happened when Henry broke with Rome?**
- **What changes did Henry's children make?**
- **What was the impact of the Reformation on Ireland?**

One of the countries where the Reformation was most successful was England. As we shall see, this success was not guaranteed. It only came about after a lot of different religious changes introduced by England's rulers in the sixteenth century.

Why did Henry VIII break with Rome?

In the 1520s, the king of England was **Henry VIII.** He ruled from 1509 to 1547. He was from the **Tudor** family and was a very intelligent but cruel ruler. At first he was an opponent of Luther's religious beliefs and had been awarded the title **'Defender of the Faith'** by the pope.

Henry was worried about who would succeed him after he died. He was married to **Catherine of Aragon** and they had one child, **Mary.** Catherine was now too old to have any more children. He wanted a boy, as he did not believe that the English people would accept a woman as a ruler.

Henry had fallen in love with **Anne Boleyn** and wanted to leave Catherine and marry her. However, there was a major problem for Henry. The Catholic Church did not permit divorce. In special cases it would grant an **annulment.** This ended the marriage on the grounds that it should never have been allowed in the first place.

The King's Great Matter

Henry asked his chief advisor **Cardinal Wolsey** to persuade the pope to grant an annulment on the grounds that Catherine had originally been married to his brother, Arthur. Marrying a brother's wife was banned by the Church. This demand became known as **The King's Great Matter.**

Pope Clement VII wanted to agree but he was in a difficult position. The Church had originally given special permission to Henry to marry his brother's wife. Now

Henry was asking the Church to say it had been wrong in the first place. Also the pope had to be very careful not to annoy Catherine's nephew, the Holy Roman Emperor, **Charles V**. The emperor was strongly opposed to the annulment.

Catherine of Aragon (1485–1536) was the daughter of King Ferdinand and Queen Isabella of Spain

What happened when Henry broke with Rome?

After a long delay the pope refused to agree to Henry's demands. Henry was very angry and decided to break with Rome. He dismissed Cardinal Wolsey and appointed **Thomas Cromwell** to introduce his policies. **Thomas Cranmer** was made Archbishop of Canterbury – the most important bishop in England. He agreed with Henry's policies. He married Henry and Anne Boleyn. Soon afterwards they had a daughter. Henry later had Anne executed. In all he married six times and had one son, Edward.

In 1534, the English parliament passed the **Act of Supremacy**. This made Henry head of the English Church, instead of the pope. The **Church of England** was now set up. Henry ordered that all English people recognise him as head of the Church.

Henry did not trust the monks to be loyal to his new Church and so he decided to close the monasteries. He had another reason for this decision – he wanted the wealth and land of the monasteries. This event was called the **Dissolution of the Monasteries**. As many monasteries helped the poor and looked after the sick, this policy was unpopular.

Although he had broken with Rome, Henry did not allow Protestant religious teachings in the Church of England. It was during the reign of his son, **Edward VI**, that the new, Protestant religious ideas were introduced to England.

The ruins of Fountains Abbey in Yorkshire. Today ruins of monasteries closed by Henry VIII are to be found throughout England, Ireland and Wales

PART 2

What changes did Henry's children make?

King Edward VI (1547–53)

On the death of his father Edward VI became the King of England, and was king for six years. He was only nine years old, so a group of leading nobles really ruled England. These men were Protestants. They allowed Thomas Cranmer to introduce Protestant beliefs into the Church of England. He wrote the ***Book of Common Prayer***. This was used in all churches. The Mass in Latin was now replaced by a service in English. People could be sent to prison if they did not attend the new services. The measures were unpopular with many ordinary English people.

Henry VIII's only son: Edward VI

The young king approved of these changes but he died at the age of fifteen in 1553. He was succeeded by Mary Tudor, who was the daughter of Catherine of Aragon.

Henry VIII's daughters: Mary I and Elizabeth I

Queen Mary I (1553–58)

Mary Tudor was queen for only five years. At first, the English people were very happy when Mary became queen. She was a strong supporter of the Catholic Church and most English people were still Catholic. However, Mary made two serious errors that damaged the Catholic cause in Britain and made her very unpopular:

- She married her second cousin, **Philip of Spain.** He was the son of Charles V and eleven years younger than her. The marriage was very unpopular in England. People were worried that Mary would be dominated by her Spanish husband.
- Mary started to persecute Protestants. About 300 people, including Archbishop Cranmer, were burned at the stake. This was the traditional punishment for heretics, but the executions shocked people. These actions earned her the nickname **Bloody Mary.**

The execution of Archbishop Thomas Cranmer. This picture came from a book called *Foxe's Book of Martyrs*. The book was widely read during the reign of Queen Elizabeth and did much to damage the reputation of Mary Tudor and Catholics in general. Do you think it is a reliable source?

Queen Elizabeth I (1558–1603)

Mary was succeeded by Elizabeth, the daughter of Anne Boleyn. She reigned for forty-five years and was called the **Virgin Queen** because she never married. She is remembered today as one of England's greatest rulers.

Elizabeth was a Protestant and quickly changed her sister's policies. She passed an **Act of Supremacy** that made her governor of the Church of England. The teachings of the Church of England (or the **Anglican Church,** as it was also known) were set out in the **Thirty-Nine Articles.**

Term

Act of Supremacy
A law that made the king or queen of England the head of the Church of England.

Church services were to be in English and the *Book of Common Prayer* was to be used. Priests were allowed to marry. She also passed a law saying that all her subjects were expected to attend Protestant services or be fined.

Her policies worked and by the time of her death England was a stronghold of the Protestant faith. Her successor, King James I, continued her policies.

Did you know?

Some Catholics hoped to replace Elizabeth with her Catholic cousin, Mary Queen of Scots. After one failed plot Elizabeth had Mary executed.

PART 2

What was the impact of the Reformation on Ireland?

Henry VIII introduced his religious changes into the areas of Ireland that were under English control. Monasteries were closed and the **Church of Ireland** was set up with Henry as its head. However, the reforms had little popular support:

- The **Gaelic Irish** were very suspicious of anything English, and remained Catholic.
- Most of the **Old English** (the descendants of settlers who had come to Ireland with the Normans) also refused to accept the new Church.

Elizabeth I's religious reforms also had little impact in Ireland. Her officials became worried that Ireland could be used as a base by England's Catholic enemies. To ensure English control it was decided to bring Protestant settlers to Ireland. This policy was continued by Elizabeth's successor, James I. We will find out more about this policy in the next section of the book – Plantations.

Religious change in Tudor England – a time of confusion!

Henry VIII	Edward VI	Mary I	Elizabeth I
Broke with Rome, made himself head of the Church but kept Catholic beliefs	Introduced Protestant reforms	Made England Catholic again and persecuted Protestants	Established England as a Protestant country – persecuted Catholics

QUESTIONS

1 Why did King Henry VIII want to end his marriage to Catherine of Aragon?
2 Why was it difficult for the pope to agree to Henry's request?
3 Why was the Act of Supremacy important?
4 Explain what the Dissolution of the Monasteries involved.
5 What was the *Book of Common Prayer*? Who wrote it?
6 What major religious change was introduced by Mary I?
7 How did Mary I earn the nickname Bloody Mary?
8 'Elizabeth I was a Protestant'. Do you agree? Give two reasons to support your answer.
9 Was the Reformation in Ireland successful? Explain your answer.
10 Write a paragraph on one of the following:
(a) The religious changes introduced by Edward VI and Mary I
(b) Elizabeth I and the Reformation

Do you understand these key terms?

King's Great Matter
annulment
Act of Supremacy
Dissolution of the Monasteries
Anglican Church

EXAM QUESTION

- Write an account of Henry VIII and the Reformation in England. (HL)

Chapter 5

The Consequences of the Reformation

Key Learning Objectives

- **What were the consequences of the Reformation?**
  - **The Counter-Reformation**
  - **Religious persecution**
  - **Religious wars**

What were the consequences of the Reformation?

In this chapter, we will look at some of the consequences of the Reformation. One of the most important was the reaction of the Catholic Church as it fought back against the spread of Protestantism. This was called the **Counter-Reformation.**

The Reformation also caused division in many countries. The sixteenth century was not a time when people accepted religious views different from their own. This sometimes meant that:

- People were not allowed to practise the religion they wanted. This is called **persecution.**
- A number of **wars** broke out: some between countries, some within countries.

Term

Counter-Reformation
A response of the Catholic Church to the spread of Protestantism.

1 The Counter-Reformation

As we saw in Chapter 1, many people had called for reform in the Church. As more and more people became Protestant it became clear that action would have to be taken to stop the spread of Protestantism.

In 1534, **Pope Paul III** (1534–49) was elected. His election was important as he was in favour of reform. He was pope for fifteen years and made two very important decisions:

1. He set up the **Council of Trent.**
2. He agreed to the formation of the **Jesuits.**

Meeting of the Council of Trent

What was agreed at the Council of Trent?

The main demand of people who hoped for reform was a **Church council.** This was a meeting of leading cardinals and bishops. People hoped that they would tackle the abuses in the Church. Pope after pope had resisted this demand as they were afraid that it would reduce their power in the Church.

Pope Paul III agreed to a council and it finally met at Trent in the north of Italy in 1545. Some, including Charles V, hoped that the council would end the split between Protestants and Catholics.

The Council met three times between 1545 and 1563. It did little to end the division in Christian Europe, but did make a lot of important decisions about **Church discipline** and **Catholic doctrine** (beliefs).

Term

Doctrine
A list of beliefs of a religious group, e.g. the Catholic Church

Church discipline

- The abuses of simony, nepotism, absenteeism and pluralism were ended and the sale of indulgences controlled.
- To solve the problem of poorly educated priests, each diocese was to have a **seminary** to train priests.
- Bishops were to make sure that priests were living good lives.

Term

Seminary
A special school that trains people to be priests.

PART 2

Catholic doctrine

- The council said clearly what a Catholic should believe.
- The council stated the reasons why it disagreed with the new Protestant beliefs, e.g. it declared that tradition and the Bible were the source of teachings, not just the Bible.
- An **index** (list) of books was drawn up. Catholics were forbidden to read books on this list.

The decisions reached at Trent brought discipline and unity to the Church. This made the Catholic Church far stronger to tackle the Protestant threat.

The Society of Jesus (the Jesuits)

The **Jesuits** were the most influential of the new Catholic religious orders set up during the Counter-Reformation. They were founded by an ex-soldier from Spain, **Ignatius Loyola.** Badly wounded after a battle, he decided to devote his life to God. Along with six others he formed the **Society of Jesus** or the Jesuits, as they became known. Pope Paul III approved the Jesuit Order in 1540.

Ignatius Loyola (1491–1556)

Loyola worked very hard to make the order successful:

- He modelled the Jesuits on an army. As head of the order he was known as the **Superior General.**
- The members were taught to be totally loyal to the pope and go wherever they were sent by him.
- Loyola wrote a book called the ***Spiritual Exercises*** to guide the Jesuits in their search for holy lives. By the time of Loyola's death in 1556 the Jesuit order had over 1,000 members.

What was the importance of the Jesuits?

Missionaries

The Jesuit Order carried out **missionary work** in Protestant lands. The activities of the Jesuits helped to win back parts of Poland, Austria and Hungary to the Catholic Church. However, the work was very dangerous. Protestant countries such as England treated them very harshly if they were captured. Jesuit missionaries also went to Asia. The most famous was **St Francis Xavier**.

Education

The Jesuits were also famous for the schools that they founded. They had advanced views on education for the time and treated the pupils well. Jesuit schools made sure that the children of the wealthy and powerful people were loyal Catholics.

> **Did you know?**
>
> Every year in Britain, **Guy Fawkes Night** (Bonfire Night) is celebrated on 5 November. This event celebrates the discovery of a plot by some Catholics to blow up King James I and the English Parliament. The plot was foiled when Guy Fawkes was arrested with barrels of gunpowder under the Houses of Parliament.

2 Religious persecution

Religious persecution was very common in Europe during the Reformation. Catholics in Protestant countries and Protestants in Catholic countries had to be careful. They could suffer fines, imprisonment or in some cases death. Many people were forced to leave their own country to practise their beliefs.

In England under Mary Tudor, some Protestants were burned at the stake. Under Queen Elizabeth, Catholics had to go to Mass secretly and faced heavy fines or imprisonment. Priests were cruelly executed if captured.

The burning of heretics at the stake by the Spanish Inquisition

What was the role of the Inquisition?

The **Inquisition** played a very important role in the Counter-Reformation. It was a **Church court** set up to try people who held views that were different to the teachings of the Catholic Church. These people were called **heretics**. The court was active in Spain, Portugal and Italy.

It had originally been founded in Spain to investigate Jews and Muslims who had converted to Christianity. When Protestant ideas began to reach Spain, it was used against them as well.

- People brought before the Inquisition were not usually told of their crimes. They or their family had to pay for the cost of their imprisonment. Torture was sometimes used to get people to confess that they were heretics.
- A person found guilty by the Inquisition could be fined, flogged, imprisoned or burnt alive at the stake. The sentences were announced at a religious ceremony called an ***auto-da-fé*** (act of faith). During the ceremony those found guilty would wear the ***sanbenito***.

> **Term**
>
> ***Sanbenito***
> A special tunic worn by those who were condemned by the Inquisition.
>
> ***Auto-da-fé***
> Religious ceremony at which the sentences passed by the Inquisition were carried out.

The Inquisition in Italy was not as harsh, but famously it tried the scientist and astronomer Galileo. The Inquisition made sure that Protestant ideas gained little support in Spain or Italy. Protestant writers condemned the Spanish Inquisition. However, they greatly exaggerated the numbers who were killed to make the Catholic Church look bad. This is an example of propaganda. Because of this, today historians are unsure how many people were executed by the Inquisition.

Did you know?

Historians have estimated that 125,000 people were tried by the Inquisition over its 350-year history. About 2,250 were executed.

What the Counter-Reformation involved

The Counter-Reformation

The Council of Trent	The Jesuits	The Inquisition
Church court that persecuted Protestants	Missionary work in Protestant countries	Decisions on discipline and church teachings

3 Religious wars in Europe, 1525–1648

Why did religious wars break out?

The spread of the new religious ideas led to a large number of wars. There were a number of reasons. Here are the most important:

- Some kings or queens saw it as their duty to protect either the Catholic or the Protestant faith.
- Most rulers would not accept two religions in their country. They persecuted religions they disagreed with and this led to war.

St Bartholomew's Day Massacre in Paris, 1572

What were the main religious wars?

The **German Protestant states** formed an alliance to resist the power of the Catholic Emperor, **Charles V**. War broke out and the struggle ended with the **Peace of Augsburg** in 1555. The treaty said that the prince of each state should decide the religion of his people.

The most serious religious war was the **Thirty Years' War** that lasted from 1618 to 1648. It was fought in Germany but it involved most of the countries of Europe. Historians think that about one-third of the population of Germany died as a result of the war.

A civil war broke out in **France** between Catholics and Protestants, who were called **Huguenots**. In 1572 Protestants were massacred in Paris. This terrible event became known as the **St Bartholomew's Day Massacre**. The war ended with the **Edict of Nantes**. This law allowed Protestants to practise their religion. At the time it was one of the few examples of religious toleration in Europe.

In the sixteenth century the **Netherlands** was ruled by Spain. Many Dutch people became followers of John Calvin. The Spanish tried to stamp out Protestantism and this led to a revolt of Protestant areas against their Spanish rulers. The war lasted for eighty years and in the end the Protestants won independence from Spain.

King Philip II of Spain was annoyed that English ships were attacking Spanish ships bringing treasure back from the New World. **Elizabeth I** was also helping the Protestants in the Netherlands. Philip decided to invade England. There was a further reason – he wanted to make England a Catholic country again. His invasion fleet, called the **Spanish Armada**, was defeated by the English in 1588.

Do you understand these key terms?

Counter-Reformation	**council**	**seminary**	***sanbenito***
persecution	**doctrine**	**index**	***auto-da-fé***

QUESTIONS

1 What two important decisions did Pope Paul III make?
2 Why were people calling for a Church council?
3 Mention one decision reached by the Council of Trent under (a) doctrine and (b) discipline.
4 Why was the Council of Trent important for the Catholic Church?
5 Explain why Ignatius Loyola was a key person during the Counter-Reformation.
6 Why was it sometimes dangerous to be a Jesuit?
7 Give two examples of religious persecution in sixteenth-century England.
8 Explain the following terms associated with the Inquisition: heretic; *auto-da-fé*; *sanbenito*.
9 Name two countries where the Inquisition operated in the sixteenth century.
10 Give two reasons why religious wars broke out in Europe during the Reformation.
11 'In the sixteenth century many wars were caused by disputes over religion.' Do you agree? Write a ten-sentence account explaining your answer.

EXAM QUESTION

› Write an account of one of the following elements of the Catholic Counter-Reformation:
  › The Council of Trent › The Court of Inquisition › The Jesuits

TIMELINE

PART 2

Section 8

Plantations

Chapter 1

Ireland in the Early 1500s

Key Learning Objectives

- **What was Ireland like in 1500?**
- **What were the laws and customs of the three parts of Ireland?**
- **What did the people of the Pale think of the lords?**

What was Ireland like in 1500?

Ireland in 1500 was very different from how it is today. Thick forests and scrub covered a lot of the country. Wild boar and wolves roamed there. Roads were just dirt tracks. There were very few bridges so it was difficult to get across rivers and streams. It was easier to travel by sea or river to get to most parts of the country.

Travel was also dangerous because of outlaws. Even men would not travel alone. To go through different parts of the country you needed the permission of the local lord.

There was no central government in Ireland. Henry VII was king of England at that time, and called himself 'Lord of Ireland'. But he only controlled a small area around Dublin. It was called **the Pale**. Powerful noble lords ruled the rest of the country.

Ireland in 1500. Was there a Gaelic or Old English lord in your area? Do any of his descendants still live there?

> ***Term***
>
> **The Pale**
> A small area of land around Dublin controlled by the king of England.

Ireland in the 1500s was divided into three sections: the area controlled by the **Gaelic lords**, the area controlled by the **Old English lords**, and the Pale. The Old English lords and the people of the Pale were descended from the Normans (see page 100).

What were the laws and customs of the three parts of Ireland?

	Gaelic Lords	Old English Lords	The Pale
Who ruled?	› Gaelic lords ruled over a clan. This was a group of people who shared the same surname such as O'Connor or McCarthy. In theory all members of the clan elected the lord from the ruling family called the **derbhfine**. In practice the new lord was likely to be the brother or son of the previous lord	› These were descended from the Norman lords who came to Ireland in the 12th century. They had been given their lands by the English king so in theory they saw them as their overlords. But in practice the **Old English** lords ruled their lands like countries. They had their own private armies and laws	› The English kings and queens still ruled this area. Most of the people were descended from the Normans. They followed English laws and customs
Language	› Irish	› Mainly Irish because they had married into Gaelic families over the centuries	› English
Law	› **Brehon law**. The Brehon (judge) was in charge of carrying out the law. The only form of punishment was the **éiric** or fine. The guilty person's family had to pay a fine to the victim's family. There were no executions or gaols	› Mostly Brehon law although they used English law when it suited them	› English **common law**. It was so called because it was common to all the English king's subjects. The king appointed judges to go from place to place and try serious crimes. Courts were held in a courthouse in the town › People found guilty were either beheaded or given long prison sentences

PART 2

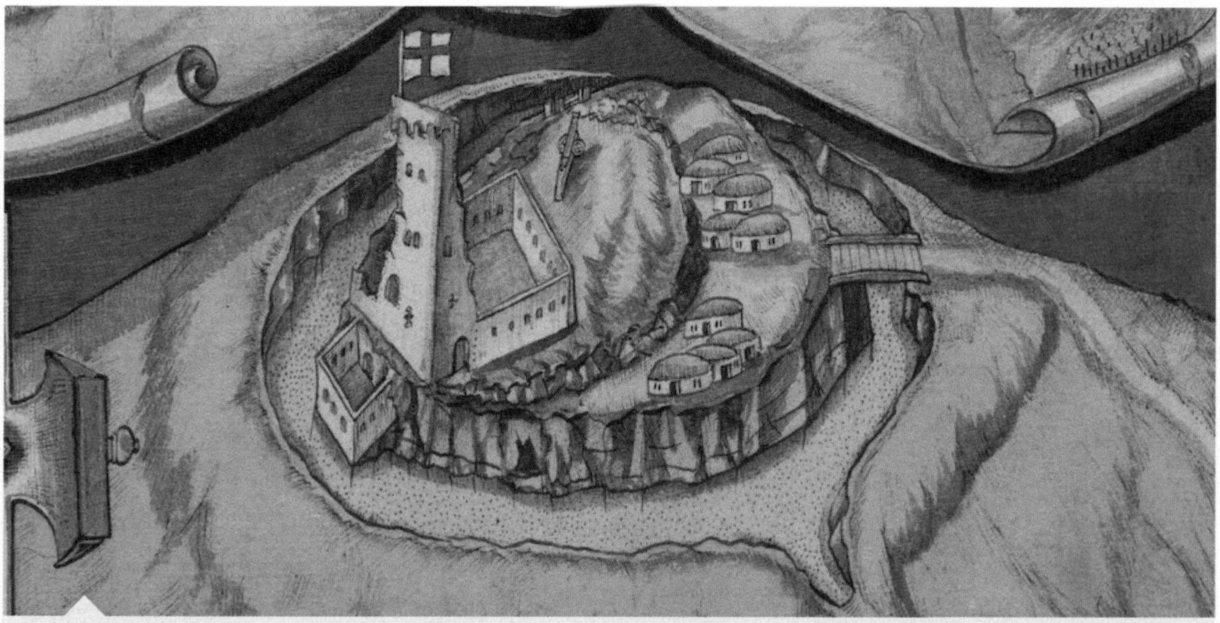

This is the castle of a Gaelic lord in the 1500s. The houses are called clocháns. Who do you think lived in them? How is this castle protected? *This image is reproduced courtesy of the National Library of Ireland [Ms 2656/5 Richard Bartlett]. www.nli.ie*

	Gaelic Lords	Old English Lords	The Pale
Marriage laws	› Wives could keep their own names and property when they married › Divorce allowed › Children born outside of marriage were entitled to a share in their father's property	› Followed Brehon law	› A wife took her husband's name and he took control of her property and money › Divorce not allowed › Children born outside marriage could not inherit their father's property
Land	› Land belonged to the whole clan. The clan's huge herd grazed on the land and a person's wealth was calculated by the number of cows they owned › Those who farmed the land had few rights but they moved from lord to lord, depending on where they could get the best deal	› They followed English law. The eldest son inherited his father's land and became the new lord. This is called **primogeniture**	› The richer people in the pale were landowners (large farmers) and merchants (in trade). The eldest son inherited the land or business › Tenants who rented the land had **leases** which fixed their rent and allowed them to farm the land for a set number of years
Dress	› Women: long tunic and a **mantle** (cloak) › Men: knee-length tunic and a mantle. They often wore a moustache and a fringe called a **glib**	› Gaelic dress	› English dress. Men and women wore shoes and English fashions such as stockings, cloaks and long gowns. The men were often clean-shaven

Do you think these drawings were done by an Irish or an English person? Give a reason for your answer

A man and woman from the Pale in 1616 drawn by the same person. How are they different from the Gaelic people on the left?

What did the people of the Pale think of the lords?

The landowners and the merchants of the Pale hated the Gaelic Irish and Old English lords. Wars were common between the various lords. That disrupted trade and made it difficult for merchants in the Pale to do business.

The Gaelic Irish often raided the Pale to steal cattle. Many Pale farmers paid 'black rent' (i.e. protection money) to the raiders to stop them coming.

A The kerns (Gaelic soldiers) arrive.

B The houses of the people are burnt.

C Their animals are stolen.

This picture is taken from a book about Ireland published in 1581

Do you understand these key terms?

the Pale	**Brehon law**	**glib**	**lease**
Gaelic lords	**common law**	**primogeniture**	**black rent**
Old English	**éiric**	**clochán**	

QUESTIONS

1. Name two powerful Old English lords and two Gaelic lords. (Look at the map on page 190)
2. Why was travelling in Ireland dangerous in the 1500s?
3. What was Brehon law?
4. Why was land very important to the Gaelic clans? Who owned it?
5. Where did an Old English lord get his land?
6. Explain two ways in which Old English lords became more like Gaelic lords.
7. What was the Pale?
8. How were the people of the Pale different from the people in the rest of Ireland?
9. What was the common law?
10. List three ways in which common law was different from Brehon law.
11. How did the people of the Pale feel about the rest of Ireland? Explain why they felt that way.

Chapter 2

The Beginning of the Plantations

Key Learning Objectives

- How did Henry VIII try to control Ireland?
- Why did the English use plantation?
- How did the plantations work?
  - Laois-Offaly
  - Munster
- What were the results of the two plantations?

How did Henry VIII try to control Ireland?

Term

Lord deputy The king's representative in Ireland.

From the time the Normans had arrived in Ireland, English kings had seen themselves as Lords of Ireland. However, they took little interest in the country.

Up to the 1530s, English kings had usually appointed one of the Fitzgeralds of Kildare as their **lord deputy**. But in 1534, **Henry VIII** broke away from the Catholic Church, as we read in see Section 7, Chapter 4. One of the Fitzgeralds, Lord Offaly (known as Silken Thomas), declared that he would defend the Pope and the Catholic Church, and rebelled against the king. Henry wanted to make himself head of the Church in Ireland as well as England, so he sent over a large army and defeated the rebels.

Surrender and regrant

But Henry still had to gain control of the other lords in Ireland. It was far too expensive to keep an army in Ireland the whole time, so he came up with an idea called **surrender and regrant**.

1. The Gaelic lords would **surrender** their lands to Henry VIII and promise to use English laws and language.
2. They would swear loyalty to the English king.
3. Henry VIII would grant back (**regrant**) the land to the lords along with English titles such as baron or earl. For example, it was in this way that the chief of the O'Neills became the Earl of Tyrone.

Henry hoped that this would make Ireland peaceful, but only forty lords took up his offer.

This picture shows a Gaelic chief and his followers surrendering to the king's deputy. Why was this ceremony held out in the open?

Why did the English use plantation?

When surrender and regrant did not work, the English decided to try a new way of bringing Ireland under their control. It was called **plantation.** It meant bringing in English and, later, Scottish people to take over the land of the Gaelic Irish and the Old English. It had a lot of advantages for the English government:

- Bringing in new settlers would be cheaper than having an English army permanently in Ireland.
- The settlers would bring English laws and customs to replace the Irish laws and customs. They would also set up towns, increase trade and improve the economy.
- Settlers would be Protestant, so plantations were a good way of spreading the Protestant religion to Ireland.

Term

Plantation
People from one country are sent to another country to take land and to live and work there.

The Laois-Offaly plantation

Queen Mary planned the first plantation in Ireland in the 1550s. Two Gaelic clans – the O'Connors and the O'Mores – were raiding the Pale and stealing cattle. The lord deputy suggested to Queen Mary that she give the land around them to English soldiers. They would farm the land and at the same time guard the borders to the Pale.

Queen Mary

How did the Laois-Offaly plantation work?

Queen Mary took land from the O'Connors and the O'Mores and organised the Laois-Offaly plantation. This is what happened:

- The land was divided into two parts.
- One-third was given back to the O'Connors and the O'Mores. It was the land nearest the River Shannon and was very boggy.
- Two-thirds was given to loyal English families. Each family got a farm of about 360 acres.

Queen Mary divided the land she had taken into two separate counties:

1. The O'Connors' territory (Laois) was called Queen's County.
2. The O'Mores' territory (Offaly) was called King's County after Mary's husband, King Philip.

In each county, Mary appointed an official called a **sheriff** to enforce the common law. Each town was to have a courthouse and a gaol, as well as a regular market where farmers could bring their crops to sell.

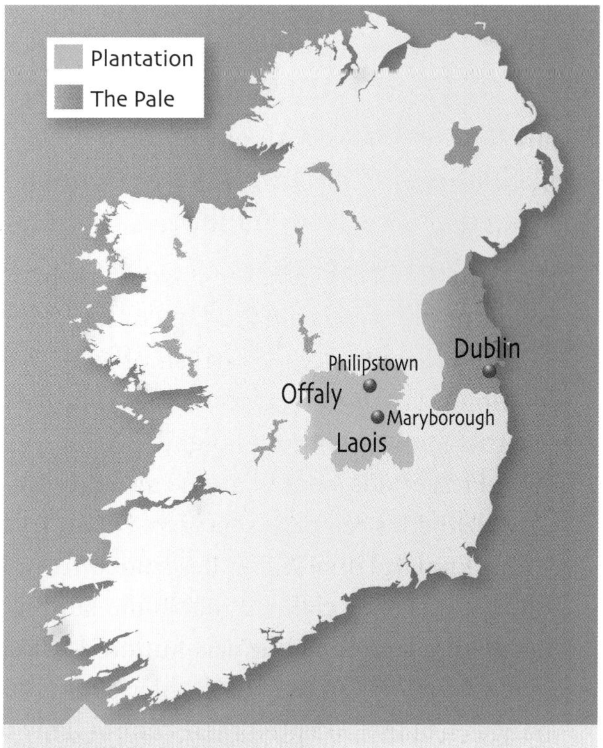

Laois-Offaly plantation (1550s)

PART 2

What were the results of the Laois-Offaly plantation?

The Laois-Offaly plantation was not a success. Only eighty-eight planter families from the Pale settled there. Nobody came from England. But this plantation became a blueprint for future plantations.

QUESTIONS

1. What was a 'lord deputy'?
2. Why did Henry VIII appoint an Englishman as lord deputy in the 1530s?
3. Explain 'surrender and regrant'. Why did Henry VIII introduce it?
4. What does 'plantation' mean?
5. Give two reasons why the English government thought plantations would be a good idea for Ireland.
6. Why did Queen Mary decide to plant Laois and Offaly?
7. Was this plantation a success? Give a reason for your answer.

Special Study: Queen Elizabeth I and the Munster plantation

The next big plantation was in Munster. Queen Mary's half-sister Elizabeth became queen in 1558. She ruled for forty five years, up to 1603.

Elizabeth was a Protestant. She didn't trust Catholics. Like most kings and queens at that time she felt that the people should have the same religion as their ruler.

Queen Elizabeth I

Why did the Fitzgeralds of Desmond rebel?

Elizabeth I quarrelled with one of the most powerful families in Ireland, the Fitzgeralds of Desmond. There were three reasons for this:

1. For hundreds of years, the Fitzgeralds had run Munster without interference from England. But Elizabeth wanted them to accept English officials who would bring common law into their territories. They would not give up their power without a fight.
2. The Fitzgeralds were Catholic and did not want to become Protestant.
3. In Elizabeth's reign, **adventurers** began to arrive in Ireland. They were men from England and Wales, descended from Norman lords who once lived in Ireland. They claimed that some land in Munster should really belong to them, even though it was hundreds of years since their families had lived there. When they took their claims to the English courts, the Queen's judges usually accepted their claims. This worried the Fitzgeralds and other lords in Munster. They could lose a lot of their lands in this way.

Term

Adventurers
English and Welsh men, descended from Norman lords, who hoped to make their fortune by getting their hands on Irish land.

In 1579, the Fitzgeralds and some other lords rebelled against Queen Elizabeth. She sent an army of 8,000 men into Ireland to crush them. For four years a vicious war raged throughout the Desmond lands. Farming land and crops were destroyed. Thousands died of starvation or fled abroad. Finally, the Fitzgeralds were defeated. Elizabeth confiscated all the land of the rebels. This amounted to half a million acres!

How did the Munster plantation work?

Elizabeth then began to plan a plantation.

- The land was divided into thirty-five estates of 12,000, 8,000, 6,000 and 4,000 acres.
- Each estate was given to a man called an **undertaker**. In return for the land he undertook (agreed):

  1. to bring in English families as servants and tenants;
  2. to build a castle and to pay for soldiers and arms to protect them;
  3. not to employ Gaelic Irish as servants or to rent land to them;
  4. to follow the Protestant religion and English laws.

An undertaker was also expected to build a town that would have a weekly market where the farmers could sell their goods.

Term

Undertaker
A man who received an estate in a plantation and undertook (agreed) to follow the rules of the plantation.

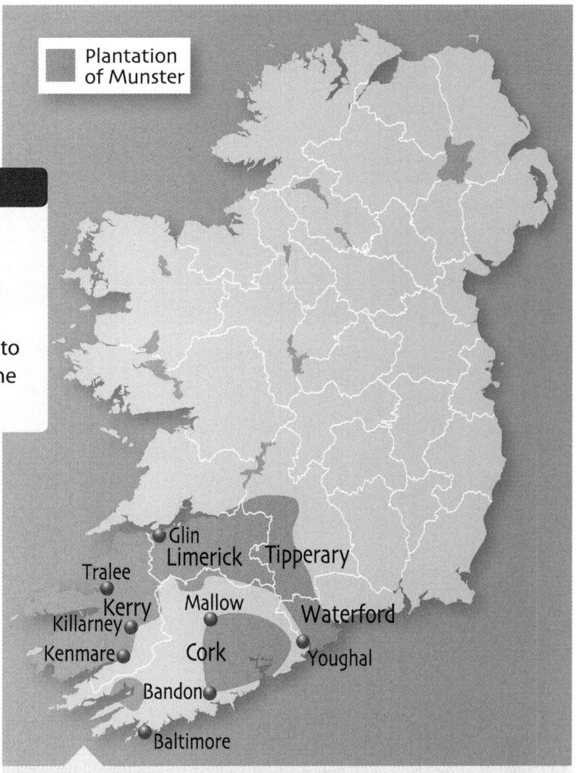

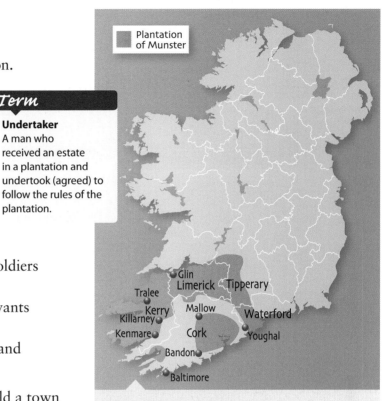

This map shows the Munster plantation (1580s). The purple dots mark the new towns that were built

What were the results of the Munster plantation?

Queen Elizabeth hoped that the plantation would make Munster English and Protestant. But it failed to achieve these aims, for the following reasons:

- Elizabeth hoped that 20,000 English settlers would come to Munster, but only 4,000 arrived.
- Many undertakers rented land to Gaelic Irish tenants who were willing to pay more rent than English settlers. They also employed Gaelic Irish servants because they were willing to work for lower wages.
- Some undertakers got huge estates which they could not defend properly. For example, **Sir Walter Raleigh**, an English explorer, got a massive 42,000 acres in Youghal, Co. Cork.

But the plantation did have some successes. The settlers built **new towns** such as Killarney, Glin and Mallow. They also developed **industries** such as timber, mining and fishing.

The plantation was restarted in the 1600s. By 1641, 22,000 Protestant settlers had made their home in Munster. Many of their descendants still live there today.

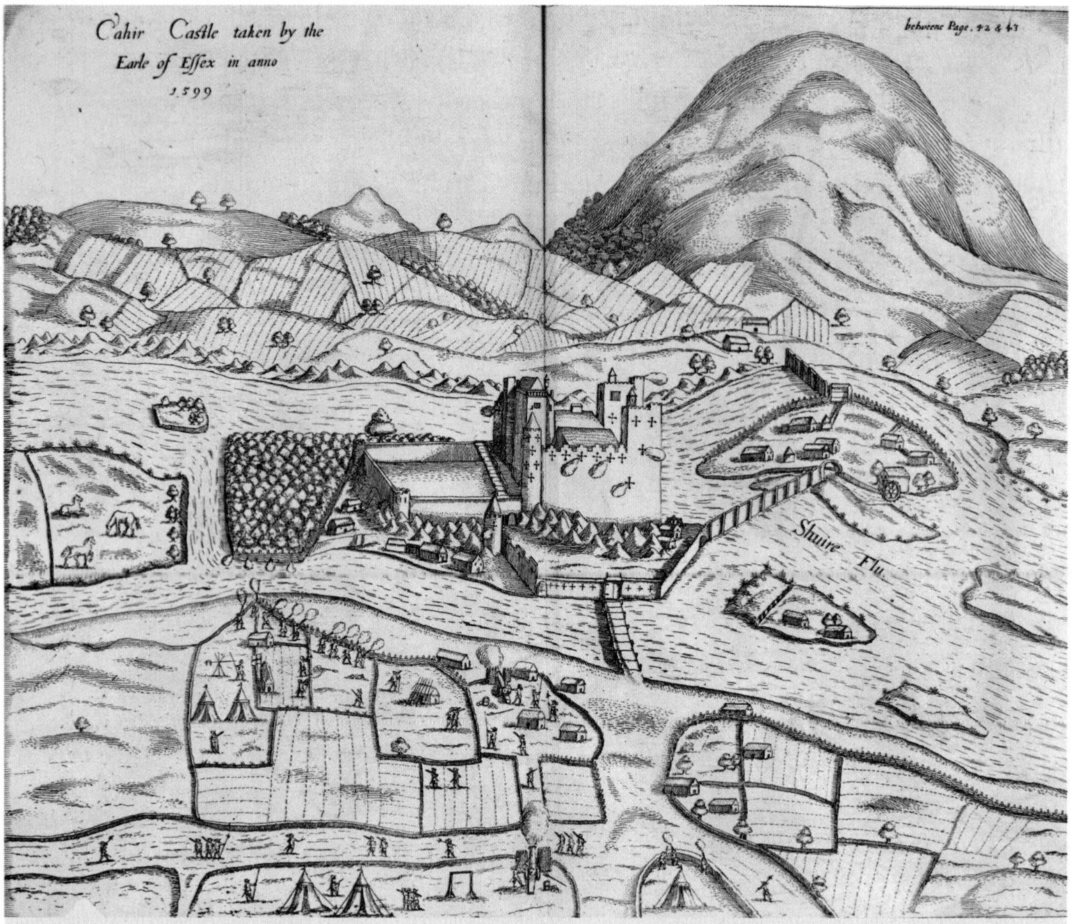
Cahir Caſtle taken by the
Earle of Eſſex in anno
1599
between Page. 42 & 43
Shuire Flu.

The new plantation around Cahir Castle in 1599. How is the castle defended? Can you see the fields and ditches that the planters have built? © *The British Library Board. G.5853 between pages 42–43*

Do you understand these key terms?

lord deputy **plantation** **adventurer** **undertaker**
surrender and regrant **sheriff**

QUESTIONS

1. Give two reasons why Queen Elizabeth was attracted to the idea of plantation.
2. Why did the Fitzgeralds rebel against Queen Elizabeth? Give three reasons.
3. How much land was to be planted in Munster? How was it divided?
4. In the Munster plantation, what was an undertaker?
5. What did an undertaker have to promise to do?
6. Why do you think undertakers had to build towns? Give two reasons.
7. Why do you think they could not have Gaelic tenants?
8. Why did they end up having Gaelic tenants?
9. List two ways in which the Munster plantation failed and two ways in which it succeeded.

Chapter 3

King James I and the Ulster Plantation

Key Learning Objectives

- **What happened in Ulster in the 1590s?**
- **How did the Ulster plantation work?**
- **What were the results of the Ulster plantation?**

Special Study: James I starts the Ulster plantation

What happened in Ulster in the 1590s?

By the 1590s, the English controlled every part of Ireland except Ulster. The ruling lords in Ulster became worried about the spread of English law to their lands. Some of them had English titles under the surrender and regrant scheme. The most powerful Gaelic lords were **Hugh O'Neill**, Earl of Tyrone, and **Hugh O'Donnell**, Earl of Tyrconnell.

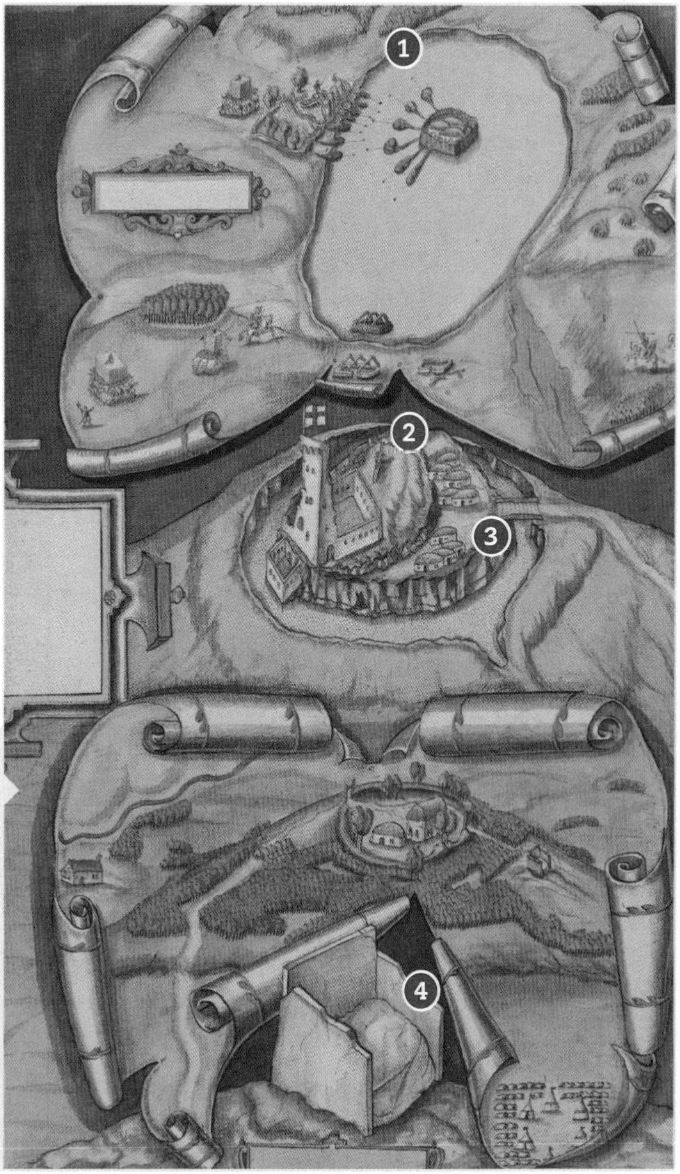

The Tullaghoge

The Tullaghoge was the place where all the O'Neill clan leaders were made chiefs. This picture was made in the early 1600s. What does it tell you about Gaelic Ulster?

1. An O'Neill crannóg under attack
2. Dungannon castle where the O'Neills lived
3. Clocháns – Gaelic Irish homes
4. Tullaghoge chair used when the O'Neill leader was made chief

This image is reproduced courtesy of the National Library of Ireland [Ms 2656/5 Richard Bartlett]. www.nli.ie

The Nine Years War (1594–1603)

At first Hugh O'Neill and other Gaelic lords went along with Queen Elizabeth and her officials. But by the 1590s English officials were telling the lords how to run their lands. Many Gaelic clans led by Hugh O'Neill joined together and went to war with the English. This was called the **Nine Years War**.

Hugh O'Neill, who was a very skilled soldier, won several battles against the English. But the Ulster lords knew they would need outside help to win the war. To get it, they claimed they were fighting for the Catholic faith against the Protestant Elizabeth. They asked the King of Spain, who was the most powerful Catholic king in Europe, to help them.

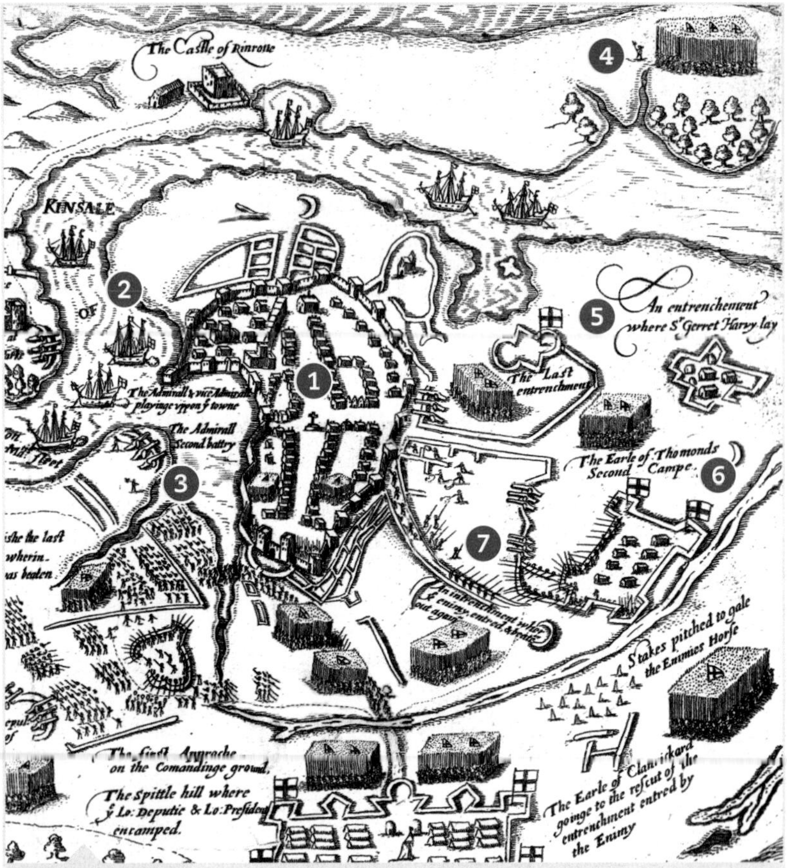

This map from the time shows the march of the O'Neills and O'Donnells to Kinsale.

1 Town of Kinsale
2 Spanish ships
3 English fort
4 Gaelic Irish came from this direction
5 English camp
6 Earl of Thomond (O'Brien)
7 Forts and trenches built by English

Reproduced courtesy of Neptune Gallery

The Battle of Kinsale, 1601

The Spanish king promised an army but it was a long time coming. At last in 1601 it arrived, but it landed in Kinsale, Co. Cork, not in Ulster. In the middle of winter, O'Neill and his army had to march south to join the Spaniards.

But an English army got there first. A fierce battle followed and the Irish and Spanish forces were defeated. O'Neill held out for two years, but he had to surrender in the end.

The **Battle of Kinsale** is famous because it was the last time Gaelic lords had a real chance to rule Ireland.

What happened after the war?

O'Neill was not harshly punished because the new king, James, wanted peace in Ireland. But most of the Gaelic lords found it impossible to accept English rule. Many got into debt too, because they didn't have the power to collect rents and taxes as they had done in the past. In 1607, most of the Gaelic Ulster lords decided to leave Ireland and go to Europe. They hoped to persuade the Spanish to send another army. This became known as the **Flight of the Earls**.

James VI of Scotland became James I of England and Ireland when Elizabeth died. He was the first *British* king

PART 2

QUESTIONS

1 Why did the Ulster leaders rebel against Queen Elizabeth?

2 Name the two strongest Gaelic lords in Ulster in the 1590s. Why did these lords have an English title?

3 Which country did they ask for help? What reason did they give for wanting it?

4 When and where did the help arrive? What battle followed and who won?

5 What was the 'Flight of the Earls'?

6 Look at the picture of Tullaghoge on page 199. Can you see the English cannons attacking O'Neill's home at the top of the picture? The English forces also smashed the Tullaghoge chair to pieces. In your opinion, why did they do this?

How did the Ulster plantation work?

With the Gaelic leaders gone, King James decided to plant Ulster. He declared that the earls of Tyrone and Tyrconnell were traitors and he took away their land. As King of Scotland, England and Ireland, he wanted to bring people from all parts of his kingdom together. He saw Ulster as a land where he could do this. By 1609 King James' plantation plan was ready.

- The land that had been taken was divided into six counties: Donegal, Derry, Tyrone, Armagh, Fermanagh and Cavan.
- He divided the area into estates of 1,000 acres, 1,500 acres and 2,000 acres – more manageable sizes than those in Munster. He would give estates to three types of planter: **undertakers, servitors** and '**loyal Irish**' (native Irish who stayed loyal to the English during the Nine Years War).

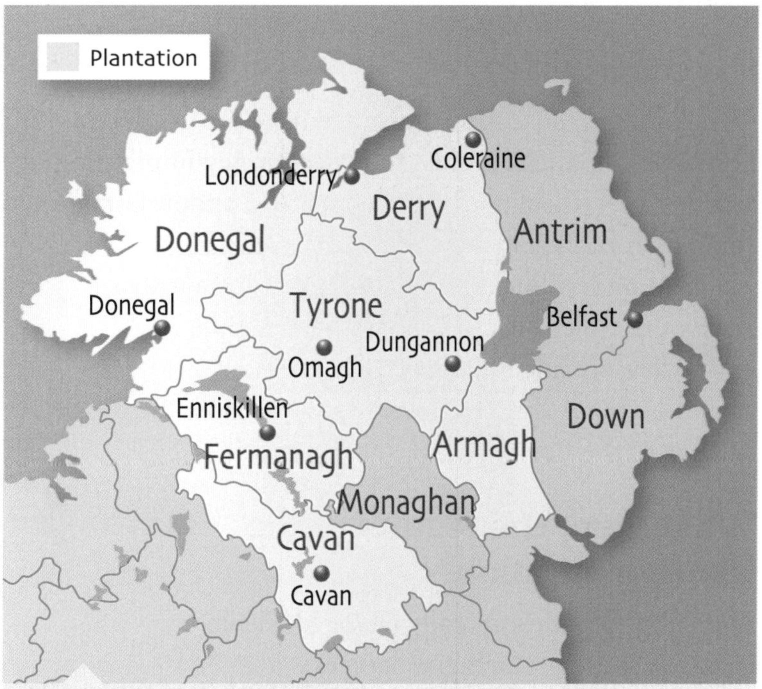

This map shows the Ulster plantation. Not all of the area shaded yellow was used. Many undertakers found it too difficult and expensive to carry out their duty to build new towns and bawns, and never developed their land. Others found they made more money by leasing part of the land to Irish tenants

Term

Servitors
Mostly English or Scottish soldiers who got land in the Ulster plantation.

This table shows the three types of settler and the conditions they had to agree to in order to get land.

Type of settler	Undertakers	Servitors got 13% of land	Loyal Irish got 14% of land
Who they were	English and Scottish landowners	Englishmen and Scots who worked for the government in Ireland. Most were soldiers	Gaelic landowners who stayed loyal to the king
What they got	Most got estates of 2,000 acres	Estates of 1,500 or 1,000 acres	Estates of 1,000 acres or less
What rent they paid to the king	£5 per 1,000 acres per year	£8 per 1,000 acres	£10 per 1,000 acres
Who they could rent land to	They must bring in English or Scottish tenants and must not rent land to Irish tenants	They could rent land to Irish tenants	They could rent land to Irish tenants

Plantation in Derry

King James made a special arrangement for Co. Derry. He persuaded twelve London companies (guilds) to invest money in planting it. They divided the land between them and renamed it Co. Londonderry. You can see the twelve companies on this map.

The London businessmen built two large towns: Derry and Coleraine. In Derry, Gaelic people had to live outside the town walls. They settled on the boggy area nearby. The area is still called the Bogside.

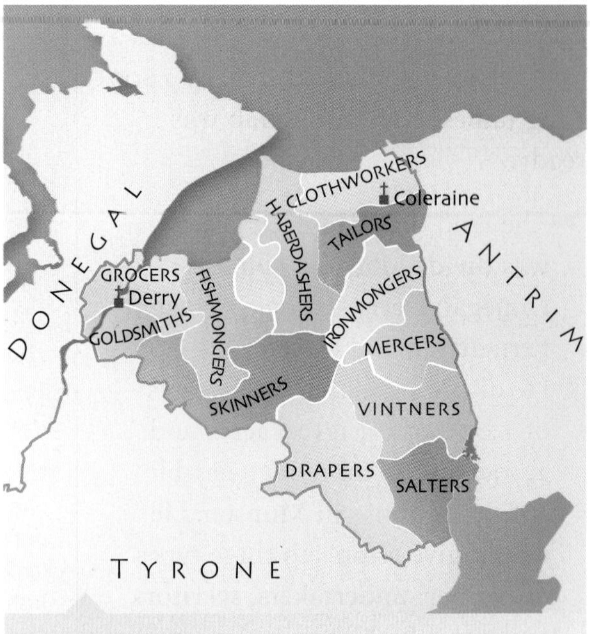

A map of Co. Derry, or Londonderry as it was called then. This map shows where each London company got land. The companies were like the medieval guilds. Can you name the work of each company? Why did the government want to bring these companies to Ireland?

What were the results of the Ulster plantation?

The Ulster plantation really changed Ulster. Here are some of the main changes:

1 New settlers

By 1640 there were about 40,000 English and Scottish adult settlers in Ulster. Gaelic Irish people remained farming the land, but very few of them owned any land.

2 New houses

The settlers drew maps of their new estates. You can see one on the next page. From these pictures we can see the kind of houses and towns that the settlers built.

3 New laws

English judges brought in common law. In the large towns there were courthouses and a gaol to house prisoners.

4 New religions

Most of the settlers were Protestant. The Scottish settlers were Presbyterian (followers of Calvin) and the English settlers were Anglican (belonged to the Church of Ireland).

5 New ways of farming and trading

The settlers cleared the forests and introduced new ways of farming. They grew more crops rather than raising cattle. They also organised markets and fairs in the towns where settlers and native Irish could sell their crops. They helped to develop trade by building roads to link the towns.

Term

Bawn
A walled courtyard built by planters for defence.

6 New towns

By 1640, the settlers had set up over twenty new towns. Some towns developed and became large and successful. Others never grew bigger than villages. The new towns were well planned. The houses were laid out in streets with a square, often called the Diamond, in the centre. A Protestant church was usually built nearby.

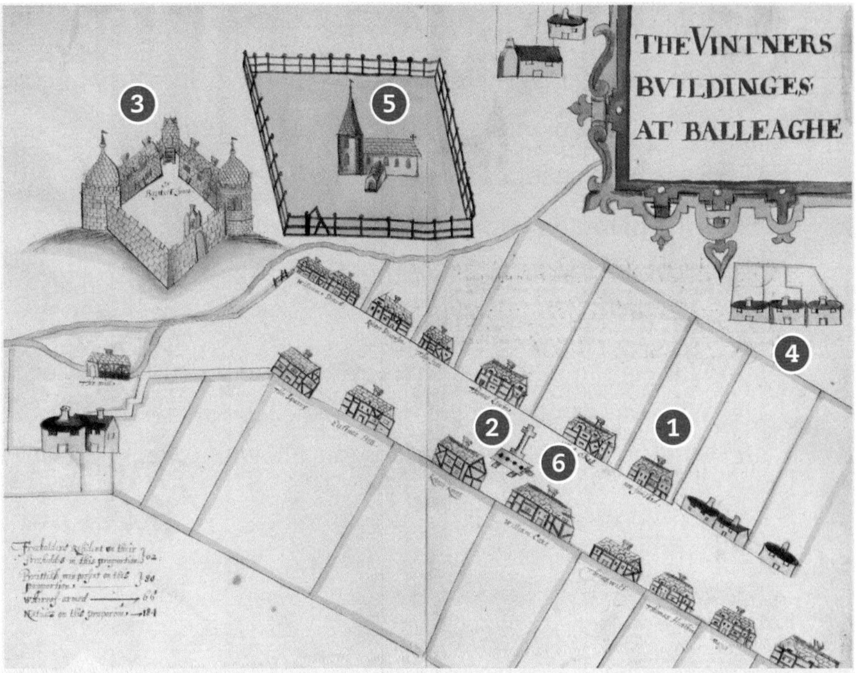

Bellaghy: a plantation village

1 The settlers' houses
2 The market square and cross
3 The undertaker's house with a **bawn**
4 Clochāns: Gaelic houses
5 Protestant church
6 The stocks

7 Problems with the plantation

The Ulster plantation was more successful than earlier plantations but there were some problems.

- Religion divided people as the settlers were Protestants and the natives were Catholic. There was also tension between the Anglican English settlers and the Presbyterian Scottish settlers.
- Many undertakers broke their agreements. They did not build proper defences and many of them took on Gaelic tenants. This meant that there were more Gaelic Irish than settlers. That was a serious threat to the planters because many of the Gaelic Irish were very bitter about losing their land. They hated the settlers and often attacked them.

The ruins of an undertaker's house. Many of these houses had orchards and gardens

Do you understand these key terms?

Flight of the Earls **servitor** **loyal Irish** **bawn**
undertaker **Nine Years War**

QUESTIONS

1 Name the king who planted Ulster.
2 What did the king hope to achieve with this new plantation?
3 Name the six Ulster counties that were planted.
4 Explain the terms undertakers, servitors and loyal Irish.
5 How did 'Londonderry' get its name?
6 One town in Co. Derry is called Draperstown. In your opinion, why is it called that?
7 Why did some planters take on Gaelic Irish tenants?
8 Explain three changes that happened in Ulster because of this plantation.
9 Was the plantation a success? Why or why not?
10 How did the Gaelic Irish and the new settlers get on?
11 Look at the table on page 202.
(a) Who had to pay the most rent? Why do you think this was?
(b) Why was some land given to Gaelic landowners?
(c) Why, do you think, were servitors allowed to have Gaelic tenants?

PART 2

SOURCE QUESTION

› Look at the map of the town on page 203 and answer the questions below.
(a) Who built this town?
(b) Where are the Gaelic houses? Why are they there?
(c) Is there anything on the map to show that the undertaker broke his agreement with the government? Explain your answer.

People in History

Write about a native Irish landowner who lost land in a plantation.

Chapter 4

The Cromwellian Plantation

Key Learning Objectives

- What was the background to Cromwell's plantation?
- Why did Cromwell come to Ireland?
- What was the plan for Cromwell's plantation?
- What were the results of the Cromwellian plantation?

What was the background to Cromwell's plantation?

The 1641 rebellion

For thirty years after the Ulster plantation there was peace in Ireland. Settlers and natives began to get on better, but there were still tensions below the surface.

In 1639, a row broke out between the king, **Charles I**, and the English parliament. Some people believed that the parliament should have more power. The supporters of King Charles were called **Royalists**, opposing them were the **Parliamentarians**.

Catholics slaughter Protestants in the 1641 rebellion. This picture comes from an eighteenth-century pamphlet. How are the native Irish shown in it? Is this source reliable?

In October 1641, some Gaelic Irish took this opportunity to attack the settlers and get their lands back. It is thought that between 4,000 and 12,000 settlers were killed. The rebellion then spread to the rest of the country. Many **Old English** also joined in.

Settlers fled from Ulster to Dublin and to England and Scotland. They told stories of how they had been robbed and mudered by the native Irish. Their stories convinced Protestants in Britain that Irish Catholics had killed over 200,000 Protestants. These British Protestants were very angry and became determined to punish the Catholics in Ireland.

In fact, the population of Ireland in 1641 was about one million. It is not possible that 200,000 Protestants were killed.

Why did Cromwell come to Ireland?

Meanwhile, the row between King Charles and the parliament led to a **civil war** in England that lasted until 1649. The leader of the parliamentary side was a brilliant general called **Oliver Cromwell.** He defeated King Charles and the king was executed. That left Cromwell free to come to Ireland.

- He wanted to punish the Catholics for the massacres of 1641.
- He also needed their land to pay the parliament's debts from the English civil war.

Oliver Cromwell was the head of the English government between 1649 and 1660

Cromwell conquers Ireland

In 1649, Cromwell brought 12,000 experienced soldiers to Ireland. He first laid siege to Drogheda. He was determined to make an example of the town. When he captured it, he slaughtered the entire population.

Cromwell then captured Wexford and other important towns. By 1653 the whole of Ireland was conquered. By then thousands of people were dead and there were many widows and orphans. The Cromwellian soldiers rounded many up and transported them to work on sugar plantations in the West Indies. The English government allowed 30,000 Irish soldiers who surrendered to leave Ireland and join foreign armies.

Did you know?

To find out how much land there was, Cromwell ordered a man called Sir William Petty to carry out a survey. It is called the **Down Survey**. It contains the first modern maps of the whole of Ireland. Petty estimated that 11 million acres of land were confiscated.

What was the plan for Cromwell's plantation?

Cromwell now planned the biggest plantation of all. In 1652 he brought in the **Act of Settlement**. Under it, people had to prove they had supported the parliament in the civil war or else lose all or part of their land. There were very few people anywhere in Ireland, either Catholic or Protestant, who could prove that, so most landowners throughout Ireland lost land.

Cromwell wanted to turn Ireland into a Protestant country.

- Wealthy Catholic **landowners** had to leave their homes and move across the River Shannon. Ordinary Catholic farmers and labourers were left alone.
- Protestant landowners were allowed to keep their land if they paid a fine.
- It is estimated that about 40,000 people had crossed the River Shannon by the mid-1650s.
- Priests were also targeted in an effort to wipe out Catholicism. Many of them were executed and a reward was offered to anyone who handed in a priest to the government.

A Catholic print showing Irish priests and bishops being tortured. How are the English presented? Is this source reliable? © *The British Library Board. G.11732 page 81*

PART 2

What were the results of the Cromwellian plantation?

- The main result was to replace Catholic landowners in Ireland with Protestants.
- In 1640 Catholics owned about 60 per cent of the land in Ireland. By 1660 they only owned 20 per cent, most of it the poorer land in Connacht.
- Although the owners of the land changed, the people who worked on it as farmers and labourers did not. They were Catholics and easily outnumbered the Protestant settlers who came to Ireland. This destroyed Cromwell's plan to turn Ireland into a Protestant country.

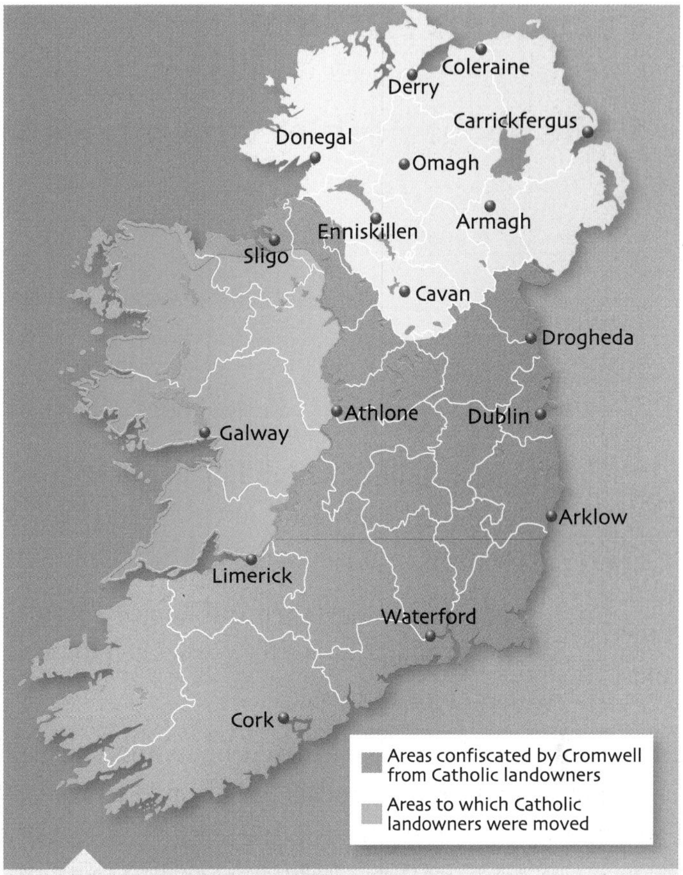

This map shows the Cromwellian plantation

QUESTIONS

1. What happened in Ireland in 1641?
2. How many Protestants were said to have been killed? About how many were in fact killed?
3. Who were the Old English? Why did they join the Gaelic Irish in this rebellion?
4. Why did civil war break out in England?
5. Name the two sides in the civil war?
6. Who was Oliver Cromwell?
7. Why did Oliver Cromwell come to Ireland?
8. What was the Act of Settlement? What did it say?
9. How did it affect Catholic landowners?
10. Give two important results of the Cromwellian plantation.

SOURCE QUESTION

- Look at these maps.

  (a) Name the plantations marked A, B and C.

  (b) Name the rulers who carried out these plantations.

  (c) What is plantation D called?

  (d) Why did that plantation not include Connacht?

  (e) In your opinion, why did plantation D include all the land around the coast?

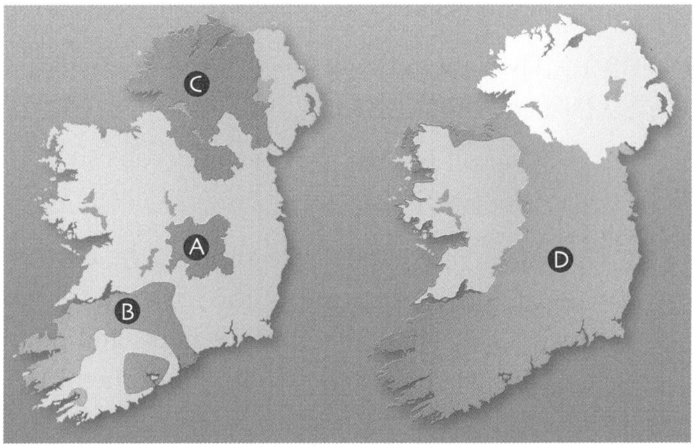

People in History

Write about a settler who received land during a plantation.

Sample Answer

A settler on a plantation

Thomas Phillips is from England. He came to Ireland in 1610 because he was granted some land in Co. Tyrone by King James I, as part of his new plantation.

He is an undertaker and he got a grant of 2,000 acres at £10 per year rent. He would never have got the chance in England to rent so much land for such a good price.

He had to swear that he would bring English tenant farmers and craftspeople with him. He hoped to persuade some of the workers and farmers from his brother's estate in England to come with him. He offered them land at a much cheaper rent. Not as many came as he needed and he had to hire some native Irish.

He also had to swear that he would promote the Protestant religion and English laws and customs in Ulster. This was not a problem for him as he is a Protestant. He would love to help the Irish people learn about his faith.

He built a village around his house and bawn. It has a Protestant church and a school. There are not many students yet but he hopes it will grow.

He based the design of the town on the two big towns, Londonderry and Coleraine. It has a square for weekly markets so that the farmers from around can come in and sell their food. It has wide, straight streets and a diamond (square) in the centre for holding markets.

They are building a courthouse and there's a new constable to look after law and order.

The soil is great for growing crops such as potatoes. They also grow flax to make linen.

He is very happy here although he is afraid that the natives might attack his family. Some of the Irish are friendly but others resent him being here. He thinks that the poets and popish priests are stirring up trouble. He would love to be rid of them!

Chapter 5

How Did the Plantations Change Ireland?

Key Learning Objectives

- How did Ireland change politically?
- How did everyday life change?
- How did religion change?

Plantations began in the 1550s and ended in the 1650s. They changed Ireland in almost every way.

How did Ireland change politically?

By 1700, almost all the Gaelic and Old English lords who had ruled Ireland in 1550 were gone. The Protestant settlers now owned 85 per cent of the land.

Land ownership in Ireland

Year	Catholic ownership
1600	90%
1640	60%
1660	20%
1720	10%

The Protestant Ascendancy

These new rulers were called the **Protestant Ascendancy**. They were the only ones who could sit in the Irish parliament. For the next 200 years they helped the British to rule Ireland.

Term

The Protestant Ascendancy
The Protestant ruling class in Ireland.

New landlords

Most of the Protestant Ascendancy were **landlords**. That means they made their money by renting their land to the (mostly Catholic) tenant farmers. The new landlords usually made a legal written agreement, called a **lease**, with their tenants. It set out clearly how much the tenant had to pay every year. That made life easier for most farmers.

The new landlords changed life in local communities.

- They often built towns on their estates and owned most of the houses and shops in them.
- They built large, elegant houses, many of which are still standing.
- They were the main employers in an area.
- They were usually the local magistrates (judges).

Estate of Colonel Pole-Cosby, Stradbally Hall, Co. Laois in the 1720s. What improvements has Colonel Pole-Cosby made to his estate? What, do you think, were the ponds used for? Can you see Stradbally village on the left of the picture?

How did everyday life change?

New Irish people

About 100,000 people came from Britain to settle in Ireland. Most settlers were ordinary farmers, not landlords. They soon mixed with the locals and became Irish themselves. The language, ideas and customs they brought with them became part of Irish life.

Changes in farming

The Gaelic way of farming, with huge herds of cattle roaming freely around the countryside, was finished. The settlers divided the land into farms and fields. They enclosed each field with a hedge and ditch. As time passed, all farmers did the same.

The settlers drained the land and cleared the forests. Many lakes and bogs disappeared. The settlers also introduced new methods of farming, and grew more crops, such as wheat.

Did you know?

The Electric Picnic takes place in the grounds of Stradbally Hall every summer.

The settlers changed how the countryside looked by introducing hedges and ditches into farming

Plantation towns

The planters built many new towns such as Derry and Killarney. These had a different layout from the medieval towns. Here is a typical plantation town.

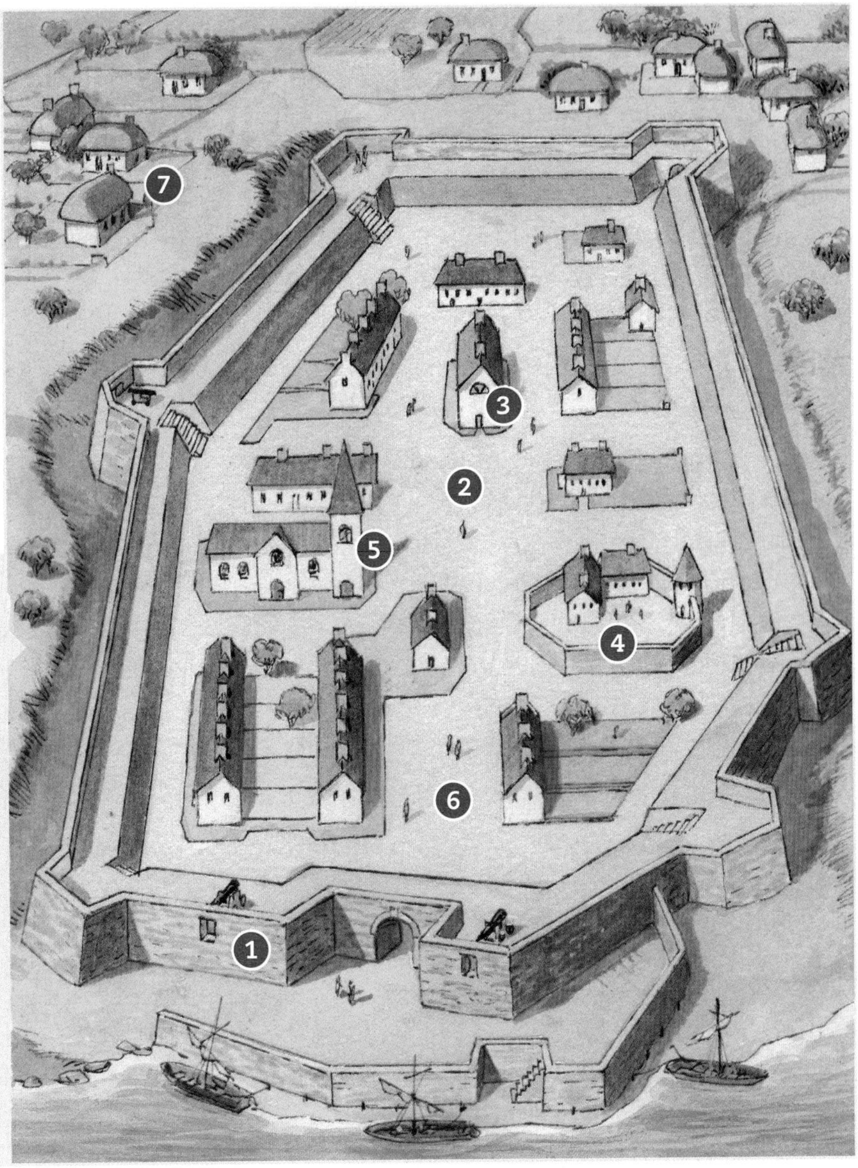

A plantation town

The square is where weekly markets were held. In Ulster it was usually called 'the Diamond'.

1 Walls
2 The square
3 Courthouse
4 Gaol
5 Protestant church
6 Wide, straight streets
7 Gaelic-style houses outside the town walls

Industry

Settlers set up new industries. **Iron** and **glass** works began in Co. Cork. Later, **linen** was made on a large scale in Ulster. They also sold the timber from the forests to make ships and barrels.

Law and order

Brehon law was forbidden and only **common law** was allowed. The king's judges travelled around the country to judge serious crimes. There was a sheriff in every county and a constable in each parish.

Did you know?

Under common law, new crimes appeared. **Witchcraft** became a crime. So did **begging**. In 1659, Dublin Corporation ordered that 'a large cage' be set up in the cornmarket for 'all beggars, idle women and maids selling apples and oranges'.

Irish customs

The English banned Irish fashions such as the glib, the Irish mantle, and harping. The Irish language was used less and by 1700 most well-educated people spoke only English.

But Irish culture remained strong. Irish music and poetry remained popular. Irish scholars, especially in Europe, wrote down the history of Ireland and old Irish legends.

How did religion change?

- The English hoped the plantations would turn the Catholic Irish into Protestants, but that did not happen. In most of Ireland the majority of the people remained Catholic. Many priests still operated in secret. Only in Ulster did the plantation produce a large number of Protestants.
- There was also tension between Catholics and Protestants. Catholics who had once owned a lot of land resented the new settlers. Protestants settlers and their descendants didn't trust the mainly Catholic population.
- In the 1700s, laws were passed to stop Irish Catholics getting power. These were called the **Penal Laws.**

Here are some examples of the Penal Laws:

- Priests could not say Mass.
- Catholic schools were banned.
- Catholics could not keep weapons.
- Catholics (and Presbyterians) were not allowed to vote or become members of parliament.

Do you understand these key terms?

Protestant Ascendancy **landlord** **lease** **Penal Laws**

QUESTIONS

1 What percentage of land in Ireland did Protestant settlers own by 1720?
2 What does 'Protestant Ascendancy' mean?
3 Why did landlords become so important in Ireland? Give three reasons.
4 How many British settlers came to Ireland between 1609 and 1660?
5 Give two ways in which a plantation town was different from a medieval town.
6 How did farming and industry change as a result of the plantations? Write down five examples.
7 Do you think the plantations were a good or a bad thing for Ireland? Give two reasons for your answer.

EXAM QUESTION

- Name a plantation you have studied and write about the effects of that plantation on two of the following:
  (a) Political control
  (b) Religion
  (c) Culture and customs. (HL)

Section 9

Revolutions

Chapter 1

The American War of Independence

Key Learning Objectives

- What was life like in the British colonies of America?
- What were the causes of the War of Independence?
- What role did George Washington play in the US War of Independence?
- What were the consequences of the US War of Independence?

In the eighteenth century, kings and queens ruled the countries of Europe. They were very powerful and were not chosen by the people. They inherited the throne after the death of their father or mother. These rulers believed that they were chosen by God. The people they ruled were called **subjects**. Some rulers were very good and therefore popular. Others were very bad or cruel and were hated by their subjects.

Some people began to question this system of government. They wanted more freedom and the right to elect their own rulers. They were influenced by writers in France and Britain who were called **Enlightenment** writers. These writers argued that the power of rulers came not from God but from their people. They argued that if a ruler was cruel or unfair their subjects had the right to replace them. When a ruler is removed or changed it is called a **revolution**.

In this section of the book, we will study how revolutionary movements grew up in three countries during the eighteenth century:

- **America**, which was part of the British Empire
- **France**, which was ruled by King Louis XVI
- **Ireland**, which was controlled by Britain.

Now let's examine how revolution broke out in America.

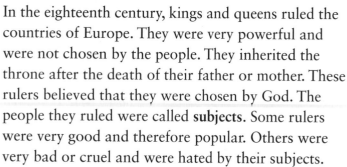

George III ruled Britain from 1760 until 1820

Term

Revolution
The successful overthrow of a government.

Rebellion
An organised attempt to overthrow a ruler or government.

What was life like in the British colonies of America?

Today the United States of America (USA) is made up of fifty states with a population of 300 million. It is the world's most powerful country.

But in 1765, Britain ruled the east coast of America where there were **thirteen colonies**. You can see the colonies on the map below. The population of these colonies was about 2.5 million.

In 1607, the British had founded their first colony, which they called Virginia. Over the next 100 years more colonies were set up.

> **Did you know?**
>
> Around 1765 Ireland and America had the same population.

- Some were started by people looking for religious freedom, e.g. Massachusetts and Pennsylvania.
- New York and Delaware were originally Dutch colonies but they became British after a war.
- Most people who settled in the colonies came from Britain, Ireland or Germany.
- The Irish settlers were mainly Protestants from Ulster. They were the descendants of the planters that you read about in the last section.

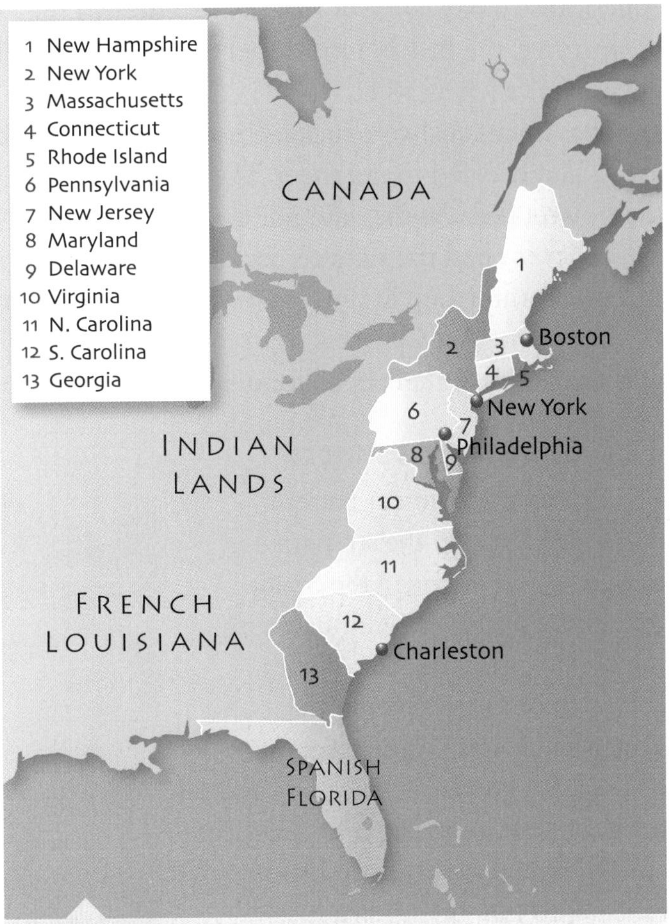

Britain controlled these thirteen colonies on the east coast of America

By 1765 the colonies were wealthy. However, there were two groups of Americans who were treated very badly. These were slaves and Native Americans.

- **Slaves** made up about one-fifth of the population – about 500,000 people. They were mainly found in the South, working on large farms called **plantations**.
- **Native Americans** (sometimes known as 'Indians') lost their land as more settlers arrived from Europe. They often attacked the settlers and were feared and hated by the Americans.

How were the colonies governed?

Each colony had an elected assembly and a governor appointed by the king. The Americans were loyal to the British king, George III. Their main enemies, the French and the Native Americans, had just been defeated in the Seven Years War (1756–63). Canada had been captured from the French. The future looked good for British America. However, this was soon to change.

Slaves working on a cotton plantation

What were the causes of the War of Independence?

The Stamp Act

There were a number of actions by the British that made many Americans unhappy. The most important was the decision to tax the colonies. The war against the French had been very expensive. The British now had to keep more troops in America to protect all the land they had conquered. They wanted the Americans to pay some of this cost. To do this they decided to tax the Americans.

Term
Act
Another name for a law.

In 1765, the British introduced the **Stamp Act**. This brought in a tax on official documents such as wills.

The Americans were furious that the British parliament, nearly 5,000 kilometres away, had decided to tax them. They were very independent and were used to deciding their own taxes. As they did not have any members in the British parliament they did not believe it had the right to decide taxes for Americans. This opposition to the Stamp Act was summed up in the slogan: 'No Taxation without Representation'.

The **Stamp Act Congress** was set up to fight the tax. It contained members from most of the colonies. Often tax collectors were attacked and forced to give up their jobs.

The Boston Massacre

The British government backed down when it saw the strength of opposition. It ended the Stamp Act, but foolishly it continued with the policy of taxing the colonies. It introduced new taxes in the **Townshend Acts**. These were **duties** or taxes on goods such as glass and tea that were imported into America.

Term
Duties
Taxes on imported goods that make them more expensive.

The Boston Massacre

The Americans reacted by refusing to buy British products. To get around paying taxes they smuggled goods. One port at the centre of smuggling was **Boston**.

In Boston, relations between the people of the town and British soldiers were poor. In March 1770, a mob of about fifty men attacked a group of soldiers with stones and snowballs. The soldiers opened fire and killed five people. This event outraged Americans, who called it the **Boston Massacre**. They saw it as an example of cruelty by the British. Some began to feel that it would be better if America controlled her own affairs. They called themselves **patriots**.

In response to the events in Boston and the refusal of Americans to buy the taxed goods, the British government took the duties off all the goods except tea. Unwilling to pay any tax, Americans refused to buy tea imported from Britain.

The Boston Tea Party

The Boston Tea Party. This picture was made close to the time it happened

The government then decided to allow cheap tea to be sold in America. The British hoped that the cut-price tea would tempt the Americans. There was one problem – the tea was still taxed.

The plan backfired. The Americans were annoyed that the British government was still trying to tax them. When ships carrying tea arrived at the port of Boston the patriots acted. Men dressed as Native Americans boarded the ships and threw the tea overboard. This event became known as the **Boston Tea Party.**

The British government was furious. It passed a series of laws that closed Boston port until the colonists paid for all the destroyed tea. General Gage was sent to Boston to restore order. He closed the local assembly when it refused to pay for the destroyed tea.

The First Continental Congress

Americans were worried by the British actions. They called the laws passed against Boston the **Intolerable Acts**. They felt that they had to work together to protect their freedoms.

Representatives from twelve of the thirteen colonies met in Philadelphia. This meeting was called the **First Continental Congress.** It called on Americans not to buy British goods until the Intolerable Acts were removed. The Congress was very important as it showed that the colonies could act together against the British government.

Term

Congress
The American name for a parliament.

The Battle of Lexington

The colonies had a long tradition of groups of volunteer soldiers that were called **militias.** They had originally been set up to defend the Americans against attack from the French or the natives. Around Boston, militias were now being prepared against the British. They were called the **minutemen** as they were ready to take action at a minute's notice.

General Gage was worried by the activities of these militias. He heard that they were storing military supplies at a place called **Concord.** On the night of 18 April 1775, he sent troops to Concord. Spies found out about his plans and warned the minutemen. At the village of **Lexington** shots were fired. There was a further battle at Concord and the British troops went back to Boston. The following day the port of Boston was surrounded by the patriots. The American War of Independence had begun.

PART 2

The Key Causes of the American War of Independence

1765 – The Stamp Act	Britain decided to tax the colonists to pay for the defence of America. American slogan: 'No Taxation without Representation'
1767 – The Townshend Acts	Taxes on imported goods
1770 – The Boston Massacre	Five civilians shot by British soldiers
1773 – The Boston Tea Party	Tea dumped overboard from ships
1774 – The Intolerable Acts	Port of Boston closed
1774 – The First Continental Congress	Met to support Boston
1775 – Battle of Lexington	First shots fired

QUESTIONS

1 Name four British colonies in America.
2 Why did the British decide to tax the colonies?
3 What was the American reaction to the Stamp Act?
4 What was the Boston Massacre? What was the attitude of many Americans to the event?
5 Why did the Boston Tea Party happen? How did the British react to the event?
6 What was the importance of the First Continental Congress?
7 Who were the minutemen?
8 Why were the events at Lexington so important in American history?

Special Study: George Washington

The War of Independence lasted from 1775 until 1781. The British called the Americans **rebels** and expected to win easily. There were a number of reasons for this:

- They did not think the Americans would make good soldiers.
- The British had a powerful navy and army.
- The American people were divided. A majority supported the patriots but over a quarter of the population remained loyal to the king. They were called **Tories** or **Loyalists**. Many fought for the British.

However, the British government were to be proven wrong.

George Washington (1732–99) is a great hero in America's history. The capital city and one of the states are named after him

The leadership of George Washington

One major factor in the success of the Americans was the leadership provided by **George Washington**. A wealthy farmer from Virginia, Washington had served in the British army in the war against the French. After 1765 he was opposed to British policies and had attended the First Continental Congress in 1774.

In 1775, the **Second Continental Congress** meeting at Philadelphia chose Washington as commander-in-chief of the American army. His bravery, good judgement and common sense were to prove vital in the years ahead.

The capture of Boston

The British had attempted to end the American siege of Boston at the **Battle of Bunker Hill** in 1775, but had failed. When Washington arrived in Boston after the battle he brought order and discipline to the American army. He began to bombard the city with cannons. In March 1776, the British army left the city. Washington had his first victory.

Did you know?

The first copy of the Declaration of Independence was printed by an Irishman, John Dunlap.

The Declaration of Independence

When the war began most Americans wanted the British government to stop taxing them. Now more and more Americans began to look for independence. One reason for this was the writing of **Thomas Paine.** He wrote a pamphlet called *Common Sense*. In it he attacked the rule of George III and called for complete independence from Britain. It was widely read and many Americans agreed with his ideas.

As a result, the Continental Congress decided to declare independence from Britain. A member from Virginia, **Thomas Jefferson,** wrote the **Declaration of Independence.** It was passed by Congress on 4 July 1776. A new nation was born, the United States of America (USA). But it had to yet win this independence.

The war was not going well for the Americans. In the summer of 1776, the British attacked Washington at New York. In the biggest battle of the war, at **Long Island,** they defeated Washington and forced him to leave the city. The British controlled the city for the rest of the war.

On Christmas Day 1776, Washington and his troops crossed the Delaware River and launched an attack on British troops at **Trenton** in New Jersey. The British troops were celebrating Christmas and the attack caught them completely by surprise. This victory lifted the spirits of Americans.

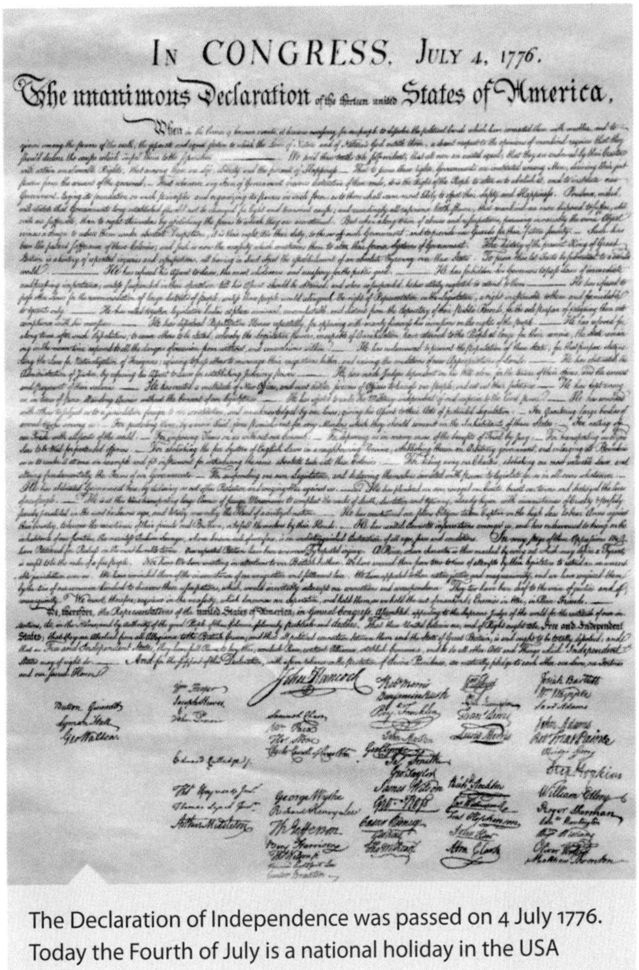
IN CONGRESS, JULY 4, 1776.

The unanimous Declaration of the thirteen united States of America,

The Declaration of Independence was passed on 4 July 1776. Today the Fourth of July is a national holiday in the USA

PART 2

Turning point

In 1777, the British defeated Washington and captured the American capital of Philadelphia. Washington was now forced to spend the winter at **Valley Forge** near Philadelphia.

At the same time the Americans had a very important victory at **Saratoga**. The Americans, led by General Gates, forced a large British army to surrender. This victory was the turning point of the war. The French were watching events in America closely. They wanted revenge after the loss of Canada. When news of Saratoga reached France, **King Louis XVI** decided to join the war in support of the Americans. French help was very important, for a number of reasons:

- The French navy could challenge the British navy off the coast of America.
- French soldiers were disciplined and well trained.
- The British were forced to pull troops out of America to defend their colonies in the Caribbean from French attack. This weakened their army in America.

Did you know?

An important figure in the War of Independence was John Barry from Wexford. He is remembered as the 'Father of the American Navy'.

The winter at Valley Forge

Meanwhile conditions at Valley Forge were very poor. Short of food and clothing, over 2,000 men died from disease. However, the remaining soldiers were trained and turned into a professional army that was a match for the British. Soldiers from Europe helped them. Much of the training was carried out by Baron Friedrich von Steuben from Germany.

Did you know?

Probably the best American general was Benedict Arnold. However, in 1780 he changed sides and fought for the British. He is the most famous traitor in American history.

The Battle of Yorktown

The British sent troops to the South where they believed there was a large number of loyalists who would fight for them. Led by General Cornwallis, they took the city of **Charleston** in 1780 and captured over 5,000 American soldiers.

After a number of further battles, Cornwallis led his troops into Virginia. He found himself trapped by Washington at **Yorktown**. A French fleet prevented help reaching Cornwallis. Outnumbered, he surrendered in October 1781. The war was over – the Americans had won!

Why did the Americans win?

- The leadership of George Washington
- Military help from the French
- Distance of the colonies from Britain – nearly 5,000 kilometres

The Battle of Yorktown. This was the last major battle of the war

The Treaty of Paris

Negotiations began in France in 1782 between the British, the Americans and the French. The Americans were led by the writer and inventor **Benjamin Franklin.** Under the Treaty of Paris the British agreed to recognise the independence of the USA. In 1783, the last British troops left New York and America was now an independent country.

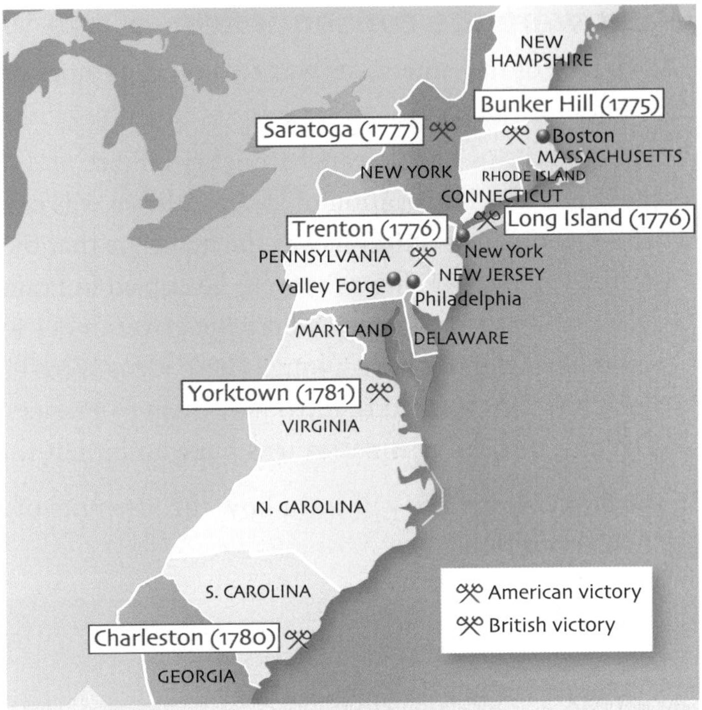

The main battles during the War of Independence

The US Constitution

The Americans now decided upon the best way to run their country.

- America would be a **republic** – there would be no king or queen.
- Each state would have a lot of control over matters such as business and education.
- Major issues such as foreign relations, money and war would be decided by the central government in the capital. This is called a **federal system.**
- Another very important decision was that the people would elect the government. This is called **democracy.**

During the war the Stars and Stripes became the American flag. The stars represent each state. As you can see, there were 13 states in 1783 and today there are 50

Washington became the first President in 1789. He served for two terms. He then retired to his farm in 1797, a rich and respected man. He died two years later and is regarded as the father of the American nation. The capital of the new nation was named Washington in his honour.

The American Congress building in Washington DC

PART 2

What were the consequences of the War of Independence?

The victory of the Americans was to have a number of important consequences, especially for France:

- The Americans had defeated a mighty empire and this inspired other peoples to do the same. The Declaration of Independence was copied by many countries.
- The American constitution was the first time that the rules for governing a country had been written down. It was soon to be copied in France and throughout the world.
- America was a democracy where the government was elected by the people. It was a republic. It did not have a king. These ideas were brought back to Europe. Returning French troops wanted to introduce them to France.
- The cost of helping America was huge and it left the French king with no money.

In the next chapter, we will learn how the attempts of the French king to raise taxes led to a revolution.

TIMELINE The Life of George Washington

1732	Born in Virginia
1775	Appointed commander-in-chief
1776	Captured Boston but defeated at New York
1777	Spent the winter at Valley Forge
1781	Defeated Cornwallis at Yorktown
1789	Became the first American President
1799	Washington died

Do you understand these key terms?

revolution	**republic**
militia	**duties**
rebellion	**federal system**
rebel	**Congress**
Act	**democracy**

QUESTIONS

1 Why did Congress choose George Washington as commander-in-chief?
2 Why was Thomas Paine an important figure during the revolution?
3 Who was the main author of the Declaration of Independence?
4 How did George Washington show good leadership at Trenton in 1776?
5 Why was the Battle of Saratoga a turning point in the war?
6 Why was Yorktown an important battle?
7 Under what Treaty did the British recognise American independence?
8 Write a paragraph on two of the following:
- The Stamp Act, 1765
- Events in Boston between 1770 and 1774
- The outbreak of the War of Independence
- The role of the French in the War of Independence
- The consequences of the American War of Independence

SOURCE QUESTION

› George Hewes was a member of the group that boarded the ships during the Boston Tea Party. Read his account below and answer the questions that follow:

Part A

It was now evening, and I immediately dressed myself in the costume of an Indian, equipped with a small hatchet... after having painted my face and hands with coal dust in the shop of a blacksmith, I repaired to Griffin's wharf, where the ships lay that contained the tea.

Part B

When we arrived at the wharf [harbour], there were three of our number who assumed an authority to direct our operations. They divided us into three parties [groups], for the purpose of boarding the three ships which contained the tea at the same time. The name of him who commanded the division to which I was assigned was Leonard Pitt.

We then were ordered by our commander to open the hatches and take out all the chests of tea and throw them overboard, and we immediately proceeded to execute [carry out] his orders, first cutting and splitting the chests with our hatchets...

Part C

In about three hours from the time we went on board, we had thus broken and thrown overboard every tea chest to be found in the ship. We were surrounded by British armed ships, but no attempt was made to resist us...

The next morning, after we had cleared the ships of the tea, it was discovered that very considerable quantities of it were floating upon the surface of the water.

Source: ***http://www.eyewitnesstohistory.com/teaparty.htm***

(a) According to Part A how did George Hewes disguise himself?

(b) From Part B why were the men divided into 'three parties'?

(c) According to Part B who was the commander of the author's division?

(d) In Part B what were they ordered to do by the commander?

(e) According to Part C how long did it take them to throw all the tea overboard?

(f) From Part C what was the reaction of the 'British armed ships'?

(g) According to Part C what did they discover the next morning?

(h) This account was written a few years after the event. Does that affect how reliable it is to a historian? Explain your answer.

Chapter 2

The French Revolution

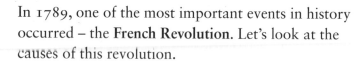

Key Learning Objectives

- **How was France ruled before 1789?**
- **Why were there demands for change in France?**
- **What events led to a revolution in France in 1789?**
- **What role did Robespierre play in the Revolution?**
- **Why was the king executed in 1793?**
- **What were the consequences of the French Revolution?**

In 1789, one of the most important events in history occurred – the **French Revolution**. Let's look at the causes of this revolution.

How was France ruled before 1789?

King Louis XVI

France was a powerful country, ruled by King Louis XVI. Louis became king in 1774 at the age of 20. He was an absolute monarch and ruled France from his beautiful palace at Versailles near Paris.

Louis believed his power came from God. He made all of the major decisions. He appointed his advisors and there was no elected parliament. A kind and generous man who loved hunting, Louis was popular with most French people. However, he found it difficult to take hard decisions. People also felt he was controlled by his wife, Marie-Antoinette. She was an Austrian princess and was not liked by the French people. Austria was traditionally an enemy of France. They believed that she wasted vast amounts of money on luxuries such as jewellery.

Louis XVI (1754–93)

The Three Estates

The people of France were subjects of King Louis and were divided into three 'Estates':

- The **First Estate** was the clergy – the bishops and priests of the Catholic Church. They numbered about 100,000 people. The Church ran schools and hospitals. It also owned over 10 per cent of the land of France. Farmers and peasants had to pay a tax to the Church called a **tithe**. This was about one-tenth of what they produced.
- The **Second Estate** was the nobles. There were about 400,000 nobles. Most were wealthy landowners and some acted as advisors to the king or as judges or generals in the army. Nobles had great power over the peasants who worked on their land.
- The **Third Estate** was the remaining 95 per cent of the population. They were also called **commoners**. The vast majority were poor workers or peasants. The rich and educated members of the Third Estate were called the **bourgeoisie**. They were businessmen, lawyers and doctors and they wanted more say in how France was governed and how taxes were raised.

This political system had been accepted in France for hundreds of years, but now people were beginning to question it.

Why were there demands for change in France?

The Enlightenment

In Chapter 1, we learned that Enlightenment writers were against powerful kings. Their ideas were very influential in France. Writers such as **Voltaire** and **Rousseau** were read by many people. Here are some of the things they wrote:

- They thought religion was superstition and did not believe that the king's power came from God.
- They were opposed to the absolute power of the king and argued that his power came from the people.
- They felt that the Church and the nobles were too powerful and that the ordinary people of France should have a greater say in running their country.

Rousseau (1712–78) was born in Switzerland. The leaders of the French Revolution were influenced by his ideas

Taxes

As in America, taxes were a major source of discontent. The tax system was very unfair.

Even though the Church was wealthy it did not pay any taxes. It gave a gift of money to the king every year.

Although the nobles were rich, they did not have to pay many of the taxes that the king collected from the Third Estate. For example, nobles did not have to pay the **gabelle**, a tax on salt. This tax was disliked by ordinary people as salt was used to preserve food.

Although most peasants were poor they had to pay taxes to their local lord. These were called **feudal dues**. The tithe paid to the Church was also very unpopular.

To make matters worse, in the late 1780s there had been a number of bad harvests and there was a food shortage. The most important food of the ordinary French people – bread – had risen greatly in price.

Did you know?

In the eighteenth century, the main reason governments collected tax was to pay for the army.

PART 2

The impact of the American revolution

Thousands of French soldiers had fought during the American War of Independence. They had been impressed by the freedoms that Americans had, and wanted to see some of them introduced into France.

Helping the Americans also had another major impact on France. The War of Independence was one of a long line of wars that France had fought in the eighteenth century. These wars were very expensive and France was now bankrupt.

King Louis XIV built the Palace of Versailles near Paris in the seventeenth century. From here, the kings of France ruled the country

What events led to a revolution in France in 1789?

The king needed to raise money and he wanted the nobles to pay more taxes. Naturally, the nobles did not want to give the king more money. They forced the king to call an **Estates General**. This was a parliament that contained members of all the Three Estates. It had not met since 1614. The nobles thought that they could control this parliament and stop reform. The Third Estate had other ideas and wanted to see reform.

The question of voting

When the Estates General met, in May 1789, members of the Third Estate wanted a role in the decisions that were to be made. To do this they needed to change the system of voting:

- In 1614, each Estate met separately and made up its mind on an issue. It then had one vote. This was called **voting by order**. The nobles and clergy hoped that this system would continue. They would be able to outvote the Third Estate by 2 to 1.
- The Third Estate wanted each member of the Estates General to have a vote. This was called **voting by head**. They knew that, with the help of some of the nobles and clergy who were sympathetic to them, they would be able to introduce reforms. As they made up the vast majority of the population, this was fairer.

The National Assembly

When they did not get their way on the issue of voting, the Third Estate refused to attend the Estates General and met separately. They said they represented the people of France and called themselves the **National Assembly**. They wanted the king to allow them to draw up a constitution for France.

The Tennis Court Oath, painted by the French artist David

On 20 June, they found the door to where they met locked. Fearing that they were about to be arrested, they met in an indoor tennis court. They swore that they would continue meeting until their demands were met. This event became known as the **Tennis Court Oath.**

The king gave in and ordered the other two estates to join with the Third Estate. France now had a parliament – the king was no longer an absolute monarch.

The Bastille

In Paris there was strong support for the National Assembly. People feared that the king and the nobles would try to crush the revolution. Rumours spread that the king's troops were marching on Paris.

An army called the **National Guard** was formed to defend the city. There was an urgent need for guns. On 14 July, after capturing muskets (guns), a crowd marched to the Bastille prison where gunpowder was stored. This medieval fortress had been used by the kings of France to imprison people who criticised them. To many it was a hated symbol of the king's power. The crowd stormed the prison.

The storming of the Bastille

This was a very important event – a symbol of the king's power had been captured by the people. The news of the fall of the Bastille was celebrated not just in France but throughout Europe.

Causes of the French Revolution

- The influence of the Enlightenment
- Bankruptcy due to wars fought in the eighteenth century
- The absolute power of the king
- Poor harvests that left ordinary people hungry
- Resistance of the nobles to tax reform
- The unfair nature of the tax system

Did you know?

There were only seven prisoners in the Bastille when it was stormed, one of whom was Irish. Every year, on 14 July, the French celebrate Bastille Day as a national holiday.

Important changes for France

Quickly, the new National Assembly made two important decisions:

- It banned the feudal system that had existed since the Middle Ages. This ended the power of the nobles.
- Influenced both by the American constitution and the views of Enlightenment writers, the Assembly issued a document known as the **Declaration of the Rights of Man and of the Citizen.** This gave the ordinary people of France more rights, such as freedom of religion, the right to free speech and the right to a fair trial.

King Louis was still on his throne but his power was greatly reduced. The three different estates were gone. The people were now equal citizens and not the king's subjects. In October, King Louis was forced to move to Paris from Versailles. The National Assembly also moved to the city.

A new slogan

In 1789, some nobles had fled France. Led by the king's brother, they organised an army and hoped to restore King Louis XVI as an absolute ruler.

But most French people supported the changes that were being introduced and the new society that they were creating. A new slogan became very popular. It reflected the aims of the revolutionaries: **Liberty, Equality, Fraternity**.

- **Liberty** for people from the rule of kings
- **Equality** of treatment for all
- **Fraternity**, i.e. brotherhood or cooperation between people

QUESTIONS

1. When and at what age had Louis XVI become king?
2. Give two reasons why Queen Marie-Antoinette was unpopular.
3. Explain briefly who the members of the First, Second and Third Estates were.
4. Why was the price of bread rising in the 1780s?
5. Why did the nobles force the king to call an Estates General?
6. Explain what the Tennis Court Oath was.
7. List two important decisions reached by the National Assembly.
8. Explain the slogan of the French Revolution.

Special Study: Maximilien Robespierre

In the French parliament, those who called for a republic were led by a lawyer from Northern France, Maximilien Robespierre. He had been elected to the Estates General in 1789. He was an opponent of the king's power and was strongly influenced by the ideas of Rousseau, the Enlightenment writer.

He became the leader of a political party called the **Jacobins**. He was very popular with the ordinary people of Paris. To them he was a hero. He was nicknamed **the incorruptible one** because of his devotion to the revolution.

Maximilien Robespierre (1758–94) was a very strong supporter of the revolution

Why was the king executed in 1793?

The Flight to Varennes

The capture of King Louis XVI and his family at Varennes in a drawing made at the time

In 1790, the National Assembly passed the **Civil Constitution of the Clergy**. Most revolutionaries disliked the Catholic Church because it had supported the king and the nobles. They wanted to reduce its power. This law brought the Church under the control of the government. Monasteries were closed and priests had to take an oath to support the revolution.

King Louis was a very religious man and he did not like the changes to the Catholic Church. He decided to leave France with his family. The king hoped to reach Belgium. It was ruled by the Austrian Emperor, who was the brother of Marie-Antoinette. On the night of 20 June 1791, the royal family left Paris, but they were captured at **Varennes** – near the border. They returned to Paris under guard.

The revolutionaries were divided about what to do with Louis. To Robespierre and many others this event showed that he was an enemy of the revolution. They argued that France must become a republic with no king.

France becomes a republic

A crucial turning point for the revolution was the outbreak of war. In April 1792, France declared war on Austria. France was soon at war with most of Europe. The kings and queens of Europe were determined to crush the revolution. The war went badly and foreign armies invaded France.

Many people suspected King Louis was hoping for the defeat of France. Revolutionaries stormed the Tuileries Palace, where the royal family lived. Mobs then broke into prisons and massacred anyone suspected of being an enemy of the revolution.

The revolutionaries decided to remove Louis from the throne. On 21 September 1792, the monarchy was abolished and France became a republic. Robespierre warmly welcomed this decision.

Term

Convention
Name of the French parliament during the Reign of Terror.

The execution of King Louis XVI

The most important issue now facing the revolutionaries was what to do with King Louis XVI. The newly elected parliament, called the **National Convention**, decided to try him for treason. They claimed he was plotting with other kings in Europe to crush the revolution.

The execution of King Louis XVI

Now called *citizen Louis Capet*, he was found guilty by the Convention in January 1793. He was sentenced to death by a small majority. Robespierre was one of those who voted for the king's execution. On 21 January, he was executed by guillotine. This action shocked many in Europe. In October 1793, his wife Marie-Antoinette was also beheaded.

Did you know?

After 1789 it was decided to introduce one form of execution – the **guillotine**. It was seen as quick and humane. Later, during the Terror, it would be nicknamed the *National Razor*.

The Reign of Terror

The Revolution now faced enemies both at home and abroad:

- The king still had many supporters who saw his son, Louis XVII, as the rightful king of France.
- The religious changes were unpopular and regions such as the Vendée were in open revolt.
- France was at war with several European countries. Their armies were invading the country.

A **Committee of Public Safety**, consisting of twelve members, was set up to protect the revolution. It was led by Robespierre and his supporters. Robespierre believed that the use of terror was needed to defeat the enemies of the revolution. Anyone suspected of disloyalty to the government was arrested. Robespierre's rule of France became known as the **Reign of Terror**.

In September 1793, a **Law of Suspects** was passed that set up a Revolutionary Tribunal (court). This tried anyone suspected of treason. Once a person was accused of being an enemy of the revolution it was assumed that the person was guilty. It was very difficult for people to prove their innocence. Executions now became very common, as priests, former nobles and many ordinary people were tried and guillotined. In six weeks 1,400 people were executed in Paris alone.

Robespierre then turned on his political opponents and had them executed. His most famous victim was his former ally, **Georges Danton**.

Term

Sans-culottes
The name given to poor men who wore long trousers instead of knee-breeches which were worn by the wealthy.

The sans-culottes

One of the major reasons why Robespierre was able to stay in power was the support of the poor people of Paris. They were called the ***sans-culottes***. To keep them happy Robespierre made sure that the price of bread was kept low.

On the battlefield Robespierre's policies were working. A large revolutionary army was created of over one million men. This army defeated the Austrian army. The rebels in the Vendée were also defeated.

Picture of a sans-culotte of the time

The fall of Robespierre

With the success of France's armies people wanted the Terror to end, but Robespierre was having more and more people executed. He lost the support of the Parisians. Members of the Convention feared they could be next. On 24 July 1794, he and his followers were arrested. In an attempt to commit suicide, Robespierre shot himself in the jaw. The next day Robespierre, his brother and other prominent supporters were executed. The Terror was over and a more moderate government called the **Directory** came to power.

Robespierre had saved the revolution but at a terrible human cost. Historians believe that up to 40,000 people were executed during the Terror.

PART 2

TIMELINE	Maximilien Robespierre
1758	Born in Arras
1789	Elected as a deputy to the Estates General
1792	Leader of the Jacobins France went to war with Austria He supported France becoming a republic
1793	Voted for the execution of the king Committee of Public Safety formed – Robespierre a leading member Called for a Reign of Terror to defeat France's enemies French army greatly increased in size
1794	Defeat of Austrian armies and rebels in the Vendée Robespierre removed from power and executed

The rise of Napoleon Bonaparte

The war with France's enemies continued. General **Napoleon Bonaparte** emerged as the most powerful man in France. Under his leadership French armies conquered large parts of Europe. In 1804 he crowned himself Emperor of France. In 1812 he made a major mistake and invaded Russia. He suffered a crushing defeat. Three years later he was defeated at Waterloo in Belgium. He was then sent to a remote island in the Atlantic where he died in 1821.

Napoleon Bonaparte (1769–1821)

What were the consequences of the French Revolution?

- Throughout Europe, many people welcomed the French Revolution. They demanded that kings and queens share power with their people as had happened in France.
- Inspired by events in France, people such as Wolfe Tone hoped to spread revolutionary ideals to Ireland. (In the next chapter, we will read about events in Ireland.)
- However, many rulers were afraid that the French Revolution would spread to their countries. They were determined to prevent this and arrested people who criticised them.
- The Reign of Terror shocked many ordinary people. These people preferred the rule of kings to the chaos of revolution.
- Because of the revolution, war broke out in Europe. This war lasted until the defeat of Napoleon at Waterloo in 1815.
- Among the lasting changes introduced during the revolution were the tricolour flag and the metric system of weights and measures.
- A new national anthem, 'La Marseillaise', was adopted – this is the French national anthem today.

Do you understand these key terms?

Enlightenment	**Estates General**	**equality**	**National Convention**
Three Estates	**National Assembly**	**fraternity**	**guillotine**
commoners	**liberty**	**Jacobins**	**sans-culottes**
feudal dues			

QUESTIONS

1 Name the party that Robespierre led.

2 Why was the Civil Constitution of the Clergy introduced?

3 What was the flight to Varennes? Why was it important?

4 Why did war break out in 1792?

5 Why was the Tuileries Palace attacked in August 1792?

6 In 1793, why was the revolution in danger?

7 During the Terror what was the Law of Suspects?

8 Why did members of the Convention turn against Robespierre?

9 Write an account of two of the following:
- The storming of the Bastille
- The events leading to the execution of King Louis XVI
- The Reign of Terror in France
- Why Robespierre fell from power
- The consequences of the revolution.

People in History

Write about a named leader involved in the French revolution during the period 1771–1815

Use the plan below to help you with your answer.

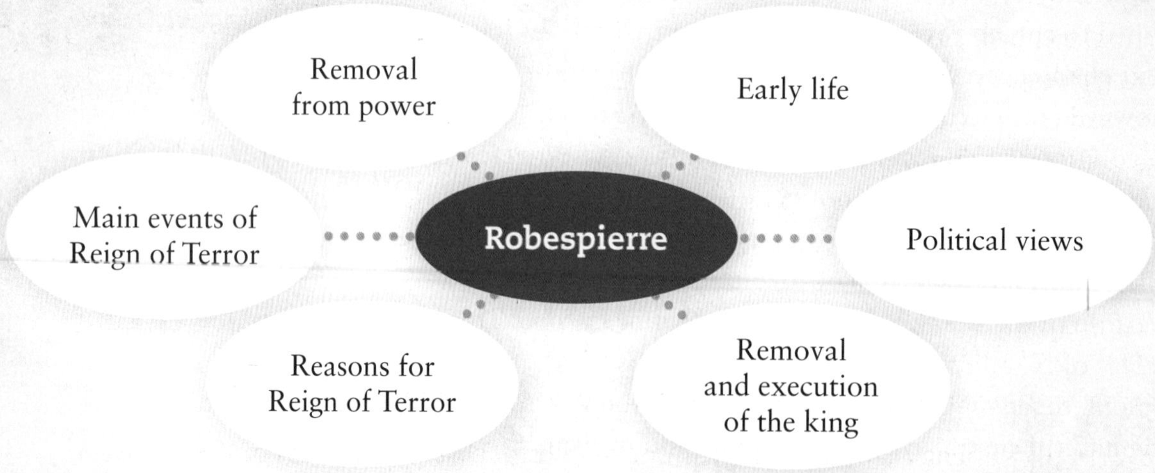

Chapter 3

The 1798 Rebellion

Key Learning Objectives

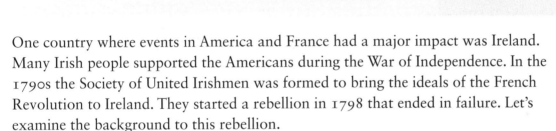

- How was Ireland governed in 1790?
- Who was Wolfe Tone and what did he do?
- Why did rebellion break out in Ireland in 1798?
- What were the main events of the 1798 rebellion?
- What were the consequences of the 1798 rebellion?

One country where events in America and France had a major impact was Ireland. Many Irish people supported the Americans during the War of Independence. In the 1790s the Society of United Irishmen was formed to bring the ideals of the French Revolution to Ireland. They started a rebellion in 1798 that ended in failure. Let's examine the background to this rebellion.

How was Ireland governed in 1790?

The Irish parliament

At the time King George III ruled Ireland. There was an Irish parliament that met in Dublin.

In 1782, weakened by the war in America, the British gave in to demands that the Irish parliament should get more power. They agreed to allow the Irish parliament to pass its own laws without first getting the approval of the British. It became known as **Grattan's parliament** after a leading figure of the time, Henry Grattan.

The Irish parliament building at College Green. It is a bank today

Why was the system of government unfair?

There were a number of serious problems with the way Ireland was governed:

- The Irish parliament was very unrepresentative. Only wealthy members of the Church of Ireland could be elected as members of parliament (MPs). Parliament was dominated by wealthy landlord families, called the **Protestant Ascendancy**.

They lived in beautiful houses and made their fortune by renting land to farmers called **tenants**.

- **Catholics** made about 75 per cent of the population. In 1793, Catholics were allowed to vote, but were not allowed to become members of parliament. This was one of the few remaining **Penal Laws**. These laws had been passed earlier in the century to stop Catholics becoming powerful in Ireland (see page 212).
- In **Ulster** there was a large number of **Presbyterians**. They also had suffered under some of the Penal Laws. For example, they were barred from parliament. They were very independent and strongly supported the Americans during the War of Independence.
- Only wealthy people could vote in elections. This was unfair as most of the population, Protestant or Catholic, were poor and therefore could not vote.
- Although the Irish parliament was in theory independent, this was not the case in reality. The king and his government made sure that the parliament did not pass any laws that they disliked.

The demand for reform

Many people wanted to reform or change the Irish parliament but the Protestant Ascendancy would not agree. They would not share power, especially with the Catholics.

Those who wanted change admired the French Revolution. In Ulster, many Presbyterians wanted to see a fairer government based on the changes introduced in France. The small town of Belfast was home to many who wanted to see reform.

Special Study: Theobald Wolfe Tone

One man inspired by events in France was a young Dublin-born Protestant lawyer, Theobald Wolfe Tone. He was born in 1763 and attended Trinity College. He was a strong critic of British control of Ireland and called for a reform of the Irish parliament. In 1791 he wrote a pamphlet called *An Argument on Behalf of the Catholics of Ireland*. This made Tone well known among people who wanted to change how Ireland was run.

Wolfe Tone (1763–98) impressed the French including Napoleon with his enthusiasm and his bravery

The Society of United Irishmen

As we have seen, there was a lot of sympathy for reform in Belfast and in October 1791 Tone attended a meeting there. At this meeting the **Society of United Irishmen** was formed. All of its members were middle-class Protestants who shared with Tone an enthusiasm for the ideals of the French Revolution. Some leading figures included **William Drennan**, **Henry Joy McCracken** and Tone's friend **Thomas Russell**.

They hoped to unite Irishmen of all religions to achieve a fairer government for Ireland through peaceful means. A branch was soon founded in Dublin by **James Napper Tandy**.

Term

Middle class
People such as businessmen, lawyers and doctors belong to this class.

The impact of war between France and Britain

As we saw in the last chapter, France and Britain went to war in 1793. The British government became very suspicious of the Society of United Irishmen. They disliked the fact that it was pro-French and in 1794 it was banned.

Leading members of the organisation decided to continue as a secret society whose members took an oath. **Lord Edward Fitzgerald** joined and was soon one of the leaders.

Lord Edward Fitzgerald (1763–98)

Not all members of the Protestant Ascendancy opposed change. Lord Edward Fitzgerald (1763–98) was from one of the most powerful families in Ireland. His father was the Duke of Leinster and owned Leinster House, which is now the Dáil. However, Lord Edward was a supporter of the French Revolution. He visited France where he stayed with Thomas Paine. Lord Edward wanted a republic in Ireland, free of English rule. He helped to organise the military preparations for the revolt in 1798.

Lord Edward Fitzgerald (1763–98)

Tension over land

In the 1790s, Ireland's population was growing very quickly and there was not enough land for them. This led to disputes over the renting of land, especially in Ulster. Catholic tenants were prepared to pay higher rents than their Protestant neighbours. This led to violence and battles between Catholic and Protestant farmers. The secret society the **Defenders** was formed to protect Catholic farmers.

Protestants formed the **Orange Order**. The Order attacked and drove hundreds of Catholics from Ulster. Catholics were scared of the Orange Order and believed the United Irishmen would defend them. Soon Catholics throughout Ireland were joining the United Irishmen in large numbers.

Did you know?

The Orange Order was set up to defend Protestants and British rule in Ireland. The name comes from the victory of the Protestant King William of Orange over the Catholic King James II in 1690. It still has many members.

Wolfe Tone and the French

Tone's aims had changed when the Society of United Irishmen was banned. We know what they were because Tone kept a detailed diary.

- He wanted Ireland to have independence from Britain and to become a republic like France.
- He believed violence would have to be used to achieve this aim.
- He also hoped to unite all Irishmen in supporting Irish freedom regardless of religion.
- Tone hoped to get the help of the French to stage a revolution in Ireland. This help would increase their chances of beating the British.

In 1795, the British discovered that Wolfe Tone had met a French spy and he was forced to leave Ireland with his family for America. Soon he left America and travelled to France to persuade the French to send an

PART 2

invasion fleet to Ireland. The French were prepared to listen as they hoped that a rebellion in Ireland would weaken their British enemy.

The French were impressed by Tone's arguments and agreed to send an invasion fleet to Ireland. A fleet of forty-three ships and 14,000 soldiers under the command of the experienced general **Lazare Hoche** left the port of Brest in December 1796. Tone was on one of the ships. The expedition was a disaster.

- Hoche's ship was separated from the main fleet.
- When the rest of the fleet arrived off Bantry Bay in Co. Cork a violent storm prevented the troops from landing.

Tone was forced to return to France. He urged the French to send another fleet to Ireland but they were not interested.

QUESTIONS

1. In 1782, what power had the British given the Irish parliament?
2. What was the Protestant Ascendancy?
3. What were the Penal Laws?
4. Why was the voting system unfair?
5. In the 1790s, why was the French Revolution admired in Ireland?
6. What was the name of the pamphlet that Tone wrote?
7. Name three men who helped to set up the United Irishmen.
8. What impact did the war between Britain and France have on the United Irishmen?
9. In Ulster why were there disputes between Catholics and Protestants over land?
10. What were Wolfe Tone's aims?

Why did rebellion break out in Ireland in 1798?

The British government realised how close they had come to disaster at Bantry Bay. The experienced French troops would probably have conquered the country. They decided to destroy the United Irishmen. Severe measures were taken:

- Anybody caught giving the oath of membership for the United Irishmen could be executed. A person who took the oath would be transported to the new penal (prison) colony of Australia for life.
- A new army called the **Yeomanry** was formed. Its members were Protestants and the government encouraged members of the new Orange Order to join.

A British officer pitch-capping a prisoner in Kildare. At the start of the 1798 rebellion rebels killed the officer in the picture

- Led by General Lake, the government started a reign of terror in Ulster where the United Irishmen were strongest.
  - Suspects were flogged.
  - Others were hung until they lost consciousness – this was called **half-hanging**.
  - One very cruel method of torture was the use of the **pitch-cap** – a cloth cap filled with tar was placed on a suspect's head and then set alight.

Despite the brutality of these methods, they worked. Ulster was now firmly under the control of the government.

What were the main events of the 1798 rebellion?

The United Irishmen plan a rebellion

The government's methods caused the leaders of the United Irishmen to set a date for a rebellion. They were afraid that the government would soon crush their movement. They also believed that French help was on the way. The day of the rising was 23 May 1798. Membership grew, and Lord Edward Fitzgerald thought he could count on 100,000 men in the event of a revolt.

Term

Loyalist
A supporter of the British government. Most Protestants were loyalists although a large number of Catholics supported the government as well.

Betrayed by spies

As the United Irishmen movement grew in size so did the number of British spies. Two of the leaders, **Leonard McNally** and **Thomas Reynolds**, were in fact passing information to the British government.

In March 1798 the government, acting on information from Reynolds, arrested the leaders of the United Irishmen. The government then started a campaign of terror in Leinster to find United Irishmen, especially in Co. Kildare.

Lord Edward Fitzgerald had managed to escape arrest, but he was captured two months later. Another spy betrayed him. He was shot during his arrest, and later died of his wounds in prison.

Causes of 1798 Rebellion

- Support for the ideals of the French Revolution
- Activities of Tone and the United Irishmen
- The unfair political system and the Protestant Ascendancy
- War between Britain and France – hope of French help
- Government's use of terror to crush the United Irishmen

The rebellion in Wexford

With the help of information from spies, the government easily crushed rebel plans to capture Dublin. At the end of May fighting started in Counties Kildare, Meath and Carlow. The rebels had some success but were crushed by superior British forces. After battles rebel prisoners were often executed. By then the rebellion had spread to the county most associated with 1798 – Wexford.

There were a number of reasons why rebellion broke out in Wexford:

- People in Wexford were terrified by reports of massacres of rebels in neighbouring Wicklow.
- There was anger at the government's use of terror to crush the United Irishmen in the county.

Led by **Father John Murphy**, the rebels attacked and captured the town of Enniscorthy. At **Vinegar Hill**, overlooking the town, they established their headquarters.

Two days later, showing great bravery, the rebels captured the town of Wexford. A local landlord and United Irishman, **Bagenal Harvey**, became the leader of the rebels. Copying the French Revolution, a Committee of Public Safety was set up to run the area controlled by the rebels.

The rebellion in Ulster

While fighting raged in Wexford the remaining United Irishmen in Ulster staged a rebellion. **Henry Joy McCracken** led a force of 6,000 men that attacked the town of Antrim. They were defeated and McCracken was later executed.

In Co. Down, rebels led by **Henry Munro** had some early victories, but the British regained control at the **Battle of Ballynahinch**. Munro later suffered the same fate as McCracken. This defeat marked the end of the rebellion in Ulster.

Did you know?

The rebels were poorly armed. They mainly used a spear-like weapon called a pike.

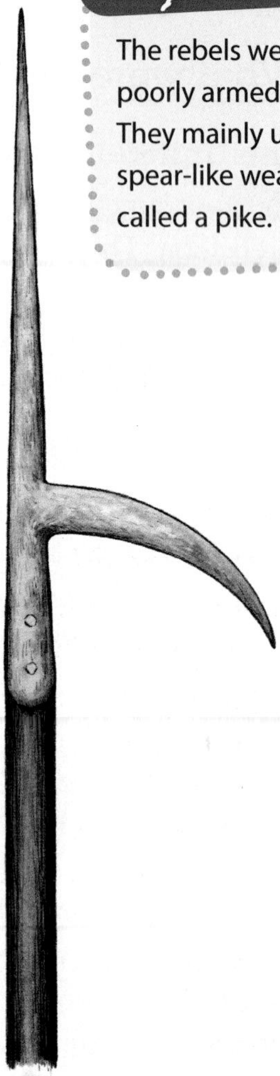

A pike

Terror

Soon the tide turned against the rebels in Wexford. Though brave, they lacked weapons, especially cannons. On 5 June, a rebel army was defeated at New Ross. After the battle the British executed rebel prisoners and in revenge the rebels did a terrible thing. They set fire to a barn at **Scullabogue** containing loyalist prisoners including women and children. A further massacre of loyalist prisoners occurred on Wexford Bridge a few days later. Most of those killed were Protestants. These killings shocked many people and Harvey resigned as leader of the rebels. **Father Philip Roche** replaced him.

The massacre of Protestants at Scullabogue. This picture comes from a nineteenth-century history of the Rebellion

The battle of Vinegar Hill, painted in about 1880. Is this a reliable source?

Did you know?

Although some of the rebel leaders were Catholic priests, the Catholic bishops condemned the rebellion and strongly supported the government.

Vinegar Hill

A rebel army was defeated at Arklow and British troops pushed into Co. Wexford. On 21 June, they attacked and captured the rebel headquarters at Vinegar Hill.

Groups of rebels continued fighting but the British were now in control. The leaders, including Bagenal Harvey, Father Roche and Father Murphy, were captured and hanged. British forces executed many rebels and transported some of them to Australia.

General Cornwallis was sent to Ireland to restore order. He offered a pardon to any rebel who surrendered. This helped to end the fighting. It seemed as if the rebellion was over but there was one major surprise in store for the British.

The year of the French

A small French army of 1,000 men under the command of **General Humbert** landed at Killala in Co. Mayo in August. At Castlebar they defeated a British force led by General Lake. Many Irishmen now joined the French army. Humbert marched to Longford.

However, at Ballinamuck, he met a much greater British force under General Cornwallis. He had no choice but to surrender. The French troops were treated well, but their Irish allies were executed. Among those captured was Wolfe Tone's brother, Matthew. He was taken to Dublin and hanged.

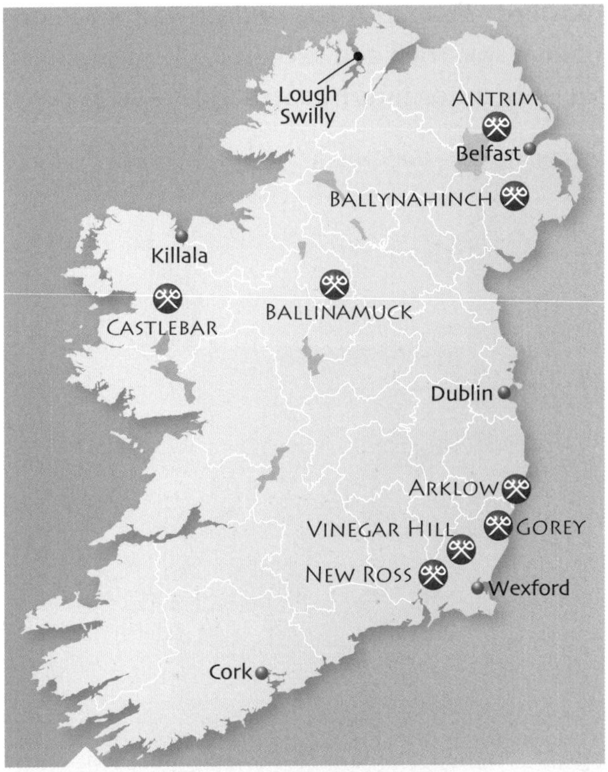

This map shows the main battles during 1798

The death of Wolfe Tone

In October, a French fleet containing 3,000 soldiers and including Wolfe Tone set sail for Ireland. It was attacked and captured by a British fleet off the Donegal coast. When the prisoners landed, Tone was recognised and taken to Dublin where he was tried. He was sentenced to death by hanging. He asked to be shot like a soldier. This request was refused and he attempted to commit suicide by cutting his throat. He died of his wounds a week later, on 19 November 1798.

Wolfe Tone served as inspiration to later generations of Irish people who wanted freedom for Ireland. He was later called the father of Irish republicanism. **Republicanism** involved the use of violence to end British rule in Ireland.

TIMELINE	Theobald Wolfe Tone
1763	Born in Dublin
1791	Admirer of the French Revolution. Helped to form the Society of United Irishmen
1795	Forced to leave Ireland for America
1796	Went to France – persuaded the French to send a military expedition to Ireland. Sailed to Ireland but failed to land
1798	Absent from Ireland for most of the rebellion. Captured after a naval battle off the Donegal coast. Committed suicide before his execution

The rebellion of Robert Emmet

A few years later, **Robert Emmet** (1778–1803), a United Irishman, organised another revolt in Dublin. He was the brother of one of the leaders of the 1798 rebellion, Thomas Addis Emmet. The rebellion in July 1803 was defeated easily. Emmet was tried and executed. He showed great bravery at his trial and this made him a hero for future generations of Irish people.

The execution of Robert Emmet, from a painting of 1883

What were the consequences of the 1798 Rebellion?

The 1798 rebellion was to have a number of important consequences for Ireland:

- It brought great death and destruction to Ireland. The British crushed it ruthlessly. It is estimated that over 30,000 people died. The vast majority were rebels and civilians who died at the hands of British troops.
- The aim of uniting Catholics and Protestants didn't succeed. In Wexford there were massacres of Protestant civilians. Many Protestants, especially Presbyterians who had been sympathetic to the United Irishmen, were shocked by these events. They became fearful of what would happen if Ireland got independence. They became strong supporters of British rule in Ireland.
- The British government wanted to make sure that a rebellion didn't happen again. They didn't want the French to use Ireland as a base to attack England. The prime minister, **William Pitt**, decided to end the separate Irish parliament in Dublin. In 1801, the **Act of Union** was passed and this closed the Irish parliament. Irish MPs now went to London.
- Many Irish people opposed the use of violence to achieve political change. They decided that the best way to improve the life of the Irish people was through persuasion. The two most popular political leaders of the nineteenth century, **Daniel O'Connell** and **Charles Stewart Parnell**, used peaceful means to try to win reform for Ireland.

TIMELINE The Main Events of the 1798 Rebellion

1791	Formation of the Society of United Irishmen
1794	United Irishmen banned
1796	French failed to land at Bantry Bay
1797	Government unleashed a reign of terror in Ulster
1798	Leadership of United Irishmen captured Rebellion began in Leinster – main centre Wexford Rebels captured Enniscorthy and Wexford Town Major defeat of rebels at New Ross Rebellion in Ulster crushed after the battles of Antrim and Ballynahinch Battle of Vinegar Hill French landed at Killala but defeated at Ballinamuck
1803	Rebellion of Robert Emmet

Do you understand these key terms?

Defenders	**Orange Order**	**Yeomanry**	**pike**
Republicanism	**Act of Union**	**loyalist**	

QUESTIONS

1. How did the British government react to the failed landing at Bantry Bay?
2. Why did the leadership of the United Irishmen decide to rebel?
3. Name two important United Irishmen who were also British spies.
4. Write a brief account of the capture of Lord Edward Fitzgerald.
5. In which counties did the rebellion begin?
6. Give two reasons why a rebellion broke out in Wexford.
7. Give the name of two battles in Ulster during 1798.
8. How was the rebellion in Wexford defeated?
9. Where did the French land in 1798? Who led them?
10. How was Wolfe Tone captured? Why is he called the father of Irish republicanism?
11. What happened in 1803?
12. Write a paragraph on two of the following:
    - The Society of United Irishmen
    - The aims of Wolfe Tone
    - Wolfe Tone and the French
    - The rebellion in Wexford
    - The consequences of the 1798 Rebellion.

EXAM QUESTIONS

- What were the reasons for the failure of the 1798 Rebellion in Ireland?

People in History

Write about a named leader involved in a revolution (America or France or Ireland) during the period 1771–1815

Use the plan below to help you with your answer.

Hint

Ireland: Wolfe Tone

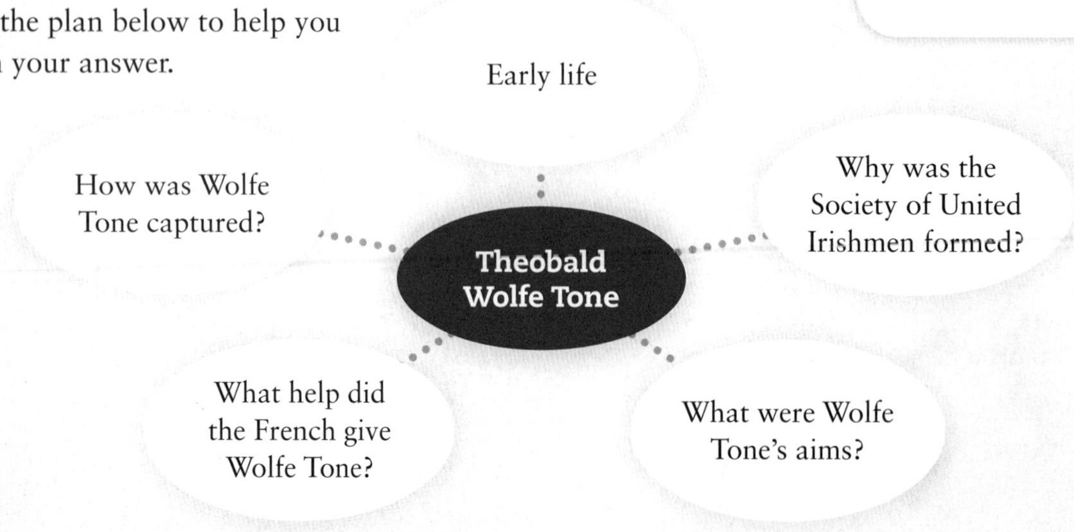

TIMELINE

PART 2

Section 10

The Industrial Revolution

Chapter 1

Industrial Revolution

Key Learning Objectives

- **Why did the Industrial Revolution begin in Britain?**

People's daily lives had changed very little since the Middle Ages. Between 1750 and 1850 huge changes took place in the way people lived and worked. Up to 1750 most goods were produced in people's homes. The invention of steam-powered machines greatly increased the amount of goods that could be produced. Most goods were now made in factories, especially in Britain. It changed the way people lived and worked. This change is called the **Industrial Revolution**. There were also major changes in agriculture and transport.

Why did the Industrial Revolution begin in Britain?

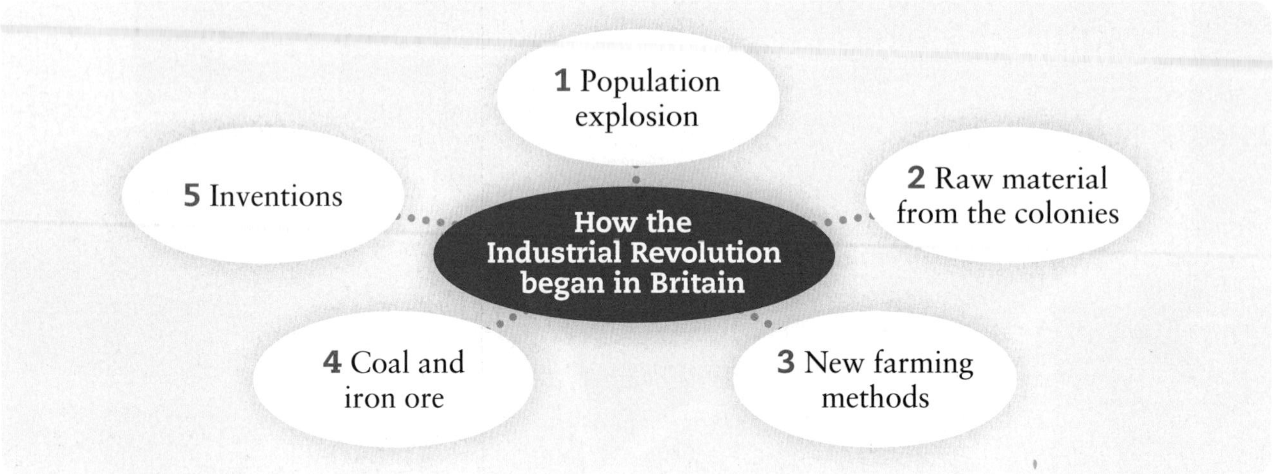

1 The population explosion

The population explosion in the eighteenth century was one of the most important causes of the Industrial Revolution. The population of Britain increased from about 5 million in 1700 to 20 million in 1850.

The causes of the population explosion:

- **Fewer famines:** As people had a wider choice of food to eat, famines were rare. This was due to new foods such as potatoes and rice being brought from other parts of the world. People were healthier and lived longer. This resulted in a decrease in the death rate and a rise in the birth rate.

- **Plagues ended:** By 1700, plagues such as the **Black Death** had disappeared. These plagues had wiped out much of Europe since 1300.
- **Medical discoveries: Edward Jenner** discovered the cure for smallpox, a disease that killed thousands of people. He saw that milkmaids caught cowpox (a mild disease) but never caught smallpox. Jenner injected cowpox into a small boy. Even though he came into contact with people with smallpox, he never caught the disease. This discovery was called **vaccination**. As a result the disease of smallpox disappeared.

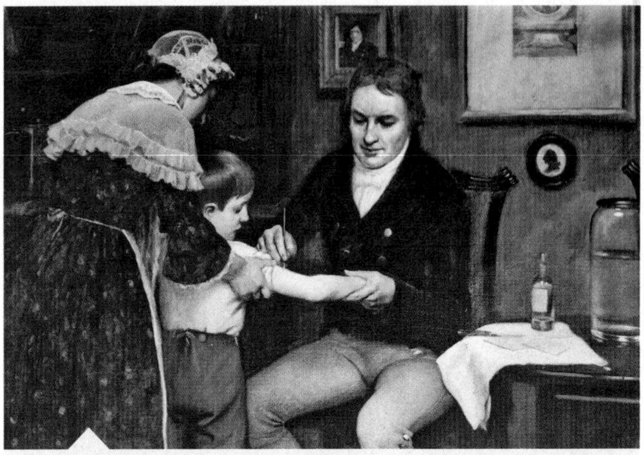

Edward Jenner vaccinating a child with cowpox

The increase in population created a **large labour force** for the factories in the industrial cities. It also meant that there was a **larger market** for the goods made in the factories.

2 Raw materials from the colonies

British colonies (countries that had been taken over by Britain) provided Britain with cheap raw materials such as cotton. They also provided a market for British products.

3 New farming methods

The new methods of farming produced a lot more food. This led to the population increasing. As a result, there were more people to work in the factories and more people to buy the manufactured products.

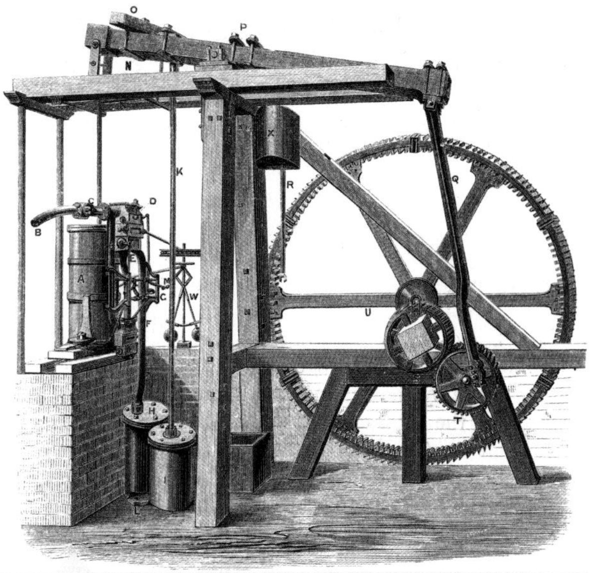

James Watt's steam engine was the most important of all the inventions of the Industrial Revolution

4 Coal and iron ore

Britain had a good supply of coal and iron. Coal was used to heat water to produce steam. Steam was used to power machines. Iron was used to make machinery.

5 Inventions

Inventors such as **James Hargreaves** produced machines for the textile industry. In 1763, **James Watt** invented the steam engine which was used to drive the machines in the factories. We will look at some of these inventions in Chapter 3.

Do you understand these key terms?

vaccination
steam engine

QUESTIONS

1. What does the term 'Industrial Revolution' mean?
2. What were the causes of the population explosion?
3. Write a paragraph on four other reasons why the Industrial Revolution began in Britain.

Chapter 2

The Agricultural Revolution

Key Learning Objectives

- **What was the Agricultural Revolution?**
- **What were the new farming methods?**
- **What were the effects of the Agricultural Revolution?**

What was the Agricultural Revolution?

Farming had not changed much since the Middle Ages. Farmers still used the **three-field or open-field system** (see Section 4, pages 70–71). Crops were grown in three large fields that surrounded a village. Each field was divided into strips. Every peasant in the village had some strips in each field. The peasants rented these strips from the landlord who owned the manor. Cattle and other animals grazed on the commons.

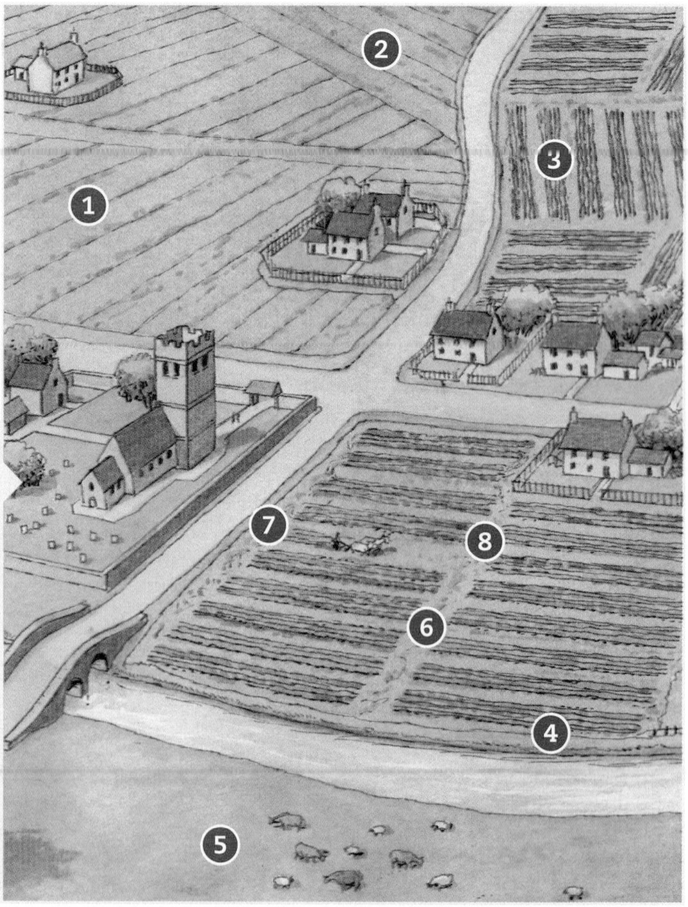

Disadvantages of the three-field system

1. Each year one field had to be left fallow (unused) so that the soil could recover
2. Farmers wasted time travelling from one field to another
3. Weeds could spread easily between strips
4. As the land was unfenced it meant that animals could wander into a field and destroy crops
5. Animal diseases spread easily
6. Land wasted between strips
7. Land wasted at end of strips where oxen turned
8. Farmers were not free to try new ideas because everyone had to grow the same crop in the same field

As the population was growing rapidly the old system of farming was unable to produce enough food. New methods were needed. The change in farming methods during the eighteenth century was called the **Agricultural Revolution**.

New farming methods

1 The four-field system

Charles Townshend introduced a new system of crop rotation, using four crops. This system had been developed in Holland during the seventeenth century. It was called the **four-field system** or **Norfolk system**, as Townshend farmed in Norfolk.

There was a cycle of crops in each field. Look at the table on **crop rotation**.

Advantages of the four-field system

- The turnips and grass restored nutrients to the soil.
- The food supply increased as no fields were left fallow.
- It now meant that cattle did not have to be killed each winter as turnips and hay were used to feed them.
- As a result, the numbers of animals increased dramatically. Fresh meat was available all year round. There was now enough meat to feed the increasing population.

2 Enclosure

Due to the popularity of the four-field system the problems of the open-field system became obvious. Landlords forced their tenants to accept a new system of farming called **enclosure**. Laws were passed in the British parliament to allow the rich landlords to enclose the land (**Enclosure Acts**). Each tenant's strips of arable (crop-growing) land and their portion of the commons were brought together into a single farm. Fences and hedges were used to enclose the farm.

Advantages of enclosure

- It reduced the spread of weeds and disease. This increased food supply and the number of cattle.
- Farmers could use new methods of farming.
- More food could be produced. This meant that tenants and landlords became better off.
- Landlords could charge higher rents.

Disadvantages of enclosure

- Small farmers were unable to meet the costs of enclosure because they could not afford to plant hedges and dig drains. Also, they could not afford the higher rents. They sold their farms and went to the towns and cities to work in the factories.
- Labourers never had land and they lost their grazing rights on the commons. The new machinery meant that many of them had no work. As a result, they moved to the industrial towns to work in the factories.

Crop rotation

Year 1	Wheat
Year 2	Turnips
Year 3	Oats or barley
Year 4	Clover or grass

Did you know?

Charles Townshend was called 'Turnip' Townshend because he used turnips when rotating crops.

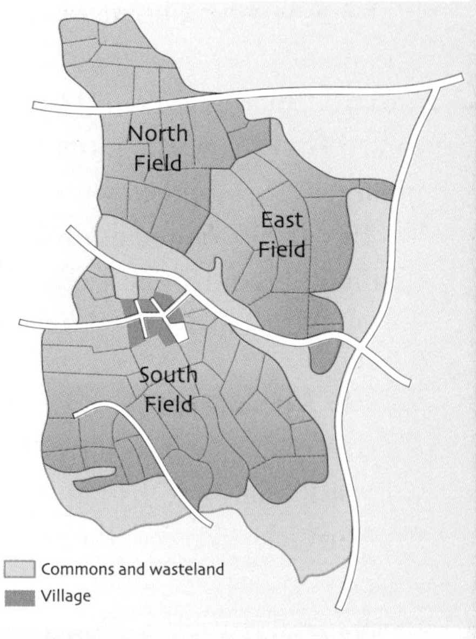

Before enclosure

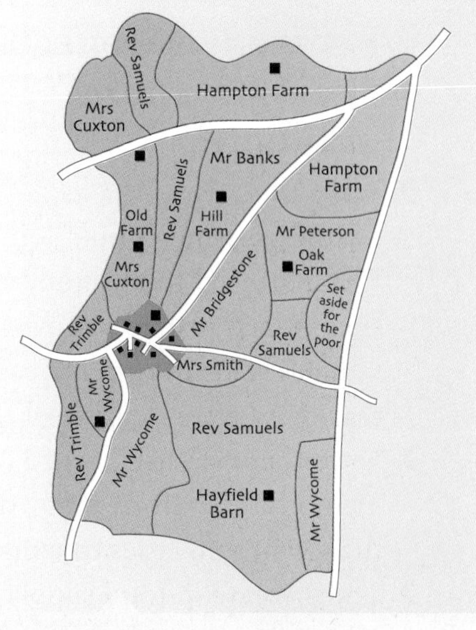

After enclosure

PART 2

3 Selective Breeding

Now that farms were enclosed, the numbers of cattle and sheep grew, as disease could not spread as easily. However, the size of the animals was still the same.

Robert Bakewell took the largest ewe and strongest ram and he bred them. This produced larger lambs. This was repeated year after year and the size of sheep increased. The size of horses and cattle also increased due to **selective breeding**. The weight of cattle and sheep more than doubled in the eighteenth century.

4 New agricultural machinery

Jethro Tull

The old way of planting seeds was by scattering them by hand. This was called **broadcasting**. Birds ate much of the seed. In 1701 **Jethro Tull** invented a **seed drill**. It was pulled by a horse or cattle. This drill made a furrow and dropped seed into it. A blade covered the seed with soil to protect it from the birds. This resulted in larger crop yields.

Tull also invented a **horse-drawn hoe** that could remove the weeds from between the crops.

Jethro Tull's seed drill made a furrow in a straight line and dropped seeds into it

Cyrus McCormick

Cereals such as wheat and barley were still harvested by hand. **Cyrus McCormick** invented a machine for cutting corn. It was called a **mechanical reaper**. It reduced the time needed for harvesting crops.

Cyrus McCormick invented a mechanical reaping machine used for cutting corn

What were the effects of the Agricultural Revolution?

- More food was produced for the growing population. The increased food supply encouraged people to have larger families. This in turn increased the rate of population growth. It meant that there were more workers available for the factories.
- Fewer people were needed on the land due to machinery and the new methods. Therefore, many of the poorer farmers and labourers went to the towns and cities to work in the factories.
- The increase in food supply meant that there was enough food to feed the growing population in the cities.

PART 2

Do you understand these key terms?

three-field system
fallow
four-field system
crop rotation
enclosure
selective breeding
seed drill
mechanical reaper

QUESTIONS

1 What were the problems of the open-field system?
2 What was the four-field system? What were the advantages of the system?
3 What was enclosure?
4 What were the advantages of enclosure? What were its disadvantages?
5 In farming, what was broadcasting?
6 What were the effects of the Agricultural Revolution?
7 Write a paragraph on Robert Bakewell and selective breeding.
8 Write a note on Jethro Tull's seed drill.

EXAM QUESTIONS

1 Give two factors that made the Agricultural Revolution possible. (HL)
2 Explain the way the Agricultural Revolution contributed to the Industrial Revolution. (HL)
3 In Britain during the Agricultural Revolution what is meant by the term 'enclosure'? (OL)

People in History

Write about a farm labourer during the Agricultural Revolution.

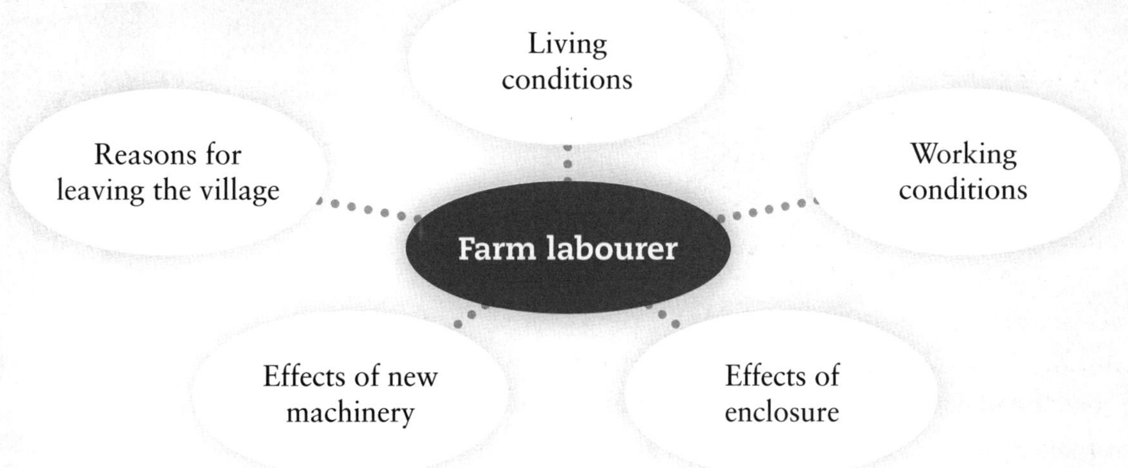

Chapter 3

The Industrialisation of Britain

Key Learning Objectives

- **What changes occurred in the textile industry?**
- **What changes occurred in the coal industry?**
- **How did the manufacture of iron change?**

The textile industry

Term

Loom
A machine used for weaving cloth.

What was the domestic system?

Before 1750, people made cloth by hand in their own homes in the countryside. Women used a **spinning-wheel** to turn wool into thread (yarn). Men wove the threads on a **loom** into cloth. These machines were small and powered by hand. This system is called the **domestic system** or **cottage industry**.

The disadvantage of this system was that it was slow and the amount of cloth produced was small. With the large increase in demand from 1750 due to the growing population, a new system was introduced. New machines were invented to produce more cloth more quickly.

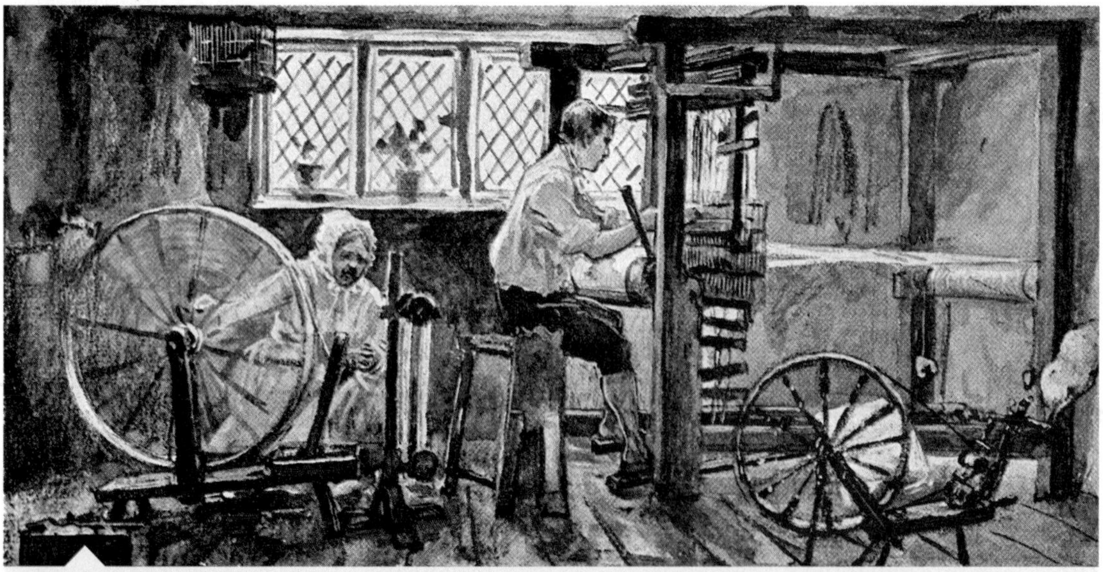

A woman working at home using a spinning-wheel in the 1750s. The man is weaving. This is an example of cottage industry. Whole families were often involved

What was the factory system?

A factory using a power loom in the mid-nineteenth century

The new machines that were invented were too big to be put into cottages. A new building called a **factory** was built to house these large machines. The machines were expensive, so only wealthy factory owners could afford to buy them. The new machines were powered by water and located beside a river. Later, they were driven by steam power.

Factories required large numbers of workers. As a result, cities grew up around the factories. The workers in the domestic system were forced to move to the cities to work in the textile mills. They produced huge amounts of cloth at a cheap price. This is called **mass production**.

New inventions in the textile industry

1733 The **weaving** of thread was boosted by the invention of the **flying shuttle** by **John Kay**. This machine was twice as fast as the previous loom. It needed three people working on spinning-wheels to keep the loom supplied.

John Kay invented the flying shuttle

1765 **James Hargreaves** invented the **spinning jenny**. It was eight times quicker than the spinning-wheel. It meant that yarn (thread) could be mass-produced.

1769 **Richard Arkwright** invented the **water frame** to further speed up the spinning process. It could spin hundreds of threads at once. It was powered by a water wheel which was turned by the river outside the factory. The water frame was a large machine and it speeded up the move to the factory system.

A spinning jenny

1779 **Samuel Crompton** invented the **spinning mule**. This invention improved spinning even further, and became very popular in the cotton mills.

1785 **Edward Cartwright** invented the **power loom**. This **weaving** machine allowed cloth to be made as quickly as yarn was being spun. It used **James Watt's steam engine** (see page 245) to speed up the process. Steam power now replaced water power in the textile industry.

Lancashire was the centre of the cotton industry. Cotton was imported cheaply from British colonies through the port of Liverpool. It was stronger than wool and it was easier to wash.

Arkwright's water frame

Crompton with his spinning mule. This painting from 1880 imagines the inventor as a romantic hero, alone in his workshop

QUESTIONS

1 What was the domestic system? What were the disadvantages of this system?
2 Why were factories built?
3 What was the advantage of the factory system?
4 What role did each of the following play in the textile industry?
(a) John Kay (b) James Hargreaves (c) Richard Arkwright
5 Write an account of how Cartwright improved weaving cloth.
6 Why did cotton become more popular than wool?

EXAM QUESTIONS

1 Name one improvement during the Industrial Revolution that you associate with each of the following: James Hargreaves, James Watt, Edward Cartwright and Richard Arkwright. (HL)
2 Name two important inventions during the Industrial Revolution in Britain. (HL)
3 Name one important invention or development of the Agricultural or Industrial Revolution and the person responsible for it. (OL)

The coal industry

There was a huge increase in the demand for coal from 1750.

- Coal was used to heat water to create steam. This steam was used to drive the machines in the factories.
- It was also used to power locomotives on the railways and steam ships.
- Finally, it was burnt to make **coke**. This was used in furnaces to **smelt** iron ore.

Term

Smelt
Separate the iron from the rock in which it is contained (see page 254).

Coke
Coal is burnt to remove harmful gases and this turns the coal into coke. Coke burns at a higher temperature in the furnace.

Coalmines

Some **seams** (layers) of coal lay near the surface and could be extracted easily. However, most seams lay deep underneath the surface. Tunnels (**mine shafts**) were dug straight down. Then tunnels were dug at right angles to the mine shaft to where the seams were. Wooden supports were put in the tunnels to prevent them from caving in. Miners used pickaxes and shovels to cut the coal at the coalface. Ropes and pulleys, powered by Watt's steam engine, brought the coal to the surface in iron cages.

A coalmine in the 1750s. Can you describe what is happening in the picture?

What were the dangers of coalmining?

Term

Collier
A coalminer.

Flooding

The presence of underground water stopped colliers from digging down too deeply. However, the invention of the steam engine meant that water could be pumped from the mine. **Watt's steam engine**, invented in 1763, had wheels that turned. It could be connected with belts to other machines and drive them along. It was powerful enough to pump water from the deepest shafts. As a result, there was a huge increase in coal production.

Many children worked in the coalmine, where working conditions were very harsh

Explosions

Carbon gas built up in a mine. When it came in contact with the naked flame of a candle, it exploded, killing many miners. However, the invention of the **Davy safety lamp** reduced this risk.

Between 1750 and 1850 coal production rose from 2 million tonnes to 50 million tonnes. This was due to the improvements in technology used in mines.

Factories were built near the coalfields, as coal was bulky and expensive to transport over long distances. Towns and cities developed around these coalfields.

PART 2

The iron industry

Iron was needed for making machinery such as steam engines and locomotives. Therefore, there was a huge increase in demand for iron.

Smelting iron

What was smelting?

Iron had to be separated from the rock in which it was contained (**iron ore**). **Charcoal** (burnt timber) was used in furnaces to extract the iron from the iron ore. Limestone was then used to get rid of impurities, which would have weakened the iron. However, a shortage of charcoal made it expensive to use.

Wrought iron

Abraham Darby used **coke** instead of charcoal to smelt the iron ore. The molten **pig iron** is beaten with a hammer to remove the impurities. This is called **wrought iron**. This was a cheaper method than using charcoal.

Puddling and rolling

In 1794, **Henry Cort** invented the **puddling and rolling method**. This made better-quality wrought iron and it was cheaper. Fifteen tonnes of wrought iron could be produced in one hour. This dramatically increased the production of wrought iron. Wrought iron was easy to shape, and was therefore ideal for making machines.

Term

Pig iron
Iron produced by smelting. At this stage it contains many impurities.

Puddlers at work. Puddling was the melting of the pig iron and stirring it to remove the impurities. Rolling was the next stage, when it was rolled out into bars of wrought iron

Steel

In the 1850s **Henry Bessemer** invented the **converter** method of making steel. A vessel was filled with liquid pig iron and some chemicals were added. A blast of hot air was passed through the mixture. This got rid of the impurities. The liquid steel was allowed to harden.

Advantages of steel

- Steel was cheaper to make.
- It was stronger than wrought iron.
- It was less likely to crack, as it was more flexible.

The use of steel improved the quality of machines and ships. The large amounts of iron and steel speeded up the development of the railways and large ships.

Steel workers turning iron into steel using the Bessemer converter method

Do you understand these key terms?

spinning-wheel	**spinning jenny**	**smelt**	**wrought iron**
loom	**water frame**	**collier**	**coke**
domestic system	**spinning mule**	**iron ore**	**puddling and rolling method**
cottage industry	**power loom**	**charcoal**	**converter**
flying shuttle	**coke**	**pig iron**	

QUESTIONS

1 Why was coal so important for the Industrial Revolution?
2 What tools did miners use to cut coal?
3 What caused explosions in the mines? How was this problem solved?
4 What was iron used for?
5 What is smelting?
6 Why was charcoal replaced by coal?
7 What were the advantages of steel?
8 Write an account of the machine that was used to prevent mines flooding.
9 Write a note on the role of each of the following in the iron industry:
(a) Abraham Darby (b) Henry Cort
10 Write a note on Bessemer's converter method.

Chapter 4

The Transport Revolution

Key Learning Objectives

- **What was the Transport Revolution?**
  - **Roads**
  - **Canals**
  - **Railways**
  - **Steam ships**
- **What were the effects of the Transport Revolution?**

What was the Transport Revolution?

There was a big increase in the movement of goods and people due to both the Industrial and the Agricultural Revolutions. The existing transport system was unable to cope with this increase. New ways of carrying people and goods were invented. Roads were also improved, making it easier to travel. This is called the **Transport Revolution**.

Did you know?

Tolls are still used today on roads, e.g. the West-Link in Dublin and the Fermoy bypass in Co. Cork.

Roads

Up to 1750 roads were dirt tracks, full of potholes, and in the winter they became muddy. People and goods travelled in carts and horse-drawn coaches. There were many breakdowns due to the rough surfaces of the roads. Travel was slow and expensive. Carts could only carry small loads.

During the Industrial Revolution there was a huge increase in the amount of raw materials and finished products that had to be transported. Major improvements had to be made to roads to cope with this increased traffic.

In the eighteenth century, roads were bumpy and travelling on them was uncomfortable

Turnpike trusts

Turnpike trusts were private companies which got permission from parliament to improve and maintain a section of road. In return, they charged people for using the road (**tolls**). They used some of the money to keep the road in good condition. In 1730 these trusts looked after 35,000 kilometres of road.

However, even these improved roads were not suited to carrying carts with heavier loads. A new type of road surface was needed.

> *Term*
>
> **Turnpikes**
> Barriers on roads where tolls are collected.
>
> **Toll**
> Money paid for travelling along a road.

Thomas Telford

Thomas Telford improved roads by:

- Digging deep foundations.
- Putting down a layer of heavy stones. Smaller stones covered this layer.
- Putting a layer of tightly packed gravel on top, which gave a smooth surface.
- Making roads high in the middle and sloping towards the sides, which allowed water to drain off.

People travelling on turnpikes had to pay a toll. What do you think is happening in this picture?

> *Did you know?*
>
> **Tarmacadam** is named after John MacAdam, but tar was not invented until after his death. MacAdam had solved the problem of how to get a smooth road surface and tar was a further improvement.

John MacAdam

John MacAdam stated that:

- There was no need for a deep foundation. A layer of small stones 30cm deep was enough.
- The carts and coaches would grind the stones on the surface to powder and the rain would wash this powder down, which would hold lower layers together.

Roads were highest in the middle to allow the rain to flow into the ditches at each side of the road. These roads were cheaper to build than Telford's.

> *Did you know?*
>
> Charles Bianconi set up a transport company using coaches called **Bianconi cars**. These transported people between towns in southern Ireland.

What were the effects of road improvements?

- The improvements in roads cut the journey time between London and Manchester from four days in 1794 to eighteen hours in 1830.
- More people wanted to travel. They did so in **stagecoaches**.
- Greater amounts of raw materials and finished products could be transported more quickly. This reduced transport costs.

The Tyburn Turnpike, London

Canals

Water transport was the cheapest way of moving bulky goods such as coal and iron. One canal barge could carry the same amount of goods as twelve horse-drawn wagons.

The **Duke of Bridgewater** could not transport coal from his coalmines to Manchester at a reasonable price. **James Brindley** built a canal from the Duke's coalfields to Manchester. It reduced the cost by half. It was called the **Bridgewater Canal**. As a result, the profits of the Duke's business rose greatly.

Canals became such a popular way of moving goods that 6,500 kilometres of canal were built by 1830. Their main advantage was that goods were transported cheaply. However, it was a very slow method of transport.

By the 1860s railways had replaced canals as the main form of transport.

The Bridgewater Canal. Notice that the canal goes *over* the bridge

Railways

Stephenson's Rocket

Watt's steam engine made possible the invention of the **steam locomotive.**

In 1804, the steam engine was adapted by **Richard Trevithick** to run on an iron track. This was called the **locomotive.**

George Stephenson built the first train carrying goods. It ran between Stockton and Darlington in 1825. In 1830, Stephenson invented a locomotive called the **Rocket.** It carried passengers between Manchester and Liverpool. Its average speed was 25 kilometres per hour.

Railway fever swept Britain. In 1842 there were 3,000 kilometres of track. By 1862 there were 18,600 kilometres.

What were the effects of the railways?

- They provided fast and cheap transport.
- Heavy goods were transported quickly over long distances.
- They gave a huge boost to the mining, iron and steel industries.
- They also boosted tourism, as people were able to go to resorts such as Bath and Brighton.
- Fresh food was transported to cities every day.
- They created many jobs.
- They led to a decline in the use of canals and road transport.

Steam ships

Up until the eighteenth century, sail had powered large ships. But steam ships started to replace sailing ships.

In the late eighteenth century a steam engine was invented for ships. In 1819, a steam ship crossed the Atlantic Ocean for the first time. It took a sailing ship about six weeks to cross the Atlantic. By 1870 a steam ship did the same journey in ten days.

The Savannah was the first steamship to cross the Atlantic Ocean in 1819

What were the effects of the Transport Revolution?

The Transport Revolution had a major effect on the Industrial Revolution.

- It meant that raw materials and manufactured goods could be transported more quickly and cheaply.
- The less time it took to carry goods from the factory to the market, the lower the cost.
- This made goods cheaper and as a result more people could afford to buy them.
- Iron and steel and coal production increased greatly due to the Transport Revolution.

Do you understand these key terms?

turnpikes **tolls** **locomotive**

QUESTIONS

1 What problems did people face travelling by road in 1750?
2 Write a note on how each of the following improved roads: (a) Telford and (b) MacAdam.
3 What were the effects of improved roads?
4 What was the problem facing the Duke of Bridgewater?
5 Who solved the Duke of Bridgewater's problem? What was the solution?
6 Mention one advantage and one disadvantage of canals.
7 Who adapted Watt's steam engine for railways?
8 Who built the first goods train?
9 Where did the locomotive called the Rocket travel between?
10 Mention four effects of the railways.
11 Write a paragraph on the effects of the Transport Revolution on the Industrial Revolution.

EXAM QUESTIONS

1 Write an account of the improvements in transport in the Industrial Revolution. (HL)
2 Give two effects of the Transport Revolution. (HL)
3 Name one new method of transporting goods during the Industrial Revolution in Britain. (OL)
4 Explain why the 1830s and 1840s were known as the Railway Age in Britain. (OL)

Chapter 5

Living and Working during the Industrial Revolution

Key Learning Objectives

- **What was life like for workers in industrial Britain in 1850?**
- **What were working conditions like in textile mills?**
- **What were working conditions like in coalmines?**
- **What reforms were brought in to improve working and living conditions?**

Special Study: Life in industrial Britain c.1850

Growth of cities

In 1750, 25 per cent of the population of Britain lived in towns and cities. By 1850 this had risen to 50 per cent. This movement of people from the countryside to the cities is called **urbanisation**. There were two main reasons for it:

- Small farmers and labourers were forced off the land due to the enclosure system (see Chapter 2, page 247).
- The domestic system could not compete with the factory system. As a result, spinners and weavers who had lost their jobs had to move to the cities to work in the factories.

There was a huge increase in the size of cities. For example, in 1750, 45,000 people lived in Manchester. By 1850 the number was 303,000 people.

Sheffield in 1745, before the Industrial Revolution

Sheffield in 1850, during the Industrial Revolution. Mention three differences between these two images

Living conditions

The rapid increase in the size of cities caused overcrowding. Some factory owners built houses for their workers near the factories. Many other families lived in a single room in larger houses. Some of these houses had twelve rooms, with a total of 100 people living in them. People had very little furniture. Some slept on straw put on the ground. There was no running water. There was a toilet and a water tap in the front yard and they were shared by everyone. Some people lived in cellars in which the walls were black with damp.

There were open drains in the middle of the narrow streets. Rubbish was thrown into the drains, which were infested with rats. Water was carried from the polluted river nearby.

The air was polluted by the smoke from the factories and by the coal being burnt in people's homes.

The diet of working class people was made up of bread, cheese, porridge and potatoes.

This is taken from a report by Friederich Engels. He describes living conditions in Manchester in 1844:

> *In one of the courts there stands at the end of the covered passage, a privy (toilet) without a door, so dirty that the inhabitants can pass into and out of the court only by passing through foul pools of stagnant urine and excrement.*
>
> *The Condition of the Working Class in England in 1844* by F. Engels

Poor people lived in terrible conditions during the Industrial Revolution. This is an engraving by Gustave Dové from 1875

Diseases

Typhoid was the most common disease. This was caused by people using dirty water for drinking and cooking. Many people also died of **tuberculosis** (TB) due to living in damp conditions. In 1832, there was a **cholera** outbreak in Britain and 56,000 died. Many people died young because of the living and working conditions.

Leisure for workers

Workers had only Sunday off. Many drank heavily to forget the harshness of their lives. They drank beer, gin or cider. Fights often broke out because of the drinking. Other leisure activities included gambling, dogfighting, cock-fighting and bare-knuckle fighting.

From 1850, workers got a half day off on Saturday. Soccer became popular in the industrial towns. The newly-formed Football Association introduced rules. This increased its popularity.

Cock-fighting and gambling were popular pastimes at this time

Education

In the first half of the nineteenth century very few working-class children went to school. They had to work in the factories or mines. Their families needed their wages to survive. The **Factory Act** of 1833 stated that children under thirteen years of age must attend school for two hours a week. Other Factory Acts reduced the number of hours that children had to work. As a result, children had more time to go to school.

The factory owners and their families

Most of the factory owners lived in the countryside where there was no pollution. They lived in large houses with expensive furniture and silverware. They had many servants including butlers, cooks and maids.

Their children were well educated. Often boys went to Oxford or Cambridge University. They later joined the family business. Girls were educated privately by tutors or governesses. Their mothers taught them good manners, painting and needlework.

The owner was paid rent for the houses that his workers lived in. He visited his factory in a horse-drawn carriage.

The wealthy families ate fish, beef, soup and chicken. They drank wine with the meal. Men drank port after dinner while women drank tea or coffee.

QUESTIONS

1 Give two reasons why so many people moved to the cities in the period 1750–1850.
2 How does Engels describe the living conditions in the city of Manchester?
3 Write a note on diseases that people caught in the cities.
4 Write an account of the leisure activities of workers in the industrial towns.
5 Write an account of living conditions in the industrial cities.
6 Write a paragraph on the life of a factory owner.

What were working conditions like in textile mills?

- The **mills** (textile factories) were five storeys high. The noise of the machines was deafening.
- Dust was everywhere and caused lung diseases.
- The air was hot and damp. Windows were kept closed to keep the air moist so that cotton threads would not break.
- People worked from 5.30am to 8pm, six days a week.
- Wages were low as there were so many people looking for work.
- There were more women and children employed than men, as their wages were lower.
- Children had to work, as the family needed their wages to make ends meet.

Did you know?

Factory workers were paid very little in the nineteenth century. Men earned about £1 per week. Women were paid only half this wage!

Children wind yarn in a textile factory in London in 1848.
What is happening in the picture?

A 'piecer' fixing a spinning machine in a cotton mill. Why do you think children were employed to do work like this? What else is happening in the picture?

- Workers were allowed forty minutes for dinner and could go to the toilet three times a day. They were fined for many offences, such as opening a window or being late.
- When people were tired they fell against the machines, which had no protection. Many were killed or lost a limb.
- Some of the children had to lean over the spinning-machines to repair broken threads. They were called **piecers.** This often resulted in serious injury.
- A supervisor beat the children if they were not working fast enough.
- People's backs became deformed or bent because they were standing all day or bending over machines.
- Machines threw off water which wet the workers' clothes. In winter, as they made their way home, their clothes became stiff due to the frost.

William Dodd was a piecer. This is his story:

The position in which the piecer stands to his work is with the right foot forward, and his right side facing the frame. In this position he continues all day. The chief weight of his body rests upon his right knee, which is almost always the first joint to give way. My evenings were spent in rubbing my knees, ankles, wrists and elbows with oil. I went to bed, to cry myself to sleep, and pray that the Lord would take me to himself before morning.

***A Narrative of William Dodd, a Factory Cripple*, 1841**

What were working conditions like in coalmines?

People worked in the mines for fourteen hours a day, in dark and damp conditions.

Boys and girls as young as five years of age worked in the mines. They were called **trappers**, because they opened and closed doors in the tunnels. This allowed air to circulate in the mine. It prevented the build-up of explosive gases.

At eight years of age, children became **hurriers**. They dragged wagons of coal from the coalface to the mine shaft. At seventeen years of age, they began digging out coal at the coalface. Women also dragged wagons loaded with half a tonne of coal along the tunnels.

What were the effects of working in the mines?

- Colliers got **miners' lung** which caused breathing difficulties. This was as a result of breathing in coal dust over a long period of time. Many died of this disease.
- Their backs became crooked because of bending over and pulling wagons.
- They had poor eyesight from working in the dark.
- Many miners were killed by floods, explosions and tunnels caving in (see page 253).

Children who worked in the coalmines, pushing and dragging wagons of coal, were called hurriers

Reforms in working and living conditions

Robert Owen

Robert Owen owned cotton mills in New Lanark in Scotland. He thought that if workers were treated well and paid a fair wage, they would work harder. This would increase the profits of the factory owner. He built good houses for his workers and set up schools for their children. To everyone's amazement he made a large profit. Some owners followed his example. However, the majority of owners were only interested in bigger profits and treated their workers badly.

Robert Owen helped to improve children's lives by building schools

Edwin Chadwick

In 1832, **cholera** killed 56,000 people. The government was worried as it killed both rich and poor people. Edwin Chadwick wrote a report about the causes of the cholera epidemic. He said that dirty water and bad drains caused many diseases, including cholera. People were shocked by his report, which described the unhealthy conditions that workers lived in. They put pressure on the government to change the conditions. Chadwick recommended that every city should have a sewage system

A cartoon from the magazine *Punch*. What point is the cartoonist making about the way the River Thames affected people in London?
© The British Library Board. Father Thames p.p.5270.ah

and a clean water supply. This would mean raising taxes. Some of the upper class objected. However, when another cholera epidemic broke out in 1848 a **Public Health Act** was passed. It stated that sewers and water pipes would be built. Local Boards of Health were set up to clean the streets. Gradually, cities became cleaner and the health of people improved greatly.

Lord Shaftesbury was responsible for passing the Factory Acts which helped to improve working conditions

The Chartists

The **Chartist movement** was founded by William Lovett in 1838. Its aim was to increase the number of working-class men who had the right to vote. The Chartists tried to persuade parliament to grant them the vote by organising huge **rallies** and signing **petitions.** Parliament ignored their petitions and the movement was a failure.

Term

Petition
A written request signed by many people and sent to those in power.

Rally
A large public meeting.

Lord Shaftesbury

Lord Shaftesbury was the man who did most to improve working conditions in mines and factories. The government was afraid that there would be a revolution in Britain just like the French Revolution (see Section 9, Chapter 2). Shaftesbury got a series of laws passed from 1830 onwards that dramatically improved working conditions.

TIMELINE	The Factory Acts
1833	Children under 13 could not work over 55 hours a week and had to attend school for two hours. Children under 9 could not work in a factory. This was a major improvement. Inspectors were appointed to make sure that the law was obeyed
1842	Women and children under 13 were not allowed work in mines
1844	Women could only work 12 hours a day and children were limited to 6.5 hours
1847	Women and children under 18 could only work 10 hours a day

Trade unions

Trade unions were made legal in 1825. They had very little success. In the 1870s they got the right to strike. As a result, the power of unions increased.

Do you understand these key terms?

urbanisation	**cholera**	**trapper**	**Chartists**
typhoid	**mills**	**hurrier**	**rally**
tuberculosis	**piecer**	**miners' lung**	**petition**

QUESTIONS

1. What was a piecer?
2. What were (a) a trapper and (b) a hurrier?
3. Describe how Robert Owen improved the lives of his workers.
4. Why was the government worried about the cholera outbreak?
5. What did Chadwick say were the causes of the cholera outbreak?
6. According to Chadwick, what were the solutions to these problems?
7. What were the terms of the Public Health Act 1848?
8. When were trade unions made legal? When did they get the right to strike?
9. Write a paragraph on working conditions in textile factories.
10. Write an account of the effects of working in the mines on people's health.
11. Write an account of how the Factory Acts improved the working conditions of factory workers and miners. Who inspired the passing of these laws?

EXAM QUESTIONS

1. Mention two serious problems faced by those living in industrial towns in England in the early nineteenth century. (HL)
2. Give two reasons why life in British cities was unpleasant around 1850. (OL)

People in History

Write about a worker in a mine or factory during the Industrial Revolution.

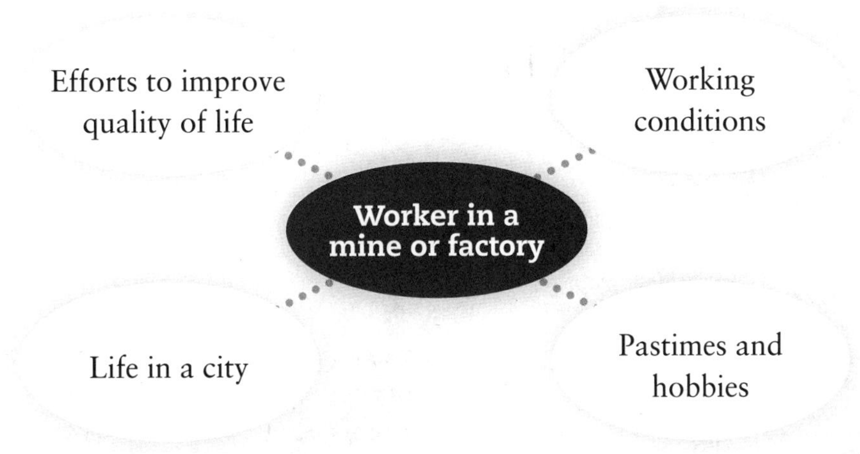

Chapter 6

Irish Society in the Nineteenth Century

Key Learning Objectives

- What was life like in Ireland in the 1840s?
- What were the causes of the Famine?
- How did the government respond to the Famine?
- What were the effects of the Famine?

Special Study: Life in Ireland in the 1840s

In 1840, Ireland was part of the United Kingdom. This meant that Ireland was ruled directly from the British parliament in London. Most of the country depended on agriculture.

There were three major groups who lived in the countryside; these were **landlords, tenant farmers** and **cottiers** (labourers).

Did you know?

In 1801, Ireland became part of the United Kingdom, after the Act of Union was passed.

1 Landlords

The landlord class was descended from the English and Scottish settlers who had received land in the plantations of the sixteenth and seventeenth centuries (see Section 8, Chapter 2). Five thousand landlords owned 90 per cent of the land in Ireland. They lived in the 'big house' with many servants. They rented out their estates to tenant farmers. These rents were the landlord's source of income.

Many landlords were **absentee landlords**, i.e. they lived mainly in England. Some landlords had no interest in their estates. A land agent collected the rent twice a year from the tenants. If a tenant failed to pay the rent, he was **evicted**.

Term

Absentee landlord
A person who owns and rents out land but lives somewhere else.

Eviction
Forcing people to leave their homes and land.

Landlords were rich and lived in big houses with servants

2 Tenant farmers

There were two different kinds of tenant farmer: large farmers and small farmers.

- **Large farmers** rented more than thirty acres. They grew wheat and barley, which they sold to pay the rent. They hired labourers to help them, especially at busy times of the year such as harvest time. They reared a few cattle and sheep. Their diet consisted of potatoes, vegetables, meat and milk.
- **Small farmers** rented between five and thirty acres. They divided their farm among their sons. As a result, the sons had very small farms, which meant that their income was low. They grew wheat and barley to pay the rent. Their food consisted of potatoes and milk.

Term

Cottier
A farm labourer.

Conacre
Land rented out to grow potatoes.

3 Cottiers (labourers)

Cottiers or **labourers** rented one acre from a farmer. They paid the rent partly by working for the farmer and partly with money. They sometimes had to rent extra land called **conacre**. On their plot of land they had their cottage and grew potatoes.

They lived in one-roomed cabins with thatched roofs. The walls were made of mud. The cabins were damp and they slept on some straw that was put on the floor. There were a million cottiers or labourers in 1845. Including their families, there were 4 million people totally dependent on the potato as a source of food.

If the potato crop failed for two years in a row the cottier class would be wiped out.

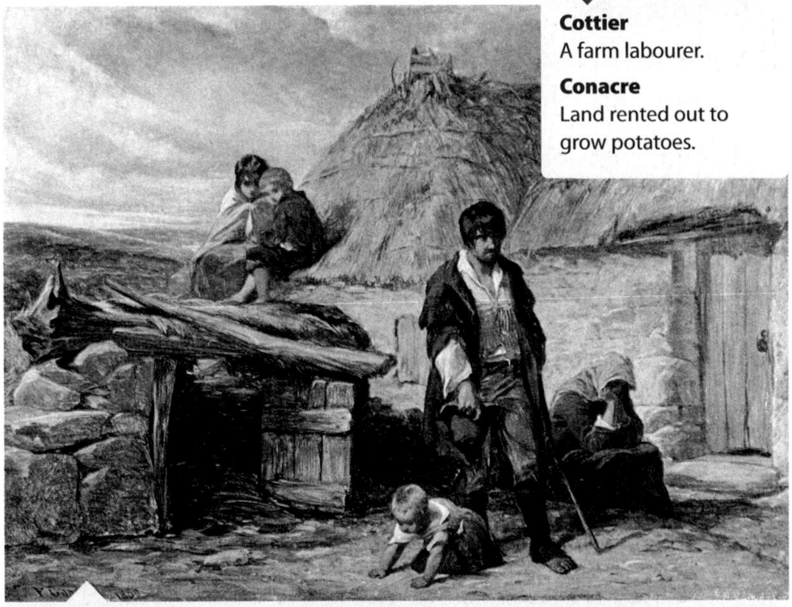

The cottiers and labourers were poor and lived in tiny cottages

Did you know?

Potatoes were grown on ridges called **lazybeds**.

PART 2

QUESTIONS

1 What was an absentee landlord?
2 What did an agent do?
3 Why would a tenant be evicted?
4 What was a large farmer?
5 Why did farmers grow barley and wheat? What was their diet?
6 How much land did a small farmer have?
7 What would happen to the cottier class if the potato crop failed two years in a row?
8 Write a paragraph on the life of a cottier.

The Famine

What were the causes of the Famine?

This image of an attack on a potato store in Galway in 1842 from a London newspaper shows how desperate people were for their main source of food

1 Rise in population

The population rose rapidly from 5 million in 1801 to 8 million in 1841. The average size of farms decreased because of the rise in population. As a result, people became poorer.

2 Subdivision

Subdivision was when a farmer divided his land among his sons. This happened because there were no other job opportunities. Most people depended on farming, as there was no industry in Ireland (except in north-east Ulster). As a result, there was less land for each son. Therefore, people became poorer. By 1845 one-third of the population depended on the potato.

Subdivision encouraged people to marry at an early age. Therefore, they had large families and more people had to be supported on the same amount of land.

3 Dependence on the potato

Cottiers depended totally on the potato as a food source. One acre could feed a family. But if the crop failed for a couple of years it would cause a famine. By 1845 the potato was the only source of food for 4 million people.

4 Potato blight

Potato blight came from Canada. It was a fungus that spread in the warm, moist weather. It could devastate a potato crop. This meant that the cottier class faced starvation.

1845: Famine in Ireland

In 1845 the potato blight arrived. It thrived in the humid conditions in Ireland that autumn. One-third of the autumn crop was lost. The first thing that people noticed was the smell from the potatoes in the fields. Then the stalks turned black. The potatoes were rotten when they were dug up. Not many died of starvation in 1845. However, blight struck again in 1846 and 75 per cent of the crop was lost.

On 11 August 1846, a priest from Co. Galway wrote to a Dublin newspaper:

> As to the potatoes, they are gone, clean gone. If travelling in the dark you would know when a potato field was near by the smell. The fields present one space of withered stalks.

In 1847 (Black '47) there was only a very small crop of potatoes as people had eaten the seed potatoes. Thousands of the poorest people died of starvation. These were the labourers or cottiers who were almost wiped out as a class.

QUESTIONS

1 What was the population of Ireland in 1841?
2 What effect did this have on farm size and people's living standards?
3 Why did a farmer subdivide his land? List two effects of subdivision.
4 How much land was needed to support one family?
5 What class depended totally on the potato as a source of food?
6 In 1845, how many people depended on the potato for food?
7 What was blight? Where did it come from?
8 What was the effect of the blight between the years 1845 and 1847?

A starving family might be forced to leave home to find food

How did the government respond to the Famine?

1 Maize

At first, the London government were slow to help the Irish people. They believed that they should not interfere. However, in 1845 the government under Sir Robert Peel bought £100,000 worth of **maize** from Canada. Local relief committees were set up to distribute the maize. It was sold at cost price to the poor, mainly the small farmers and labourers. It fed one million people. This helped reduce the impact of the Famine in 1845. It was very hard to eat, as it was not cooked properly. It was nicknamed **Peel's Brimstone**.

2 Public Works scheme

The government set up the **Public Works scheme** to allow the poor to earn money to buy food. They gave grants to build roads, piers and drains.

After the crop failures in 1846 and 1847, 3 million people who depended totally on the potato faced starvation. 750,000 people were on the Public Works scheme. Many were too weak to work on these schemes.

Did you know?

The reason that the government did not give out free food was that they were afraid that people would become lazy.

3 Workhouses

Because there was no food, many people were now forced to go to the **workhouses**. These had been introduced under the **Poor Law Act** in 1838.

- Ireland was divided into 130 Poor Law Unions.
- The local landlords and farmers had to pay the **poor rate**. This was a tax that was used to build a workhouse, and pay the costs of running it, in each Poor Law Union.

Term

Workhouse
Large building where poor people were given basic accommodation and made to work.

Only the desperate went to the workhouse. Families were split up when they entered them. They were not allowed to meet. They hated the workhouse as they were humiliated and treated almost like criminals.

But people had nowhere else to go, so the workhouses were soon overcrowded. By 1847 there were 200,000 people in the workhouses, which normally held 100,000. Many people died of diseases such as typhoid, cholera and famine fever. These diseases spread very quickly in the overcrowded conditions.

There were terrible scenes outside the workhouse where people were desperate for food

4 Soup kitchens

Irish politicians asked the government to set up soup kitchens outside the workhouses to help those who could not be catered for inside. They refused, but were forced to change this decision in 1847. However, thousands had died by this time. The local ratepayers had to pay for the cost of the soup kitchens. Three million people benefited from this scheme.

The Quakers set up soup kitchens like this one to help the starving people

Private charities

The **Quakers** and some landlords also set up soup kitchens to give free food to the starving people. They saved many lives. Newspaper reports abroad resulted in a great deal of help being given to Ireland to feed the starving. Nineteen countries sent money. The British Relief Association collected £400,000.

Term

Quakers
A Protestant group known for its opposition to war and its practical good works.

QUESTIONS

1 Why was the government slow to intervene?
2 What measures did Sir Robert Peel take in 1845 to help the Irish people? How successful were these measures in 1845?
3 What was the Public Works scheme?
4 What were workhouses, and what role did they play during the Famine?
5 Why did the government refuse to set up soup kitchens?
6 Why was the government forced to set up soup kitchens in 1847? How effective were they?
7 Write a short account of the role of private charities in famine relief.

What were the results of the Famine?

1 Fall in population

The population fell by 2 million between 1845 and 1850. One million died and one million emigrated. Cottiers were almost wiped out as a class. This decline in population and emigration continued after the Famine. By 1901, the population had fallen to 4.6 million.

2 End of subdivision

The law was changed after the Famine to ban subdivision. Now only the eldest son got the land. The other sons and daughters had to move to the cities or emigrate to find work. The eldest son only took over the farm after his father died. As a result, the size of families got smaller, as he married later. This added to the decline in the population.

3 Decline in the Irish language

It was the Irish-speaking areas of the west and south-west which suffered most from death and emigration. The Irish language continued to decline after the Famine, as people needed to speak English if they were going to emigrate.

4 Emigration

Between 1846 and 1850, one million people emigrated. Some were helped by their landlords to emigrate. Most went to America.

However, many people sailed in **coffin ships**. These were ships that were in poor condition. They were overcrowded and many people died on the voyage to America. Some of the ships sank at sea, drowning all on board. Thousands died of fever in the overcrowded conditions. When ships reached America many were not allowed to dock, as there was fever on board.

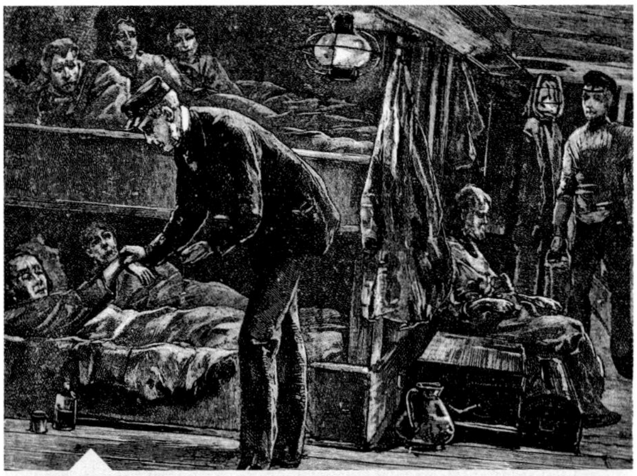

Many people died from fever on the coffin ships because of the bad conditions

5 Anti-British feeling

Many people blamed the British government for the Famine. Also, ships left Ireland full of livestock and crops such as wheat and barley, while the country was starving. This led to much bitterness against the government, as they did not prevent the export of this food.

This bitterness increased support for those who wanted to drive England out of Ireland by force. Emigrants never forgot this and supported groups like the **Irish Republican Brotherhood** (IRB) who wanted to stage a rebellion against the British in Ireland (see Section 11, Chapters 2 and 3).

6 Agriculture changed

There was a change in agriculture, away from the traditonal growing of crops.

Many landlords went bankrupt (lost all their money), as tenants could not pay their rents. They had to sell their estates. The buyers saw the estates as an investment and they evicted tenants to make way for more profitable farming such as cattle-rearing and dairy farming. The size of farms increased.

The falling population also allowed landlords to increase the size of farms. Bigger farms meant that there was an increase in living standards among farmers.

PART 2

Do you understand these key terms?

absentee landlord	**eviction**	**potato blight**	**poor rate**
tenant farmer	**conacre**	**Peel's Brimstone**	**Quakers**
cottier	**subdivision**	**workhouse**	**coffin ship**

QUESTIONS

1 What effect did the Famine have on the population of Ireland?
2 What was the long-term impact of the Famine on the population?
3 What were the effects of the ending of subdivision?
4 Which parts of Ireland were hardest hit by the Famine?
5 Why did the Irish language continue to decline after the Famine?
6 What action of the British government caused much bitterness among Irish emigrants?
7 What was the long-term effect of this bitterness?
8 Explain two effects that the Famine had on agriculture.

EXAM QUESTIONS

1 Explain three of the following terms: cottier; conacre; lazybeds; eviction.
2 What measures were taken during the 1840s to help the victims of the Famine in Ireland? (HL)
3 Why were Irish people in such fear of living in the workhouse? (OL)
4 Write about a landlord in Ireland in 1850. (People in History)

SOURCE QUESTION

(a) Describe how the Great Famine affected the size of farm holdings.
(b) What size of holding decreased most in numbers?
(c) Using what you have learnt about the Great Famine, what happened to those who had to leave their farms?

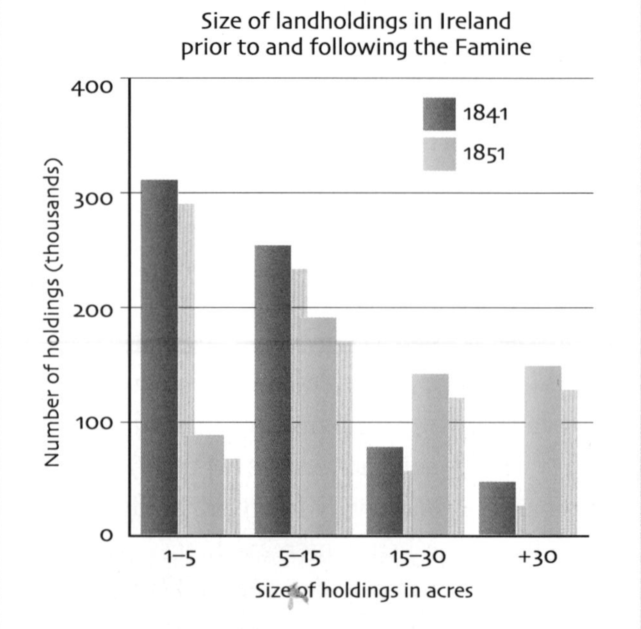

TIMELINE

PART 3

Section 11

Political Developments in Twentieth-Century Ireland

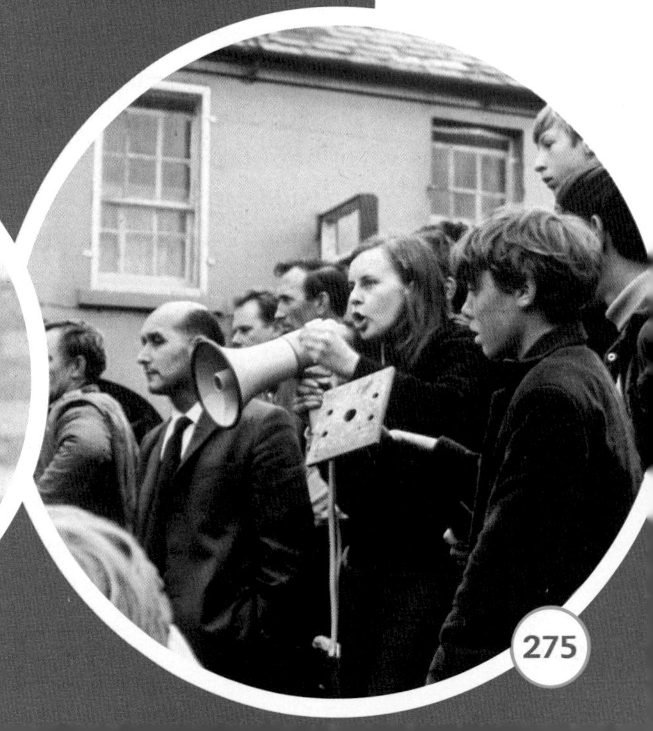

Chapter 1

Ireland 1900–14

Key Learning Objectives

- What was the political situation in Ireland before the Home Rule crisis?
- What was cultural nationalism?
- What was the impact of cultural nationalism?
- What was the Home Rule crisis, and what were its main events?

What was the political situation in Ireland before the Home Rule crisis?

Act of Union

The Act of Union in 1801 meant that Ireland was part of the United Kingdom (UK). Ireland, England, Scotland and Wales were all ruled from the Westminster parliament in London. Ireland had 105 MPs in Westminster. The **viceroy** represented the king in Ireland.

John Redmond was leader of the Home Rule Party

Nationalists

The majority of Irish Catholics were **nationalists**. They wanted **Home Rule.** That meant having their own parliament in Dublin, which would govern Ireland's local affairs, such as education and health. Westminster would control trade and foreign affairs. They felt that Ireland was being ruled badly by Westminster. Laws were passed for the benefit of the UK, but no account was taken of their effect on Ireland.

The **Home Rule Party** represented the nationalists. Their leader was **John Redmond**. They had about eighty MPs at Westminster.

Irish Republican Brotherhood

A small minority of nationalists wanted more independence than Home Rule would bring. They wanted a **republic**. This meant that Ireland would be independent of Britain.

Many of these extreme nationalists belonged to the **IRB (Irish Republican Brotherhood)**. This was a secret society that wanted to gain independence by using violence. However, in 1910, there was no hope of republicans staging a rebellion as they had very little support.

Term

Republic
A country not ruled by a monarch, where power rests with the citizens who vote.

Unionists

Most Protestants were **unionists**. That means they supported the union with Britain. They were a small minority in the country except in the north-east of Ulster. They didn't want a Home Rule parliament because:

- They were afraid that a parliament in Dublin with a Catholic majority would **discriminate** against them. They believed that 'Home Rule is Rome Rule'.
- They believed that a Dublin parliament would be bad for business, especially for industries such as shipbuilding and linen. These industries relied on free access to the British market, i.e. no taxes on their exports. Home Rule might put this access in danger.

In Westminster, the **Unionist Party** represented the unionists. Their leaders were **Edward Carson** and **James Craig**.

Term

Discrimination
Treating a group of people unfairly.

Sir Edward Carson, leader of the Unionist Party, speaking at a unionist meeting

Larkin and the ITGWU

Many workers in towns and cities were poorly paid and lived in appalling conditions in slums. **Jim Larkin** set up a trade union called the **ITGWU** (Irish Transport and General Workers' Union) in Dublin. Its aim was to fight for better wages and working conditions for Irish workers. It had 10,000 members in 1913. James Connolly was in charge of the Belfast branch of the union.

The success of the union worried the employers in Dublin. The employers were led by William Martin Murphy. They decided to destroy the ITGWU by telling their workers that they had to leave their union or lose their jobs. In August 1913, Larkin called the workers out on strike. The employers hit back by locking out their workers until they left the union. The **Lockout** lasted for five months.

James Connolly set up the **Irish Citizen Army** in 1913 to defend workers from attacks by the police during the Lockout. Connolly wanted a **socialist** revolution.

In the end, the union was defeated. The workers left the union and returned to work. Larkin left for America.

Jim Larkin speaking at a strike meeting in O'Connell Street, Dublin. © *RTÉ Stills Library*

Term

Socialism
A social system that promotes equality among citizens through shared ownership of land and industries.

What was cultural nationalism?

In the late nineteenth and early twentieth centuries a new type of nationalism emerged: **cultural nationalism**. Cultural nationalists stressed the cultural differences between Ireland and Britain. They came to feel that Ireland should have its own government because it had a different culture from that of Britain.

At the same time, many Irish people were adopting more and more of English culture as the nineteenth century progressed. This is called **Anglicisation**.

Term

Anglicisation
The spreading of English culture, i.e. language, games and customs.

PART 3

- More people were speaking English and the Irish language was in decline.
- English was necessary if people were emigrating to Britain and America. The Irish-speaking areas suffered most from emigration. Parents encouraged their children in these areas to learn English.
- Many Irish people were playing English games such as cricket, soccer and rugby.

Did you know?

In 1900, only 14 per cent of people in Ireland spoke Irish.

Cultural nationalists were worried that there would soon be little difference in culture between Britain and Ireland. In that case, the Irish would not be able to claim the right to rule themselves. So they set up movements to encourage Irish culture.

What was the impact of cultural nationalism?

The GAA (Gaelic Athletic Association)

In 1884, **Michael Cusack** set up the **GAA** in Thurles. Its aims were:

- To increase the numbers of people playing hurling and Gaelic football, and to draw up rules for the games
- To organise competitions.

Clubs were established in almost every parish. Competitions were organised and the first All-Ireland was played in 1887. It made people proud of their parish. It was the first experience that Irishmen had of running a democratic organisation. It was the most successful of the cultural movements.

Gaelic League

In 1893, **Eoin MacNeill** and **Douglas Hyde** started the **Gaelic League**. Its main aim was to stop the decline in the Irish language. It promoted the language by:

- Setting up an Irish language newspaper called *An Claidheamh Solais* (Sword of Light)
- Training teachers called *timiri* who went all over the country teaching people the Irish language
- Encouraging Irish dancing and music.

It slowed down the decline of the language.

Douglas Hyde and Eoin MacNeill, who started the Gaelic League

Increase in support for the IRB

Both the GAA and the Gaelic League attracted people who wanted to end British influence in Ireland. People like **Patrick Pearse** felt that only an Irish government could preserve the Irish language. They became attracted to organisations that wanted to use violence to drive the British out of Ireland. These movements produced many of the leaders of the 1916 Rising, e.g. Patrick Pearse and Thomas MacDonagh. Many of its members switched from supporting Home Rule to become members of the IRB.

Did you know?

Patrick Pearse was a member of the Gaelic League. He loved the Irish language. He set up an all-Irish school at St Enda's in Rathfarnham.

QUESTIONS

1. What was the Act of Union?
2. What was Home Rule?
3. Write a paragraph on the extreme nationalists.
4. Write an account of Larkin and the ITGWU.
5. Why did James Connolly set up the Irish Citizen Army?
6. What did cultural nationalists want?
7. Why were the Irish losing their culture?
8. Which organisation benefited from the GAA and the Gaelic League? How did it benefit?
9. Write a paragraph on each of the following: (a) Gaelic League and (b) GAA.

The Home Rule crisis 1912–14

At Westminster there were two major parties.

1. The **Liberal Party** was led by Herbert Asquith. He was the prime minister in 1910.
2. The **Conservatives** (Tories) were led by Andrew Bonar Law. They supported the unionists and were against Home Rule.

In the 1909 Budget, the Liberal government increased taxes on the rich. The House of Lords, which was dominated by the Conservatives, defeated the bill. This was the first time a budget had been rejected by the House of Lords. Asquith called a general election on the issue of the House of Lords **veto.**

The results of the election meant that the Liberal Party needed the support of the Home Rule Party if they were to continue in government. Redmond demanded Home Rule as the price for his support.

First Asquith passed the **Parliament Act, 1911.** This ended the veto of the House of Lords. They could reject a bill twice, but it would become law the third time. This meant that the Third Home Rule Bill, which was passed in the House of Commons in 1912, would become law in 1914 in spite of strong Conservative opposition in the House of Lords.

Term

Veto
The right of the House of Lords to reject bills passed by the House of Commons.

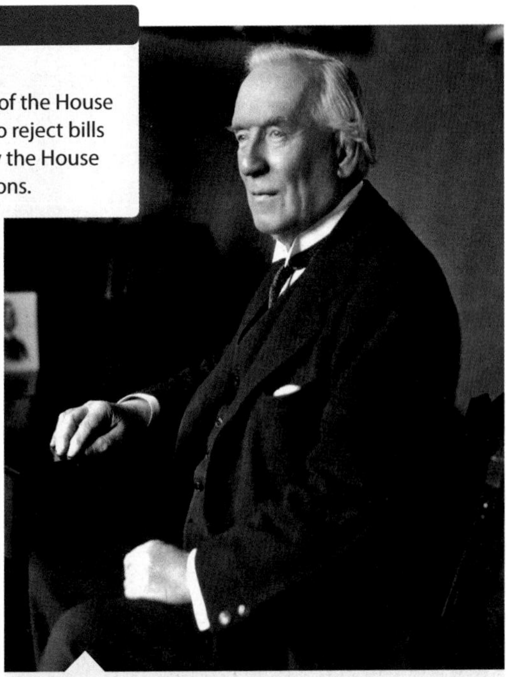

Herbert Asquith was leader of the Liberal Party

Did you know?

In March 1914 many British officers threatened to resign if they were ordered to act against the UVF to enforce Home Rule in Ulster. This was known as the **Curragh Mutiny**.

How did Ireland react?

Nationalists were delighted that success was at hand in getting Home Rule. Unionists were very disappointed.

- The unionists, led by James Craig and Edward Carson, organised demonstrations. The most famous was the signing of the **Solemn League and Covenant** in 1912. They promised to use every means possible, including violence, to prevent Home Rule being imposed on them.
- The **Ulster Volunteer Force** (UVF) was set up to train men to resist through force. They had 100,000 men in 1914. Guns and ammunition were imported through Larne, Co. Antrim.

Carson signs the Solemn League and Covenant in Belfast City Hall

Irish Volunteers

Nationalists were afraid that this unionist threat would force the British government to back down and stop Home Rule. As a result, in 1913 they formed the **Irish Volunteers**, led by **Eoin MacNeill**, to make sure that Home Rule would be granted. However, unknown to MacNeill, many of the leaders of the Volunteers were also in the IRB. They hoped to use the Volunteers in a fight for total independence (Irish Republic). The Volunteers imported guns through Howth in 1914.

John Redmond inspecting the Irish Volunteers.
This image is reproduced courtesy of the National Library of Ireland [INDH12B]

Threat of civil war

Ireland now had two armed forces and there was a real threat of civil war. Asquith persuaded Redmond and Carson to talk. He also persuaded Redmond to agree to **partition**.

However, Carson and Redmond could not agree on how many counties would be ruled by the Unionists in Ulster. Carson wanted six counties, whereas Redmond would only agree to four counties. (These were the counties with a unionist majority, i.e. Derry, Antrim, Armagh and Down.)

Term

Partition
Dividing a country into two parts.

The outbreak of World War I

When Germany invaded Belgium in August 1914, Britain declared war. World War I had begun. It was decided to postpone Home Rule until after the war. Both Redmond and Carson urged their volunteers to join the British army.

Do you understand these key terms?

viceroy	**republic**	**Anglicisation**	**veto**
nationalists	**unionists**	**lockout**	**partition**
Home Rule	**discrimination**	**socialism**	

QUESTIONS

1 What were the two main parties in Westminster?
2 Before 1911 why would a Home Rule bill be defeated?
3 What was the Parliament Act? What effect did this act have on Ireland?
4 Write an account of the unionists' reaction to the threat of Home Rule.
5 What was the Solemn League and Covenant?
6 How did nationalists react to the setting up of the UVF?
7 Why did IRB members join the Irish Volunteers?
8 What was partition?
9 What did Redmond and Carson disagree about?
10 How did the outbreak of World War I affect Home Rule?

EXAM QUESTIONS

1 Explain one reason why unionists wanted to remain part of the UK. (OL)
2 Mention two reasons why unionists opposed Home Rule. (HL)
3 Write an account of the Home Rule crisis, 1912–14. (HL)

Chapter 2

The 1916 Easter Rising

Patrick Pearse, one of the leaders of the 1916 Rising

Key Learning Objectives

- What was the background to the 1916 Rising?
- What were the main events of the 1916 Rising?
- Why did the Rising fail?
- What were the effects of the Rising?
- Why did support for Sinn Féin increase?

What was the background to the 1916 Rising?

World War I begins

In August 1914, World War I began and Home Rule was postponed until the war ended. Thousands of Ulster unionists joined the British army to show their loyalty to the king. At Woodenbridge, Co. Wicklow, Redmond, the Home Rule leader, asked the Irish Volunteers to join the British army. He hoped this would influence the negotiations for Home Rule after the war. This speech caused a split in the Volunteers. 170,000 Volunteers agreed with Redmond. They were known as the **National Volunteers**.

National Volunteer officers outside the courthouse in Waterford.
This image is reproduced courtesy of the National Library of Ireland [PWP2600]

Term

Western Front
Trenches in France that stretched from the English Channel to the Swiss border.

However, 11,000 Volunteers, led by MacNeill, disagreed. They kept the name **Irish Volunteers**. They wanted to stay in Ireland to ensure that the British government would not break its promise of granting Home Rule.

England's difficulty is Ireland's opportunity

As Britain's attention was focused on fighting on the **Western Front**, the IRB (Irish Republican Brotherhood) saw this as an opportunity to win independence for Ireland. A military council was set up in 1915 to plan the **Rising.** Its members included Patrick Pearse, Thomas Clarke and Joseph Plunkett.

Did you know?

30,000 National Volunteers joined the British army. Another 30,000 Ulster Volunteers formed the 36th Ulster division in the British army.

James Connolly was invited to join the council when the IRB discovered that he was planning a rebellion with the Irish Citizen Army. He wanted to set up a socialist republic in Ireland.

James Connolly, a leader of the Rising, believed in a socialist republic

Casement goes to Germany

Roger Casement went to Germany to seek German support for an Irish Rebellion and buy guns. The Rising was planned for Sunday, 23 April. The weapons were to arrive off the coast of Kerry. Unfortunately, the ship, called the *Aud*, which was carrying the arms, was captured by the British navy.

The *Aud* was used for gunrunning

Roger Casement. After the *Aud* was captured he was arrested and later hanged

Misleading MacNeill

The IRB had only a few hundred members. Therefore, it needed to get the support of the 11,000 Irish Volunteers to have any chance of a successful rebellion. The IRB controlled most of the leading positions in the Irish Volunteers, unknown to its leader Eoin MacNeill. Joseph Plunkett forged a document (called the **Castle Document**) which stated that the government was going to arrest the leaders of the Volunteers. MacNeill told the Volunteers to get ready to resist.

Setbacks

MacNeill found out on Easter Saturday that the *Aud* had been captured. He also discovered that the Castle Document was a forgery. He cancelled the plans for fighting. This order was published in the Sunday papers. This ended any hope of a country-wide Rising.

The Rising

On Sunday morning the leaders of the rebellion met. They knew that there was no hope of success but they decided that they would go ahead anyway. They were influenced by the idea of **blood sacrifice**.

Term

Blood sacrifice
This was the idea that deaths (the spilling of blood) would inspire the Irish to fight for independence.

Joseph Plunkett, one of the leaders of the Rising.
This image is reproduced courtesy of the National Library of Ireland

PART 3

They decided that the rebellion would start the next day. On Easter Monday, 24 April 1916, the Volunteers and the Irish Citizen Army (1,500 in total) seized key buildings around Dublin, including the GPO, the Four Courts, Boland's Mills and the College of Surgeons (see map). They failed to take Dublin Castle, which was the headquarters of the British in Ireland.

The GPO was the headquarters of the Rising. Pearse read the **Proclamation of the Irish Republic** outside the GPO to puzzled onlookers. It was signed by the seven members of the Military Council: Thomas J. Clarke, Seán McDermott, Thomas MacDonagh, P.H. Pearse, Eamonn Ceannt, James Connolly and Joseph Plunkett.

The British were caught by surprise. However, there were 6,000 British soldiers in the city by Tuesday. On Wednesday the gunship, *Helga*, came up the Liffey and shelled Liberty Hall. The GPO was shelled by guns in Trinity College. On Friday, Pearse ordered the evacuation of the GPO because it was on fire. They moved to houses in Moore Street. On Saturday, Pearse ordered the Volunteers to surrender. The rebellion was over.

James Connolly lies wounded in the GPO. *The Birth of the Republic* by Walter Paget. National Museum of Ireland

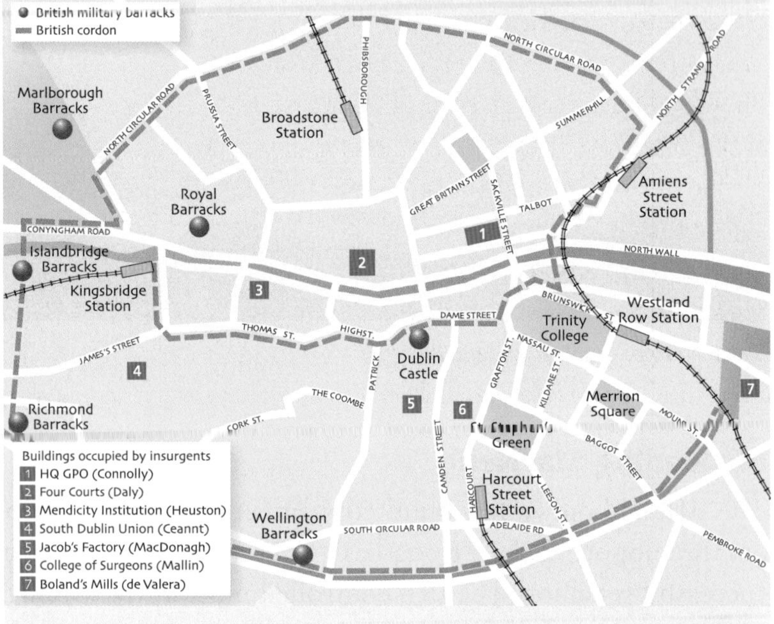

This map shows the key buildings used during the Rising

Why did the Rising fail?

1 There was no countrywide rebellion, which meant that the British could concentrate their forces in Dublin.
2 The decision to take over key buildings in the centre of Dublin made it easy for the British to surround them. Bad tactics!
3 The rebels were heavily outnumbered by the British forces, whose soldiers were more experienced and better armed.

Did you know?

Eamon de Valera was the commander of the Volunteers at Boland's Mills.

What were the effects of the Rising?

Around 3,000 people were arrested. Ninety people were sentenced to death by secret military courts between 3 and 12 May. Fourteen of the leaders were executed in Kilmainham Gaol. All the signatories of the Proclamation were shot.

As the executions were carried out over those ten days, public opinion began to change.

British troops man a barricade during the Rising

Why did public opinion change?

During the Rising and immediately after it the people were angry with the rebels. This was due to the damage caused to the city and the loss of earnings of many workers. However, the executions – especially that of the seriously wounded Connolly – caused people to sympathise with the rebels. Also 2,000 people were imprisoned, most of whom were innocent. This increased the public's sympathy. The British soon recognised the change in public opinion and stopped the executions. Those who were sent to **internment** camps were released within a year. They had become republicans while in the internment camps in Britain.

However, the damage was done and **historians see this moment as a turning point in Irish history**. Most people no longer wanted Home Rule, but now demanded total independence from Britain, i.e. an Irish republic.

Term

Internment
Imprisonment without trial.

Did you know?

Among the leaders of the Rising who were not executed were: Eamon de Valera because he was an American citizen, and Countess Markievicz because she was female.

The effects of shelling on the GPO during the Rising

QUESTIONS

1. Why did Redmond want the Volunteers to fight in World War I?
2. What effect did this request have on the Volunteers?
3. Why did the IRB plan a rising during World War I?
4. Name three members of the Military Council. Why did they bring in James Connolly?
5. Write an account of Casement's role in the preparations for the Rising.
6. Why did the Military Council deceive MacNeill? How did they deceive him?
7. Why did MacNeill cancel plans for the fighting?
8. Why did the IRB decide to go ahead, with no hope of success?
9. Apart from the GPO, mention two buildings occupied by the rebels during Easter Week, 1916.
10. How did the ordinary people of Dublin react immediately after the Rising?
11. Why do historians see this event as a turning point in Irish history?
12. Write an account of the main events of Easter Week.
13. What were the main effects of the Rising?
14. Why was the Easter Rising a military failure?

PART 3

Why did support for Sinn Féin increase?

Arthur Griffith set up **Sinn Féin** in 1905. He wanted to win more independence than Home Rule would give. He hoped to achieve this by peaceful means.

Before the 1916 Rising, Sinn Féin had very few supporters, but it was the party to benefit most from the change in public opinion after the Rising. The British had wrongly called it a 'Sinn Féin rebellion'. In fact, Sinn Féin did not take part in the Rising.

Home Rule was no longer seen as enough by most nationalists. In 1917, nationalists who favoured complete independence from Britain joined Sinn Féin. The party was also strengthened by the release of those interned in Britain, especially **Michael Collins** and **Eamon de Valera**.

In 1917, Griffith stepped aside and let Eamon de Valera become leader. The **aims of Sinn Féin** were:

1. To set up a republic, completely independent of Britain
2. To set up a parliament in Dublin called the **Dáil**, independent of Westminster. The Dáil would elect a government and set up an alternative administration to the British one.

Did you know?

Michael Collins was from Co. Cork. He fought in the GPO during the Rising. When he was released he used his organisational ability to build up Sinn Féin and the Volunteers.

Michael Collins in uniform during the Civil War, 1921. *This image is reproduced courtesy of the National Library [INDHo403]*

Support for Sinn Féin was boosted by events in 1917 and 1918.

- The British announced plans to introduce **conscription** into Ireland. All Irish parties opposed this plan, but Sinn Féin got most of the credit when the British dropped the plan.
- The British arrested Sinn Féin leaders such as de Valera and Griffith. This increased support for Sinn Féin.
- Sinn Féin won four **by-elections**.

Term

Conscription
Being forced to join an army.

Term

By-election
When an MP dies or retires an election is held to replace them.

Sinn Féin leaders at the first Dáil Éireann. In the front row are Michael Collins, Cathal Brugha, Arthur Griffith, Eamon de Valera, Eoin MacNeill and William Cosgrave

PART 3

1918 general election

Term

Franchise
The right to vote.

A general election was called when World War I ended in November 1918. This was the first election for ten years and the change in the **franchise** rules meant a lot of young men and women over thirty were voting for the first time. This favoured Sinn Féin as it was seen as a young and dynamic party. The Home Rule Party was seen as old and tired.

The results of the 1918 general election were dramatic (see table). Sinn Féin won 73 seats, whereas the Home Rule Party won only 6. Now Sinn Féin was the voice of nationalist Ireland. The Unionist Party won 26 seats and would have a major say in future events in Ireland.

Arthur Griffith, founder of Sinn Féin

Party	Before	After
Sinn Féin	7 MPs	73 MPs
Home Rule	78 MPs	6 MPs
Unionists	18 MPs	26 MPs

Do you understand these key terms?

National Volunteers
Irish Volunteers
Western Front
blood sacrifice
internment
Sinn Féin
Dáil
conscription
by-election
franchise

QUESTIONS

1. Why did Sinn Féin benefit most from the Rising?
2. What were the aims of Sinn Féin in 1917?
3. Who became president of Sinn Féin in 1917?
4. What actions of the British government in 1918 increased support for Sinn Féin?
5. What were the results of the 1918 general election?
6. Why did the change in franchise help Sinn Féin?

EXAM QUESTIONS

1. Write down one fact about the 1916 Rising. (OL)
2. What were two consequences of the executions in 1916? (HL)
3. Give two reasons why Sinn Féin won the 1918 election. (HL)
4. Why was the Home Rule Party unsuccessful in the 1918 election? (HL)

Chapter 3

The First Dáil and the War of Independence 1919–21

Key Learning Objectives

- **What happened in the first Dáil?**
- **What were the main events of the War of Independence?**

The first Dáil

Term

Dáil
The parliament set up in Dublin by Sinn Féin TDs who refused to take their seats in Westminster.

On 21 January 1919, the **Dáil** met for the first time in the **Mansion House** in Dublin. It declared Ireland a republic. Only twenty-seven TDs were present, because many of them were in prison. In April, Eamon de Valera became President (head of government). He appointed the following ministers:

- Arthur Griffith as Vice-President and Minister for Home Affairs
- Cathal Brugha as Minister for Defence
- Michael Collins as Minister for Finance
- Countess Markievicz as Minister for Labour (see also Section 13, Chapter 5).

In June 1919, de Valera went to America to try to persuade the American government to recognise the Irish Republic. He failed, but managed to raise $4 million for the fight for independence.

Griffith took control in de Valera's absence. Sinn Féin set up an alternative government in opposition to the British:

- Collins organised a loan of £350,000. This, together with the American money, paid for weapons and the costs of running the government.
- Sinn Féin courts were set up to replace British courts.
- Many local councils switched their support to the Dáil.

The first Dáil, the Sinn Féin Parliament, opened at the Mansion House, Dublin, in 1919.
This image is reproduced courtesy of the National Library of Ireland [EAS1745]

The War of Independence

The War of Independence began on 21 January 1919 at Soloheadbeg in Co. Tipperary. This was the same day the First Dáil met. Two constables from the **Royal Irish Constabulary (RIC)** were killed by a group of Volunteers led by Dan Breen. The Volunteers were by this time renamed the **IRA (Irish Republican Army)**. The IRA attacked RIC barracks located in the countryside. As a result, the RIC retreated to the towns, leaving the countryside under the control of the IRA.

Term

RIC
The police force in Ireland.

Collins' spy network

Michael Collins was the Director of Intelligence in the IRA. He had a network of spies throughout the country, including railway men and office clerks. He even had spies in Dublin Castle, the headquarters of the British administration in Ireland. He also set up a group of assassins called **'the Squad'**. They murdered anyone who was a British spy. These murders were very effective in preventing the British from finding out the plans of the Volunteers.

Dan Breen, leader of the Third Tipperary Brigade. © *RTÉ Stills Library*

Guerrilla warfare

Term

Guerrilla warfare
A type of fighting that consists of surprise attacks and ambushes.

The IRA used **guerrilla warfare** against the British. This involved ambushing British convoys of lorries, then disappearing into the countryside. As they didn't wear uniforms they could hide among the ordinary people. This made it very difficult for the British to capture them. Also their knowledge of the local countryside meant they could disappear very quickly. Local commanders such as **Dan Breen** (Tipperary) and **Tom Barry** (West Cork) operated independently. As the war got worse, the IRA formed **flying columns**. These were groups of full-time Volunteers (twenty or more members) who moved from place to place to help the local commanders set up ambushes.

West Mayo Brigade flying column, 1920–21. *Reproduced courtesy of Military Archives, Defence Forces Ireland*

PART 3

Black and Tans

Due to the successes of the IRA then, the RIC needed help. In the spring of 1920 former British soldiers were sent to Ireland. They were called the **Black and Tans.**

Later, ex-army officers called **Auxiliaries** were recruited. The Black and Tans and Auxiliaries soon became very unpopular due to their ruthlessness. This increased support for the IRA among the ordinary people.

Did you know?

The Black and Tans got their nickname from the fact that they wore army khaki trousers and RIC dark green jackets.

Revenge attacks

Sometimes when a policeman was killed the British forces hit back by terrorising the local people. Houses were burned, towns were smashed up and prisoners were shot. This also increased support for the IRA. In December 1920, the Black and Tans burned Cork city. This was revenge for an IRA ambush near Cork.

A woman outside her house, which had been burned by the Black and Tans in Mitchelstown, Co. Cork. *This image is reproduced courtesy of the National Library of Ireland [HOGW118]*

The truce

Term

Truce
A ceasefire.

People in Britain were embarrassed by the behaviour of their forces in Ireland. Pressure was put on their government to end the war. The IRA was short of arms and members. A **truce** was agreed; it began on 11 July 1921.

TIMELINE	The main events of the War of Independence
March 1920	British forces murdered the Lord Mayor of Cork, Thomas MacCurtain
1 November 1920	Kevin Barry, an 18-year-old student, was hanged for taking part in an ambush in which a British soldier was killed
21 November 1920	Collins' Squad killed 13 British intelligence agents In retaliation the Auxiliaries entered Croke Park looking for the killers among the crowd. Dublin and Tipperary were playing a football match. They opened fire and killed 14 people. These events are known as Bloody Sunday
28 November 1920	Tom Barry and the West Cork brigade ambushed and killed 17 Auxiliaries in Kilmichael. The Black and Tans then burned part of Cork
25 May 1921	The IRA burned the Custom House in Dublin. However, 80 IRA men were killed or captured
Early summer 1921	The IRA was under severe pressure. It was running out of arms and had lost a lot of men

Did you know?

The Hogan Stand in Croke Park is named after the Tipperary captain, Michael Hogan, who was killed on Bloody Sunday.

Do you understand these key terms?

Dáil	**guerrilla warfare**	**Auxiliaries**
RIC	**flying column**	**truce**
IRA	**Black and Tans**	**Bloody Sunday**

The delegation had two main aims:

1 To set up a republic so that Ireland would be completely independent from Britain
2 To end partition so that the Northern Ireland state would cease to exist.

The British delegation was led by the prime minister, David Lloyd George. The British wanted:

1 Ireland to stay within the British Commonwealth, as they were afraid that other members of the Commonwealth would also leave if Ireland were successful
2 To protect the state of Northern Ireland rather than risk unionist violence.

Talks dragged on until December. Finally, Lloyd George issued an ultimatum to accept the following terms or 'there would be immediate and terrible war'.

Term

British Commonwealth
An association of countries consisting of the UK and its colonies.

Dominion
A self-governing state within the British Commonwealth where the king was head of state.

What were the terms of the Treaty?

1 Ireland would be called the Irish Free State
2 The Free State would not be a republic but part of the **British Commonwealth**. This is called **dominion status**. The king would be head of state and TDs would have to take an oath of loyalty to the king
3 The British would have three naval ports in Ireland: Lough Swilly, Cobh and Berehaven
4 The Governor-General was to be the king's representative in the Free State
5 A **Boundary Commission** was to be set up to decide the border between Northern Ireland and the Irish Free State. There would be a representative from both Northern Ireland and the Free State. There would be an independent chairman

Lloyd George had assured the Irish delegates that, as a result of the Boundary Commission, areas of Northern Ireland that had a nationalist majority would join the Free State, i.e. Fermanagh and Tyrone.

Collins knew that the IRA was in no fit state to restart the War of Independence. He reluctantly signed the Treaty with the other Irish delegates on 6 December 1921.

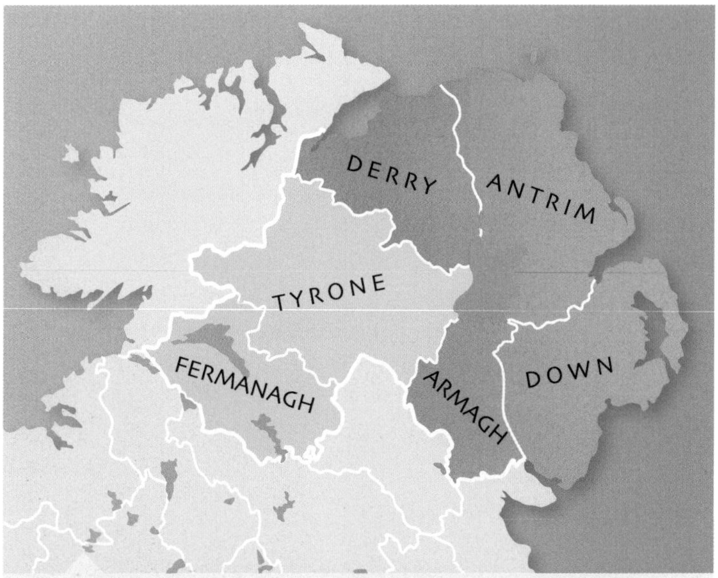

On this map the counties in orange had a unionist majority, the counties in green had a small nationalist majority. The six counties together make up Northern Ireland

PART 3

What was the reaction to the Treaty?

The Treaty split both Sinn Féin and the IRA down the middle. De Valera was annoyed that Collins and Griffith had not consulted him before signing the Treaty. The Dáil met to debate the terms of the Treaty. TDs spoke with great passion on both sides of the argument.

The main arguments in favour of the Treaty

1. It gave Ireland more independence than Home Rule would have.
2. As Collins stated, 'It was a stepping stone to greater independence'. Once the British had left it would be easier to work towards full independence.
3. If the war started again the IRA would be beaten. It was the best deal that could be got!

The main arguments against the Treaty

1. The Treaty didn't give Ireland the republic that the IRA had fought for.
2. Republicans could not swear an oath of loyalty to the king.
3. As Ireland was so close to Britain it would be easy for the British government to interfere in Irish affairs, as the king was head of state.

The Dáil voted on 7 January 1922 (see table). Those against the Treaty left the Dáil, led by de Valera. Griffith replaced him as President.

Dáil vote on the Treaty, January 1922	
For the Treaty	64 TDs
Against the Treaty	57 TDs

Rory O'Connor led the battle at the Four Courts. Here you see the PRO (Public Records Office) being destroyed at the beginning of the Civil War. © *RTÉ Stills Library*

The Civil War

An irregular prisioner captured by Free State troops. *This image is reproduced courtesy of the National Library of Ireland [HOG106]*

What were the causes of the Civil War?

- The Treaty caused much division in the country. It divided families. It divided the IRA so much that the two sides were prepared to fight each other.
- When the British army began to pull out of their barracks, both pro- and anti-Treaty IRA took them over. The pro-treaty IRA were called the **Free State Army**. The anti-treaty IRA called themselves **Republicans**, but were usually known as **Irregulars**.
- The Irregulars, led by **Rory O'Connor**, took over the Four Courts, but at first Collins left them alone as he wanted to avoid a civil war.
- In the general election of June 1922 a majority of the people voted in favour of the Treaty. This gave Collins the confidence to face up to O'Connor.
- When the anti-Treaty forces in the Four Courts kidnapped General O'Connell of the Free State army, it gave Collins the excuse he needed to attack the Irregulars in Four Courts.

What were the main events of the Civil War?

On 28 June 1922, Collins used artillery (big guns) borrowed from the British to fire on the Four Courts. This was the start of the Civil War. Within two days, the Irregulars in the Four Courts had surrendered. The Irregulars were defeated in Dublin within a week.

The Irregulars retreated to Munster where their support was strongest. They set up the **Munster Republic**. Liam Lynch was their chief of staff. The Irregulars used guerrilla warfare tactics against the Free State troops. They gradually took control of Munster.

On 12 August 1922, Arthur Griffith died of a stroke. Ten days later Michael Collins was killed in an ambush at Béal na Bláth in West Cork.

In August 1922, **William T. Cosgrave** became the new head of the Free State government. Kevin O'Higgins was now in charge of law and order. He passed a **Special Powers Act** that allowed them to execute Irregulars for offences such as having a gun.

De Valera tried to get the Irregulars to stop fighting as he saw there was no hope. In May 1923, the Irregulars agreed to a ceasefire.

PART 3

What were the results of the Civil War?

- £30 million worth of damage had been caused. Cities, towns, roads and railways were damaged. This caused huge disruption to the economy.
- Almost 600 people had been killed.
- The nation was left divided and bitter for decades afterwards.
- The two major parties of the Free State had their origins in the Civil War: Cumann na nGaedhael (renamed Fine Gael in the 1930s) was pro-Treaty; Fianna Fáil was the anti-Treaty party.

Do you understand these key terms?

British Commonwealth	**Free State Army**	**Republicans**
dominion	**Irregulars**	**Munster Republic**

QUESTIONS

1. What were the terms of the Government of Ireland Act?
2. Name two members of the Irish delegation. What were their main aims?
3. Name the leader of the British delegation. What were their main aims?
4. What were the terms of the Treaty?
5. Why did the Irish delegation agree to sign the Treaty?
6. What were the main arguments in favour of the Treaty?
7. What were the main arguments against the Treaty?
8. What was the result of the Dáil vote?
9. What event started the Civil War?
10. What was the Munster Republic?
11. What were the results of the Civil War?

EXAM QUESTIONS

1. Explain the following terms: Government of Ireland Act 1920; dominion status; Irregular forces. (HL)
2. Give an account of the Anglo-Irish Treaty, 1921. (HL)
3. Give two reasons why there was a civil war in Ireland during the years 1922–23. (HL)

Chapter 5

Cumann na nGaedhael in Government 1923–32

Key Learning Objectives

- **What were the challenges facing the new government?**
- **What were the achievements of the Cumann na nGaedhael government?**
- **Why did the Cumann na nGaedhael government become unpopular?**

What were the challenges facing the new government?

In January 1923, the pro-Treaty TDs of Sinn Féin changed their name to **Cumann na nGaedhael**. Their leader was William T. Cosgrave. The anti-Treaty TDs kept the name of Sinn Féin. In May 1923 Cumann na nGaedhael won the general election. Sinn Féin refused to take their seats in the Dáil, so the Labour Party became the main opposition in the Dáil.

When Cumann na nGaedhael won the Civil War they set about the task of running the country. They faced many challenges.

- The economy was in ruins after five years of fighting.
- There was great bitterness on both sides as a result of the Civil War.
- The biggest threat was that a large minority did not recognise the Free State and threatened its very existence.

William Cosgrave, leader of Cumann na nGaedhael

Sinn Féin in 1922

Pro-Treaty › Cosgrave	**Anti-Treaty** › de Valera
Cumann na nGaedhael (1922–33)	Sinn Féin (1922–26)
Fine Gael (since 1933)	Fianna Fáil (since 1926)

Achievements of the Cumann na nGaedhael government

Term

Constitution
The rules by which a country is governed.

The Constitution

The **constitution** was based on the Treaty.

- There were two houses of parliament: **Dáil Éireann** and **Seanad Éireann**.
- Members of the Dáil had to swear an oath of allegiance (loyalty) to the king as head of the Commonwealth.
- The Governor-General was the king's representative in the Irish Free State.
- Women were given the same voting rights as men.

Did you know?

Garda Síochána means guardians of the peace.

Law and order

The main task was to restore law and order.

- The Minister for Home Affairs (Justice), Kevin O'Higgins, set up a new police force called the **Garda Síochána**. The well-trained force was widely accepted as they were unarmed, and law and order returned.
- Many IRA members still posed a threat to peace. O'Higgins introduced **Public Safety Acts** in 1923 and 1924 which enabled the government to imprison IRA members. These Acts ended this threat.
- The biggest threat to the state came from the **army**. The government planned to reduce the size of the army. A group of army officers demanded that the government abandon these plans. They also condemned the government for failing to bring the Irish Free State closer to a republic. The government considered this to be **mutiny**. The officers involved were arrested. From then on the army was never a threat to the state. This was a major achievement of the Cumann na nGaedhael government.

Kevin O'Higgins, founder of the Garda Síochána

Newly formed Gardaí on parade at the Depot, Phoenix Park, 1923. *This image is reproduced courtesy of the National Library of Ireland [HOG72]*

The economy

The government believed that agriculture was more important than industry, as most of Ireland's exports were agricultural products sent to Britain. To increase food exports to Britain, the quality of eggs, meat and butter was improved.

The **ACC** provided loans to farmers to modernise their methods. However, very few farmers took out these loans. Low taxes minimised farmers' costs. This meant that they were able to sell more in the British market. By 1930, agricultural exports were at their highest for years. However, due to low taxes the government had very little money to help the poor in Irish society.

Term

ACC
Agricultural Credit Corporation

The Shannon Scheme

Industry grew slowly as it was unable to compete with its British rivals. One of the major problems facing industry was the lack of a cheap energy source. As a result, the government built a hydroelectric power station on the Shannon. This was called the **Shannon Scheme**. It was built by Siemens, a German firm, and cost £5 million. It provided cheap electricity. The ESB (Electricity Supply Board) was set up to distribute the electricity around the country.

By 1930, there were 13,000 more people employed in industry than in 1922.

The huge turbines under construction at the Shannon hydroelectric scheme at Ardnacrusha, Limerick. *This image is reproduced courtesy of the National Library of Ireland [INDH1143]*

Relations with Northern Ireland

In 1924, the **Boundary Commission** was set up to decide the border between the Irish Free State and Northern Ireland. In the Free State most people expected that large areas of Northern Ireland where Catholics had a majority would become part of the Free State.

Eoin MacNeill represented the Free State, J.R. Fisher represented Ulster Unionists and the independent chairman was Judge Richard Feetham of South Africa. It was reported in the *Morning Post* newspaper that the Free State would not acquire large areas of the North and that they would lose small parts of East Donegal (Protestant majority). There was uproar in the Free State and MacNeill resigned. Cosgrave hurried to London and an agreement was reached which left the border unchanged. This was a major blow to Cumann na nGaedhael.

Meeting of the Irish Boundary Commission: Mr Fisher (Northern Ireland), Mr Justice Feetham (South Africa, Chairman), and Eoin MacNeill (Irish Free State)

PART 3

Relations with Britain

The main aim of the Cumann na nGaedhael government was to increase the country's independence from Britain. It wanted the Free State to be recognised as an independent country by the rest of the world. As a result, the Free State joined the **League of Nations** (see page 329) in 1923. It also appointed its own ambassadors. This upset Britain as all Commonwealth countries were represented by the British ambassador abroad.

However, as the Free State was part of the British Commonwealth, with dominion status, its independence was limited. With the help of other Commonwealth members such as Canada, the government put pressure on Britain to increase the independence of the dominions. The British gave in to their demands. In 1931, the **Statute of Westminster** was passed. As a result:

- The Dáil could pass any laws without interference from Britain.
- All dominions could change laws that the British had made for them without the approval of Britain. This meant that the Free State could get rid of the Treaty as it had been passed into law at Westminster. Cosgrave stated that they would not alter the Treaty. However, de Valera would take advantage of this law when he came to power in 1932.

Founding of Fianna Fáil

Eamon de Valera formed the Fianna Fáil Party in 1926. How many women do you see in this photo of Fianna Fáil TDs?

Anti-Treaty Sinn Féin TDs would not swear an oath of loyalty to the king. This meant that they could not enter the Dáil. This was bad for democracy. In 1926, Eamon de Valera proposed to the Sinn Féin party that they would enter the Dáil if the oath were removed. He was afraid that they would lose support in elections if they did not take their seats in the Dáil. This proposal was defeated and de Valera left Sinn Féin and set up **Fianna Fáil**. Among those who joined him was Seán Lemass. When Kevin O'Higgins was murdered by the IRA, Cosgrave introduced the **Electoral Amendment Act** 1927, which stated that all TDs must take the oath or give up their seats. After this Act, de Valera took the oath and entered the Dáil.

Why did Cumann na nGaedhael become unpopular?

Between 1927 and 1932 the Cumann na nGaedhael government became more unpopular. This was due to:

- The Depression, which was caused by the **Wall Street Crash** and which led to high unemployment.
- Cutting teachers' salaries and reducing old age pensions.

As a result, Fianna Fáil became more popular.

Term

Wall Street Crash
In October 1929 shares on the US stock exchange fell. The US economy collapsed and this caused a worldwide economic depression.

PART 3

General election, 1932

In 1932, Cosgrave called a general election. The government wanted to be judged on its record. However, Fianna Fáil promised to:

1. Break up the Treaty
2. Put tariffs (taxes) on imports to encourage more Irish industry (more jobs)
3. Build houses for people living in slums
4. Improve pensions for poor people.

Fianna Fáil won the election and with the support of the Labour Party became the government. People wondered if Cosgrave would hand over power peacefully. He was a democrat and quietly stepped aside. This showed that democracy was safe, which was one of the main achievements of the Cumann na nGaedhael government.

Do you understand these key terms?

Cumann na nGhaedhael
constitution
dominion status
Garda Síochána
mutiny
ACC
Boundary Commission
Electoral Amendment Act
Statute of Westminster
Fianna Fáil
Wall Street Crash

QUESTIONS

1. Mention three challenges that the Free State government faced in 1923.
2. Mention three actions that the Cumann na nGaedhael government took to restore law and order.
3. Write a note on how Cumann na nGaedhael improved agriculture.
4. Why was the Shannon Scheme set up?
5. Give two reasons why the army mutiny happened.
6. Why were people in the Free State disappointed with the findings of the Boundary Commission?
7. What were the terms of the Statute of Westminster?
8. What was the most important effect of the Statute of Westminster?
9. Why had the Cumann na nGaedhael government become unpopular by 1932?
10. What was Fianna Fáil's programme for government?

EXAM QUESTIONS

1. Explain the following terms: army mutiny; Boundary Commission; Electoral Amendment Act; Statute of Westminster; dominion status. (HL)
2. Write an account of each of the following:
   (a) Relations between Britain and Ireland 1923–32
   (b) The Shannon Scheme. (HL)
3. Describe the main achievements of the Cumann na nGaedhael government 1923–32.

Chapter 6

Fianna Fáil in Government 1932–39

Key Learning Objectives

- **What were the achievements of the Fianna Fáil government?**
  - **Changing the Treaty**
  - **Economy**
  - **Law and order**

Achievements of the Fianna Fáil government

Changing the Treaty

The leader of Fianna Fáil was **Eamon de Valera**. As soon as he came to power he began to change the Treaty. The Statute of Westminster allowed him to get rid of:

- The oath of loyalty (allegiance) to the king.
- The Governor-General, James MacNeill; he was so undermined by the actions of the Fianna Fáil government that he resigned. The office was later abolished.
- The king as head of the Irish Free State; the Dáil agreed to this in 1936.

1937 Constitution (Bunreacht na hÉireann)

As a result of all these changes, de Valera decided to introduce a new constitution in 1937. Some of its main terms were as follows:

- The Free State was renamed Ireland (in Irish *Éire*).
- The head of state was to be a president who was to be elected for seven years.
- The head of government was to be called the **Taoiseach**.
- Articles 2 and 3 claimed control over the whole island of Ireland and not just the twenty-six counties. (This angered unionists in Northern Ireland who saw it as a threat to their state's existence.)

Did you know?

The chief of the clan in Celtic Ireland was called the Taoiseach.

Eamon de Valera and members of the cabinet during the introduction of the 1937 Constitution

Economy

The Economic War

The Irish government collected **land annuities** from farmers and paid them to Britain. De Valera kept the money to invest in Irish industries. This resulted in a trade war between Britain and the Free State, which was called the **Economic War**.

The British put a **tariff** (tax) of 20 per cent on Irish cattle exports. This had a disastrous effect on Irish agriculture, as cattle exports fell. De Valera retaliated by putting a 5 per cent tariff on imports from Britain.

The **Anglo-Irish Agreement** ended the Economic War in 1938. Its terms were that:

- The land annuities were abolished and the Irish government had to make a one-off payment of £10 million.
- Both governments reduced their tariffs.
- The **Treaty ports** (Cobh, Berehaven and Lough Swilly) were given to the Free State. This was important as it allowed the Free State to stay neutral in World War II.

Term

Land annuities
In the late 1800s, the British government loaned money to Irish tenants to buy their farms. The land annuities were the annual repayments of these loans, by the Irish to the British.

Term

Tariff
Taxes imposed on imported goods.

Economic policy

Fianna Fáil's economic policy was to get the Free State to produce its own goods instead of depending on imports. To do this it put tariffs on foreign imports to make them more expensive than Irish goods. This is called **protectionism.** It allowed Irish industry to develop. This policy was successful as the number of workers in industry rose from 111,000 in 1931 to 166,000 in 1938.

Fianna Fáil provided for the poor by giving **unemployment assistance.** Pensions were provided for widows and those with disability. Also 100,000 houses were built for those living in slums like those in Dublin.

Term

Fascist
A supporter of fascism, where a strong ruler runs a country and there are no elections. See Section 12, Chapter 2.

Law and order

1 The Blueshirts

When Fianna Fáil entered government they released all IRA prisoners from gaol. The IRA began to attack Cumann na nGaedhael meetings in revenge for imprisoning them. The **ACA** (Army Comrades Association), set up by ex-members of the Free State army, provided protection at these meetings. After riots between the ACA and the IRA, de Valera sacked the Garda Commissioner, **Eoin O'Duffy** in 1933.

Eoin O'Duffy then became leader of the ACA. They changed their name to the **National Guard.** He organised them into a **fascist**-style organisation, and they adopted the fascist salute. They were called the **Blueshirts** due to their uniform.

The Irish fascist leader Eoin O'Duffy inspecting his Blueshirts

In August 1933, O'Duffy organised a march in Dublin. De Valera was afraid that there would be an attempt to overthrow his government (like Mussolini in Rome, see Section 12, Chapter 2) and banned the march. He outlawed the Blueshirts.

De Valera didn't take any steps against the IRA. As a result, Cosgrave was afraid that de Valera was going to establish a **dictatorship**. He decided to join with O'Duffy to stop this happening.

In 1933, Cumann na nGaedhael united with the National Guard to form **Fine Gael**. O'Duffy was appointed leader. He was totally unsuited to the leadership of a political party. He allowed the Blueshirts to attack the Gardaí and threatened to invade Northern Ireland.
In 1934 Fine Gael voted to sack O'Duffy and elected Cosgrave as their leader again.

Term

Dictatorship
A form of government where all the power is in the hands of one person.

2 The IRA

The IRA felt that de Valera was not making enough progress towards a thirty-two county republic. De Valera was forced to outlaw the IRA after it committed several murders. In 1939 the IRA started a bombing campaign in Britain that killed five people. In response de Valera introduced a law against the IRA called the Offences Against the State Act.

Achievements of Fianna Fáil

- Stopped paying land annuities to the British government
- Improved industry
- Moved Ireland closer to becoming a republic by dismantling the Treaty
- Got back Treaty ports
- Defeated the Blueshirts
- Restrained the IRA

QUESTIONS

1 Why was de Valera able to dismantle the Treaty?
2 Write a paragraph on how de Valera dismantled the Treaty.
3 List three of the terms of the 1937 Constitution.
4 What were land annuities?
5 What was the main aim of Fianna Fáil's economic policy?
6 Describe two achievements of the economic policy of Fianna Fáil.
7 What action did de Valera take against the Blueshirts in 1933?
8 Why was Fine Gael formed in 1933?
9 Why was O'Duffy unsuitable as a political leader?

Do you understand these key terms?

Taoiseach
land annuities
tariff
Economic War
Treaty ports
protectionism
Blueshirts
fascist
dictatorship
Fine Gael

EXAM QUESTIONS

1 Explain each of the following terms: Blueshirts; internment; tariff. (HL)
2 Give two reasons for the economic war between Britain and Ireland in the 1930s. (HL)
3 Write an account of Ireland under de Valera, 1932–39. (HL)

Chapter 7

The Emergency 1939–45

Key Learning Objectives

- **Why and how did Ireland stay neutral?**
- **How did the government deal with the problems of the Emergency?**
- **What were relations like with the Allies?**
- **What were the results of World War II for Ireland?**

Why and how did Ireland stay neutral?

The Emergency

World War II began on 3 September 1939, when Britain declared war on Germany. All political parties in Ireland supported neutrality. The Dáil passed the **Emergency Powers Act** to ensure that Ireland remained neutral. It gave the government enormous powers. Newspapers were censored, so there was no news about the war that might favour one side. Weather forecasts were not allowed as they might help either side in military operations such as bombing. The period of World War II was known as **The Emergency** in Ireland.

Term

Neutral
A country that doesn't take part in a war. It favours no side.

Why did the government choose neutrality?

1. If Ireland became involved in the war it could result in widespread destruction and loss of life.
2. People did not want to fight on the side of Britain because of partition.
3. It would show that Ireland was independent of Britain.

What were the threats to neutrality?

The main threat to neutrality came from the IRA. In 1939, the IRA started a bombing campaign in Britain. They got in contact with Germany, and several German spies were sent to Ireland. All of them were arrested. De Valera was afraid that the activities of the IRA would put Irish neutrality at risk by giving Britain an excuse to invade Ireland. As a result, he imprisoned over 500 IRA members.

How did the government deal with the problems of the Emergency?

Defence forces

In 1940, the Irish army had increased to 37,000 men. The government also set up the **Local Defence Force** (LDF), which eventually numbered 250,000. The aim was to train young people to fight in case Ireland was invaded. They were a part-time force and they were poorly equipped.

A Local Defence Force march in Waterford

Food supplies

Due to Ireland's neutrality, Britain limited the goods such as tea that it carried to Ireland. **Seán Lemass** was appointed Minister for Supplies. He set up Irish Shipping Ltd to bring essential supplies from abroad. However, there were still severe shortages due to German U-boat (submarine) activity at sea. As a result, **rationing** was introduced. People were given ration books for goods such as tea, flour and butter.

Farmers were ordered to grow more wheat for flour. This was called the **Compulsory Tillage Scheme**. But despite these measures there was still great hardship.

The government rationed the amount of food and other goods people could buy during the shortage. This ensured that everyone got a fair share

Fuel shortages

- Petrol was very scarce and available only to doctors and priests.
- In Dublin, gas was used for cooking, but it was rationed. Men called **glimmer men** were appointed to ensure that people used only the amount of gas and electricity that was allowed.
- Coal was scarce, as Britain needed all her coal during the war. Trains were powered by turf from the Irish bogs rather than by coal, but the trains took much longer to complete a journey.
- People from towns and cities went out to the bogs in summer to cut enough turf to provide heat for the winter.
- Many factories were closed due to the lack of energy and raw materials. Many of those who lost their jobs emigrated to Britain to find work.

What were relations like with the Allies?

Britain was unhappy with Ireland's decision to stay neutral. When Churchill became prime minister of Britain in 1940 he wanted the former Treaty ports to be used as naval bases to protect **convoys** bringing vital supplies to Britain. De Valera refused, as it would endanger Ireland's neutrality. Churchill promised de Valera that he would reunify Ireland if it entered the war on Britain's side. De Valera rejected this idea partly because he felt that Churchill would not be able to deliver reunification due to the strength of unionist opposition. When the Allies began using Northern Ireland's ports as naval bases the threat of Britain taking over the Treaty ports by force disappeared.

Term

Convoys
Groups of cargo ships with warships to protect them against German U-boats.

After the Americans entered the war in 1941, they were also against Ireland being neutral. The Americans were afraid that the South was full of German spies who observed American troops in Northern Ireland.

Pro-Allied neutrality

One of the main reasons why the Allies didn't invade the South was because Irish neutrality favoured the Allies.

- When Allied pilots crashed they were sent back over the border to Northern Ireland. German pilots were imprisoned.
- Fire brigades were sent to Belfast after it had been bombed in 1941.
- Weather reports were sent secretly to the British.
- 50,000 Irishmen joined the British army.

Very few people were aware of this, even the British ambassador in Dublin. This was to ensure that there was no threat to Irish neutrality.

The Germans were unable to invade Ireland, as Britain would have to be taken over first.

In 1941, German bombers hit the North Strand area of Dublin. Twenty-eight people were killed and 300 houses were damaged.

Houses in the North Strand area of Dublin were destroyed by German bombs in WWII. Some people have suggested that this was a deliberate act, but it may also have been a simple mistake

End of World War II

The war ended in May 1945. De Valera maintained his policy of neutrality to the very end. When Roosevelt, the American president, died he went to the US embassy to express his condolences. Similarly, when Hitler died he went to the German embassy to express his condolences. This angered the Allies. After the war, Churchill stated in a speech that Ireland should be grateful that the Allies had not invaded. De Valera's response was that Ireland had fought Britain for 800 years on her own just as Britain had been on her own against Germany. His speech was highly praised in Ireland.

Results of World War II in Ireland

- Ireland escaped the death and destruction that occurred in Europe.
- The economy suffered greatly and it took several years for it to improve.
- The neutrality policy widened the gap between Northern Ireland and the South, making unification even more unlikely. The British were grateful to the North for its vital role in the war and would support the wishes of the unionist population.

Do you understand these key terms?

the Emergency
Emergency Powers Act
neutral
Local Defence Force
rationing
Compulsory Tillage Scheme
glimmer men
convoys

QUESTIONS

1 What was the period of World War II known as in Ireland?
2 Why was Ireland neutral during World War II?
3 Describe how de Valera dealt with the IRA.
4 What measures did the government take to defend the country?
5 Who was appointed Minister for Supplies?
6 What was the role of the 'glimmer men'?
7 Write a note on relations between Ireland and Britain during World War II.
8 Why did Britain or Germany not invade Ireland during World War II?
9 What did de Valera do in 1945 that showed his neutrality? What was the reaction of the Allies?

EXAM QUESTIONS

1 Give an account of life in Ireland during the Emergency. (HL)
2 Mention two ways in which Irish neutrality favoured the Allies. (HL)

Chapter 8

Ireland 1950–66

Key Learning Objectives

- **How was Ireland governed in the 1950s?**
  - **The First Inter-Party government (1948–51)**
  - **Economic policy**
- **How was Ireland governed in the Lemass years?**
  - **Economic policy**
  - **North–South relations**
  - **Cultural policy**

How was Ireland governed in the 1950s?

The First Inter-Party government (1948–51)

Life did not improve after the war ended in 1945. There were still food shortages, so rationing continued. Unemployment and emigration were high. Fianna Fáil was blamed for all these problems.

Seán MacBride set up a new party called **Clann na Poblachta** in 1946. Its republican policies attracted some followers from Fianna Fáil. When there was a general election in 1948 Fianna Fáil lost power. A **coalition** government called the **First Inter-Party government** replaced them. Its leader was John A. Costello of Fine Gael. The parties in the coalition included Fine Gael, Labour and Clann na Poblachta.

Term

Coalition
A government formed with more than one political party.

Seán McBride. Can you read what is written on the posters behind him?

What were the achievements of the First Inter-Party government?

- The First Inter-Party government declared Ireland a **republic** in 1949. Ireland was now totally independent of Britain and no longer a member of the Commonwealth.
- It secured better prices for agricultural exports in an Anglo-Irish trade agreement.
- It brought electric power to many more rural areas, which helped modernise Irish agriculture.

- It set up the **IDA (Industrial Development Authority)** to support and develop export-led businesses in Ireland. It later changed its role to focus on attracting foreign companies to Ireland.

Noel Browne, Minister for Health

Noel Browne was a member of Clann na Poblachta. As Minister for Health, his priority was to eliminate **tuberculosis** (TB), which killed 3,000 Irish people a year. He built special hospitals, organised mass X-rays and brought in the new BCG vaccine to get rid of the disease. The number of deaths fell to 300 a year.

Browne wanted to introduce free medical care for all mothers and their children up to sixteen years of age. This was called the **Mother and Child Scheme**.

Noel Browne, Minister for Health, with his family

Opposition came from doctors who felt it would end the privacy of the doctor–patient relationship. More importantly, the Catholic Church objected to the scheme. They felt that the state was interfering in private family matters. Other members of the government supported the Catholic Church. Browne resigned. The government lost its majority in the Dáil and it called a general election. Fianna Fáil was returned to power.

Economic policy

The economy struggled during the 1950s. Fianna Fáil's economic policy (1951–54) of imposing tariffs on imports failed to deal with the economic problems. Irish industry was inefficient and was confined to the small, home market.

Factories closed down and unemployment increased. As a result, 50,000 people a year emigrated during the 1950s looking for work.

In 1954, the **Second Inter-Party government** came to power. However, it was no more successful than previous governments in dealing with Ireland's economic problems. In 1957, Fianna Fáil returned to power. There was an atmosphere of despair in the country.

As the result of mass emigration, Irish communities flourish in the USA where the St Patrick's day parade is a big event

PART 3

How was Ireland governed in the Lemass years (1959–66)?

Economic policy

In 1959, Eamon de Valera retired as Taoiseach and Seán Lemass took over. Lemass realised that the economic policy had not worked and that a new approach was needed. He appointed younger ministers such as **Donough O'Malley** and **Jack Lynch**. They were open to new ideas.

A civil servant, **T.K. Whitaker**, drew up a plan to deal with the economic crisis, called the **First Programme for Economic Expansion**.

Did you know?

In 1955, Ireland was admitted to the United Nations. Entry had been blocked by the Soviet Union because of Ireland's neutrality during World War II.

Its main points were:

1 To attract foreign industry into Ireland by:
   - Offering them **grants** to set up here
   - Not taxing their profits
   - Providing the facilities these industries needed by building industrial estates.
2 To give grants to Irish firms to make them more efficient and thus enable them to export their goods.

Seán Lemass was Taoiseach from 1959 to 1966

This strategy was very successful. In the 1960s many firms from America, Britain and Japan came to Ireland. The IDA was given the job of attracting these industries to Ireland.

Employment went up and emigration went down. For the first time since the Famine the population increased in the 1960s.

In 1965, the **Anglo-Irish Free Trade Agreement** was signed. It removed all tariffs on Irish industrial exports to Britain.

Between 1960 and 1968 over 600 firms set up in Ireland.

Free education

Lemass saw that Ireland needed an educated workforce. Only 30 per cent of children went to secondary school in 1960. Donough O'Malley, Minister for Education, announced that school fees for secondary schools would be abolished in 1967. This would mean **free secondary education for all children**. As a result there was a huge increase in the numbers of children attending second level. This was also helped by free school transport for all second-level pupils. These policies helped create a well-educated workforce to fill the new jobs provided by foreign companies.

Term

Grant
A sum of money given by government for a special purpose

North–South relations

Lemass believed that the best chance for Ireland's reunification lay in the South becoming so wealthy that the unionists in the North would want to join. He improved relations between the two states and stopped attacking partition. He accepted the invitation of the new prime minister of Northern Ireland, **Terence O'Neill**, to visit Belfast. They encouraged cooperation in areas such as tourism and agriculture. O'Neill visited Dublin at a later date. Extreme unionists such as Ian Paisley were horrified by this development. The start of the Troubles in 1968 brought an end to this cooperation (see Chapter 11).

Terence O'Neill (left), the prime minister of Northern Ireland, with Seán Lemass

Cultural policy

RTÉ

RTÉ was launched as the national television service in 1961. This led to a change in the attitude of society, as Ireland was exposed to British and American cultures. Political and church leaders had their views challenged. On *The Late Late Show* there were debates on social issues such as contraception and divorce. Advertisements brought about changes in lifestyle and fashion. It has been argued that television was a major factor in the decline of traditional Irish culture. By 1970, over 50 per cent of Irish homes had a television.

The Catholic Church

At the beginning of the 1960s, the Catholic Church dominated Irish society. However, changes were happening within the Church. In 1959, the new pope, John XXIII, called a **Vatican Council** of bishops to modernise the Catholic Church. It brought in many changes, such as the Mass being said in a country's native language. The debate within the Church encouraged ordinary Catholics to question the Church's teachings. This greatly lessened the influence of the Church on Irish society.

In 1966, Lemass retired. He had helped bring about major changes in the Irish economy and in Irish society.

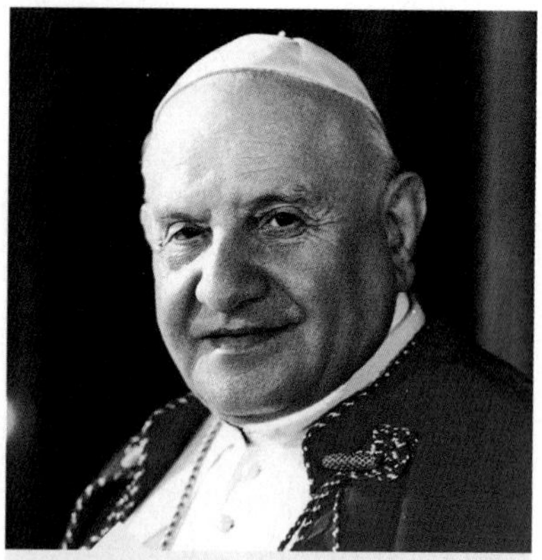

Pope John XXIII

Do you understand these key terms?

Clann na Poblachta
coalition
IDA (Industrial Development Authority)
grant
tuberculosis
Mother and Child Scheme
First Programme for Economic Expansion
Anglo-Irish Free Trade Agreement
Vatican Council

QUESTIONS

1 Why did Lemass appoint younger ministers? Name two of them.
2 What was Lemass' new economic plan called?
3 List three ways in which the economic plan tried to attract foreign industry.
4 Why was the First Programme for Economic Expansion a success? Explain your answer.
5 What was free education? Which minister introduced it? What were the effects of free education?
6 Write an account of North–South relations in the 1960s.
7 How did RTÉ change Irish society?
8 Write a note on changes in the Catholic Church in the 1960s.
9 Write an account of the 1960s in the Republic of Ireland.
10 Give an account of Seán Lemass as Taoiseach, 1959–66.

EXAM QUESTIONS

1 Name two political parties that were part of the First Inter-Party government, 1948–51. (HL)
2 Mention one national project promoted by Dr Noel Bowne as Minister for Health.
3 Give two ways in which Seán Lemass as Taoiseach improved the standard of living in Ireland. (HL)

Chapter 9

Ireland 1966–2000

Key Learning Objectives

- What were the main events of Jack Lynch's first government?
  - The EEC
  - The arms trial
- What economic problems did Ireland face in the 1970s?
- How was Ireland governed in the 1980s?
- How was Ireland governed in the 1990s?

The Jack Lynch years

Joining the European Economic Community (EEC)

In 1966, **Jack Lynch** succeeded Seán Lemass as Taoiseach. Lynch's greatest achievement was to negotiate Ireland's entry into the EEC in 1973. Agriculture benefited most from this as farmers' incomes doubled between 1973 and 1978. This was due to the **Common Agricultural Policy** (CAP), which gave grants to farmers to invest in modern farming methods and machinery. The CAP guaranteed high prices for their produce.

However, industry was unable to compete with foreign companies when tariffs were lowered. Many factories were forced to close.

Ireland benefited from EEC grants to improve roads and education. This laid the foundations for the economic boom of the 1990s (Celtic Tiger). Money was also given to aid the poor regions such as the west of Ireland.

Jack Lynch succeeded Seán Lemass as Taoiseach in 1966. He had two terms in office, 1966–73 and 1977–79

The arms trial

Violence broke out in Northern Ireland in 1969. This was the start of a sustained period of violence called the **Troubles** (see Chapter 11). Protestants attacked Catholic areas in Belfast, burnt their houses and drove them out. Some ministers wanted the Irish army to intervene in the North. However, Lynch refused, as it would create a 'blood bath'.

Lynch sacked two ministers, **Charles Haughey** and **Neil Blaney**. They were accused of using public money to import arms for the IRA. These arms were to be used by nationalists in the North to protect themselves. The ministers were tried for illegally importing arms, but were found not guilty.

Charles Haughey and Neil Blaney leaving the arms trial at the Four Courts

What economic problems did Ireland face in the 1970s?

Fianna Fáil was defeated in the 1973 general election. The party had been in power for sixteen years and people wanted a change. **Liam Cosgrave** led the national coalition government of Fine Gael and the Labour Party.

However, the **Arab-Israeli War** led to a worldwide **oil crisis**. Oil prices soared. This created huge economic problems, such as **inflation** (prices going up) and **unemployment**.

Term

Inflation
The rise in price of goods and services.

To cope with the crisis, the coalition government borrowed money from foreign banks. Ireland's foreign debt became bigger and more people were out of work. As a result of the failure of the coalition government to solve these problems, Fianna Fáil won the general election in 1977.

The new government increased spending, which boosted the economy and reduced unemployment. However, the **second oil crisis**, 1978–79, increased oil prices and caused more unemployment. **Charles Haughey** took over from Lynch as Taoiseach in 1979. He failed to cut back government spending. This resulted in more borrowing, inflation and unemployment.

Queue outside a Social Welfare office in the 1970s

Sunningdale Agreement, 1973

Talks were held between the British government, the Irish government, the Unionists and the SDLP (main nationalist party in Northern Ireland). In December 1973, an agreement was reached. This was called the **Sunningdale Agreement**. (For more information see Chapter 11.)

Ireland in the 1980s

There were many changes in government during the 1980s. However, most of them were unsuccessful in dealing with the economic crisis.

Economic problems

There was a major rise in unemployment, emigration and inflation. As a result, the government had to cut back on spending in areas such as health and education.

In 1987, the new Fianna Fáil government, led by **Charles Haughey**, began to deal successfully with the economic problems facing the country.

- The government, trade unions and employers agreed a plan to help the economy develop. This was called **social partnership.** Workers were given tax cuts in return for low wage increases over the following three years.
- The government introduced very severe **cutbacks** in government spending. This was the beginning of the solution to Ireland's economic problems.

Charles Haughey became leader of the Fianna Fáil government in 1987

Northern Ireland

The Troubles continued, with little sign of a solution. In 1985, Taoiseach **Garret FitzGerald** and British prime minister **Margaret Thatcher** concluded an agreement called the **Anglo-Irish Agreement.** (For more details see Chapter 11, page 325.)

Garret FitzGerald met Margaret Thatcher, prime minister of Great Britain, at the Anglo-Irish summit

Ireland in the 1990s: the Celtic Tiger

The Irish economy grew faster than any other economy in Western Europe from the mid-1990s onwards. In this period Ireland became known as the **Celtic Tiger.** Major computer companies such as Intel and Hewlett-Packard were attracted to set up in Ireland. This investment was due to a well-educated workforce, low corporation tax (see page 404) and the fact that Ireland was a member of the EU.

Term

Celtic Tiger
This was a phrase used to describe Ireland during the period of rapid economic growth that began in the 1990s.

Do you understand these key terms?

Common Agricultural Policy
Troubles
oil crisis
inflation
unemployment
social partnership
Celtic Tiger

QUESTIONS

1. What was Jack Lynch's greatest achievement as Taoiseach?
2. Describe how agriculture benefited from Ireland's entry to the EEC.
3. What were the 'Troubles'?
4. Why did some ministers want to intervene in the North? What happened?
5. Why did Jack Lynch sack two ministers?
6. List two reasons why Fianna Fáil lost the 1973 general election.
7. Which parties were in the national coalition led by Liam Cosgrave?
8. What effects did the oil crisis have on the Irish economy?
9. How did the national coalition deal with the economic crisis? How successful were they?
10. Describe how Fianna Fáil dealt with the economy 1977–80.
11. Write a paragraph on the problems facing the Irish economy in the 1980s.
12. Name the Taoiseach and the British prime minister who signed the Anglo-Irish Agreement in 1985.
13. What measures did the Haughey government take in 1987 to deal with the problems in the economy?

Chapter 10

Northern Ireland 1920–45

James Craig was the first prime minister of Northern Ireland

Key Learning Objectives

- What was Northern Ireland?
- How was Northern Ireland governed under James Craig?
  - Sectarianism
  - The economy
- What was Northern Ireland's role in WWII?

What was Northern Ireland?

In 1920, the **Government of Ireland Act** was passed (see Chapter 4, page 292). A new state was formed called Northern Ireland. There were six Ulster counties in the new state (see map). A Home Rule parliament was set up in Belfast.

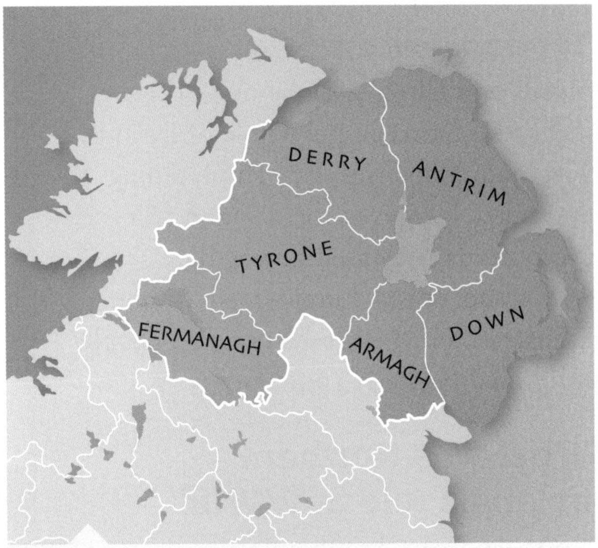

Map of Northern Ireland showing the six counties

What did the unionists get?

1. Northern Ireland was still part of the United Kingdom (UK). Westminster had control over trade and most taxes. Northern Ireland was represented by twelve MPs at Westminster.
2. Northern Ireland had control over local affairs such as health and education.
3. Unionists were permanently in government. They had a 3:1 majority in seats.

What did the nationalists want?

The nationalists who lived in Northern Ireland wanted to be part of the Irish Free State. They supported the Nationalist Party or Sinn Féin. However, as they had no hope of being in government they were hostile to the Northern Ireland state.

How was Northern Ireland governed under James Craig?

James Craig (Lord Craigavon) said that Stormont was 'a Protestant parliament for a Protestant people'. Unionists saw the nationalists as a threat to the Northern Ireland state. They feared that they would be forced into a united Ireland by the Free State helped by the nationalists in the North. This is why they treated the nationalists so harshly.

Sectarianism

Craig was prime minister until 1940. His policies discriminated against Catholics.

- The **Royal Ulster Constabulary** (RUC) was a mainly Protestant police force. They were backed up by the **B-Specials**, which was a reserve police force who were all Protestants. They treated the nationalists very unfairly.
- In local council elections, each part of a city or town was divided into areas called **wards**. Each ward elected councillors. The boundaries of the wards were drawn to ensure that more unionist councillors were elected than nationalists. This is called **gerrymandering**. In Derry, the Catholics were the majority of the population, but the unionists still held the majority of the seats on the city corporation.

Term

Sectarianism
Being treated unfairly because of your religion.

Gerrymandering
Rearranging voting districts for the benefit of a political party.

Nationalists suffered discrimination in areas such as:

1. **Housing:** Protestants rather than Catholics were given local authority housing, because unionists (Protestants) dominated local councils.
2. **Jobs:** Catholics found it hard to get jobs in the civil service or in companies like Harland and Wolff (shipbuilding). This caused high unemployment among nationalists.

The economy 1920–39

North-east Ulster was the only industrial centre in the whole of Ireland. The main industries were shipbuilding and linen. However, the demand for these goods decreased during the 1920s and 1930s. Employment in both industries fell. As a result, 50,000 people emigrated between 1926 and 1937.

Harland and Wolff dockyard in Belfast in the 1930s

What was Northern Ireland's role in WWII?

Northern Ireland took an active part in World War II because it was part of the UK. The war created a boom for its industries which resulted in:

- **No unemployment**. There were many well-paid jobs. 1,500 planes (Shorts' factory) and 170 ships (Harland and Wolff) were built in Belfast.
- A revival of the **linen industry**, because linen was used in making uniforms and parachutes.

A textile worker operating a machine at an Ulster linen factory

PART 3

- Large amounts of money were spent on improving roads and ports. These were needed to cater for the huge numbers of American troops in Northern Ireland.
- American troops used the North as a training ground after they entered the war in 1941. They were preparing for D-Day.
- British and American ships used Derry as a base to patrol the North Atlantic. This allowed vital supplies from America to arrive in the UK.

The bombing of Belfast

In April and May 1941, the Luftwaffe (German airforce) bombed Belfast. About 1,100 people were killed and over 56,000 houses were destroyed. De Valera sent fire brigades from Dublin to help put out the fires. The prime minister, John Andrews, was blamed for the poor defences. He was eventually forced to resign in 1943 and Sir Basil Brooke (Lord Brookeborough) replaced him.

The bombing of Belfast was also known as the Belfast Blitz

What were the results of Northern Ireland's role in WWII?

1. The contribution of Northern Ireland to the war effort meant that the link with Britain was strengthened.
2. World War II widened the gap between the North and the South, as the South had been neutral during the war.

Do you understand these key terms?

sectarianism
Royal Ulster Constabulary
B-Specials
gerrymandering
Belfast Blitz

QUESTIONS

1. What were the terms of the Government of Ireland Act?
2. Why did unionists want a Home Rule parliament in Northern Ireland?
3. Who was the first prime minister of Northern Ireland?
4. Why were the nationalists treated harshly by the unionists?
5. What is gerrymandering?
6. What were the main industries in Northern Ireland?
7. Why did these industries suffer a fall in demand for their products?
8. Why did the war create a boom in industry?
9. Write an account of the bombing of Belfast in 1941.
10. What were the effects of Northern Ireland's involvement in the war?

Chapter 11

Northern Ireland 1945–2000

Key Learning Objectives

- What was the welfare state and what were its effects?
- What was the civil rights campaign and how did the Protestants react to it?
- What were the main events of the Troubles?
- What were the main terms of:
  - The Sunningdale Agreement, 1973
  - The Anglo-Irish Agreement, 1985
  - The Good Friday Agreement, 1997

  and how successful were they?

What was the welfare state?

After the war there was a general election in Britain in 1945 and the Labour Party won. They introduced the **welfare state**. This meant that the state provided to all citizens:

1 Free **healthcare** (National Health Service)
2 Free secondary **education** for all children
3 Better old-age **pensions** and unemployment pay.

Thousands of new houses were built in Northern Ireland.

What were its effects?

The welfare state had a major effect on the lives of poor people, both Catholic and Protestant.

- They had decent housing and healthcare.
- The children of poor families gained most. If they passed an exam at eleven (the 'eleven–plus') they got a free grammar school place. This would give them a good chance of going to university. Catholics and Protestants benefited equally.
- The free education system produced a new type of leadership for the nationalists. Educated Catholics were not prepared to accept being second-class citizens. This created the **civil rights movement** in the 1960s, with leaders like **John Hume**.

As a result of the welfare state, both Catholics and Protestants had a much higher standard of living than people in the Republic. Many Catholics were not prepared to give up all the advantages of living in the North for the sake of reunification. They began to change their views of the Northern Ireland state.

Lemass meets O'Neill

In 1963 **Terence O'Neill** succeeded Lord Brookeborough as prime minister of Northern Ireland. He wanted relations with the Catholics to get better. He also improved relations with the Republic. He had two meetings in Dublin and Belfast with the Taoiseach, Seán Lemass. More extreme Protestants such as the **Orange Order** and Ian Paisley were horrified by O'Neill's soft approach towards the Catholics. They were afraid that this would endanger the North's link with Britain.

What was the civil rights campaign?

Nationalists were disappointed that O'Neill did not end discrimination against them. In 1967, the **Northern Ireland Civil Rights Association** (NICRA) was formed. Its aim was to end discrimination against Catholics. They demanded:

- One person, one vote in local elections
- An end to discrimination in jobs and houses.

They staged peaceful marches to highlight their aims. Major figures in the campaign for civil rights included Gerry Fitt, John Hume and Bernadette Devlin.

How did the Protestants react to it?

Often, when there was a NICRA march, **Ian Paisley** organised a counter-demonstration. This resulted in riots. The RUC and B-Specials attacked the civil rights marchers. Pictures of RUC attacks on peaceful marchers were shown on TV throughout the world. This embarrassed the British government. They forced the Unionists to agree to civil rights for the Catholics.

Demonstrators, including John Hume (second from right), during a civil rights march protest in Derry

Protestant loyalists, members of the Orange Order, parade in the streets of Belfast

Bernadette Devlin, a major campaigner for civil rights, addresses a civil rights rally

Discrimination ended in areas such as housing and in local elections (gerrymandering). The B-Specials were disbanded. O'Neill was forced to resign when he lost the support of his party because because he had to accept these reforms.

Ian Paisley (left)

The Troubles

Term

Apprentice Boys
A society that commemorates the siege of Derry in 1689, in which the Protestants faced a Jacobite (Catholic) army.

The Troubles began in 1969:

- Rioting broke out in the Catholic Bogside area of Derry. This was caused by a march by the **Apprentice Boys** in Derry. The Catholics blocked off the Bogside area, using barricades. The **Battle of the Bogside** took place between the police and Catholics.
- In Belfast, Catholic areas were attacked by Protestant mobs helped by the police. Many Catholics were burnt out of their houses and many went south to the Republic.
- Northern Ireland was on the brink of civil war.
- As a result, the British army was sent in to protect Catholic areas from Protestant attacks.

Emergence of the Provisional IRA

The IRA had not defended Catholic areas in Belfast and this resulted in a split in the IRA.

- The **Official IRA** was socialist and favoured peaceful methods.
- The **Provisional IRA** wanted a united Ireland, using violence.

Battle of the Bogside. Who do you think are in the foreground of this picture, and what are they wearing?

The Provisionals (**Provos**) planted bombs and shot at the British army and the RUC. British soldiers were heavy-handed when searching Catholic homes for arms. As a result Catholics turned against the British army.

Two Protestant paramilitary groups, the **UVF** (Ulster Volunteer Force) and the **UDA** (Ulster Defence Association), began to attack Catholics. The death toll rose dramatically.

Internment

In 1971, the prime minister, Brian Faulkner, introduced **internment** in an effort to stop the violence. Over 300 people were imprisoned without trial; all of them were nationalists. However, violence increased, as did support for the IRA.

Bloody Sunday, 1972

A march to protest against internment took place in Derry on Sunday, 30 January, 1972. Thirteen unarmed Catholics were shot dead by the British army. This became known as **Bloody Sunday**. As a result, violence increased. In response, the British government imposed **direct rule** from Westminster. The Stormont parliament was suspended. **William Whitelaw** became the first Secretary of State for Northern Ireland.

Term

Direct rule
Northern Ireland was ruled directly from Westminster.

A young Catholic rioter throws a stone at a British armoured jeep in Derry in March 1972 during a rally protesting against the events of Bloody Sunday

The Sunningdale Agreement, 1973

The British hoped direct rule would not last very long. They began talks with the Unionist Party, the SDLP (the new nationalist party in Northern Ireland) and the Irish government. In December 1973, an agreement was reached. This was called the **Sunningdale Agreement**. Its terms were:

- To set up a **power-sharing government**. This meant that there was a coalition government between the Unionists and the SDLP. Brian Faulkner (Unionist leader) was prime minister and Gerry Fitt (SDLP leader) was deputy prime minister.
- To set up a **Council of Ireland** consisting of politicians from both sides of the border, who would consult on Northern policies.

Most unionists opposed sharing power with the nationalists. In 1974, Protestant workers staged a general strike organised by the Ulster Workers' Council that paralysed Northern Ireland's economy. This resulted in the fall of the power-sharing government. The violence continued throughout the rest of the 1970s.

Protestant workers opposed to the Sunningdale Agreement went on strike. Here they are blockading Stormont

PART 3

QUESTIONS

1 What was the welfare state? How did it affect Northern Ireland?
2 What was the long-term effect of free education for nationalists?
3 Why did extreme unionists oppose O'Neill?
4 Why were nationalists disappointed in O'Neill?
5 How did O'Neill improve relations with the Irish Republic?
6 What were the aims of the Northern Ireland Civil Rights Association?
7 What was the reaction of Paisley and the RUC to NICRA's marches?
8 What effect did internment have?
9 What happened on Bloody Sunday?
10 Who was the first Secretary of State for Northern Ireland?
11 Write an account of the Sunningdale Agreement. Why did it fail?

EXAM QUESTIONS

› Give an account of
(a) Political developments in Northern Ireland, 1963–71
(b) The Civil Rights Movement in Northern Ireland.

The hunger strikes

IRA prisoners in the **Maze Prison** (H-Blocks) demanded that they be treated differently from criminals. They wanted to be treated as **political prisoners** (with political status). They also wanted to wear their own clothes. The British prime minister, Margaret Thatcher, refused these demands. As a result, some of the prisoners went on **hunger strike** in 1980. **Bobby Sands** was the first. The British did not give in. Bobby Sands died after sixty-six days on hunger strike. Nine other prisoners died later. Eventually the hunger strikes were called off. The IRA prisoners didn't get political status. However, there was a huge increase in support for the IRA.

Bobby Sands, who died on hunger strike

Anglo-Irish Agreement, 1985

In 1985, the Irish government, led by **Garret FitzGerald,** persuaded the British prime minister, Margaret Thatcher, that the best hope of ending violence in Northern Ireland was to involve the Irish government in bringing about a solution. This resulted in the **Anglo-Irish Agreement**. The main terms were:

- The Irish Republic had a role in the internal affairs of Northern Ireland.
- The Irish Republic agreed that unification would only happen if a majority of people in Northern Ireland voted for it.

Unionists protested; they didn't want the Irish Republic having any say in the internal affairs of Northern Ireland. However, the British government stood firm and ignored the unionist demonstrations.

The agreement laid the foundation for further progress in Northern Ireland. The decision of British governments to support this agreement helped bring about the IRA ceasefire in 1994.

The bombing of the Grand Hotel in Brighton by the IRA in 1984. Margaret Thatcher had a narrow escape

Good Friday Agreement, 1998

In 1997, the Labour Party won the general election in Britain. The new prime minister, **Tony Blair,** was committed to bringing peace to Northern Ireland. He was helped by the fact that the Unionist Party leader, **David Trimble,** was willing to talk to Republicans. These men, helped by John Hume (SDLP), Gerry Adams (Sinn Féin) and Bertie Ahern (Taoiseach), succeeded in reaching an agreement on Good Friday, 1998.

The main terms of the **Good Friday Agreement** were:

- An elected Assembly in Northern Ireland
- A government elected by the Assembly in which the Ulster Unionists, Sinn Féin and the SDLP agreed to share power
- Articles 2 and 3 to be removed from the Republic's constitution (these claimed control over the six counties of Northern Ireland). This was accepted in a referendum.

Violence decreased dramatically. In 2007, the IRA finally 'put their guns beyond use'. **Ian Paisley** (Democratic Unionist Party) was elected First Minister (prime minister) and **Martin McGuinness** (Sinn Féin) was elected Deputy First Minister. A power-sharing government was formed.

Ian Paisley and Gerry Adams sit side by side in 2007 to announce the beginning of the power-sharing government

Do you understand these key terms?

welfare state
civil rights movement
Orange Order
NICRA
the Troubles
Apprentice Boys
Battle of the Bogside
Provisional IRA
UVF
UDA
internment
Bloody Sunday
power-sharing
hunger strike

QUESTIONS

1 Why did the Maze prisoners go on hunger strike?
2 What was the reaction of the British government?
3 How many hunger strikers died?
4 What was the effect of these deaths?
5 Why did the British agree to the Anglo-Irish Agreement of 1985?
6 What were the terms of the agreement?
7 What was the long-term effect of the agreement?
8 Name five people involved in the negotiation of the Good Friday Agreement.
9 What were the terms of the Good Friday Agreement?
10 What happened in 2007?

EXAM QUESTIONS

1 Give one reason why unionists opposed the Anglo-Irish Agreement, 1985. (HL)
2 Write an account of a poltical leader in Northern Ireland after 1920. (HL)

People in History

Write about a named political leader in Ireland, North or South, during the period 1922–85.

Use the plan below as a guide.

Early life

Main aims

Named leader

Results of these policies

Policies

Tip

Remember to give the leader's name and the name of his party.

TIMELINE

PART 3

Section 12

International Relations in the Twentieth-Century

Chapter 1

Europe after World War I

Key Learning Objectives

- Why was there a communist Revolution in Russia in 1917?
- What were the aims of the Allies at the Paris Peace Conference?
- What was agreed in the Treaty of Versailles?
- What were the problems with the treaty?

The period between 1920 and 1945 was one of the most dramatic in history. It saw the growth of fascism and communism and the biggest war ever – World War II. In this part of the course we will look at the following topics:

- The rise of fascism in Italy and Germany
- The drift to war in the 1930s
- The main events during World War II

To help us understand the background to these events, we must first look at World War I and the peace treaty agreed after the war called the **Treaty of Versailles.**

Term

World war
A war fought by a large number of countries on a number of different continents. World War I was fought in Europe, Asia and Africa.

Central Powers	The Allies
Germany	Britain
Austria-Hungary	France
Turkey	Russia (defeated in 1917) Italy (joined the war in 1915) USA (joined the war in 1917)

World War I

World War I started in August 1914 and lasted until November 1918. The table on the right shows the two groups of countries involved.

In the west soldiers lived in trenches and fought in very poor conditions. Two of the most famous battles were **Verdun** and the **Somme.** Over 10 million soldiers were killed during the war and countless others were wounded.

German soldiers in their trench await an attack. Machine guns made it very difficult for soldiers to advance. New weapons such as planes, tanks and poison gas were widely used during World War I

Why was there a communist Revolution in Russia in 1917?

During the war Russia suffered a number of heavy defeats at the hands of the Germans. Many Russians blamed the government of **Tsar Nicholas II**. In February 1917, he was overthrown after a revolt in the capital, St Petersburg. The new government made a major mistake by continuing the unpopular war against Germany. This provided an opportunity for **Vladimir Lenin,** leader of the **Bolshevik Party**. He believed in **communism.** He called for an end to the war, better conditions for the workers and for land to be given to peasants.

Term

Tsar
Title of the emperor of Russia.

Bolshevik Party
The party led by Lenin. It was later renamed the Communist Party.

In October 1917, Lenin led a successful revolution and he became the ruler of Russia. His government ended the war with Germany. He allowed workers to take control of their factories and gave land to the peasants. Russia was now called the **Union of Soviet Socialist Republics** (**USSR**). Many called it the **Soviet Union** for short. The new government was brutal. Hundreds of thousands of its opponents were executed, including the Tsar and his family.

Across Europe, reactions to the revolution in Russia were very different:

- Many workers hoped that they could bring **communism** to their own country. Communist parties gained a lot of support.
- On the other hand, many people feared that there might be a communist revolution in their country.

As we shall see in later chapters, this fear would contribute to the growth of fascism.

Vladimir Lenin (1870–1924)

Term

Communism
A political movement which aims to create an equal society, where all property is owned by workers and peasants.

Soviets
Workers' and soldiers' councils that controlled the cities in Russia in 1917.

Did you know?

As the war ended a terrible form of the flu spread throughout the world. Between 1918 and 1919, it infected over one-fifth of the world's population and killed between 50 and 100 million people. Known as the Spanish flu, it was the deadliest outbreak of disease ever!

What were the aims of the Allies at the Paris Peace Conference?

World War I ended in 1918 when the Central Powers surrendered. The victorious Allies met in Paris to draw up a peace **treaty**. The Allies argued over how to treat Germany:

- The French, led by **Georges Clemenceau,** looked for revenge. They wanted to make sure they could never be attacked by Germany again. They also demanded that Germany compensate France for the cost of the war.
- The USA did not agree with the French. They did not want a harsh treaty. The US president, **Woodrow Wilson,** came up with the **Fourteen Points** programme, which set out the basis for a post-war peace. His main aim was to set up an international organisation called the **League of Nations.** He hoped this would preserve world peace in the future.
- Britain wanted to weaken the German navy and to make Germany pay for the war. The British Prime Minister, **David Lloyd George,** felt that some of the French demands were too extreme.
- The Italians, led by **Vittorio Orlando,** wanted the land in the Austrian Empire that they had been promised for joining the war in 1915. However, the USA said that it was not fair to give some of this land to the Italians as the people living there were not Italian.

Term

Treaty
An agreement between countries. The contents are called **articles**.

League of Nations
An international organisation that was set up to preserve world peace.

The Big Four at the peace conference, from left to right: Vittorio Orlando, David Lloyd George, Georges Clemenceau and Woodrow Wilson

The Treaty of Versailles

By June 1919, after much discussion, the Treaty of Versailles was ready. The Germans protested, but were threatened with war if they did not accept it. On 28 June 1919, they reluctantly signed in the Hall of Mirrors in the Palace of Versailles near Paris.

What was agreed in the Treaty of Versailles?

- The German army was limited to 100,000 men. Germany was not allowed to have **conscription**. It was forbidden to have tanks or planes and its navy was greatly reduced in size.
- Germany was not permitted to station troops in the **Rhineland** – a region that bordered France.
- As the map shows, Germany lost land to France, Poland and Denmark. The German colonies in Africa and Asia were taken by the Allies.
- Austria was not allowed to join with Germany, even though it wanted to do this.
- The **War Guilt Clause** blamed Germany for causing the war. The Allies used this to get money out of the Germans. They had to pay compensation to the Allies known as **reparations**. The amount was set at £6.6 billion.
- The **League of Nations** was set up to keep the peace and prevent war in the future.

Term

Conscription
A law which forces all men to serve in the armed forces for a period, usually after they leave school.

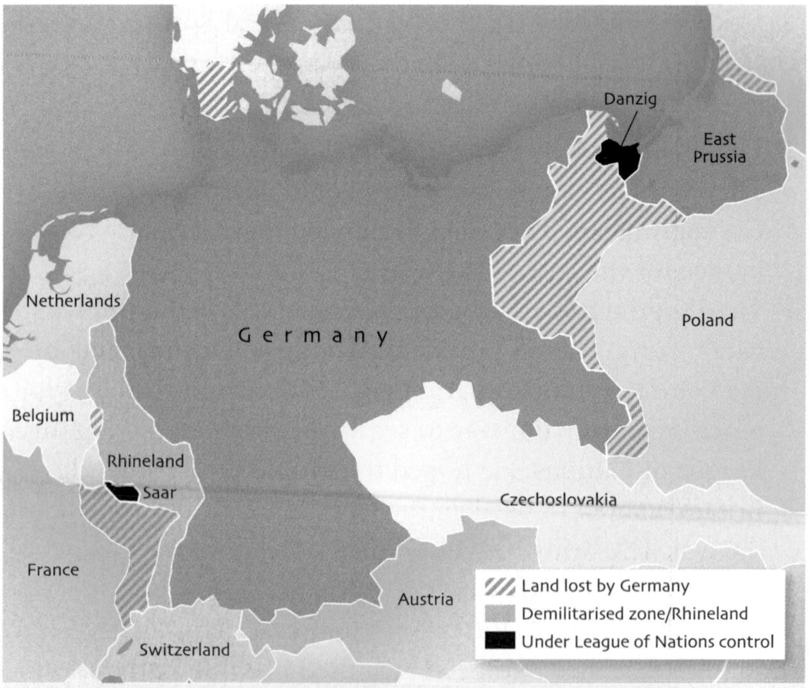

Land lost by Germany as a result of the Treaty of Versailles

PART 3

What were the problems with the treaty?

The Allied leaders hoped that the treaty would help to prevent war breaking out in the future. This was not to be the case. There were a lot of problems with the peace settlement that would cause unrest later. Here are some of the most important problems:

1 The Germans were outraged by the treaty. They attacked the loss of land, especially to Poland. They also pointed out that millions of Germans were living in countries outside Germany, such as Czechoslovakia. They were very annoyed by the War Guilt Clause, which they felt was unfair. They hoped that one day the treaty would be torn up. In Chapter 3 we will learn how dissatisfaction with the treaty was to contribute to the growth in support for the Nazis.

2 The Italians were also unhappy. They were angered that Italy had not got all the land it had been promised for entering the war. Many felt they had been cheated. In Chapter 2 we will learn how this unhappiness helped to bring Benito Mussolini to power.

3 The **US Senate** rejected the Treaty. Therefore, the USA did not join the League of Nations. As a result the League became a weak organisation. It lacked an army and failed completely to stop Hitler or Mussolini in the 1930s.

Do you understand these key terms?

world war	**treaty**
communism	**League of Nations**
tsar	**conscription**
Bolshevik Party	**War Guilt Clause**
soviet	**reparations**

QUESTIONS

1 How long did World War I last?
2 Why was the tsar overthrown in Russia?
3 Explain how Lenin came to power in Russia in 1917.
4 How did the French and the USA disagree over the treatment of Germany?
5 Name three countries that gained land at Germany's expense.
6 What did the Treaty of Versailles say about the German army?
7 Write an account of two of the following:
(a) The aims of the leaders at the Paris Peace Conference
(b) The main points of the Treaty of Versailles
(c) Reaction to the treaty in Germany and Italy
8 Do you think the Treaty of Versailles was too harsh? Give two reasons to support your answer.

Research topic

Choose a topic from World War I. It could be an important battle, a famous general, conditions in the trenches, or a new weapon that was used.

Chapter 2

Mussolini's Italy 1922–45

Key Learning Objectives

- Why was fascism popular after World War I?
- How did Mussolini come to power?
- How did Mussolini become a dictator?
- What was life like in Mussolini's Italy?
- What was Mussolini's Foreign Policy?

In 1922, **Benito Mussolini** became the first fascist ruler in Europe. Before we examine his career we need to look at what fascists believed in and why their ideas became so popular after World War I.

Why was fascism popular after World War I?

Fascists believed in a strong ruler or **dictator** who would bring order and control. **Fascism** drew a lot of its support from ex-soldiers, businessmen and landowners. These people knew that if the fascists came to power they would ban other parties, not allow political criticism and end free elections.

There are a number of reasons that explain why people supported fascism in Italy and Germany:

- Many Germans and Italians were unhappy with the Treaty of Versailles. People were ready to listen to politicians who criticised the peace treaty.
- Many people believed that their countries should be powerful. This was called **nationalism**. Mussolini and Hitler promised to make Italy and Germany great powers.
- There were a lot of economic problems. A great many people were out of work, especially in Germany, after the **Wall Street Crash** of 1929 (see page 300). There was a belief that **democracy** had failed to deal with the serious economic problems.
- People were afraid of communism. This was a growing popular movement in both countries. Some feared that a democratic government would not be able to stop a communist revolution. Only a dictator could take the ruthless measures necessary to crush communism.

Term

Dictator
A person who controls a country and makes all of the major decisions.

Fascism
A poltical system where a strong ruler has complete control over a country and there are no elections.

Nationalism
Strong loyalty to your own country, often with the belief that it should become more powerful.

Democracy
A political system where the government is chosen by the people in an election.

Mussolini – the inventor of fascism

The Italian fascist symbol. The word fascism comes from a bundle of rods called a *fasces*. It was a symbol of authority in Ancient Rome

The man who invented fascism was the Italian journalist and politician, **Benito Mussolini**. He was born in central Italy in 1883. He was a socialist to begin with, but the outbreak of World War I changed his views. He wanted Italy to join the war, and set up his own newspaper, *Il Popolo d'Italia* (The People of Italy) to call for Italian involvement in the war.

After the war, Italian governments faced a number of problems:

- Many people were out of work and there were a lot of strikes. Some workers hoped to stage a communist revolution.
- There was also widespread unhappiness with the peace treaty that ended World War I. Most Italians believed that they should have received more land.

Mussolini saw his chance to enter politics. In Milan he set up his own political party called the **Fasci Italiani di Combattimento** (the Italian Fighting League). At first it had little support and won no seats in the 1919 **general election**.

Term

General election
National vote for a new government usually held every four or five years.

How did Mussolini come to power?

Over the next few years Mussolini's support rose dramatically. There were a number of reasons for this:

- His criticism of the peace treaty and his desire to make Italy a great power were popular among former soldiers.
- After the war there were a number of weak **coalition** governments that failed to tackle Italy's problems. Mussolini promised to end political chaos and bring order to Italy.
- For many Italians, Mussolini and his supporters seemed to be the only defence against a communist revolution. Mussolini had uniformed followers called the *squadristi*. They were nicknamed the **Blackshirts** because of the colour of their uniform. They fought street battles with communists throughout Italy.

Mussolini takes part in the March on Rome. Why are so many of his followers wearing uniforms?

Mussolini's anti-communism caused many leading businessmen to finance his party. In 1921, Mussolini changed the name of his party to the **National Fascist Party** and he was elected to parliament.

PART 3

The march on Rome

In October 1922, Mussolini announced that unless he was appointed prime minister his followers would march on Rome and seize power. Hoping to avoid civil war, **King Victor Emmanuel III** refused to use troops to crush the fascists. Instead he appointed Mussolini as prime minister. At the age of 39 Mussolini was the youngest person ever to become prime minister of Italy. He and his followers then marched into Rome.

How did Mussolini become a dictator?

Although Mussolini was now prime minister his government contained a large number of non-fascists. Over the next few years he gradually took control of Italy and became a dictator. Here is how he did it:

- In 1923, the **Acerbo Law** was passed. It said that the party that got the most votes would receive two-thirds of the seats in parliament.
- The following year, 1924, Mussolini's National Fascist Party won the election and now dominated the Italian parliament.
- Soon after the election a leading socialist, **Giacomo Matteotti**, was murdered. Many people thought that Mussolini was involved in the murder. Mussolini was in trouble but the king refused to remove him from power.
- Mussolini announced his intention to establish a dictatorship and in 1926 all other political parties were banned.
- A secret police was set up and thousands of his political opponents were arrested. He was now called **Il Duce** (the leader).

Term

Propaganda
Use of posters, film, radio and newspapers to present news and information that portrays an event or person in a particular way for political purposes.

What was life like in Mussolini's Italy?

Despite the brutality of some of Mussolini's followers, his government was not nearly as cruel as Adolf Hitler's or Joseph Stalin's (see page 341). Before 1939 it seems that he was genuinely popular with most Italians. This was helped by his use of **propaganda**. Posters, newspapers and films portrayed Mussolini as tirelessly working for the good of the Italian people.

The young were taught to be loyal to him. Boys were encouraged to be soldiers and girls were expected to be good mothers. Boys were encouraged to attend after-school youth movements such as the **Balilla** that was set up for eight- to fourteen-year-olds.

A number of popular measures were introduced. New motorways, called *autostrade*, were built. The vast **Pontine Marshes** outside Rome were drained and new towns built there. Mussolini's greatest achievement was the understanding he reached with the Catholic Church.

Two propaganda pictures. What image of Mussolini's Italy does each picture try to create?

What were the Lateran Pacts?

Since 1870, there had been a dispute between Italian governments and the Catholic Church. This was over the independence of the pope in Rome. Mussolini knew that if he solved this dispute it would gain him great support, as most Italians were Catholic. The Church preferred fascism to communism and was prepared to talk to Mussolini.

The agreement reached was called the **Lateran Pacts**, named after the palace in Rome where it was negotiated. Under the agreement:

- The **Vatican City**, ruled by the pope, was recognised as independent.
- **Catholicism** became the official religion of Italy.

As a result of the agreement, Mussolini's popularity soared both in Italy and among Catholics throughout the world.

QUESTIONS

1. Give two reasons why people supported fascism after World War I.
2. What problems did Italy face after World War I?
3. Why did many Italians support Mussolini's party after 1919?
4. Who were the *squadristi*?
5. Why was the March on Rome an important event?
6. What was the Acerbo Law?
7. List two measures Mussolini took to establish a dictatorship.
8. What message did the fascists give to (a) boys and (b) girls?
9. What were the Lateran Pacts of 1929 and why were they important for Mussolini?

What was Mussolini's foreign policy?

Mussolini wanted to make Italy a great power. He hoped to recreate the glories of Ancient Rome. He once said, 'I want to make Italy great, respected and feared.' When he came to power he got Yugoslavia to agree to hand over a disputed town. He then took a hard line in a dispute with Greece. These actions were popular with the Italian people.

At first he was an opponent of **Adolf Hitler**. In 1934, he rushed troops to the Austrian border to stop a Nazi takeover of that country.

The invasion of Abyssinia

Mussolini wanted an empire in Africa, like Britain and France. In 1935, he invaded **Abyssinia** (modern-day Ethiopia). He wanted to show the world how powerful Italy was. His action was greeted with great enthusiasm in Italy.

There was a major problem for Mussolini, however: Abyssinia was a member of the League of Nations. Mussolini ignored League demands that he withdraw his troops. The League called on its members not to trade with Italy. This response annoyed Mussolini and he now turned to Hitler as an ally.

In October 1936, Italy and Germany formed an alliance that was called the **Rome–Berlin Axis**. Relations between the countries were strengthened with the **Pact of Steel**, signed in 1939.

Italy and World War II

Mussolini had exaggerated how powerful the Italian army was. When war broke out in 1939, Italy was too weak to support Germany. In June 1940, as France was about to surrender, Italy declared war. Italian troops did not perform that well during the war. Mussolini's armies attacked British forces in North Africa and invaded Greece. In both cases, they suffered crushing defeats. German troops had to be sent to rescue the Italians.

In 1943, the Italians and Germans in North Africa were defeated. Allied troops invaded Italy. Now very unpopular, Mussolini was removed from power by the king. Italy changed sides and joined the Allies.

Mussolini now ruled the north of Italy. This was called the **Salo Republic**. He was no longer a mighty dictator, but needed the support of the Germans to stay in power.

Near the end of the war, in April 1945, he tried to flee to Switzerland, but he was captured. He was executed along with his mistress. Their bodies were displayed in a public square in Milan. With his death the fascist movement ended in Italy.

This is an Italian World War II poster published by the government of Mussolini's Italian Social Republic (Salo). It says: 'Here are the liberators' and it shows the Statue of Liberty as an angel of death, with Italian cities destroyed after US bombing'.

TIMELINE Mussolini's Italy

1919	Formation of the first Fascist Party
1921	Mussolini won thirty-five seats in parliament
1922	Mussolini appointed PM after the March on Rome
1924	Fascists won the general election. Murder of Matteotti
1926	All political parties except the Fascist Party banned
1929	Lateran Pacts signed with the Catholic Church
1935	Italy invaded Abyssinia
1936	Rome–Berlin Axis signed with Hitler
1940	Italy entered World War II
1943	Mussolini removed from power. Ruled north of Italy for the Germans
1945	Mussolini captured and executed

QUESTIONS

1. What were Mussolini's main foreign policy aims?
2. Between 1933 and 1935 what was Mussolini's attitude to Hitler?
3. Why did the Italians invade Abyssinia in 1935?
4. What was the reaction of the League of Nations to the invasion?
5. Name the two agreements that Mussolini reached with Hitler.
6. How did the Italian army perform in World War II?
7. Why was Mussolini removed from power in 1945?

Do you understand these key terms?

fascism
dictator
nationalism
democracy
general election
Blackshirts
Acerbo Law
propaganda
Balilla
Lateran Pacts
Rome–Berlin Axis
Salo Republic

SOURCE QUESTION

› Read the following account of the death of Mussolini from the *Guardian* newspaper, 30 April 1945, and answer the questions that follow.

> Mussolini, with mistress, Clara Petacci, and twelve members of his Cabinet, were executed by partisans [soldiers opposed to Mussolini] in a village on Lake Como yesterday afternoon, after being arrested in an attempt to cross the Swiss frontier. The bodies were brought to Milan last night. A partisan knocked at my door early this morning to tell me the news.
>
> We drove out to the working-class quarter of Loreto and there were the bodies… under the same fence against which one year ago fifteen partisans had been shot by their own countrymen.
>
> Mussolini was caught yesterday at Dongo, Lake Como, driving by himself in a car with his uniform covered by a German greatcoat. He was driving in a column of German cars to escape observation but was recognised by an Italian Customs guard. The others were caught in a neighbouring village.
>
> This is the first conspicuous [obvious] example of mob justice in liberated Italy. The opinion expressed this morning by the partisan Commander-in-Chief, General Cadorna, was that such incidents in themselves were regrettable. Nevertheless, in this case he considered the execution a good thing, since popular indignation [anger] against the Fascists demanded some satisfaction.

(a) Who was executed along with Mussolini?
(b) How had Mussolini been arrested?
(c) Where were the bodies taken to after the executions?
(d) Where had Mussolini been caught and how was he disguised?
(e) What was the attitude of the Commander-in-Chief of the partisans to the execution?

EXAM QUESTIONS

1 Explain two of the following terms relating to Mussolini's rule in Italy, 1922–1943: Acerbo Law; Blackshirts; Lateran Treaty; Rome–Berlin Axis.

2 Write an account of two of the following:
(a) How Mussolini established his dictatorship in Italy
(b) Mussolini's foreign policy 1922–39
(c) Italy and World War II.

3 'Until Italy entered the war Mussolini was a popular ruler of Italy.' Do you agree? Give three reasons to support your answer.

Chapter 3

Nazi Germany 1933–39

Key Learning Objectives

- How did Adolf Hitler come to power?
- Why was communism so popular in the 1930s?
- How did Stalin control the Soviet Union?
- How did Hitler become a dictator?
- How did Hitler maintain power?
- How did the Nazis treat the Jews?

What was the Weimar Republic?

Term

Weimar Germany
The name given to the period of German history between 1918 and 1933.

After World War I, German politicians met at the town of **Weimar** to draw up a new democratic constitution. Germany became a republic. The new government had no choice but to sign the Treaty of Versailles in 1919.

However, there were a lot of people who did not like the new government:

- Some Germans did not like democracy and wanted a return to the good old days before the war when Germany was ruled by Kaiser (emperor) Wilhelm II.
- Many blamed the government for accepting the treaty and plotted to overthrow it.
- There was also a shortage of food and large numbers of people had no jobs. Communists wanted to copy events in Russia and stage a revolution in Germany.

Between 1919 and 1923, there were a number of unsuccessful attempts to overthrow the government. The last one was led by **Adolf Hitler.**

How did Adolf Hitler come to power?

Adolf Hitler was born in **Braunau am Inn,** Austria, in 1889. After school he went to **Vienna.** Vienna had a large Jewish population and Hitler probably developed his hatred for the Jewish people while living there.

In 1913, he moved to Germany and joined the army when World War I broke out. He was a brave soldier and was awarded the **Iron Cross First Class.**

On the right is Hitler during World War I with his pet dog

Hitler had been shocked by the German defeat in World War I. He did not believe that Germany had really been defeated, but had been betrayed by Jews and communists. He also attacked the politicians for signing the Treaty of Versailles.

Hitler speaking to an attentive crowd in 1934

The formation of the Nazi Party

After the war, Hitler joined the **German Workers Party**. He soon discovered that he had a gift for **oratory** (public speaking). He soon became the leader of the party. In 1920, he renamed the party the **National Socialist German Workers Party** (NSDAP). It became known as the **Nazi Party**.

Hitler copied a lot of ideas from Mussolini's Fascist Party:

- He had followers who were called the **Sturm Abteilung** (SA) or the **Brownshirts** on account of their brown uniforms. A smaller group, called the **Schtuzstaffel** (SS), was formed to act as a personal bodyguard for Hitler.
- He also took the title of **Der Führer** (the leader) and a right-arm salute was adopted.
- The party held marches and rallies and fought street battles with its political opponents.

The Beer Hall Putsch

In 1923, Germany was close to economic collapse. The government stopped paying reparations to the French. The French then occupied the **Ruhr**, which was the industrial centre of Germany. This led to a massive rise in prices (**hyperinflation**). Very quickly over one in five Germans had no job.

Hoping to take advantage of the situation, Hitler decided to copy Mussolini and try to seize power. His attempted rebellion in the ciy of Munich (the Beer Hall Putsch) failed. He was sentenced to five years in prison. While in prison he wrote his autobiography, *Mein Kampf* (My Struggle).

In this book, he outlined his main political aims:

- Tear up the Treaty of Versailles and make Germany a great power.
- Create a Third Reich (empire) that united all German speakers throughout Europe.
- Destroy communism and socialism.
- Remove all Jews from Germany. He believed that the Germans were a master race and the Jews were the enemies of the German race.

In 1924, Hitler came out of prison. The economy was now doing well. There was little support for Hitler's extreme views. In the 1928 election, the National Socialists only won twelve seats in the **Reichstag** (German parliament).

Why did support for Hitler increase?

The fortunes of the Nazi Party soon changed dramatically. How did this happen?

- In 1929 the **Wall Street Crash** occurred (see page 300). Stocks and shares suddenly lost value in the USA. Many businesses closed and this led to the **Great Depression.** In Germany, this caused unemployment to rise sharply.
- The government failed to deal with the crisis, and by 1932 there were over 6 million people without a job in Germany.
- Many Germans lost faith in democracy. They turned to the two extreme parties: the Nazis and the communists. Support for both parties grew quickly.
- The growth of the communists scared many Germans and they voted for the Nazis. The Nazi Party won 107 seats in the 1930 election. This was their first major success in elections.
- Political violence became very common as the Nazis and the communists fought each other on the streets.
- Hitler made many speeches throughout Germany, further increasing support for the party. In the July election of 1932, the Nazi Party became the largest party in the German parliament (see the diagram on the right).

Term

Great Depression
A period of high unemployement in the 1930s in America and Europe.

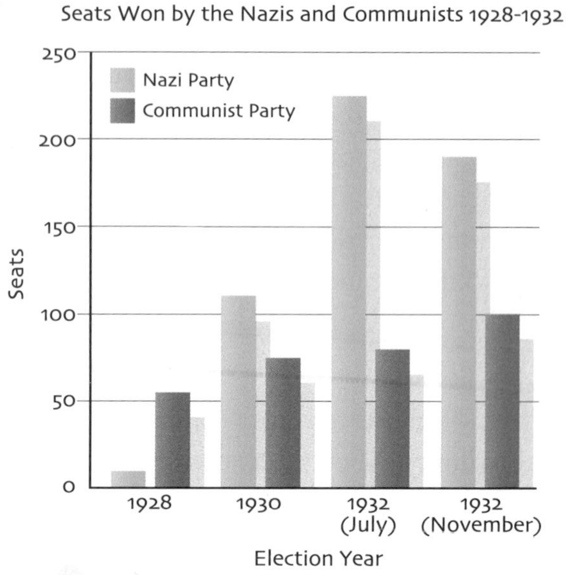

The number of seats won by the Nazis and communists grew fast as the economy got worse. In the election of July 1932 a majority of Germans voted for the Nazis or the communists who were both opposed to democracy

Why did people vote for Hitler?

- Fear of communism
- Economic problems, especially unemployment
- Hatred and resentment of the Treaty of Versailles
- Hitler's leadership and the use of propaganda
- Loss of confidence in democracy

Hitler becomes Chancellor

President Hindenburg appointed Hitler the **Chancellor** (prime minister). He did not like Hitler or the Nazis but his advisors persuaded him to change his mind. On 30 January 1933, Hitler became the Chancellor of Germany. There were very few Nazi ministers in his first government. Many thought that once he was in power Hitler would become more moderate. How wrong they were!

Hitler passing a crowd in his car. What does this picture show about the attitude of Germans to Hitler?

Case Study: Communism – Stalin's Russia

Why was communism so popular in the 1930s?

As the **Great Depression** spread, many people lost their jobs. It seemed as if democracy and capitalism had failed them.

They looked at what was happening in the Soviet Union. **Stalin** had succeeded Lenin in 1924. He introduced **Five Year Plans** to industrialise and modernise the country. Many great factories and building projects were constructed.

Poster praising Stalin. How is Stalin presented in this poster?

Workers had jobs and apartments. On the surface, Stalin was creating a fairer and happier society. Western visitors were impressed by what they saw: communism seemed to work.

Propaganda gave the impression of a contented and loyal population. Stalin controlled all of the communist parties in Europe and they also said how great things were in the USSR.

How did Stalin control the Soviet Union?

The truth was very different: Stalin used **terror** to control his people on a scale that had never been witnessed before.

- His police, the **NKVD**, kept a very close eye on the people. Anybody, guilty or innocent, could be arrested at any time, anywhere!
- People who were suspected of opposing his policies were executed or sent to vast prison camps called **gulags**. Millions died in the gulags.
- He created a man-made famine to defeat opposition to his policies in the Ukraine. Historians estimate that 5 million people died as a result. A further 5 million wealthier farmers called **kulaks** were killed or sent to camps.
- Many of the great building projects, such as the Moscow underground that so impressed visitors, were built using slave labour.
- In an event known as the **Great Purge**, Stalin had hundreds of thousands of members of the Communist Party shot. Most leading generals were also killed.

Historians are not sure how many people were killed on the orders of Stalin, but it is estimated to be about 20 million.

Did you know?

The English novelist, George Orwell, was so opposed to Stalin's actions that he wrote a famous book condemning him, called *Animal Farm*.

QUESTIONS

1 Explain why some people were not prepared to accept the new democratic government formed in 1919.
2 How did Hitler copy Mussolini?
3 What did Hitler attempt to do in 1923?
4 Mention two of Hitler's views outlined in *Mein Kampf*.
5 Why did the Nazi Party have little support between 1924 and 1929?
6 What effect did the Wall Street Crash have on the German economy?
7 Why was the 1930 election important for the Nazi Party?
8 Give three reasons why Germans voted for the Nazi Party.
9 Who appointed Hitler as Chancellor of Germany?
10 How did Stalin control the Soviet Union?

How did Hitler become a dictator?

It took Mussolini four years to take full control of Italy. Hitler was the dictator of Germany within six months. Here is how he did it:

1 The Nazis took control of the police. The Brownshirts were now free to beat up and in some cases kill political opponents. The secret police (the **Gestapo**) was established to keep an eye on the population.
2 On 27 February 1933, the German parliament building, the **Reichstag**, was set on fire. Hitler claimed the fire was a signal for a communist revolt. There was no evidence for this claim but that did not matter. The Communist Party was banned and over 10,000 people were arrested.
3 In March 1933, the German parliament passed a law called the **Enabling Act**. This gave Hitler the power to pass laws without getting them approved by parliament. He was now a dictator.
4 He then acted swiftly to crush democracy. Political opponents were beaten up or killed. All other political parties and the trade unions were banned by the summer of 1933.

Hitler was now **Der Führer**, the leader of Germany.

Did you know?

Historians have long wondered whether the Nazis themselves set fire to the Reichstag. Most now accept that Dutch communist Marinus van der Lubbe was the sole culprit.

How did Hitler maintain power?

Concentration camps

One feature of Nazi rule in Germany was the **concentration camps**. They were designed for opponents of the regime. The SS, led by **Heinrich Himmler**, was given control of the camps. The first one was at **Dachau** near Munich. Others soon followed throughout Germany. Conditions were harsh and the prisoners were at the mercy of their guards. Torture was common. As we shall see later in the section, the camps were used in the persecution of the Jews of Europe.

Term

Concentration camps
Prisons used for political prisoners and later the Jews of Europe.

PART 3

The Night of the Long Knives

One problem Hitler faced was how to deal with the growing power of the Brownshirts (SA). The organisation had over 2 million members. Its leader, **Ernst Röhm**, talked about the SA becoming the new army of Germany. This worried army generals. Röhm had also made a lot of enemies within the Nazi Party, who were jealous of his power. They persuaded Hitler that Röhm was plotting against him. He decided to act and destroy the power of the SA.

On 30 June 1934, the leaders of the SA were arrested and most were shot. The Nazis took advantage of this action to kill other political enemies as well. This event became known as the **Night of the Long Knives**. Most Germans believed Hitler when he said the Brownshirts were planning a revolt. To them the SA was the ugly face of the Nazi regime. They were happy that Hitler had taken action against them.

Why did the Germans support Hitler?

There is no doubt that Hitler was popular with most Germans. They were prepared to accept the terror and the camps. Here are some reasons for this popularity:

- His **foreign policy** successes made most Germans very proud. We will read about them in the next chapter.
- Hitler's **economic policy** worked – unemployment was cured in Germany. The Nazis also organised cheap holidays and leisure activities for workers. Many workers who had voted for the communists or socialists were now happy they had jobs and food.
- **Propaganda** played a very important role. Under the direction of **Josef Goebbels**, the Nazis were very successful at getting their message across to the German people. One popular slogan was '**Ein Volk** (one people), **ein Reich** (one empire), **ein Führer** (one leader)!'
- **Newspapers** were only allowed to report the news that the Nazis approved. Cheap radio sets were sold so that as many people as possible could hear Hitler speak. Parades and rallies were organised. The most famous was held at **Nuremberg** every year.

A Nazi propaganda poster. It reads 'Yes! Leader, we follow you!'

Dr Josef Goebbels,
Minister of Propaganda

Herman Goering,
Head of the Airforce

Heinrich Himmler,
Commander of the SS

PART 3

Controlling young people

Like Mussolini, Hitler wanted to make sure that young people would be loyal to the new government. The teaching of history was changed to reflect Nazi views. Teachers had to give the Nazi salute to their classes.

The Nazis made sure that all boys and girls attended Nazi youth groups:

- At the age of 14 boys joined the **Hitler Youth**. This became the largest youth organisation in the world.
- At the same age, girls became members of the **League of German Maidens**.
- Boys were trained to be the future soldiers of Germany while girls were expected to become good mothers. The young were also taught to hate one particular group in Germany – **the Jews**.

Did you know?

Hitler talked about creating a **Third Reich** (empire). The First Reich or Holy Roman Empire ended in 1806. The Second Reich lasted from 1871 until 1918.

How did the Nazis treat the Jews?

The Nazis taught the Germans to think of themselves as superior to other races. They were the master race or the **Aryans**. They said that the Jews were the enemies of the master race. Hitler also blamed the Jews for the defeat in World War I and for many of Germany's problems after the war.

Jews made up less than 1 per cent of the population, about 500,000 people. They were very successful in business, medicine and law. Many of the best professors in German universities were Jewish. Most Jews felt themselves to be German and were dismayed at the policies of the new government.

At first the main aim of the Nazis was to get the Jews to leave Germany. They made **anti-semitism** an official policy.

Term

Third Reich
Nazi-controlled Germany between 1933 and 1945.

Term

Anti-semitism
Hatred of and discrimination against Jewish people.

- In 1933, a boycott of Jewish shops was organised.
- Jews were not allowed to work for the government.
- Anti-Jewish signs were put up throughout the country.
- Many Jews were forced to sell their businesses at a fraction of their value.
- In 1935, the **Nuremberg Laws** were passed. They made it illegal for Germans and Jews to marry or to have sexual relations with each other.

What was Kristallnacht?

In 1938, a German diplomat in Paris was shot by a Jewish student. The Nazis took revenge on the Jewish community in Germany. On the night of 9–10 November, Jews throughout Germany were attacked.

- Every synagogue (the Jewish place of worship) in Germany was destroyed.
- Jewish property and shops were damaged.
- Ninety-one Jews were murdered. Over 30,000 were arrested and sent to concentration camps.
- The Jewish community was then fined 1 billion marks for the murder of the German diplomat. This was to pay the insurance bill for the damage caused on Kristallnacht.

The event was called **Kristallnacht** (the Night of Broken Glass). Over 80,000 Jews left Germany in the following month.

As we shall see in Chapter 5, during World War II the Nazis went further and decided to murder the Jews of Europe.

The synagogue destroyed during Kristallnacht

Did you know?

One of the Jewish people who left Germany was Anne Frank. Her family went to Holland. When the Germans invaded Holland her family went into hiding. She kept a diary of her experiences. She was later captured and died in a Nazi concentration camp.

TIMELINE Nazi Germany

1919	Hitler joined the German Workers Party
1923	Hitler attempted to overthrow the government – Beer Hall Putsch
1929	Wall Street Crash – unemployment became a serious problem in Germany
1930–32	Nazis support increased dramatically
1933	Hitler appointed Chancellor – Enabling Act passed. First anti-Jewish measures passed and concentration camps opened
1934	Night of the Long Knives
1935	Nuremberg Laws passed
1938	Kristallnacht – night of violence against the Jews of Germany

Do you understand these key terms?

Weimar Republic
Nazi Party
Brownshirts
Sturm Abteilung (SA)
Schtuzstaffel (SS)
Beer Hall Putsch
hyperinflation
Reichstag
Wall Street Crash
Great Depression
gulag
kulak
Chancellor
Gestapo
concentration camp
Hitler Youth
League of German Maidens
Third Reich
anti-semitism
Aryan
Nuremberg Laws
Kristallnacht

PART 3

QUESTIONS

1 How did the Nazis take advantage of the Reichstag fire?
2 What happened to other political parties in Germany?
3 Where was the first concentration camp opened and which organisation ran the camps?
4 What were conditions like in the camps?
5 Why did Hitler have the leaders of the Brownshirts executed?
6 What was the role of Josef Goebbels?
7 Why did the Nazis want to control the young people of Germany?
8 Why did Hitler hate the Jews of Germany?
9 What actions did the Nazis take against Jews in 1935?
10 Why, do you think, did the emigration of Jews from Germany increase in 1938 and 1939?
11 Write an account of two of the following: (a) How the Nazis came to power in Germany (b) How the Nazis established a dictatorship in Germany (c) Young people in Nazi Germany

EXAM QUESTIONS

1 Write an account of one of the following:
(a) Nazi propaganda (b) Nazi economy (c) The Nazis and the Jews.
2 Explain two of the following terms relating to Hitler's rule in Germany: Enabling Act; Nuremberg Laws; Night of the Long Knives; the SS

People in History

A member of the Nazi Party describes how Hitler came to power in Germany.

Use the plan below as a guide.

Hitler coming to power

- Problems faced by Weimar Germany
- Hitler's aims
- How did Hitler become Chancellor?
- The effect of the Wall Street Crash on Germany
- Who supported the Nazis?
- Increased support for the Nazis – election 1932

Chapter 4

The Drift to War 1933–39

Key Learning Objectives

- What were the main aims of Hitler's foreign policy?
- How did he put his policies into effect?
- What was the attitude of the British and the French?
- What events led to the Munich Conference of 1938?
- What events led to the outbreak of war in 1939?

On 1 September 1939, German troops attacked Poland and World War II started. Who was to blame for this war? The answer is one man: Adolf Hitler. It was his decisions that led directly to the outbreak of war. In this chapter we will look at the actions he took and see why the British and French did not try to stop him until it was too late.

What were the main aims of Hitler's foreign policy?

1 As we have seen, Hitler wanted to tear up the **Treaty of Versailles** and make Germany a great power again. This view was supported by nearly all Germans, who hated the treaty as well. Here are some of the main things the Germans disliked about the treaty:
   - The restrictions placed on the size of the German army
   - The fact that Germany had lost territory to Poland, in particular the town of Danzig
   - The ban on German troops entering the Rhineland, which was part of Germany. This area was called the **demilitarised zone**

2 Hitler wanted to unite German speakers living outside Germany into a **Greater Germany**. He was an Austrian and he wanted to see the country of his birth become part of Germany.

3 He hoped to create a German empire in Eastern Europe at the expense of Poland and Russia. He called this **Lebensraum** (living space) because he planned to move out the local people and replace them with Germans.

Hitler believed that the French and British were weak and wanted to avoid another war. He was prepared to use the threat of violence to get his way, as he believed that the two countries would back down rather than go to war.

Did you know?

The Austrians were German-speaking and there were large numbers of Germans in Czechoslovakia, Poland, Romania and Hungary. Most had originally been part of the Austrian Empire that had collapsed at the end of World War I.

How did he put his policies into effect?

Rebuilding the German military

Hitler started by removing the limits the Treaty of Versailles had placed on the German army. Hitler ordered secret **rearmament** and he left the League of Nations. In 1935, he felt strong enough to publicly announce the reintroduction of **conscription.** This meant there would be more men in the German army than were permitted under the Treaty of Versailles. He increased the size of the German navy and built up an airforce called the **Luftwaffe.** This was commanded by one of Hitler's loyal supporters, **Herman Goering.** Britain and France protested, but took no steps to stop Hitler rearming.

Term

Rearmament
Rebuilding the German military forces.

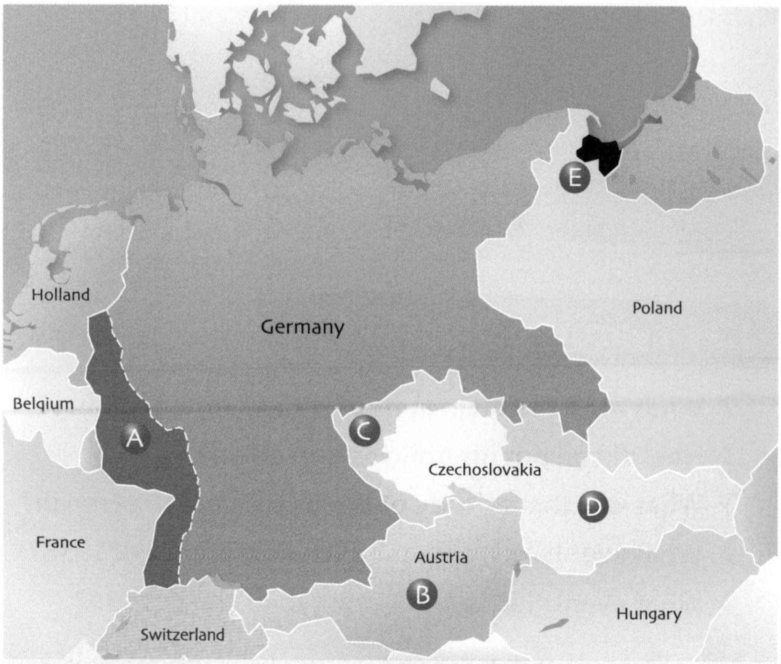

Hitler's foreign policy – the path to war. **A** – Rhineland. **B** – Austria. **C** – Sudetenland. **D** – Rest of Czechoslovakia. **E** – Danzig

The occupation of the Rhineland

People now expected Hitler to send troops into the Rhineland. This is marked A on the map above. The question was how the British and French would react. In March 1936, German troops crossed the River Rhine and were greeted by cheering crowds.

An important part of the Versailles agreement had been broken, but the French and British did nothing. Hitler had gambled and won. He was now prepared to take more risks.

A few months later he formed an alliance with Mussolini that was known as the **Rome–Berlin Axis.**

German troops enter the Rhineland in 1936. In your opinion, what is the attitude of the crowds?

What was the attitude of the British and the French?

Why did the French and the British do nothing when German troops entered the Rhineland? There were a number of reasons but these were the most important:

- The French thought the German army was bigger than it actually was. They did not want to risk war over the Rhineland. They would also not act without the support of the British.

Neville Chamberlain. His policy of appeasement was popular in Britain

- The British felt that the Treaty of Versailles was too harsh. There was some sympathy for German actions. The memory of the suffering of World War I was very strong and they did not want another war.
- Many British politicians were more worried by Stalin and the threat of communism.

In 1937, there was a new prime minister in Britain, **Neville Chamberlain**. He thought that by agreeing to Hitler's demands he could prevent war. His policy was called **appeasement**. Hitler saw it as weakness and he took advantage of the British wish to avoid war.

What events led to the Munich Conference of 1938?

Austria – the Anschluss

Marked B on the map opposite, Austria was a German-speaking country with a large Nazi Party. In 1934, some Austrian Nazis had attempted to take over the country. They were easily defeated, and Mussolini rushed troops to the border to prevent a Nazi takeover. Now, however, Mussolini was allied to Hitler and the Austrians were on their own.

In February 1938, Hitler forced the Austrian Chancellor, **Kurt von Schuschnigg**, to bring leading Austrian Nazis into his government. Schuschnigg tried to stop the Nazi influence increasing and Hitler forced him to resign. The leader of the Austrian Nazis replaced him and German troops were 'invited in' to restore order.

Hitler was greeted by enthusiastic crowds as he travelled through Austria. He proclaimed that Austria would become a province of Germany. This event became known as the **Anschluss** (joining together). Britain and France did not protest, even though it was forbidden by the Treaty of Versailles.

Did you know?

Hitler liked to take a major foreign policy decision on a Saturday when people were not working in other countries. These became known as Hitler's 'Saturday Surprises'.

The Sudetenland

The lack of reaction by the British and the French to events in Austria led Hitler to take more risks. His next target was the **Sudetenland**. This was the German-speaking region of Czechoslovakia. It is the area marked C on the map opposite. Hitler encouraged the Germans living there to campaign for independence. German propaganda accused the Czechs of treating the Sudeten Germans very badly. Throughout the summer the crisis got worse as fears of a German attack on Czechoslovakia grew.

Mussolini and Hitler in Munich, in 1938. They had been allies since 1936

The Munich Conference

Neville Chamberlain twice flew to Germany to try and stop war by using **diplomacy**. It seemed that he had failed when Mussolini proposed a conference of Britain, France, Italy and Germany. This took place in Munich. Czechoslovakia was not invited to the conference. On 29 September 1938, they agreed to hand over the Sudetenland to Germany.

Europe breathed a sigh of relief. War had been prevented. Hitler promised that this was his final demand. Chamberlain was welcomed home by cheering crowds. He said that he had brought back peace with honour. However, he had failed. War had only been delayed.

Term

Diplomacy
Negotiations between countries.

What events led to the outbreak of war in 1939?

The end of Czechoslovakia

In March 1939, Hitler encouraged the Slovaks to break away from Czechoslovakia. The Czech president went to Berlin, where he was threatened that if he did not allow German troops to occupy the Czech lands, Prague would be bombed. He agreed and Hitler sent troops into the Czech lands (marked D on the map on page 348).

British public opinion was outraged. This was not German land. Chamberlain abandoned appeasement. He guaranteed British support for Poland if Germany attacked her.

The Danzig crisis

It was clear to everyone that Poland would be Hitler's next target. All Germans resented losing land to Poland at the end of World War I. Part of Germany was cut off from the rest of the country by Polish land. Hitler now demanded the return of the German-speaking town of **Danzig**. Look at the map on page 348, where Danzig is marked E.

The Poles refused and another crisis developed during the summer of 1939.

Hitler and Stalin

One man watching events very closely was Joseph Stalin. The communist ruler of the Soviet Union had been a sworn enemy of Adolf Hitler. However, he did not trust the British or the French. He had not been invited to the Munich Conference. He believed that the Western Allies were encouraging Hitler to attack the Soviet Union.

The signing of the Nazi–Soviet Non-Aggression Pact. In the centre is von Ribbentrop, the German Foreign Minister, signing the pact. To the right is Stalin and on the left his Foreign Minister, Molotov

Hitler now offered Stalin an alliance. He wanted Soviet **neutrality** when he attacked Poland. He promised Stalin a lot of land in Eastern Europe. Stalin agreed. The world was shocked to learn of the agreement reached between the two countries on 23 August 1939. Under the **Nazi–Soviet Non-Aggression Pact** the two former deadly enemies were now friends. They promised not to attack each other. Secretly they agreed to divide Poland between them.

Did you know?

One country missing from events in this chapter is the USA. The reason for this was that in the 1930s the policy of the USA was **isolationism** – this meant staying out of European affairs.

War!

Poland was doomed. On 1 September 1939, German troops attacked Poland. Britain and France demanded that the Germans stop the invasion. When the Germans refused, they declared war on 3 September. World War II had started.

TIMELINE The Steps to War

1933	Germany left the League of Nations
1935	Hitler reintroduced conscription
1936	German troops entered the Rhineland. Rome–Berlin Axis formed with Mussolini
1938	The Anschluss: Austria became part of Germany Munich conference gave the Sudetenland to Germany
1939	Germany occupied the Czech lands Nazi–Soviet Non-Aggression Pact Germany attacked Poland – start of World War II

Do you understand these key terms?

Lebensraum	**Luftwaffe**	**Anschluss**	**neutrality**
rearmament	**appeasement**	**diplomacy**	**Non-Agression Pact**

QUESTIONS

1. Outline two aims of Hitler's foreign policy.
2. In 1935, how did Hitler build up his military power?
3. What action did Hitler take in March 1936?
4. Give two reasons why the British did not want to take action against Hitler.
5. Why did Hitler want to make Austria part of Germany?
6. Why did Hitler want the Sudetenland region of Czechoslovakia?
7. Give one important result of the German occupation of the Czech lands in March 1939.
8. Why was Stalin unhappy with the actions of Britain and France?

QUESTIONS

9 On what date did World War II break out?

10 Write an account of two of the following:
- Main foreign policy decisions taken by Hitler between 1933 and 1936
- Appeasement and the Munich Conference
- The Nazi–Soviet Non-Aggression Pact.

11 'It was the actions of Adolf Hitler that led to World War II'. Do you agree? Give four reasons to support your answer.

SOURCE QUESTION

- The two sources below are British reactions to the Munich Agreement. Study them and answer the questions that follow.

Source A

We have suffered a total and unmitigated defeat ... you will find that in a period of time which may be measured by years, but may be measured by months, Czechoslovakia will be engulfed in the Nazi régime. We are in the presence of a disaster of the first magnitude ... we have sustained a defeat without a war, the consequences of which will travel far with us along our road....

Winston Churchill to the House of Commons, 5 October 1938

Source B

Be glad in your hearts. Give thanks to your God. People of Britain, your children are safe. Your husbands and your sons will not march to war. Peace is a victory for all mankind. If we must have a victor, let us choose Chamberlain. For the Prime Minister's conquests are mighty and enduring – millions of happy homes and hearts relieved of their burden. To him the laurels.

Daily Express, 30 September 1938

(a) According to source A, what did Churchill expect to happen to Czechoslovakia?
(b) What was Churchill's opinion of the Munich Agreement? Explain your answer.
(c) Why did the *Daily Express* say to its readers 'be glad in your heart'?
(d) In source B what was the attitude of the *Daily Express* to the prime minister, Neville Chamberlain?
(e) From your study of history, which of the two views of the Munich Agreement was more accurate?

Chapter 5

World War II 1939–45

Key Learning Objectives

- Why were the Germans successful in 1939 and 1940?
- Why did the British win the Battle of Britain?
- What was Operation Barbarossa?
- What were the main turning points of World War II?
- How did the Allies defeat Germany?
- What was the Final Solution?
- How did the Allies win the War in the Pacific?
- What were the results of the war?

We saw in the last chapter that World War II started when Hitler invaded Poland in September 1939. It is estimated that over 50 million people were killed during the course of the war. The table on the right shows it involved all of the main countries in the world. Historians call the two sides in the war the Allies and the Axis.

The Allies	The Axis
Britain and her empire	Germany
USA (from 1941)	Italy
France	Japan
USSR (from 1941)	Hungary
China	Romania

Why were the Germans successful in 1939 and 1940?

Blitzkrieg

Hitler wanted to avoid the trench warfare of World War I. His army came up with a new tactic called **Blitzkrieg** (lightning war).

1. Without warning German planes would destroy enemy targets on the ground.
2. Then large numbers of tanks would smash through their defences.
3. Enemy troops would find themselves surrounded and be forced to surrender.

Term

Blitzkrieg
German military tactics involving heavy bombing from the air and rapid tank movements on the ground.

The Poles were the first to experience this new tactic. They fought bravely but were no match for the Germans. The Polish capital, **Warsaw**, was heavily bombed. To make matters worse, they were also attacked from the east by the Soviets. After three weeks Poland was defeated. The Poles were to suffer terribly at the hands of both the Germans and the Soviets.

How was France defeated?

German tanks waiting to cross through the Ardennes region and into France, 1940

Although they went to war to support Poland, Britain and France did little to help. They didn't attack Germany. There was no fighting in the West and it was soon nicknamed **'the phoney war'**. In April 1940 this calm was shattered when the Germans invaded **Denmark** and **Norway**. The following month **Belgium**, **Holland** and **France** were attacked.

The French thought that the Germans would have great difficulty breaking through the **Maginot Line** that protected their border with Germany. However, the Germans avoided this by attacking through a wooded, hilly area called the **Ardennes**. The French had thought this area was too difficult for tanks to go through and had left it unprotected.

Although the French had more tanks, the Germans made better use of their tanks. The Germans advanced quickly and French soldiers surrendered in large numbers.

Italy now entered the war on the side of Germany and attacked France. German forces entered Paris and France surrendered in June. The Germans occupied the north of the country. The Germans allowed a French government to be formed in the south of the country. It became known as **Vichy France** after its capital at Vichy. It was led by **Marshal Pétain**.

The rescue at Dunkirk

Painting by Charles Cundall, British official war artist, showing the evacuation of British, French and Belgian soldiers from Dunkirk in 1940

The **British Expeditionary Force** had been sent to help the French. They were also defeated and were trapped at **Dunkirk** on the channel coast. In a major naval operation, called **Operation Dynamo**, the British managed to rescue over 300,000 British and French soldiers from the beaches at Dunkirk. The British used over 900 ships, including fishing boats and yachts, to get the men off the beaches.

In May 1940 Neville Chamberlain had been replaced as prime minister by **Winston Churchill** – a determined enemy of Adolf Hitler. For the British it was a bleak time as the country stood alone against the might of Nazi Germany.

Why did the British win the Battle of Britain?

Hitler's plan to invade Britain was called **Operation Sea Lion.** For this invasion to be successful Germany needed control of the air. To achieve this, Hitler had to destroy the British airforce. On 13 August 1940, German attacks on the **Royal Air Force** (RAF) began. Waves of Luftwaffe planes bombed airfields and radar installations throughout Britain. The **Battle of Britain** had started.

The RAF was stretched to the limit as it tried to stop the German attacks. Pilots had little rest, as they were involved in constant **dogfights** against the German fighter planes and bombers. British Spitfires and Hurricanes fought German ME 109s and ME 110s.

Both sides suffered heavy losses, but by the middle of September the RAF had won the Battle of Britain. The Germans had failed to get control of the air.

There were three main reasons for this:

- The Germans made the mistake of bombing London and this gave the RAF time to recover and reorganise.
- The use of **radar** allowed the British to predict the arrival of German attacks.
- The **Spitfire** was an excellent fighter and superior to German planes.

Term

Radar
A device that used radio waves to detect approaching planes.

Hitler called off the invasion of Britain. The Germans now switched to night-time bombing of British cities. In all, the RAF lost over 1,000 planes and 510 pilots were killed. The Germans suffered heavier losses: 1,700 Luftwaffe planes were shot down and nearly 3,500 airmen killed or captured.

Spitfire planes flying in formation over Britain

The Blitz

The bombing of London and other cities was called the **Blitz.** It lasted until May 1941. Hundreds of German bombers dropped highly explosive bombs and **incendiaries** (bombs designed to start fires). By the end of the Blitz, London had been attacked nineteen times and about 40,000 civilians had been killed. People sought shelter wherever they could find it. In London, many went to the **Underground stations.** Conditions there were very overcrowded. Other UK cities such as **Birmingham, Liverpool, Coventry** and **Belfast** suffered heavy casualties as a result of German bombing.

The main leaders during World War II (from left): Adolf Hitler; Benito Mussolini; President Roosevelt; Joseph Stalin; and Winston Churchill

PART 3

Operation Barbarossa

Why did Hitler invade Russia?

While the Blitz was raging Hitler was already turning his attention to the East. He had decided to attack the USSR. He wanted to create a vast German empire on land taken from the Soviet Union. He expected to defeat the Red Army easily.

The Germans assembled the largest invasion force in history:

- Over 3 million soldiers, 4,000 planes and 4,000 tanks were prepared for the attack.
- The force was divided into three separate armies – Army Groups North, Centre and South.

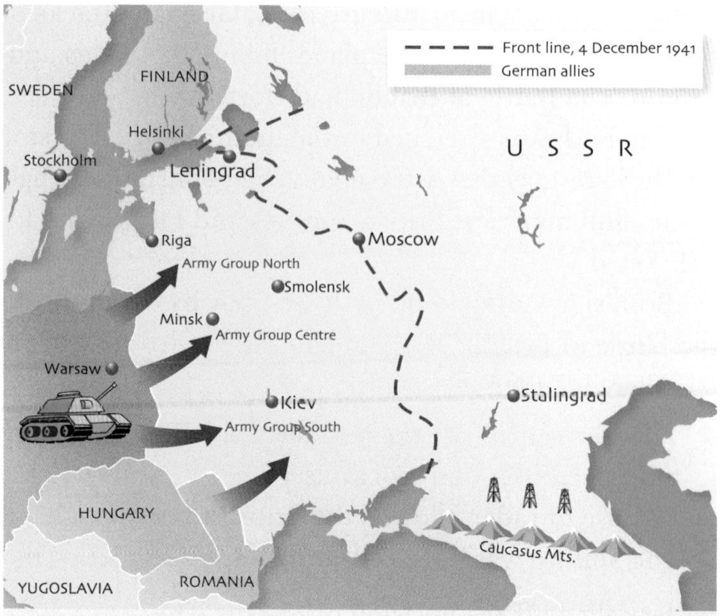

This map shows the German advance into Russia

The attack had been originally scheduled for May 1941, but it was delayed for a month when German troops invaded **Greece** and **Yugoslavia**.

Codenamed **Operation Barbarossa**, it began on the morning of 22 June 1941. Stalin refused to believe warnings about the invasion and the Germans caught the Russians by surprise.

Did you know?

German troops surrounded Leningrad for 900 days. It is estimated that one million people died during the siege.

What happened during Operation Barbarossa?

The Soviets had far more tanks and planes than the Germans but their troops were poorly led. Although the ordinary Soviet soldier fought with great bravery, the **Red Army** suffered defeat after defeat. By December, a staggering 4 million soldiers had been killed or captured by the Germans. The Germans surrounded **Leningrad** and were closing in on **Moscow**.

Despite their successes, the Germans found fighting in the USSR very tough:

- The Russians adopted a **scorched earth policy**. This meant that as they retreated they destroyed anything of use to the Germans such as factories or railway lines.
- Rain in October turned the roads into a sea of mud that made movement very difficult.
- As the Germans advanced they suffered heavy loses that could not be replaced.

German troops in Russia. They were poorly prepared for the extreme cold of the Russian winter

PART 3

- As the winter set in the Germans experienced a new enemy – the cold. They were not prepared for the extreme temperatures and did not have winter clothing. Temperatures dropped to –40°C. Petrol froze and tanks would not start. The German army lost more men to frostbite than to fighting the Soviets.
- In December, taking advantage of the cold, the Soviets launched a counter-attack. The Germans were forced to retreat and Moscow was saved.

Did you know?

Most historians regard Operation Barbarossa as Hitler's greatest military mistake of World War II.

Why did the USA enter the war?

On 7 December 1941, Germany's ally Japan attacked the main US Pacific base at **Pearl Harbour** in Hawaii. Japan wanted to build an empire in Asia and this had been opposed by America. They hoped that the attack would lead to a quick victory. Instead they woke a sleeping giant. The USA, led by **President Roosevelt**, entered the war against both Japan and Germany. Germany was now facing the might of the USA, the USSR and Britain.

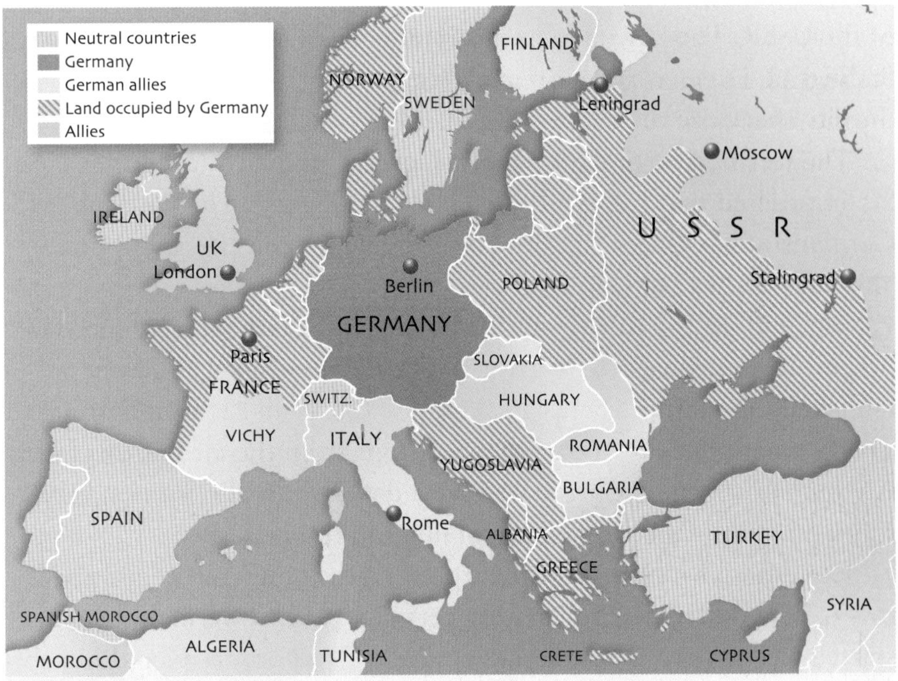

This map shows German-occupied Western Europe in the summer of 1942

QUESTIONS

1. What did Blitzkrieg tactics involve?
2. Which major Polish city was bombed by the Germans?
3. Which countries did Germany invade in 1940?
4. Give one reason why the Germans captured France in 1940.
5. Why did the Battle of Britain start?
6. What was the Blitz?
7. Why did Hitler want to invade the USSR in 1941?
8. In Russia, how successful were the Germans up to December 1941?
9. Which event saw the United States enter the war?

What were the main turning points of World War II?

In 1942, the Allies won two major battles that were to prove very important in turning the tide of World War II.

A Russian woman stands among the ruins of Stalingrad

1 Stalingrad

In the summer of 1942 the Germans advanced towards the oilfields in the south of the USSR. The key town in this region was **Stalingrad.** Hitler was determined to capture the city that bore the name of his enemy.

The German Sixth Army, led by **General Paulus**, attacked the city. Stalin ordered that the city be defended at all costs. The Russians and Germans now engaged in a bloody struggle for the city. Every street and building was fought over.

Meanwhile, the Red Army, led by **General Zhukov**, were secretly preparing a massive counter-attack. On 19 November 1942, they launched **Operation Uranus** and trapped the Sixth Army at Stalingrad. The Germans decided to supply the troops from the air but this failed. Attempts to rescue the army were also defeated by the Soviets. Hitler refused to allow the Germans in Stalingrad to break out.

Conditions worsened for the troops as the temperature dropped to –30°C. Food and supplies were very scarce. The German defenders started to starve to death. Seeing no hope, Paulus surrendered in February 1943. The Germans had lost an army of 300,000 men. This victory was the decisive turning point of the war and a massive confidence boost for the Russians.

Did you know?

One feature of the struggle for Stalingrad was the use of snipers. This can be seen in the film *Enemy at the Gates*. The film was based on the story of a famous Soviet sniper, but the German sniper in the film probably never existed.

2 El Alamein

In 1941, German troops called the **Afrika Corps** were sent to North Africa to help the Italians. They were led by **General Rommel**. He had won a number of victories over the British. By 1942, the German forces had reached **El Alamein** in Egypt where their advance was halted.

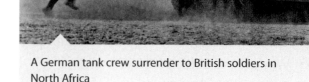

A German tank crew surrender to British soldiers in North Africa

The British **Eighth Army**, under **General Bernard Montgomery**, prepared to attack the Germans. Montgomery built up a two-to-one advantage in both tanks and men. He also had new American **Sherman tanks** which were better than German tanks.

In October, he attacked the German troops with 200,000 men. The fighting was fierce, but after two weeks Rommel was defeated. At the same time, American and British troops landed in **Algeria** and **Morocco**. The Germans were forced to retreat to **Tunisia**.

How did the Allies defeat Germany?

Throughout 1943 and 1944, the Allies had a number of important successes:

1. In May 1943, German and Italian troops in North Africa surrendered to the Allies. Allied troops then invaded **Italy**. Hitler's ally Mussolini was removed from power.
2. The Allies won the war at sea. German submarines called **U-boats** had posed a major threat to Allied shipping. By the summer of 1943 this danger was removed partly through the breaking of the German codes.
3. On the Eastern Front, the Germans launched an offensive at Kursk in July 1943. The Soviets defended fiercely and the largest tank battle of the war resulted. The Red Army won and the Germans were forced to retreat.
4. In 1944, the Russians drove the Germans from the USSR and entered Poland. At the same time, the Allies landed in France. The Third Reich was doomed.

Famous generals of World War II: General Eisenhower, General Montgomery, General Rommel

Did you know?

In US military planning, the day of attack is called D-Day and the time H-Hour. The original day of attack was 5 June 1944, but it had to be called off because of bad weather.

D-Day

Stalin had long put pressure on the Allies to land in France to relieve the pressure on the Soviets. The plan for the invasion was called **Operation Overlord**. The Allies decided to land at **Normandy** – you can see it on the map. The preparations were made in great secrecy. A deception operation was carried out to persuade the Germans that the attack was going to happen near **Calais** – the closest port to Britain.

The invasion force, commanded by **General Eisenhower**, consisted of American, British and Canadian troops. The five beaches targeted were given the codenames **Utah, Omaha, Juno, Gold** and **Sword**.

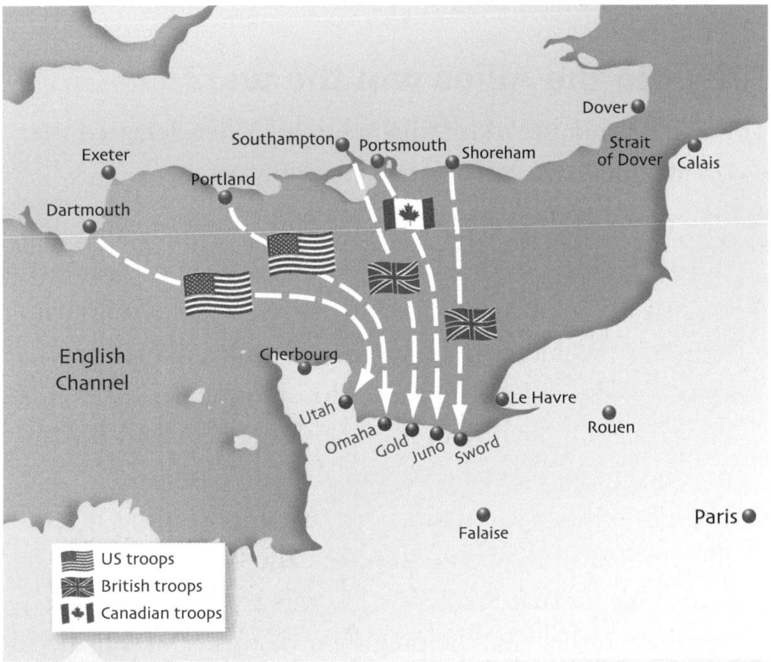

A map of the Allied landing at Normandy, showing the different beaches

The armada of over 7,000 ships and landing craft assembled for the invasion was the largest in history. Special tanks known as **funnies** were constructed in order to destroy the beach defences. **D-Day**, the day of the invasion, was on 6 June 1944. Along the Normandy coast, 156,000 soldiers were landed. Overhead they were protected by more than 10,000 planes.

Fighting in Normandy was difficult. The countryside with woods and hedgerows, known as the **bocage**, gave the German defenders plenty of cover. By August, helped by overwhelming air superiority, the Allies had destroyed the main German army at **Falaise**. Paris was then liberated and German troops were driven from France.

Why did Germany surrender?

By 1945, Germany was in a hopeless position. Cities such as **Berlin** and **Dresden** were destroyed from the air. Many Germans put their faith in new weapons such as the V2 rocket, but they made little impact.

German soldiers were still fighting well, but they could not stop Russian and Allied troops advancing towards Berlin. Millions of refugees were fleeing the advancing Red Army.

In March 1945, the Allies crossed the **River Rhine**. The following month the Russians launched a massive attack on Berlin. On 30 April 1945, with Soviet troops only a few hundred metres away, Hitler committed suicide. He was succeeded by **Admiral Donitz** who quickly surrendered to the Allies. The 8th of May 1945 was celebrated as VE Day (Victory in Europe) throughout Europe.

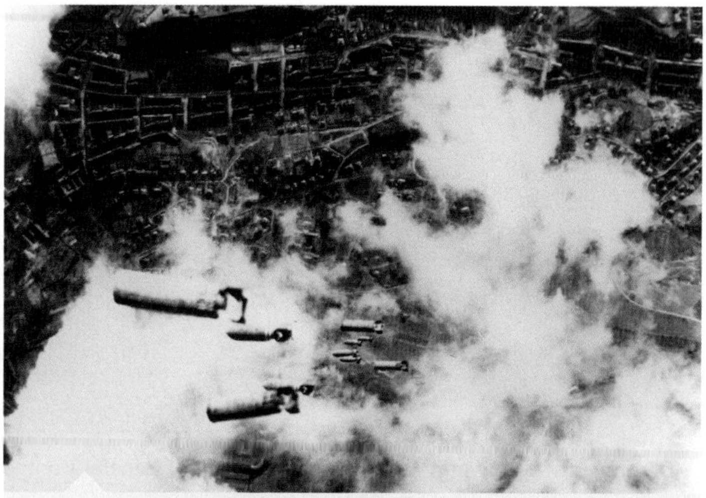

Bombs being dropped from Lancaster bombers during an air raid on Dresden in February 1945. About 25,000 people died during the bombing of Dresden

Why did the Allies win the war?

There are a number of reasons why the Allies defeated the Germans. Here are some of the most important:

- The Germans and their allies had far too many enemies. The British Empire, the USA and the USSR were too powerful.
- America concentrated on defeating Germany. American factories produced vast amounts of tanks, planes, trucks and ships for the Allies. The Ford Motor company made more military equipment than Italy. Both the USA and Russia produced more tanks and planes than Germany.
- The bombing of Germany was very important as it reduced the amount of military equipment the Germans could build. It also meant that the Luftwaffe was trying to stop the bombers rather than helping their troops. This left the Allies with complete control of the air on both fronts.

Did you know?

The July Plot

There had been little resistance to the Nazis in Germany, but as the war worsened many officers had lost faith in Hitler. Some had plotted to kill him. Colonel Claus von Stauffenberg planted a bomb in Hitler's headquarters on 20 July 1944. It exploded but Hitler survived. The plot failed and Stauffenberg was later executed. Hitler took terrible revenge on anyone involved in the attempt to kill him.

PART 3

- Throughout the war Hitler interfered with the decisions of his generals. For example, he refused to allow troops to retreat at Stalingrad. As a result, hundreds of thousands of soldiers, who could have lived to fight another day, were captured or killed.
- The most important factor, however, was the Red Army. The Soviets had far more men, tanks and planes. The Germans suffered most of their dead and wounded fighting the Soviet Army.

Term

Ghetto
Part of a city where a minority group was kept separate.

What was the Final Solution?

As Allied troops advanced they uncovered evidence of the extermination of the Jewish people, or the **Holocaust** as it became known.

As we saw in Chapter 3, the Nazis had persecuted German Jews. When the war began the Nazis began to round up the Jews in Poland. Many were shot and others were placed in **ghettos** such as the Warsaw Ghetto where they could be easily controlled.

Throughout Nazi-controlled Europe, Jews were forced to wear a yellow **Star of David** for identification. During the invasion of Russia, special SS troops called **Einsatzgruppen** rounded up Jews and shot hundreds of thousands.

In 1942, the Nazis decided to kill the Jewish population of Europe. This was estimated at 11 million. The Nazis called their policy the **Final Solution**. The head of the SS, **Heinrich Himmler**, was in charge of this secret policy. Here is what happened:

- Jews were moved from the ghettos by train to special **extermination camps** such as **Auschwitz, Majdanek** and **Treblinka**.
- Here the old and the young were gassed in fake shower units (gas chambers) using **Zyklon B** gas. Their bodies were then burned.
- The able-bodied were worked until they were murdered or died of disease. Some prisoners were also subjected to medical experiments.

Auschwitz – prisoners at the most infamous of the terrible Nazi death camps

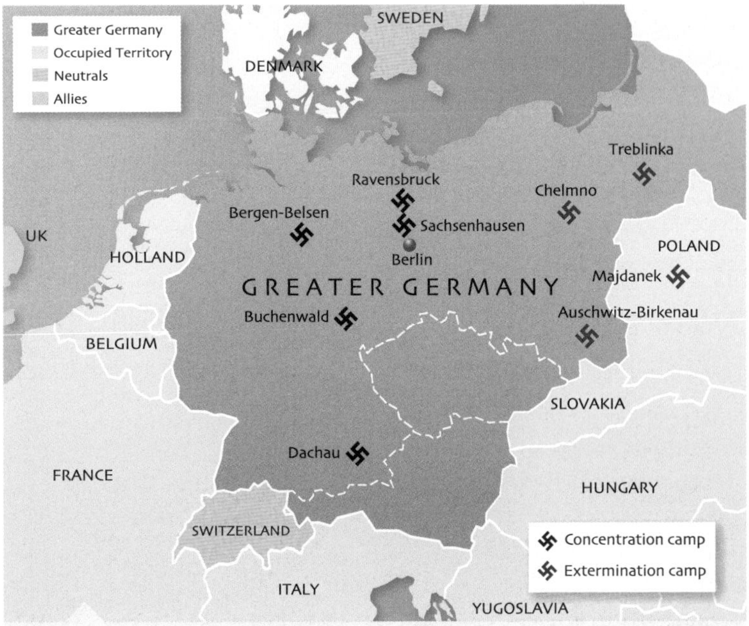

This map shows the location of the Nazi concentration and extermination camps

PART 3

It is estimated that up to 6 million Jews perished during the Holocaust. More than a million died at Auschwitz alone. Other than Jews, Roma (gypsies), Poles and Russian prisoners of war were murdered at these camps.

After the war, Nazi leaders were prosecuted for this and other crimes at **Nuremberg**. A number were hanged. However, **Himmler**, **Goering** and **Goebbels** had cheated justice by committing suicide.

How did the Allies win the War in the Pacific?

As we read earlier in the chapter, the Japanese attack on Pearl Harbour in December 1941 led to war with the USA and Britain. At first, the Japanese were very successful. They conquered large parts of the French and British Empires in Asia. They also captured many islands in the Pacific.

The turning point came at the **Battle of Midway** in June 1942. The US navy sank four Japanese aircraft carriers. After this battle the USA invaded a large number of Japanese-held islands as the Americans advanced towards Japan. By the summer of 1945, the USA was ready to invade Japan.

The US military feared that an invasion of Japan could result in the death of hundreds of thousands of US soldiers. There was now another option for America. In a top-secret project called **Operation Manhattan** scientists had developed an **atomic bomb**. The new US president, **Harry Truman**, decided that it should be dropped on Japan to force her to surrender.

In August 1945, bombs were dropped on **Hiroshima** and **Nagasaki**. These bombs were the most powerful weapons ever seen and destroyed both cities. At Hiroshima over 90,000 people were killed instantly. The Japanese surrendered and World War II was finally over.

Did you know?

The bomb dropped on Hiroshima was nicknamed Little Boy, and the Nagasaki bomb was called Fat Man.

The terrible destruction of Nagasaki, caused by the atomic bomb

PART 3

What were the results of the war?

As you can see from the table below, World War II resulted in millions of deaths. The majority of those killed were civilians. The war had a number of important results:

1. The countries of Eastern Europe were controlled by the USSR and became communist. They were to suffer under this system until 1989.
2. After the defeat of Germany, the USA and the USSR were now the two most powerful countries in the world. They did not trust each other. A period of tension developed between them called the **Cold War**. We will find out more about the Cold War in the next chapter.
3. Britain and France were very weak after the war. They both had large empires in Africa and Asia, and now the peoples of their empires demanded independence. This process was called **decolonisation**. Chapter 8 will look at the experience of one country, India, in detail.
4. Many people in Europe were determined that there would never be another war in Europe again. This feeling was very strong in France and Germany. It led to closer European cooperation and the foundation of the **EEC** (European Economic Community). Go to Chapter 7 to read about closer European cooperation.

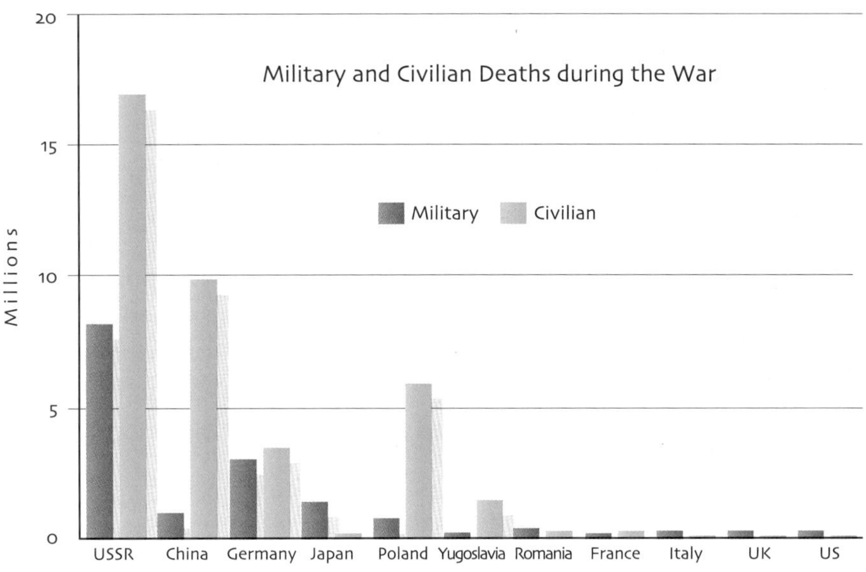

The Soviet Union suffered many more deaths than France, the UK and the US combined

TIMELINE World War II – the Main Events

1939	Germany invaded Poland, using Blitzkrieg tactics Britain and France declared war
1940	Germany conquered Denmark, Norway, Holland, Belgium and France Churchill became British prime minister British troops were evacuated at Dunkirk Battle of Britain German bombing of London and other British cities (the Blitz)

TIMELINE World War II – the Main Events

1941	German troops sent to North Africa Germany attacked Russia (Operation Barbarossa) Japanese attacked Pearl Harbour. USA entered the war, led by President Roosevelt
1942	Battle of Stalingrad began Germans were defeated at the Battle of El Alamein
1943	German forces surrendered at Stalingrad Italians and Germans surrendered in North Africa Battle of Kursk Mussolini removed from power. Italy declared war on Germany Allies defeated the U-boats
1944	D-Day landings at Normandy German forces were driven from the USSR
1945	Western Allies crossed the River Rhine and Soviets attacked Berlin Hitler committed suicide and the Germans surrendered Atomic bombs were dropped on Hiroshima and Nagasaki

Do you understand these key terms?

Blitzkrieg
phoney war
Vichy France
British Expeditionary Force
Operation Dynamo
Operation Sea Lion
Battle of Britain
radar
the Blitz
Operation Barbarossa
Red Army
scorched earth policy
Operation Uranus
U-boats
Operation Overlord
D-Day
Final Solution
extermination camps
Operation Manhattan
atomic bomb

QUESTIONS

1. Why did the Germans resume their offensive in 1942 in Russia?
2. How were the Germans defeated at Stalingrad?
3. Why were German troops sent to North Africa in 1941?
4. Why was the Battle of Kursk important?
5. What was the major result of the Allied invasion of Italy?
6. Why did Stalin put pressure on the USA and Britain to invade France?
7. Which city was liberated in August 1944?
8. Why were millions of German civilians fleeing the advancing Russians?
9. What were ghettos?
10. Which battle was the turning point in the war in the Pacific?
11. Why did the Americans drop the atomic bomb on Japan?

QUESTIONS

12 Write an account of three of the following:
(a) Early German success in the war up to May 1940
(b) The Battle of Britain
(c) Operation Barbarossa
(d) The Battle of Stalingrad or El Alamein
(e) D-Day
(f) The Holocaust

13 'By 1945 the Germans had been completely defeated.'
Write an account explaining the reasons for their defeat.

14 Do you think the US bombing of Hiroshima and Nagasaki was justified?
Write 200 words explaining your answer.

SOURCE QUESTION

› Extract from Hitler's architect Albert Speer's account of Hitler's visit to Paris after the fall of France in 1940.

We drove through the suburbs directly to the great Opéra building. It was Hitler's favourite and the first thing he wanted to see. A white-haired attendant accompanied our small group through the deserted building. Hitler seemed fascinated by the Opéra, went into ecstasies about its beauty, his eyes glittering with excitement.

The attendant, of course, had immediately recognised the person he was guiding through the building. In a business-like but distinctly aloof manner, he showed us through the rooms. When we were at last getting ready to leave the building, Hitler whispered something to his adjutant, Brückner, who took a fifty-mark note from his wallet and went over to the attendant standing some distance away. Pleasantly, but firmly, the man refused to take the money.

Afterward, we drove past the Madeleine, down the Champs Elysées, on to the Trocadéro, and then to the Eiffel Tower, where Hitler ordered another stop. From the Arc de Triomphe we drove on to Les Invalides, where Hitler stood for a long time at the tomb of Napoleon.

The end of our tour was the church of Sacré Coeur on Montmartre. Here he stood for a long time surrounded by several powerful men of his escort squad, while many churchgoers recognised him but ignored him. After a last look at Paris we drove swiftly back to the airport. Afterwards he said, 'It was the dream of my life to be permitted to see Paris. I cannot say how happy I am to have that dream fulfilled today.'

Source: 'Hitler Tours Paris, 1940', www.eyewitnesstohistory.com (2008).

(a) Name two places visited by Hitler on his tour of Paris.
(b) Give two pieces of evidence from the document that suggest Hitler was not a welcome visitor to Paris.
(c) What evidence is there that Hitler was deeply satisfied with his visit to Paris?
(d) From your study of World War II, what was Vichy France?

Chapter 6

The Cold War 1945–92

Key Learning Objectives

- **What were the origins of the Cold War?**
- **What was the Berlin Blockade, and what were its consequences?**
- **What was the Korean War, and what were its consequences?**
- **What was the Cuban Missile Crisis, and what were its consequences?**
- **How did the Cold War end?**

As we saw in the last chapter, one of the important consequences of World War II was the development of the **Cold War** between the USA and the USSR. They were the most powerful countries in the world and were called **superpowers**. They were very suspicious of each other's actions and became bitter rivals.

Term

Superpower
The USA and the USSR had the power to destroy the world and this made them more powerful than any other countries in history.

What were the origins of the Cold War?

- The two countries had different political and economic systems. The table below shows the major differences:

	USA (Capitalism)	USSR (Communism)
Government	› Governments were chosen in free elections where people could vote for different political parties. This is called **democracy** › Citizens were free to express opinions on political matters	› There were no free elections and only the Communist Party was allowed. This is called a **dictatorship** › The **secret police** were used to spy on the people › The government controlled what people watched, listened to or read. This is called **censorship**
Economy	› Businesses and property were privately owned	› Businesses were owned and managed by the government

- Even before World War II ended, the two countries began to disagree on what to do after the Nazis were defeated. For example, the USA wanted to see a freely elected government in Poland. The Soviets, on the other hand, wanted Poland to have a communist government. This would mean the USSR could control Poland.
- In 1945 the Red Army controlled Eastern Europe. This let Stalin impose a communist government not only in Poland but also in

Did you know?

The USSR stands for the Union of Soviet Socialist Republics – it was often called the Soviet Union for short. Its army was called the Red Army.

Bulgaria, Romania, Czechoslovakia and Hungary. The term 'the **Iron Curtain**' was used by Winston Churchill to describe this spreading communist control and the division between Western and Eastern Europe. The countries under Soviet control became known as **satellite states**, as they were dominated by the USSR.

- The USA became alarmed at the growth of communism in Europe. President Truman decided that he had to act. In 1947 he announced the **Truman Doctrine**. The USA would give military aid to any country resisting communism. This policy was called **containment** and became the main aim of the USA during the Cold War: to stop (contain) the spread of communism throughout the world.
- There were serious economic problems in Europe after the war. Communism was attractive to many people who had no food or jobs. The USA realised that military aid alone was not enough to stop the spread of communism. Truman's foreign minister, **General Marshall**, announced massive economic aid for Europe. This became known as **Marshall Aid**. It was offered to the countries of Eastern Europe, but Stalin forced them to refuse it.

When the USA introduced Marshall Aid to Germany this caused the first major crisis of the Cold War – the **Berlin Blockade**. Let's look at what happened.

Did you know?

The term Cold War was first used in 1947. As there was no actual fighting, the Cold War never became a 'hot' war.

Term

Containment
To stop the spread of communism throughout the world.

Harry S. Truman (1884–1972) succeeded Roosevelt as president in 1945. He played a crucial role in both the Berlin Blockade and the Korean War

Did you know?

A feature of the Cold War was the use of propaganda. Radio, newspapers, TV and films were used to get the message across – we are the good guys and they are the bad guys!

Special Study: the Berlin Blockade

What were conditions like in Germany after World War II?

As a result of the war, Germany had been completely defeated and its cities destroyed. Millions were homeless and there were few jobs. To make matters worse, there were over 12 million **refugees**. These were German civilians who had been forced to flee from countries such as Poland and Czechoslovakia.

As you can see from the map on the right the country was divided into four zones. The USA, Britain, France and the USSR each had a zone. Although it was located in the Soviet zone, Berlin was also split into four occupation zones.

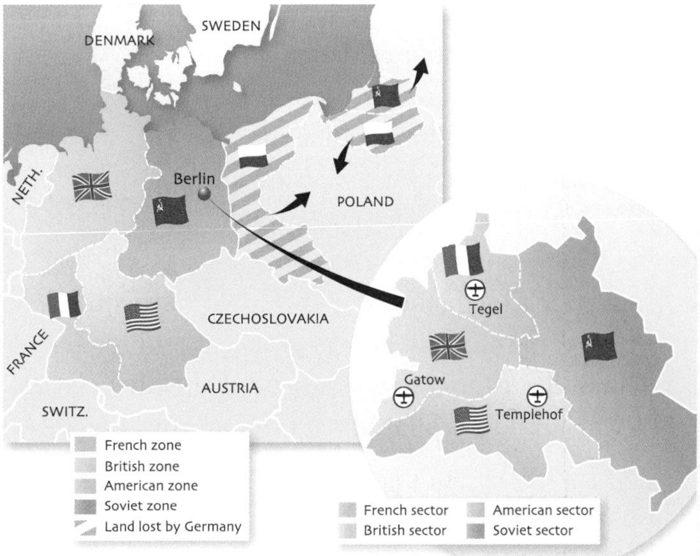

This map shows how Germany was divided into four zones, controlled by the French, British, Americans and Soviets. Berlin was also divided into four sectors

What was the background to the crisis?

The USSR and the USA disagreed on how to treat Germany.

- The USA wanted to rebuild the German economy and introduce democracy. They persuaded the British and the French to agree to join their three zones together to form West Germany. At the same time, their zones in Berlin were joined together to form West Berlin. In June 1948, as part of the Marshall Aid programme, a new currency, the **deutschmark**, was introduced into West Germany.
- Stalin wanted to keep Germany weak and divided. He wanted to establish a communist state in the Soviet zone. Stalin was particularly worried about the presence of the Allied zones in Berlin. He knew that West Berlin, with economic support from the USA, would become much richer than the Soviet zone.

When the new currency was introduced into the Western zones of Berlin, Stalin acted. He decided to drive the Allies out of Berlin.

Stalin ordered the closing of all road, water and rail access to the city. There was no way of travelling by land into the city. This is called a **blockade**. The only way in was by air. Stalin thought that the West would not remain in Berlin if the land access was cut. The American response caught him by surprise.

What was the Berlin Airlift?

Children watch a plane landing during the airlift. Some planes dropped sweets for the children as they landed

In keeping with its policy of containment, America was determined that it would not be driven from West Berlin. With the support of the British, the USA decided to fly supplies to Berlin. The Americans called it **Operation Vittles**. It became known as the **Berlin Airlift**. It lasted 320 days.

On average, planes were landing in Berlin every three minutes. Each plane carried between 10 and 20 tonnes of supplies. The 2.5 million people in West Berlin depended on the airlift for food such as milk and flour. Coal was brought in to heat homes. The Soviets did not attack the planes as they knew that would lead to war.

In May 1949, Stalin admitted defeat and reopened the routes into West Berlin.

The **Berlin Blockade** was over, but the divided city was to remain at the centre of the Cold War until the collapse of communism in 1989.

What were the effects of the crisis on superpower relations?

1. **Containment** had worked and the spread of communism had been halted in Europe. In 1949, the USA, Canada and most Western European nations formed the **North Atlantic Treaty Organisation** (NATO) to oppose the USSR.
2. The USA and the USSR were now enemies and any dispute between them might lead to war, with terrible consequences, as both sides now possessed nuclear bombs.

3 The division of Germany now seemed permanent. West Germany became the **Federal Republic of Germany**, while the East became the **German Democratic Republic.**

4 The West Germans were very impressed by the aid that the Americans gave to Berlin. West Germany became a loyal ally of the USA during the Cold War. It was allowed to have an army, and joined NATO in 1955. The **Warsaw Pact** alliance of the communist countries was formed in response to this event.

Soon the rivalry between the superpowers spread to another part of the world – Korea.

QUESTIONS

1. What was the Truman Doctrine?
2. Why was Marshall Aid important?
3. What were conditions like in Germany after World War II?
4. How did the USA and the USSR differ over what to do with Germany?
5. Why did Stalin cut off road and rail links to Berlin? Explain your answer.
6. Why did the Americans decide to fly supplies to Berlin?
7. Was the airlift a success? Give evidence to support your answer.
8. Give two results of the crisis on superpower relations.

Special Study: the Korean War 1950–53

Although their country had protected West Berlin, many in the USA felt that they were losing the Cold War. They were worried by two events in 1949:

1 The Soviets tested their first atomic bomb. Both superpowers now had the bomb. An **arms race** soon developed between the two countries. If war did break out both sides had the power to destroy the world.

2 China became communist under the leadership of **Mao Tse Tung.** The defeated opponents fled to the island of **Taiwan.** The USA refused to recognise the communist government of China. Many Americans felt they had lost China and wanted strong action against any future communist threat.

Soon events in Korea were to show the US determination to stop any further communist successes.

Term

Arms race
Rivalry between the USA and the USSR to have more and better weapons than the other.

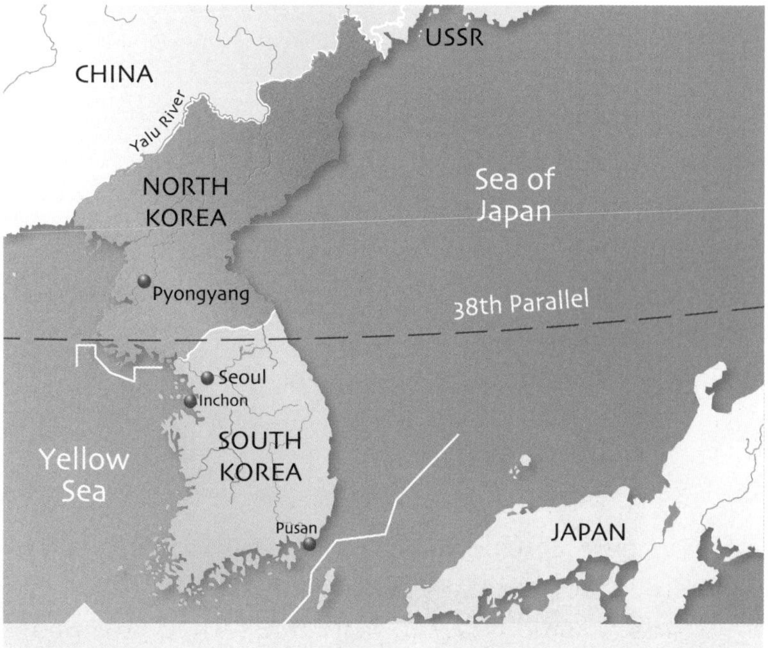

This map shows North Korea and South Korea. Korea was divided between the USA and the USSR along the 38th parallel (latitude) after World War II

PART 3

Why did the war start?

Korea had been a Japanese colony. After Japan's defeat in World War II it had been divided into two. The border was drawn along the **38th parallel.** The USSR controlled the North, and America the South. As with Germany, no agreement could be reached on reuniting the two parts. Instead two countries were set up:

- The Republic of Korea, led by **Syngman Rhee**
- The Communist People's Republic of Korea, led by **Kim Il Sung.**

The North put pressure on Stalin to approve an invasion of the South. At first he didn't agree, as he didn't want war with the USA. He eventually agreed and Soviet officers drew up plans for the attack. Stalin hoped for a quick victory for the North.

In June 1950, troops from the North invaded the South to reunify the country under communist control. Within weeks North Korea's forces controlled the peninsula except for the city of **Pusan.**

How did the USA react to the invasion of South Korea?

President Truman had to act to stop South Korea becoming communist. He called on the **United Nations** (UN) to send troops to help defend the country against communist aggression. Luckily for Truman, the USSR was boycotting the United Nation's Security Council and did not veto (stop) his request.

A UN military force was quickly sent to defend South Korea. Although this army contained soldiers from sixteen nations, most were American. It was under the command of the US General **Douglas MacArthur**, a very popular World War II hero.

In September, MacArthur's forces made a daring landing at **Inchon** behind North Korean lines. They achieved complete success and defeated the North Koreans.

Did you know?

The United Nations had been set up after World War II to preserve peace. The **Security Council** made the most important decisions. Five countries had the power to block any action taken by the Security Council: USA, UK, France, China and the USSR.

United Nations (UN) troops in Korea

General Douglas MacArthur

Why did the Chinese get involved in the war?

UN troops then invaded North Korea and advanced quickly towards the border with China. The Chinese government was worried at the American advance. They were alarmed at the prospect of a US-controlled Korea on their border.

China warned the Americans that they would not allow US troops to reach the **Yalu River**, which marked the border between North Korea and China. In November the Chinese attacked with over 300,000 troops. They drove the UN forces back across the border, although their advance was halted by a UN counter-attack.

MacArthur then began openly criticising the President's tactics of limiting the war to Korea. He wanted to attack China. Truman dismissed MacArthur and replaced him with **General Ridgway**.

Did you know?

After the war, two-thirds of the Chinese prisoners of war held by the UN didn't want to go back to communist China. They asked to go to Taiwan instead.

How did the war end?

Both sides now found it difficult to advance. The USA relied on air power and bombed North Korean targets, killing a large number of civilians. The USSR sent military aid to both the North Koreans and the Chinese, but did not get involved in the actual fighting.

In November 1951, peace talks began but they dragged on for two years. The major reason for this was the attitude of Stalin. He was quite happy to allow the war to continue as it was a drain on US manpower and resources.

When Stalin died in 1953 the new leaders in the USSR agreed to a ceasefire. Over 2.5 million people had been killed, most of them civilians. A **demilitarised zone** (DMZ) was created along the pre-war border between the countries.

Term

Demilitarised zone (DMZ)
An area from which troops are forbidden.

What were the effects of the war on superpower relations?

1. The Korean War was a victory for the US policy of containment. An attempt to spread communism had been stopped.
2. Even though they were great rivals, the USA and the USSR did not go to war with each other. Truman would not allow China to be attacked directly. The Soviets aided both North Korea and China but did not attack US forces.
3. The Cold War was no longer confined to Europe. A crisis in any part of the world could lead to a clash between the two superpowers. The USA was now committed to stopping the spread of communism throughout the world.

QUESTIONS

1. What two events worried the USA in 1949?
2. After World War II why was Korea divided into two countries?
3. What role did the USSR have in the invasion of South Korea?
4. What was the reaction of President Truman to the invasion?
5. Who was appointed commander of the invasion force?
6. Explain why the Chinese became involved in the war.
7. Explain why the war ended in 1953.
8. What were the results of the Korean War on superpower relations?

Special Study: the Cuban Missile Crisis

What were superpower relations like in the 1950s?

After Stalin's death, **Nikita Khrushchev** became the leader of the USSR. Although a committed communist, he was more moderate that Stalin. He wanted East and West to live side by side. He called this policy **peaceful coexistence.**

Relations improved briefly, but in 1956 Khrushchev sent troops into **Hungary** to crush a revolt against Soviet control. The **arms race** continued. Both countries developed missiles that could travel thousands of miles. They were very powerful and could destroy a city instantly.

The Berlin Wall being constructed in 1961. The Wall was the most famous symbol of the Cold War

Why was the Berlin Wall built?

In 1961, a meeting in Vienna between the new US President, **John F. Kennedy**, and the Soviet leader Khrushchev went very badly. Khrushchev thought he could bully the younger Kennedy. Worried by mass emigration from East Germany, he tried to force the Allies out of Berlin. When this failed, the Soviets built a wall in Berlin to stop **East Germans** fleeing to the West. Called the **Berlin Wall**, it became a symbol of division between East and West.

Both men were now very suspicious of each other's intentions. This suspicion was to contribute to the worst crisis of the Cold War.

Why did a crisis develop over Cuba?

In 1959, after a successful revolution, **Fidel Castro** came to power in Cuba. Castro introduced communism. This worried the Americans, as Cuba was so close to the USA. The USA banned trade with Cuba. In 1961, an American-backed attempt to overthrow Castro was defeated at the **Bay of Pigs**.

Castro now turned to Khrushchev for support. The Russians agreed to buy Cuba's main export: **sugar**. The Soviets also secretly began to install missiles on the island. Khrushchev did this for two main reasons:

- He was very pleased to have a communist ally so close to the USA, and he wanted to protect Cuba against American attack.
- The Soviets boasted that they had hundreds of long-range missiles that could hit the USA. This was propaganda. In fact, they had very few. The USA had far more. The Soviets hoped that by placing missiles with shorter ranges on Cuba they could catch up with the USA.

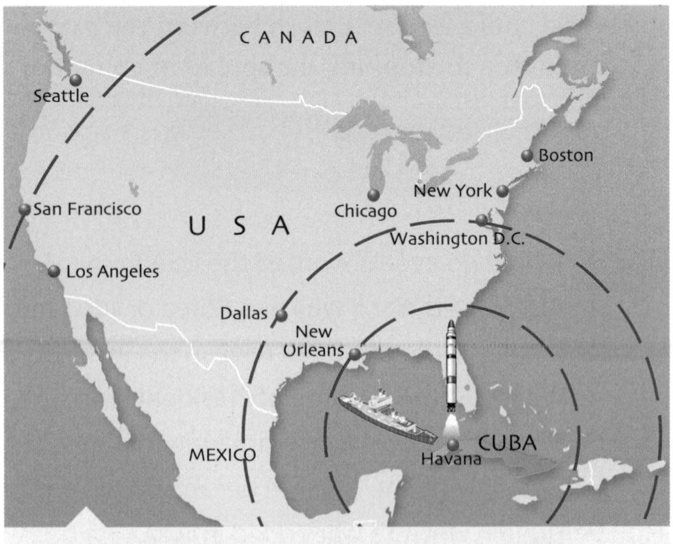

This map shows the ranges of the different Soviet missiles on Cuba

PART 3

What action did President Kennedy take?

Khrushchev hoped he could place the missiles on the island secretly, but the Americans soon found out what was happening. Special planes, called U-2s, took photographs of the missile bases.

The presence of Soviet missiles so close to America was completely unacceptable to the USA. As you can see from the map on the page opposite, nearly all American cities were in range of the missiles. President Kennedy had to act. He set up a special committee of senior advisors to decide what to do. The committee met in secret, as Kennedy did not want the Soviets to know that he had found out about the missiles in Cuba.

A P2V Neptune US patrol plane flying over a Soviet freighter during the Cuban missile crisis in 1962

Many of President Kennedy's advisors, including some generals, urged him to attack the missile sites or invade Cuba. Kennedy did not want to do this as it could have led to war with the USSR. Instead he decided to stop Soviet ships travelling to Cuba. This would prevent more missiles reaching the island. This is called a **blockade**. He hoped that his response would allow for negotiations and thereby prevent war.

On 22 October 1962, he went on TV and told the world about the Soviet missiles. He said he was going to **quarantine** Cuba. At the same time the US army was prepared for the possibility of war. He warned the Soviets that he would attack the USSR itself if any missiles were fired from Cuba.

Did you know?

When you want to stop the spread of a disease you put a person in **quarantine** – or isolate them from other people.

How was war prevented?

Throughout the world people were worried. There was panic buying in the shops. World War III seemed likely at any moment, and that would mean nuclear destruction. However, like Kennedy, Khrushchev didn't want war. He ordered the Soviet ships to slow down as they approached Cuba. The crisis was not over, however. The USA had to get the Soviets to pull their missiles out of Cuba.

Kennedy sent his brother **Robert** to negotiate with the Soviet ambassador to the USA. An agreement was reached that ended the crisis:

- The Soviets agreed to withdraw their missiles from Cuba.
- The Americans promised not to attack Cuba.
- Secretly the USA also agreed to withdraw their nuclear missiles from Turkey – a country that bordered the USSR.

The crisis was over. Kennedy had handled events very well. He had forced the Soviets to withdraw their missiles from Cuba without starting a war.

The leaders involved in the Cuban Missile Crisis: John F. Kennedy (USA) and Nikita Khrushchev (USSR)

What were the effects of the crisis on superpower relations?

1. The crisis scared both superpowers. The USA and the USSR had come very close to war. They realised that they would have to cooperate in the future to prevent war.
2. A **hotline** was set up between the White House and the Kremlin to improve communication in a future crisis.
3. As a sign of improved relations both countries agreed to stop testing nuclear weapons on land or at sea. This was called the **Partial Test Ban Treaty**.

Did you know?

Another area of superpower competition was in space exploration – the **Space Race**. The Soviets put the first satellite and the first man into space. However, the USA won the race when they landed a man on the moon in 1969.

How did the Cold War end?

Although the Cold War continued for another twenty-seven years, the superpowers never went to war. There were serious tensions, though, especially over the Middle East, Eastern Europe and the arms race.

In 1985, **Michael Gorbachev** came to power in Russia. He wanted to improve relations with the USA and allow greater freedoms for people in communist countries. Events moved very quickly.

- The USA and the USSR cooperated to end the arms race.
- In 1989, the peoples of Eastern Europe forced their communist governments to agree to elections.
- In November 1989, the East German government opened the Berlin Wall and allowed their citizens to travel freely.
- The following year the division of Germany ended. Gorbachev did not try to prevent this happening.
- In the USSR, communism collapsed and the country ceased to exist. It was replaced by a large number of independent countries including Russia, the Ukraine, Lithuania and Estonia.

Crowds celebrate the opening of the Berlin Wall in 1989. To many people this event marked the end of the Cold War

TIMELINE The Cold War 1945–63

1945	Defeated Germany divided into four zones Soviets began to place communist governments in Eastern Europe Atomic bombs used against Japan
1947	Truman doctrine and Marshall Aid
1948	Start of the Berlin Blockade (June 1948 – May 1949)
1949	USSR tested its first atomic bomb China became communist
1950	Outbreak of the Korean War
1953	Death of Stalin and the end of the Korean War
1956	Soviet troops invaded Hungary
1961	The Berlin Wall was built
1962	Cuban Missile Crisis
1963	Partial Test Ban Treaty

Do you understand these key terms?

Cold War
superpowers
Iron Curtain
satellite states
Truman doctrine
containment
Marshall Aid
Berlin Blockade
deutschmark
Berlin Airlift
NATO
Warsaw Pact
arms race
United Nations (UN)
UN Security Council
peaceful coexistence
Cuban Missile Crisis
Berlin Wall
quarantine
Partial Test Ban Treaty
Space Race

QUESTIONS

1. What happened in Berlin in 1961?
2. How did the USA oppose Fidel Castro's government in Cuba?
3. Give one reason why the USSR put missiles on Cuba.
4. What options did President Kennedy have to stop the Soviets?
5. Why did many people feel that there would be war?
6. What agreement was reached between the sides to end the crisis?
7. What were (a) the hotline and (b) the Partial Test Ban Treaty?
8. Write an account of one of the following:
   (a) The importance of the Berlin Blockade during the Cold War
   (b) Why the USA sent support to South Korea
   (c) The consequences of the Korean War on superpower relations.
9. In your opinion, how did President Kennedy handle the crisis over Cuba? Give three reasons to support your answer.

EXAM QUESTIONS

1 Explain two of the following terms: containment; Marshall Plan; satellite states; Iron Curtain.

2 Write an account of a named major crisis in the Cold War between the USA and the USSR during the period 1945–63.

SOURCE QUESTION

› Study this cartoon about the Cuban Missile Crisis and answer the questions that follow:

Source: *Daily Mail*, 29 October 1962. *Supplied by Llyfrgell Genedlaethol Cymru / National Library of Wales. Reproduced by permission of Solo Syndication*

(a) Name the two leaders depicted in the cartoon. What countries do they represent?
(b) What are the the two leaders sitting on?
(c) Describe what is happening in the cartoon.
(d) In your opinion what is the attitude of the cartoonist to the crisis? Give a reason to support your answer.

People in History

Write about a news reporter describing one of the crises during the Cold War, 1945–1963.

Use the plan below as a guide.

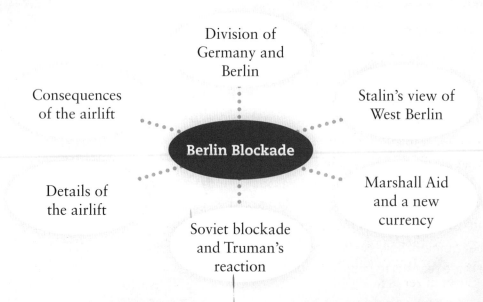

Berlin Blockade

- Division of Germany and Berlin
- Stalin's view of West Berlin
- Marshall Aid and a new currency
- Soviet blockade and Truman's reaction
- Details of the airlift
- Consequences of the airlift

Chapter 7

Moves Towards European Unity

Key Learning Objectives

- **Why was there a movement towards European unity after World War II?**
- **What were the main steps in the formation of the EEC?**
- **How has European cooperation increased since 1957?**

Why was there a movement towards European unity after World War II?

- The rivalry between France and Germany had helped to cause two world wars. If hatred and rivalry could be turned into friendship and cooperation, then another war might be avoided.
- It was important to spread democracy and respect for **human rights**. Dictators such as Hitler, Mussolini and Stalin caused great suffering by ignoring human rights. Hitler had started World War II and killed Jews. Democratic governments don't usually do things like that.
- Many poor people had voted for fascist or communist parties because these parties gave them hope for a better future. Democratic governments needed to work together to improve the economies. This would ensure their people had jobs, houses, education and healthcare, and so they would not be tempted to support fascists or communists in the future.

Term

Human rights
Basic rights, such as freedom of speech or freedom from wrongful imprisonment, which are thought to belong to all people.

Jean Monnet (1888–1979)

Who were the leaders who supported unity?

After World War II, three men worked for greater European unity.

- **Jean Monnet** was a French businessman who after the war was asked to take charge of the French economy.
- **Robert Schuman** was also French and had fought in the Resistance against the Germans. After the war he became a leading French politician.
- **Konrad Adenauer** was a German politician who had opposed the Nazis. In 1949 he became Chancellor (prime minister) of the new West German republic.

Robert Schuman (1886–1963)

Konrad Adenauer (1876–1967)

What were the main steps in the formation of the EEC?

After 1945 a number of organisations were set up to promote **greater cooperation** among European countries:

- The **Council of Europe** was formed by ten European countries, including Ireland. Its aim was to encourage democracy and respect for human rights. Members agreed to the **European Convention on Human Rights**, which set out the basic freedoms that all citizens were guaranteed, such as freedom of speech.
- The **Organisation for European Economic Cooperation** (OEEC): The USA feared that the Soviet Union planned to conquer Western Europe. To prevent that, the Americans gave money called **Marshall Aid** to European governments to help their economies recover from the war. The OEEC was set up to distribute the money. As a result of this investment, the economies of Western Europe recovered quickly from the war.
- The **Benelux Union** was formed by Belgium, the Netherlands and Luxembourg. These countries decided to work together to rebuild their economies. Goods, people and money could pass freely between them. This was called a **customs union.** The union was a success and by 1950 these countries had become prosperous.
- After the success of the Benelux Union, Jean Monnet and Robert Schuman suggested that France and Germany share their coal and steel industries. This became known as the **Schuman Declaration.** It was an extraordinary idea for these two old enemies. The German Chancellor, Konrad Adenauer, agreed and Italy and the Benelux countries joined as well. In 1951, these six countries formed the **European Coal and Steel Community** (ECSC). It proved to be a great success.

Term

Common Market
A group of countries that agree to have no barriers to trade between them. It was also a name commonly used to describe the EEC.

Guaranteed price
A good price that farmers would always be paid for their produce.

The Treaty of Rome

The six members of the ECSC then decided to cooperate in other economic areas. After talks, they signed the **Treaty of Rome** in March 1957. This set up the **European Economic Community** (EEC). The countries agreed the following:

- People, goods and services could pass freely among the six countries. This was called the **Common Market.**
- A **Common Agricultural Policy** (CAP) was set up to give farmers **guaranteed prices** for their produce.
- Under a **Social Policy,** richer countries would give money to help poorer areas.
- A promise was made to work for political as well as economic unity.

To establish the EEC, the Treaty of Rome was signed by France, West Germany, Italy and the Benelux countries on 25 March 1957

PART 3

QUESTIONS

1 Why was there growing support for European unity after World War II?
2 Name three of the men who helped to start the search for European unity.
3 Why was the Organisation for European Economic Cooperation important?
4 Write a short account of the European Coal and Steel Community.
5 Give two important decisions agreed under the Treaty of Rome.

How has European cooperation increased since 1957?

The growth of the European Union

The United Kingdom (UK) refused to join the EEC when it was set up. It had close economic and political ties with its empire and the USA.

But by 1960, the UK had lost its empire and its economy was not doing well, while the EEC prospered. The British government applied to join in 1961. This was important for Ireland as 90 per cent of Irish trade was with the UK. The Taoiseach in 1961 was Seán Lemass. He also applied to join.

However, the French President, **General de Gaulle**, twice blocked the UK's entry. He felt it was too close to the USA, which he did not trust. This meant that Ireland could not join either.

After de Gaulle resigned in 1969, the UK and Ireland (along with Denmark) were admitted into the EEC on 1 January 1973. Over 70 per cent of the Irish people voted yes for membership in a **referendum**.

Term
Referendum
A vote held to get the opinion of the people on an important issue.

Since then, more countries have joined the **European Union** (EU), as it is now known.

- Greece, Spain and Portugal joined in the 1980s.
- Austria, Finland and Sweden became members in 1995.
- The biggest group of new members came from Eastern Europe. When communism fell in 1989, the countries of Eastern Europe became democracies. All applied to join the EU, although it took a while for their economies to become strong enough. Many became members in 2004, e.g. Poland and the Czech Republic. Romania and Bulgaria became members in 2007. Croatia joined in 2013.

How were decisions reached in the EEC?

By the 1970s the main decision-making institutions of the EEC had been agreed by the member states:

The Council of Ministers	The European Commission	The European Parliament	The European Court of Justice
It consists of government ministers from the member states. They decide on the policies that the EEC will follow	Each country has one member. The Commission proposes changes to the Council of Ministers and carries out their decisions	Each country elects a number of members to the Parliament, in proportion to the size of their population	Its job is to see that the members obey the rules of the Union

PART 3

The Maastricht Treaty

Until the 1980s, the members of the EEC concentrated on developing **economic cooperation.** In 1979 the **European Monetary System** was introduced. The members agreed to try to reduce inflation and keep the value of their currencies in line with each other.

Then in 1985, a Frenchman, **Jacques Delors,** became head of the European Commission. Between 1985 and 1995 he encouraged many changes in the Community. This led to two important agreements:

Jacques Delors was head of the European Commission

1. The **Single European Act** was signed in 1986. Under this Act members agreed to bring their taxation systems into line and to remove any remaining barriers to trade and the free movement of people. It also increased the power of the European Parliament.
2. The **Maastricht Treaty** was signed at Maastricht, Holland in 1992. Here are some of the things that were agreed:
   - The Treaty changed the name of the EEC to the **European Union.** All people in the EU were now **European citizens.**
   - There were to be much **closer political ties,** with greater cooperation in foreign policy. Member states would work together in security and justice.
   - A timetable for a common (shared) currency was agreed. This currency, the **euro,** was introduced in twelve countries on 1 January 2002.
   - A **Social Chapter** brought in policies about pay and conditions for workers.

The euro symbol. Why do you think there are 12 stars?

How has the EU changed Europe?

The EU has had a great impact on the countries of Europe:

- There has not been a major war between members in sixty years.
- All countries in the EU must be democracies and this helped to stop any growth of dictatorships.
- The EU created a huge market of nearly half a billion people who move freely and trade freely among member states.

This map shows the countries that are members of the EU in 2014

TIMELINE Moves Towards European Unity 1949–92

1949	Council of Europe founded
1951	European Coal and Steel Community set up
1957	Treaty of Rome signed – European Economic Community created
1961	Ireland and the UK apply to join the EEC
1963	De Gaulle refuses to allow the UK to join
1973	Ireland and the UK join the EEC
1986	Single European Act agreed
1992	Maastricht Treaty signed – name changed to the European Union

Do you understand these key terms?

human rights
Council of Europe
European Convention on Human Rights
OEEC
customs union
ECSC
Schuman Declaration
EEC
CAP
guaranteed price
Council of Ministers
European Commission
European Parliament
European Court
European Union
European Monetary System
euro
Social Charter

QUESTIONS

1. Why could the UK not join the EEC in the 1960s?
2. Why did Ireland apply to join in 1961?
3. Was Irish entry into the EEC popular in 1973? Give a piece of evidence to support your answer.
4. Name six countries that joined the EEC in the 1980s and 1990s.
5. Write a short paragraph on the Maastricht Treaty.

EXAM QUESTIONS

1. Explain two of the following terms: Benelux Union; ECSC; CAP; Treaty of Rome, 1957.
2. Write an account of the growth of the European Union since 1957.

PART 3

Chapter 8

Asian Nationalism: India

Key Learning Objectives

- **How did the British control India?**
- **What role did Gandhi play in the struggle for independence?**
- **What impact did World War II have on British rule in India?**
- **Why was India divided into two countries?**
- **What happened when the British left?**
- **What were relations like between Pakistan and India after 1947?**

In this chapter we will look at how India gained its independence from British rule. We will also learn what happened to the country after the British left in 1947 – this is called the **post-colonial experience.**

Before 1945 nearly all of the countries of Africa and Asia were controlled by European countries. When a European country controlled an African or Asian country it was called a **colonial power**. The country it controlled was called a **colony**. One such country was India, which was ruled by Britain. Can you see it on the map?

Term

Colonial power
A European country that controlled an Asian or African country. The country they control is called a **colony**

After World War II most European countries were in debt and did not have the money to control their colonies. Many colonies wanted to rule themselves, and demanded **independence**. This is the story of how India got its independence from Britain.

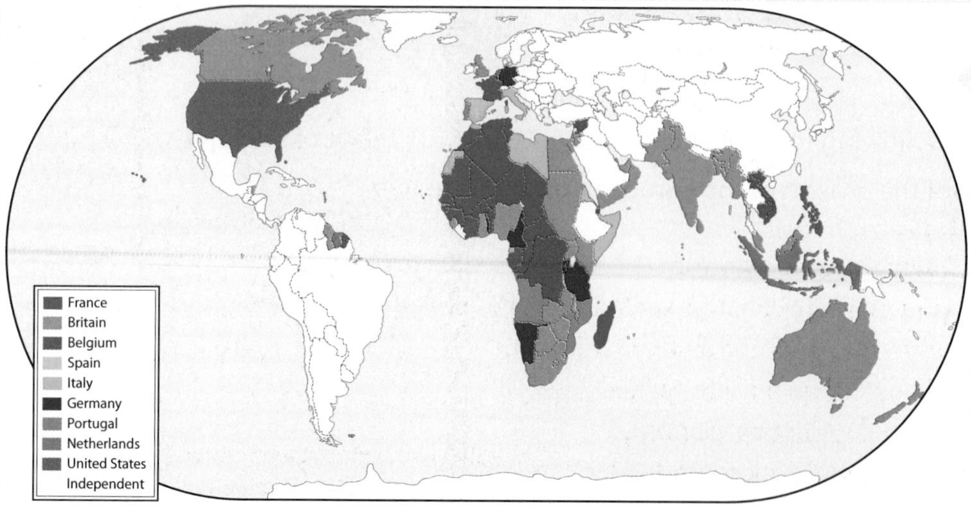

The European and American empires on the eve of World War II. The British Empire is marked in pink

How did the British control India?

British merchants first travelled to India in the late sixteenth century during the Age of Exploration (see Section 6). The **British East India Company** was set up to control trade with India. This company had an army and soon conquered most of the country. In other parts of India native princes were allowed to rule their people as long as they obeyed the British.

India was a very large country with mountain ranges and deserts. It was also divided by religion. Most of the population were Hindus while about one quarter were Muslims. The majority of the Muslims lived in the north-west (Punjab and Kashmir) and the north-east (Bengal). There had been a long history of distrust between Hindus and Muslims.

After a revolt by Indians in 1857 the British government took direct control of the country from the East India Company. From then on British India was called the **Raj**. For the British, India was the most important part of their vast empire. They called it 'the Jewel in the Crown'.

Term

Raj
Hindi (Indian language) word that means 'rule'.

Although the British built railways and improved the economy most Indians were desperately poor and could not read and write. Many Indians were unhappy with British rule. They disliked the way the British treated them and they wanted to control their own affairs.

Mahatma Gandhi (1869–1948)

What role did Gandhi play in the struggle for independence?

Mohandas Gandhi, more than any other person, was responsible for India's freedom. What is extraordinary about his story is that he achieved this without using violence.

Gandhi was born in 1869. He came from a wealthy Hindu family. He studied law in London and his first job was in South Africa. Here he fought to get more rights for Indians in many legal battles.

He returned to India in 1914 and joined the **Congress Party**. This was a political party that wanted **Home Rule** for India.

Term

Home Rule
Government of a country by its own people as a **dominion** within the British Empire.

Gandhi believed firmly in the idea of non-violence, or **truth-force** as he called it. He persuaded the Congress Party to campaign for complete independence using peaceful protest such as marches and strikes. Gandhi wore peasant clothes and was regarded by many Indians as a saint. He earned the title **Mahatma** or 'great soul'. Next to Gandhi, **Jawaharlal Nehru** was the most widely known leader. He was popularly known as **Pandit** or 'teacher'.

Mahatma Gandhi outside 10 Downing Street, the British prime minister's house, in 1931

PART 3

The Salt March to Dandi, 1930

Gandhi organised boycotts of British goods and British courts. He planned mass protest demonstrations. The most famous one was the **Salt March**. The British controlled the price of salt and they kept the prices high. Since people needed salt to preserve their food, this made a lot of Indians angry. Thousands of them went with Gandhi on a 400-kilometre protest march to Dandi on the Indian Ocean. There they evaporated the seawater to make their own salt. In the end, the British gave in and lowered the price of salt.

Gandhi also fought for the rights of women and an end to the **caste system**.

The Salt March to Dandi in 1930 forced the British to reduce the price of salt

Did you know?

Hindus believed that people were divided into higher and lower castes. At the bottom were the **untouchables** who did all the manual work.

QUESTIONS

1. What is Home Rule?
2. Give two reasons why European countries began to give up their colonies after World War II.
3. What was the name of the British organisation that controlled trade with India?
4. What was the Congress Party?
5. What was truth-force?
6. Give an account of the Salt March to Dandi.

What impact did World War II have on British rule?

There were few protests about British rule during World War II. The British fight against the Japanese was aided by over two million Indians who joined the British army. Even though the British beat the Japanese their hold on India had been weakened for a number of reasons:

- The cost of the war had reduced Britain's military and economic power in both Europe and Asia.
- Japanese victories over the British at the start of the war had shown that British power could be challenged.
- After the war the United States and the USSR were the world's most powerful nations. They were opposed to colonialism and the British Empire.

After the war there were elections in Britain and the new Labour government led by **Clement Attlee** announced that it planned to withdraw from India. There was great excitement in India at the prospect of an end to British rule.

Why was India divided into two countries?

As the reality of independence came nearer the divisions between Muslims and Hindus grew. Congress was a mainly Hindu party. This alarmed Indian Muslims who feared they would be treated badly in a Hindu-dominated India. They set up the **Muslim League** to defend the rights of Muslims in India.

The League was led by **Muhammad Ali Jinnah.** He called for British India to be divided into separate Hindu and Muslim states. Jinnah called the Muslim state **Pakistan** (the land of the pure).

Gandhi and the Congress Party were against this demand as they hoped to keep India united as one country. Gandhi said, 'Before partitioning India my body will have to be cut into two pieces.'

Muhammad Ali Jinnah

- The Congress Party wanted a single Indian state.
- The Muslim League wanted a separate state for Muslims.

What was the British response?

The British hoped to keep the country united, but they soon realised that this was impossible. In 1946 **elections** throughout India confirmed that Muslims wanted their own state.

In August 1946 violence between Hindus and Muslims broke out in the city of **Calcutta**. Soon it spread throughout India. Gandhi worked hard to end the violence. He went to live in an area where there was lot of violence. As a result Nehru represented the Congress Party in the negotiations that led to Indian independence.

In one riot in Calcutta almost 5,000 people were killed

Lord Mountbatten was in charge of negotiations on the British side. He was a famous admiral in World War II and a relative of the British royal family. In June 1947 these negotiations led to the **Mountbatten Plan.** British India would be split (or **partitioned**) into two countries, India and Pakistan (see map on the next page). The British also announced that they would leave India earlier than expected – in August 1947.

Term

Partition
When a country is split to form two separate states.

Mountbatten (centre), with Nehru (left) and Jinnah (right)

What happened when the British left?

After partition in 1947, the violence between Hindus and Muslims got worse. The border areas were the most badly affected. **Kashmir** was 75 per cent Muslim, but remained in India. **Punjab** had been split in two by the new border. About 7 million refugees fled from Pakistan to India and as many from India to Pakistan. Hundreds of thousands were brutally killed on the way.

Did you know?

When colonial powers give up their colonies it is called **decolonisation**.

Crowds of refugees on the move between India and Pakistan. About 14.5 million people left their homes

Gandhi tries to bring peace between the two sides

Gandhi tried to stop the violence. He had been against partition, but at the last minute he accepted it in 1947 as something that Muslims wanted. He believed that if the Hindus didn't accept it there would be civil war.

Gandhi said there had to be tolerance on both sides. He vowed he would fast until death if the killings continued. Gandhi insisted also that the Indian government should pay Pakistan the 550 million rupees (€50 million) that were due to them after partition. He was strongly against a plan to deport all Muslims to Pakistan.

Did you know?

About 5 per cent of Indians were Sikhs. They lived mainly in the border areas.

In January 1948, Gandhi was shot by **Nathuram Godse**. He was a Hindu fanatic who believed that Gandhi was too pro-Muslim. The assassination had such an effect on people that the widespread killings between Muslims and Hindus stopped. His death was mourned throughout the world. His peaceful methods were to influence later leaders such as Martin Luther King and Nelson Mandela.

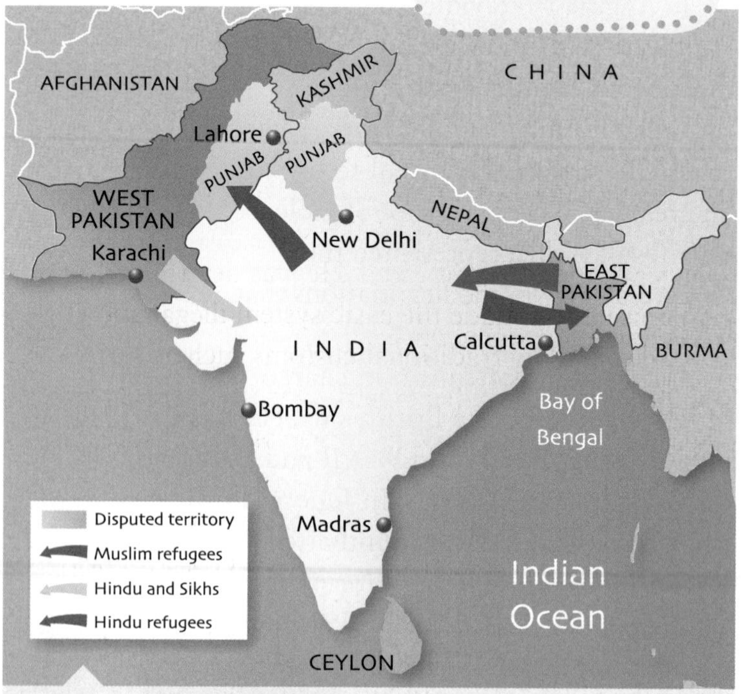

This map shows the partitioning of India in 1947. Pakistan was divided into West Pakistan and East Pakistan

Did you know?

As many as 500,000 people were killed in the 6 months following independence in India. Some historians think the death toll may have been as high as 1 million.

India's post-colonial experience

What were relations like between India and Pakistan after 1947?

Since independence relations between India and Pakistan have been poor. The main dispute has been over **Kashmir**. This province was claimed by both countries and in October 1947 war broke out between them. This lasted until the United Nations arranged a ceasefire that divided Kashmir between the countries. There were further wars over Kashmir in 1965 and 1999.

As you can see from the map opposite, East Pakistan was separated from the rest of Pakistan by about a thousand miles. It was very poor, and people in East Pakistan grew angry that the politicians in West Pakistan were giving them little say in how the country was run. After elections in 1970 violence broke out in East Pakistan, and West Pakistan sent in the army to restore control. The Indians helped East Pakistanis to defeat the West Pakistani army. In 1971 East Pakistan became the newly independent state of **Bangladesh**.

Indian soldiers patrol along a barbed wire fence near Baras Post on the border between India and Pakistan, December 2003

The new India

India had a lot of problems to face after independence. In 1947 it had a population of 400 million. By 2000 this had grown to one billion people and this has caused poverty and social problems.

Pandit Nehru (1889–1964) became the first prime minister of independent India. He was determined to modernise it. He made the caste system illegal and he tried to outlaw traditional customs such as sati. **Sati** (or suttee) was when a widow was expected to commit suicide by throwing herself on her husband's **funeral pyre**.

India is a country with many languages and different cultures. As a result it has suffered at times from violence between different communities. Over 3,000 Sikhs were killed in anti-Sikh riots when two Sikhs assassinated the Indian Prime Minister **Indira Gandhi** in 1984.

Term

Funeral pyre
A wooden structure on which a dead body is burnt as part of a funeral rite.

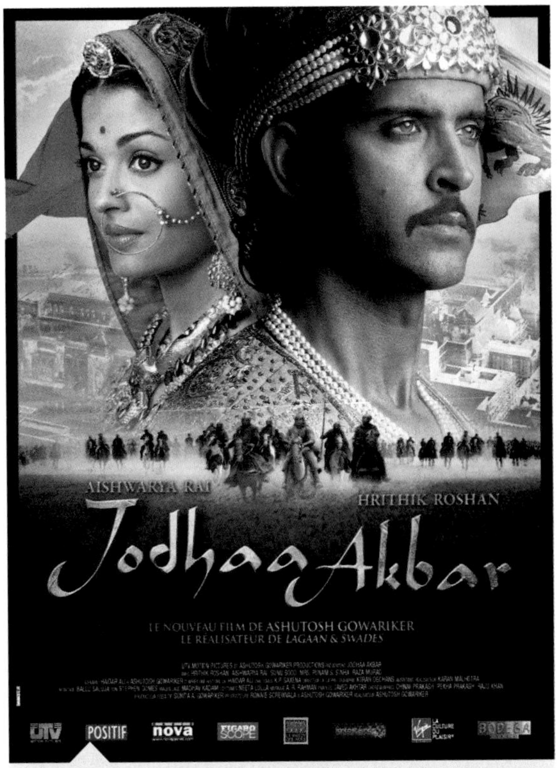

A poster from a Bollywood film. Bollywood is the Hindi-language film industry based in Mumbai (Bombay)

Despite all these problems, India has had many successes. It has remained a strong democracy. Dams and steelworks were built and free education was brought in for all children. India is now one of the biggest industrial nations in the world. It is the largest exporter of rice and has a hugely successful computer and film industry.

Did you know?

Many Indian films have words and whole phrases in English. Indians call this Hinglish.

Do you understand these key terms?

colonial power	**Raj**	**untouchables**	**Partition**
post-colonial experience	**Home Rule**	**Hindu**	**Mountbatten Plan**
independence	**Mahatma**	**Muslim**	**sati**
	caste system		

QUESTIONS

1. What effect did World War II have on British rule in India?
2. Give two reasons why the British decided to leave India.
3. What was the Muslim League and what did it want?
4. How did India finally get its independence from Britain?
5. Did that bring peace to India? Explain your answer.
6. Name three problems faced by India since its independence.
7. Give three ways in which the Indian state has been very successful.

EXAM QUESTIONS

1. Why did European countries begin to give up their colonies after 1945?
2. Give an account of the struggle for independence of a named African or Asian country after 1945.
3. In the case of a named African or Asian country, write an account of the challenges it faced after achieving independence in the period after 1945.

TIMELINE

PART 3

Section 13

Ireland: Social History

Chapter 1

Changes in Rural Ireland 1900–2000

Key Learning Objectives

- How did rural life change during the twentieth century?
  - Housing
  - Work
  - Everyday life

A century of social change

A huge change took place in the way people lived their everyday lives between 1900 and 2000. The houses people lived in, the clothes they wore, how they earned their living, how they travelled and what they did in their spare time – all these aspects of life changed over a hundred years. In this section we will look at how and why all these things changed.

How did rural life change during the twentieth century?

About 70 per cent of Irish people lived in rural areas in 1900.

Housing

Most people were small farmers or **labourers** who lived in three-roomed thatched houses like the one on the right. There was no electricity, no running water, no toilet and no central heating. People had large families, so it was common for four or five children to share one room and one bed.

Term

Labourer
Someone who worked for farmers.

A thatched house in Kerry in the early twentieth century

A kitchen c.1900

1 Stone floor
2 Open fire
3 Crane over the fire with a pot hanging from it
4 Water barrel
5 Súgán chair
6 Door to the bedroom

Can you spot five differences between this kitchen and a modern kitchen?
This image is reproduced courtesy of the National Library of Ireland

Here is a typical kitchen from that time. This is where meals were cooked, clothes washed, butter made and meat prepared. There were no fridges, so food had to be stored in a hole in the ground or the wall.

Wealthy farmers usually lived in houses with two storeys, set back from the road. There would be three or four bedrooms and a **parlour**. This was a good room used for special occasions such as when the priest or vicar visited.

This picture shows a typical house belonging to a wealthy farmer

How did rural housing change?

In the 1940s and 1950s local councils built **county council cottages** for labourers. There were four rooms with a slate roof. They were built on an acre of land. You still see many around today.

It was not until the 1960s that people began to build modern **bungalows**. They usually had three bedrooms and were built with concrete blocks. In the 1990s **dormer**-style houses became popular.

A 1960s bungalow

A 1990s dormer

What differences do you see between these houses and the pre-1950s houses? The biggest change was the fact that these houses had electricity.

PART 3

What was the effect of rural electrification?

In 1951 the **rural electrification scheme** began. Three million electricity poles were put up, bringing electricity to every home in rural Ireland.

Electricity brought enormous changes to the way people lived. This was especially true for women. In 1900, there was no electricity. Women washed and ironed clothes by hand. In the 1960s people started to use washing machines and electric cookers. In the 1980s vacuum cleaners and dryers became common.

Did you know?

The bringing of electricity to rural areas was called **rural electrification**. Many people were against it as they thought it would be far too dangerous to have in their houses!

A paraffin lamp

Ploughing a field using horses and a hand-held plough

Did you know?

Before electricity people used candles and, later, paraffin lamps to light up the house. The lamps would have to be cleaned every day.

Work

In 1900 most people who lived in rural Ireland were farmers.

- Nearly all work was done by hand.
- Since most farms were small the whole family helped out.
- Men used horses to plough the land, to sow crops and to reap them.
- Women milked cows, made butter and raised chickens, ducks, geese and turkeys.
- Neighbours helped each other at harvest time when crops had to be saved quickly. In parts of Ireland this was called the **meitheal**.

How did rural work change?

Today most people who live in rural areas no longer work on farms. They commute to towns and cities and work in factories, shops or offices.

In the 1950s tractors and other machines became common and farming changed a lot.

- Work was no longer done by hand.
- Horses almost disappeared.
- Machines such as combine harvesters and silage makers allowed farmers to do much more work by themselves.
- Electric milking machines did away with the need to milk cows by hand.
- Farms became much bigger and the old meitheal system of neighbours helping each other died out.

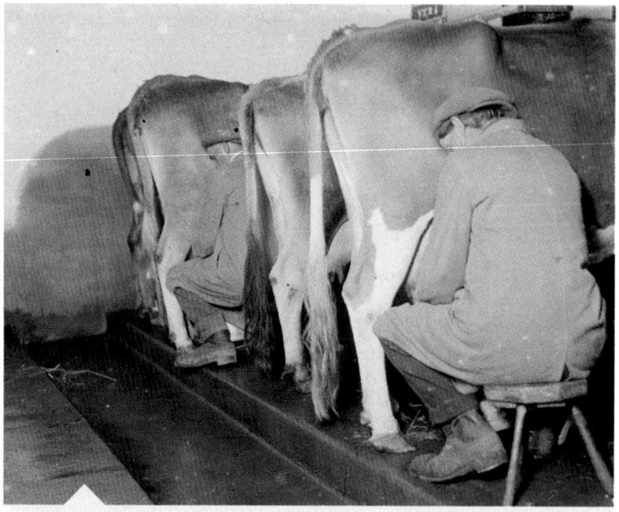

Milking cows by hand. In general, farms were smaller so there were fewer cows to milk

What was the effect of joining the EU?

Ireland joined the European Economic Community (now the European Union) in 1973. This really helped farmers. The **EEC** brought in two policies to increase farmer income:

- The **Common Agricultural Policy** (**CAP**) guaranteed good prices for farm produce.
- The **Social Fund** gave grants to improve living standards in poor farming areas.

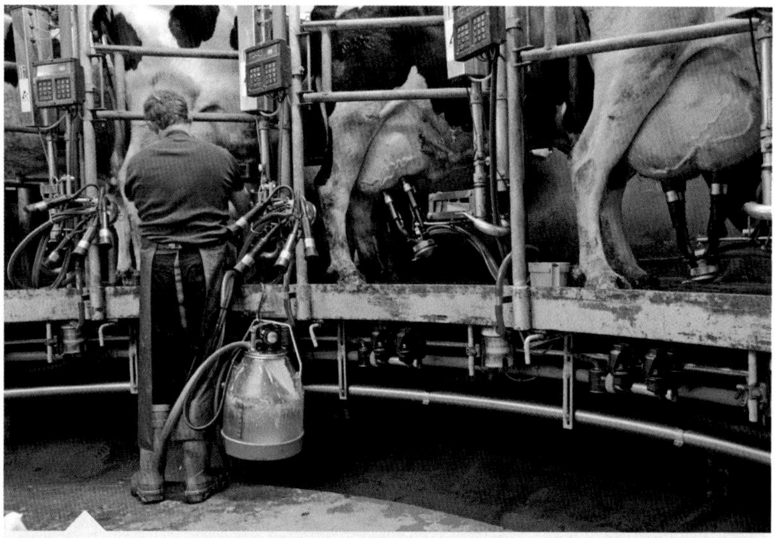

Milking cows using a milking machine

Farmers got better prices for their produce and they had a bigger market for it in Europe. Above all, CAP grants meant that more farmers were able to stay on the land, which helped slow down **emigration** (see page 403).

Everyday life

- **Food:** Farming families produced most of the food they ate, e.g. potatoes, vegetables and eggs. Women baked bread every day and made butter with milk from the family's cows. Now people buy in most of their food.
- **Shops:** People went to the small local shops for a few groceries such as meat, flour, tea and sugar. Now people go to shopping centres or big towns to shop. The small local shops have almost disappeared.
- **Class distinction:** In the early 1900s, there was a lot of class distinction between these different social groups. Sons and daughters were expected to marry into the same social class. A son of a large farmer who wanted to marry the daughter of a labourer or small farmer could find himself cut off by the family. This snobbery lasted until the 1960s.

PART 3

Religion

Religion had a huge influence on people's lives. Almost 93 per cent of people living in the **Irish Free State** in 1922 were Catholics. They went to Mass every Sunday. Most hospitals and schools were run by the Catholic Church.

Church leaders had a big influence on politics and society. In the 1930s **divorce** and **contraception** were made illegal because they were against Christian teachings. Sex before marriage was seen as a sin. If a girl got pregnant before she married, the whole family could be shunned. These girls were often sent away to homes and their babies given up for adoption.

The **Ne Temere** decree issued by the Catholic Church in 1908 meant that in Ireland the children of mixed Catholic and Protestant marriages had to be reared as Catholics. This was one of the reasons why there was a huge drop in the numbers of Protestants living in the Republic of Ireland by the 1960s.

The **Second Vatican Council** in the 1960s (see page 312) began to modernise the Catholic Church, and Irish society changed too. Television helped to spread new ideas and attitudes. From the 1970s Church teachings had less influence on how people lived their lives. In the 1990s news stories about child abuse and sex scandals also undermined the Catholic Church.

Nevertheless, the visit of Pope John Paul II to Ireland in 1979 showed how important the Catholic Church still was in Ireland. It continues to have a strong influence on Irish society, especially in schools and hospitals.

Did you know?

Contraception did not become legal in Ireland until 1980. Divorce was made legal in 1996.

Did you know?

The **Eucharistic Congress** was the biggest international event organised in Ireland before World War II. It was a Catholic festival celebrating Holy Communion. Over a million Catholics from Ireland and abroad attended the celebrations.

A million people attended the Mass in Phoenix Park during the Pope's visit to Ireland in 1979

TIMELINE Rural Life in the Twentieth Century

	1900–60	1960–2000
People	› 70 per cent of people lived in rural areas and worked on the land › Huge **class distinction** between rich and poor farmers	› Only 30 per cent of people live in rural areas › Many only farm part time › Less snobbery › Many people who live in rural areas work in nearby towns and cities
Housing	› Most houses were small thatched cottages made of stone › No running water or electricity › Three rooms. No bathroom	› In the 1960s **rural electrification** brought light, pumps, washing machines and other electrical goods › Bathrooms built › From the 1970s farmers built modern houses › Three- or four-bedroomed **bungalows** became common › In the 1990s **dormer houses** became popular
Standard of living	› Poor prices for goods › Many farmers' children emigrated (between 20,000 and 40,000 each year)	› In 1973 Ireland joined the **EEC** › EEC membership, **CAP** and **Social Fund** gave farmers better incomes
Work	› Most farm work was done with horses and human labour › All the family helped › **Meitheal** system	› Tractors and other machines reduced the need for labour › Large milking parlours, silage balers and combine harvesters reduced it further
Food	› Farmers grew much of the food they ate and bought the rest locally › Mainly Irish-produced food in the shops	› People buy food in supermarkets › Farmers had to compete with food from other parts of EU and elsewhere
Religion	› Religion very important in everyday life › Church had a huge political and cultural influence › Divorce and contraception illegal	› Religion less important in everyday life › Contraception and divorce made legal

Do you understand these key terms?

labourer	**bungalow**	**meitheal**	**Social Fund**
parlour	**dormer house**	**Common Agricultural Policy**	**class distinction**
county council cottage	**rural electrification**		

QUESTIONS

1 What percentage of Irish people lived in the countryside in 1900?
2 Why are there fewer people living in the country now? Give two reasons.
3 List six ways in which a house nowadays is different from one in the early 1900s.
4 Give two ways in which electricity changed life in rural areas.
5 List four ways in which farming has changed since 1900.
6 Do you think women help out as much on farms now? Give two reasons why or why not.
7 When did Ireland join the EEC? Give two ways the European Union has benefited Ireland.
8 Give two examples of how everyday life has changed in rural areas.
9 What do you think is meant by 'class distinction'?
10 Write an account of how rural life has changed since 1900, under the following headings: houses; standard of living; food; farming; rural electrification; the EU.

SOURCE QUESTION

› Look at the picture of a village in 1900 and answer the questions that follow.

This image is reproduced courtesy of the National Library of Ireland [LROY04085]

(a) List five things that are different from what you would see in a rural village today.
(b) Where did most people get their food from in this village?

Chapter 2

Changes in Urban Ireland 1900–2000

Key Learning Objectives

- **How did life in urban Ireland change in the twentieth century?**
  - **Population**
  - **Shops**
  - **Housing**
  - **Work**

Did you know?

About 70 per cent of people now live in urban areas.

How did urban life change in the twentieth century?

Population

In 1900, only 30 per cent of Irish people lived in cities or even big towns. Even by the 1930s only one in six Irish people lived in a city. Look at the difference between the populations of some of the Irish cities then and now. Is there anything that surprises you?

Population of Irish cities

	Belfast	Dublin	Cork	Limerick	Galway
1901	400,000	350,000	76,000	38,000	13,000
2001	276,459	506,211	119,418	52,539	72,414

(Source: *CSO* and 2001 *UK Census*)

Note: These figures are city-centre populations only. They don't include the suburbs.

Term

Suburb
A residential area built on the outskirts of a city or large town.

Shops

Towns looked different in 1900. Look at this picture of a typical street taken about 1900.

Most people still lived in the city centres, although richer people were beginning to move out to the **suburbs** where there was more space and the air was cleaner.

Kenmare, 1946. What differences can you see between this street and how a street looks today?

There were no supermarkets or shopping centres in 1900. People did their shopping in their local corner shops. Tailors and dressmakers still made a lot of people's clothes and **cobblers** did a roaring trade either selling or mending shoes.

The streets were often dirty from horse and other animals' droppings. In Dublin, for example, there were as many as 6,000 cows housed in yards in the middle of the city. Cows and cattle were driven through the streets of all major towns up to the 1960s.

Cows being driven through Killorglin in 1913

By the 1920s, **department stores** had become popular. They were family-owned, like Roches Stores and Clerys. Supermarkets were not common in Ireland until the 1970s. Shopping centres outside city centres have become widespread since the 1990s.

Housing

There was a huge divide between rich and poor city people in 1900. This divide can clearly be seen from the kind of houses people lived in.

Did you know?

£1 in 1900 would buy about as much as €130 would today.

Rich people such as doctors and bankers lived in large houses. These houses had large back gardens and cellars as well as rooms for one or two servants.

A wealthy person's house in Dublin. If the owner moved out, houses like this were often divided up among poorer families

Middle-income people rented their houses. Some of these people were quite well-off and earned between £300 and £500 a year.

Trades people or skilled workers earned about £80 a year. They often lived in houses that were called '**two up, two down**' because they had two bedrooms upstairs and a living room and kitchen downstairs. There was a small yard outside with a toilet and a water tap in it.

Typical two up, two down houses where skilled workers lived

Poor people lived in **slums**. These were often **tenements**, which were big old houses in the city. They had belonged to wealthy people before they had moved to the suburbs and now each room was rented out to poor families. Over one-third of people in cities lived in tenements.

Term

Tenement
An old house that several families lived in.

As many as eight families lived in one of these houses. There was usually only one water tap and one toilet out in the backyard, which was shared by everyone. This meant that up to ninety people were sharing the same facilities!

Not surprisingly, diseases such as cholera (from bad drinking water) and TB spread like wildfire.

McGee's Court, Dublin, 1948

Did you know?

In the early 1900s **tuberculosis** (TB) was so common in Ireland that it was known as the 'white plague'. It killed 12,000 people a year.

How did urban housing change?

In the 1930s, local councils began to build better houses for people. They were called **corporation houses**. Slums were cleared and a lot of people in city centres were moved out to big estates in the suburbs such as **Crumlin** in Dublin or **Glanmire** in Cork. There were often as many as 800 houses in these estates. They were built in long, straight lines and looked dreary. Some people found them lonely, but it was seen as a great achievement to clear the slums.

Term

Corporation house
A house built by the local council.

After the 1960s, many middle-class people began to buy their own homes. They also moved further out from the city centres into the suburbs. Most moved to estates with **semi-detached houses**. Wealthier people moved into detached houses.

Housing estate

PART 3

All these new houses had central heating and running water. Most had three bedrooms. On the down side, people had a much longer commute to work and crime and drug-taking began to become problems in big suburban estates.

Waiting for the bus: commuting to work in the city. Can you see the old telephone box on the left?
© RTÉ Stills Library

People began to move to the suburbs in the 1960s

Work

In the early 1900s about a third of workers living in towns were unskilled. They picked up work where they could as **carters**, dockers, labourers or washerwomen. The pay was terrible and they had no trade union until 1908. Some people had regular work in shops, offices or factories.

Middle-class families employed at least one **servant** to help with the housework, and it was common to employ a **nanny** to look after the children. Many girls worked as domestic servants. Most of these jobs were poorly paid, and they often had to work twelve hours a day.

Working-class women worked, whether married or single. They were employed in factories like **Jacob's** in Dublin or they did laundry. In Northern Ireland many women worked in the **linen factories**.

Term

Carter
Someone who delivered goods around the city using a horse and cart.

How did urban work change?

In the 1950s, the **IDA** (Industrial Development Authority) began to promote Irish industry abroad (see page 310). In the 1960s the economy began to improve, and so did working conditions. People became members of trade unions. Free second-level education was brought in in 1967, so the working population of Ireland is now better skilled. Most people work in **multinational companies** or **service industry** jobs in shops, banks, hotels and restaurants.

Term

Multinational company
A company that operates in more than one country.

Service industry
An industry that provides a service to people, such as food or transport.

TIMELINE Urban Life in the Twentieth Century

	1900–45	1945–2000
Population	› Cities were compact (population of Dublin 350,000) › Most people lived in the centre and walked to work › The well-off lived in the **suburbs**	› In the 1940s cities began to expand › New **council estates** were built on the outskirts › Buses and cheaper cars made **commuting** possible › From the 1970s **private housing estates** were built
Shops	› People bought most of the things they needed in **small local shops** › In the 1920s family-owned **department stores** became popular	› In the 1950s **supermarkets** opened. They offered a wide choice of goods, often at low cost › Since the 1990s many **shopping centres** have opened
Housing	› Only the rich owned their own homes › Middle-income people rented houses › Unskilled workers lived in one-room **tenements** › **1931 and 1932 Housing Acts** meant that councils began to provide houses for poorer people	› Middle-income people began to buy their houses in new estates in the suburbs › Councils built houses with three bedrooms, a bathroom and garden to rent to tenement dwellers › **Corporation houses** were built in the suburbs of cities, e.g. Crumlin in Dublin and Glanmire in Cork › From the 1970s councils began to sell corporation houses to the people renting them › By 2000 over 80 per cent of families owned their own homes
Work	› Outside Belfast, few Irish towns or cities had industries › Most jobs were in transport and services such as shops, banks and offices › About a third of people living in towns were unskilled › From 1930s small new industries developed on the outskirts of some towns	› In the 1950s the **Industrial Development Authority (IDA)** gave government grants to Irish industries to help them develop › The first **industrial estates** were built in Irish towns › By the 1990s **multinational companies** employed thousands of people in IT and chemical industries › More jobs followed in **service industries** such as shops and call centres › 1990s: For the first time immigrants looked for work in Ireland

Do you understand these key terms?

suburb	**tenement**	**semi-detached house**	**service industry**
department store	**tuberculosis**	**carter**	**industrial estate**
'two up, two down'	**corporation house**	**multinational company**	
slum	**council estate**		

QUESTIONS

1 In the early 1900s, were there more or fewer people living in the city centres than there are now?

2 Where did the rich people live?

3 Most people rented their homes in 1900. True or false?

4 What was a 'two up, two down'? Who lived in them?

5 Give three details about life in city slums in the early 1900s.

6 What change happened in government housing policy in the 1930s?

7 Name two council estates that were built in the 1930s.

8 'Women did not work outside the home before 1945.' True or false? Explain your answer.

9 Look at the chart below and answer the questions that follow.

Percentage of workers in each sector in Ireland

	Agriculture	Industry	Services
1926	53%	13%	34%
1971	26%	31%	43%
1996	10%	27%	63%

(a) What kind of work did most people do in Ireland in 1926?
(b) Give two reasons why this has changed.
(c) How have work patterns changed in towns?

SOURCE QUESTION

› Here is one woman's memory of her Dublin tenement.

> I had four sisters and three brothers. Me mother's sister had twenty-one children! We grew up in one little room and six of us slept in one bed. And we had no bedclothes; we mostly slept with me daddy's overcoats over us. Sure the bed was loaded with bugs and hoppers and you'd be scratching yourself...
>
> *Maggie Murray, born 1913*

(a) What was a tenement?
(b) What does Maggie mean by bugs and hoppers, do you think?
(c) What does this description tell you about life in the tenements?

PART 3

Chapter 3

Changes in Work and Leisure 1900–2000

Key Learning Objectives

- How did work conditions change in the twentieth century?
- How did leisure change in the twentieth century?

How did work conditions change in the twentieth century?

Wages

There was an enormous difference in the wages that different people got in the early 1900s. In the table below there are some examples of the average earnings of people per year.

Did you know?

£52 a year in 1900 is equivalent to about €20,000 a year now.

A family earning £500 a year could afford to own a yacht. Middle-class families would struggle to make ends meet on £250 a year, while a man earning less than £50 a year would find it very difficult to provide for a family.

For most people working in Ireland wages remained low in comparison with other countries until the 1960s. Unemployment was high and most young people emigrated to either Britain or the US to find work. 400,000 people out of a population of three million left Ireland in the 1950s alone.

Irish people on their way to Britain by ferry

Job	Earnings in 1900	Job	Earnings in 1900	Job	Earnings in 1900
Judges	£3,500	Carpenters	£150	Unskilled labourers	£52
Senior civil servants	£2,000	Local doctors	£120	*Maids	£10
Barristers	£800 to £1,000	School teachers	£100	*Cooks	£18
Jewellers	£300	*Eason employees	£70–100		

*Includes accommodation

In the 1960s the **IDA** (see page 310) gave generous grants to encourage foreign companies to come to Ireland. Low rates of **corporation tax** were used to attract multinational companies to Ireland. The economy picked up, and wages increased steadily during the 1960s.

Term

Corporation tax
A tax paid by a company.

Working hours

People worked very long hours in the early 1900s. It was normal for shops to be open until 8pm and people often worked twelve-hour days.

Workers in factories and shops were entitled to Sunday and one half-day off each week. They also got bank holidays off, but they got no annual holidays. In rural areas most people worked on farms and they had no official holidays. This left very little time for leisure.

Since 1945, the amount of time off people get has increased. Now people have a right to twenty-eight days' annual leave and most people work an eight-hour day.

How did leisure change in the twentieth century?

Home entertainment

In 1900 most people made their own fun. Many workers earned so little they could barely afford food and rent and had nothing left for entertainment. Even middle-income people could not afford to go out much.

The most popular entertainment was **visiting a neighbour's house.** People sat chatting by the fire and exchanged news. Sometimes they played music and sang, or played cards and games.

Wealthy people held **formal balls** to which the guests came in evening dress. Often they went on until dawn. Usually there would be an orchestra to play music for the dances.

Seafront, Kingstown (Dun Laoghaire) 1900. Why do you think most people seem to be well dressed?
© *RTÉ Stills Library*

How did home entertainment change?

The invention of electricity and electronic communication changed entertainment at home forever.

- In the 1920s, people began listening to the **wireless** (radio).
- In the 1960s, **televisions** became available. People began to stay at home to watch TV and they went visiting less. At first, most people had access to only one channel, but in the 1980s multi-channel access became widespread.

A family watching television in the 1960s. The picture was in black and white

› In the 1990s, **computers** and the **Internet** began to appear in homes. People played computer games, surfed the net or chatted online.

Public entertainment

In 1900 many people enjoyed a night out at a **music hall** in the cities. These venues put on **variety shows** that had many different acts. They included singers, comedians, jugglers and acrobats.

There were also **theatres** that put on plays. In Dublin, the **Abbey Theatre** was set up in 1904 to put on Irish plays. Outside the cities, small companies of travelling actors visited towns and villages to put on plays.

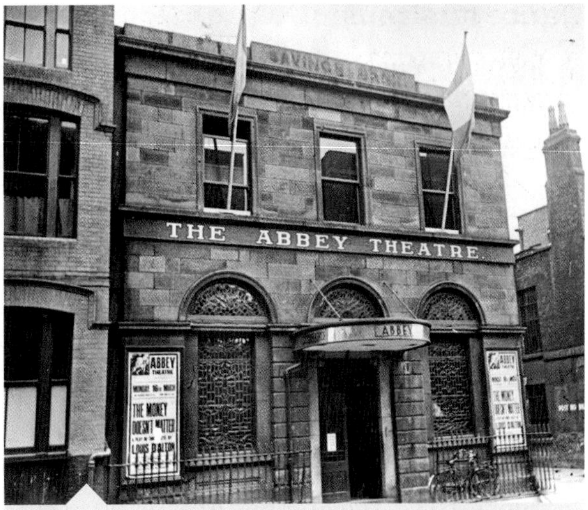

The Abbey Theatre in Dublin in the early 1900s

Film

› The first full-time **cinema** opened in Dublin in 1909. By 1916 there were 149 cinemas around the country.

› Until the 1930s the films were silent. They showed dramatic and romantic stories that thrilled the viewers.

› A pianist was employed to play music to add to the drama of the film.

› Film stars such as **Charlie Chaplin** and **Mary Pickford** became household names.

› Cinema tickets were cheap and many people went to the cinema several times a week.

› Going to the cinema was very popular until the 1960s, when competition from TV reduced the size of audiences.

› In the 1980s **video recorders** were invented and in the 1990s **DVDs** became available. This meant that people could watch films in their own homes.

› Many big cinemas closed down. Others were divided into several smaller cinemas.

Film poster from the 1940s

Going to the cinema was a popular pastime from the 1920s until the 1960s.
© RTÉ Stills Library

Dance and music

- In 1900 people had dances in their houses or at **crossroads** in country areas.
- In the 1920s **dance halls** began to appear. They were most popular between the 1940s and the 1960s.
- **Showbands** such as The Dixies and The Bachelors attracted big followings. They played the tunes that people heard on the radio.
- **Jazz** and **swing** were popular in the 1940s, and **rock and roll** in the 1950s and 1960s.
- In the 1970s **discos** began to replace dance halls.

Dances such as the jive were really popular. Everybody learned to dance

Sports

- **Betting games** like horse racing, dog racing and coursing (hunting hares with dogs) were popular.
- Organised team sports had begun in the late nineteenth century. Cricket, soccer and rugby were the first.
- In the 1880s an Irish sporting organisation, the **Gaelic Athletic Association** (GAA), was set up. It organised inter-parish and inter-county competitions.
- In the 1930s, as more people had the time and the money, crowds at the matches got bigger.

Did you know?

Some Catholic bishops were against public dancing. They felt it would lead to immoral behaviour between young couples. Some priests smashed dancing platforms or tried to limit the hours dance halls operated.

The **Tailteann games** were like mini-Olympic Games in which only people of Irish background took part. They were held in Croke Park between 1924 and 1932.
This image is reproduced courtesy of the National Library of Ireland [INDH2602]

Changes

Watching sport is more popular now. Radio broadcasts and later television brought the big matches to everybody. Now people can watch their favourite sports on TV while sitting at home.

As public transport improved and car use increased people got less exercise and became unfit. To make up for this, more people are now playing sports or taking some form of exercise such as jogging to improve their fitness.

European Championship, 1988. Which two countries are playing in this soccer game?

Going on holiday

In 1900 only wealthy people went abroad on holiday. For most people a day at the seaside was the best they could hope for. This had changed totally by 2000.

- People had far more free time and better wages so they could afford to go on holidays.
- In the 1960s, aeroplanes became more common, and since the 1990s flying has become cheaper. That has put foreign holidays within reach of more people than ever before.

TIMELINE Work and leisure in the Twentieth Century

	1900–45	1945–2000
Working conditions	› 1900: Huge difference between the wages of rich and poor › Long working hours and no annual holidays › A 12-hour working day was common › Low wages left little to spend on leisure	› 1945: Working hours reduced › Holiday entitlements extended › 1960s: Wages improved for everyone › An 8-hour working day was common › People entitled to 28 days' holiday a year › More time and money for leisure activity
Entertainment	› 1900: People entertained at home › Occasional visits to **music hall**, theatre or travelling show › 1909: First **cinema** opened in Dublin › 1920s: **Dance halls** started. Jazz music popular › 1920s: Cinemas in many towns. People went several times a week › 1930s: **Radio** became popular	› 1950s: **Showbands** played latest pop music › 1960s: **TV** in many homes. Some cinemas closed › People stopped visiting neighbours as much › 1970s: **Discos** replaced dance halls › 1990s: Computer games and the **Internet**
Sport	› 1900: Team games common, but not many could afford a ticket to watch a match › 1930s: **Radio broadcasts** made sport more popular	› 1970s: People watched sport on **TV** › 1990s: More people involved in sport to stay fit › All kinds of new sports, e.g. snooker, synchronised swimming
Holidays	› 1900: Only the rich could afford foreign holidays › Poorer people might enjoy a day at the seaside	› 1960s: Better wages allowed more people to take holidays › 1990s: Cheap flights meant that nearly everyone could holiday abroad

Do you understand these key terms?

corporation tax	**variety shows**	**showband**	**rock and roll**
wireless	**video recorder**	**jazz**	**GAA**
music hall	**dance hall**	**swing**	**Tailteann games**

QUESTIONS

1 Look at the list of wages people got in 1900 on page 403. Are there any wages that surprise you?

2 How many people emigrated from Ireland in the 1950s? Why was emigration so high until the 1960s?

3 What helped to increase employment in the 1960s?

4 Why did people have so little leisure time in 1900? Give two reasons.

5 Give two examples of how people provided their own entertainment.

6 When did television first come to Ireland? How did it affect people's lives?

7 Give two entertainment options that people had outside their homes in 1900.

8 What were the first films like?

9 Name three styles of music that were popular in the twentieth century. Say when they were popular.

10 Which sports were popular in the early 1900s?

11 Why has sport become more popular?

12 Give two reasons why more people are going on holiday now.

SOURCE QUESTION

› Look at this picture of Tramore, Co. Waterford, around 1900, and answer the questions below.

(a) What differences can you see between this beach in 1900 and a modern beach scene?

(b) What do you think the boxes on wheels were for?

This image is reproduced courtesy of the National Library of Ireland [LROY00092]

EXAM QUESTIONS

1 Give three major changes in entertainment during the twentieth century.

2 What are the main changes in the world of work since 1945?

3 Write about five changes in sport and leisure that have happened in Ireland since 1945.

Chapter 4

Changes in Transport and Communications 1900–2000

Key Learning Objectives

- **How did transport change during the twentieth century?**
- **How did communications change during the twentieth century?**

How did transport change during the twentieth century?

Term

Transport
The way people or goods are carried from one place to another.

One of the biggest changes in the twentieth century has been in the way people travel. In 1900, most people walked if they wanted to go somewhere locally. Sometimes people rode a horse or a donkey, or travelled by horse and cart.

There were also trams, bicycles, trains and cars. But these were too expensive for most people to use every day.

Roads

Most roads were bad in 1900. They often followed old tracks and were sometimes steep and narrow. They also had a poor surface. In the 1920s, they began to improve after the government introduced **road tax**. They were widened and **tarmac** was laid. Since the 1990s **motorways** have become common in Ireland.

A road in Youghal in 1900

The same road in the late twentieth century

Look at these pictures of Youghal and compare them. What differences can you see?

Trams

In the cities, trams ran on tracks through the streets. The first trams were pulled by horses, but around 1900 electric trams began to replace them. It cost a penny a mile to travel on them, which was still too expensive for most people.

From the 1940s fewer and fewer people used the trams because they travelled by bus or car. The old lines were covered over. Now new ones are being built, for example the **Luas** in Dublin.

A tram in Dalkey in 1901. There were 330 trams working in Dublin in 1911. © *RTÉ Stills Library*

Trains

If you wanted to travel a long distance you would go by train. In 1900, trains were powered by steam and there were lots of them.

Ireland had over 5,500 kilometres of railway tracks. Most trains were slow, stopping at every town and village. But they were cheap. Country people used these local trains to go to towns to shop and to sell goods such as eggs and poultry. People in cities went by train for a day out at the seaside.

In the 1950s trains powered by diesel were introduced, but railways were already becoming less popular. Most **branch lines** in Ireland were closed in the 1950s and 1960s, leaving only the main network. People were buying cars or using buses.

Since the 1990s, however, more people are using commuter trains like the DART in Dublin, or high-speed InterCity trains.

Term

Branch line
A single-track railway line that served rural areas.

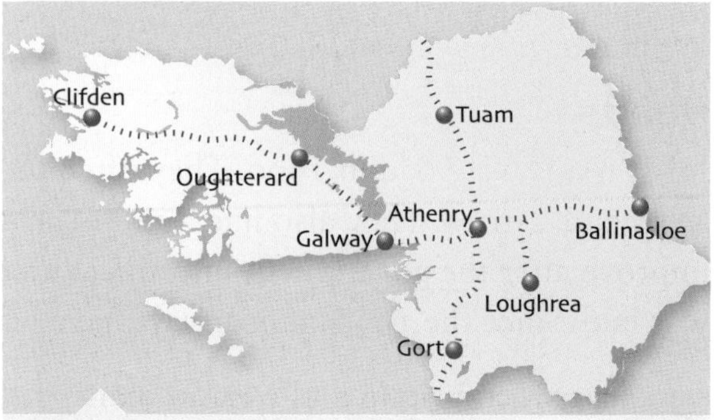

Look at this map of the Galway area c.1900. How many railway lines were linked to Galway station?

The DART (Dublin Area Rapid Transit) now carries 80,000 people a day

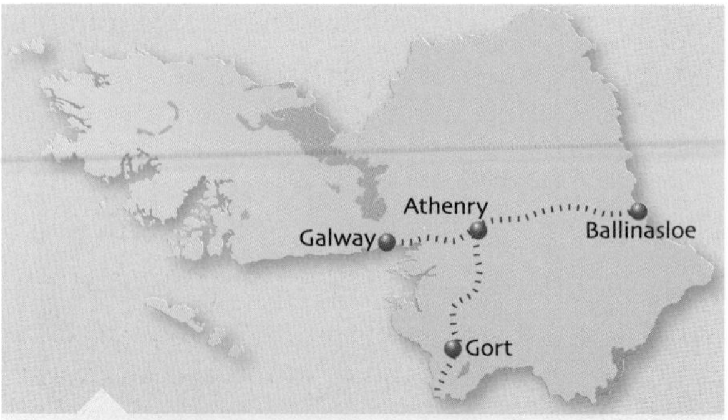

Look at the modern map. Why, do you think, are there fewer railway lines now?

Bicycles

Cycling became more and more popular with young people in the early 1900s. Both women and men cycled and that was one reason why women's skirts began to get a little shorter after 1900. It was common for people to cycle 40 to 50 kilometres in a day to attend a match or to visit friends.

Did you know?

The average cost of a bicycle in 1900 was £5.

Some women wore bloomers to go cycling but this shocked a lot of people. They said that women were trying to look like men!

Motor cars

Cars did exist in 1900, but a new car would cost at least £500 in 1900 (the equivalent of about €70,000 now). The average working-class wage was about £60 a year, so it is no surprise that there were only 250 cars registered in Ireland in 1903.

The speed limit for cars in 1900 was about 15 kilometres per hour. Apart from the speed limit, there were no rules of the road. There were no road markings or road signs.

After World War I cars became cheaper. Henry Ford introduced the **Model T**, which cost about £125. Other makers followed Ford's example. This meant that many middle-income people could afford a car. By the late 1960s, most families had a car and by the 1990s many households had two cars.

Ford assembly line. Why was it cheap to produce a car on an assembly line like this?

Travelling by sea

In 1900, the only way of leaving Ireland was on a **steamship**. There were more ferry routes between Britain and Ireland than there are now. For example, you could travel by boat from Limerick to Glasgow. Ships also called at Queenstown (Cobh) to pick up people going to the USA. Some of these ships were huge luxury **liners** such as the Belfast-built *Titanic*.

These huge liners crossed the Atlantic in about five days. Wealthy people travelled in great luxury. Poorer people, most of them emigrating to a new life in America, travelled in **steerage**, where sleeping accommodation had to be shared.

A dance floor in a luxury liner

Luxury liners continued to cross the Atlantic until the 1960s. Then aeroplanes replaced them. Today liners are mainly used for holiday cruises.

Travelling by air

The first Aer Lingus plane, the Iolar, 1936. Would it have cost much to travel in this plane?

Flying machines were new and very exciting in the early 1900s. In 1903 the Wright brothers became the first men to travel in a machine that was heavier than air. The first **transatlantic flight** by Alcock and Brown landed in Clifden, Co. Galway in 1919.

Regular passenger flights began in the 1930s. The Irish Government set up **Aer Lingus** in 1936. Its first regular route was between Dublin and Bristol. The plane, which was called the *Iolar*, carried five passengers!

Ireland was the first stopping-off point for planes travelling from America to Europe. The first regular transatlantic passenger route was set up at **Foynes** on the Shannon in 1938. The planes were **flying boats** that could land on water. By the 1960s, jet engines meant that planes could now fly directly to Europe and did not need to land in Ireland.

Since the 1990s, flying has become cheaper with **low-cost airlines** like Ryanair. Now people can travel to New York for a weekend shopping trip.

TIMELINE Transport in the twentieth century

	1900–45	1945–2000
Getting around	› Most people walked everywhere › Some took horse-drawn **cabs** › Some travelled on electric **trams**	› Fewer people walking › Petrol-driven **buses** replaced trams › Horse transport becoming rare
Roads	› Made with stone and gravel, no signs or markings › In 1909 motor cars were taxed. The money was used to improve roads	› **Tarmac** and concrete gave roads a smooth surface › Road signs and traffic lights became common › **Motorways** built in the Republic in the late 1990s
Bicycles and cars	› Bicycles newly invented. First cheap transport, cost £5 › Cars expensive and unreliable › Roads bad, petrol hard to find	› Cars became cheaper › Number of garages selling petrol grew › Cars became so common that roads became congested and dangerous for cyclists
Long-distance travel	› Trains within Ireland, ships to go abroad › 1903 first aeroplane flight › 1919 first transatlantic flight › Regular passenger flights began in the 1930s	› Many railway lines closed by the 1970s › People travelling more by car › Planes replaced ships for most long journeys › From the 1950s jet engines made planes faster

QUESTIONS

1. List four different ways you could travel in 1900.
2. Why did roads begin to improve?
3. Why did people stop using trams and trains?
4. What kind of transport did young people prefer?
5. Why did cars become cheaper to buy?
6. How did people travel outside of Ireland in 1900?
7. How long did it take to get to America?
8. What was the name of the first Aer Lingus passenger plane? How many people did it carry?
9. What are flying boats?
10. Why was the invention of jet engines so important?

How did communications change during the twentieth century?

Term

Communications
How people keep in touch with one another.

Letters and telegrams

Most people in 1900 communicated with each other by letter. A penny stamp on a letter would take it to any part of the United Kingdom. The post was fast. A letter posted anywhere in Ireland reached its destination the next day.

In an emergency, people sent telegrams. These were short messages, tapped out in **Morse code** and sent along the telegraph wires to your local post office. From there a 'telegraph boy' carried it to your house. People stopped sending telegrams when phones became more common in the 1970s.

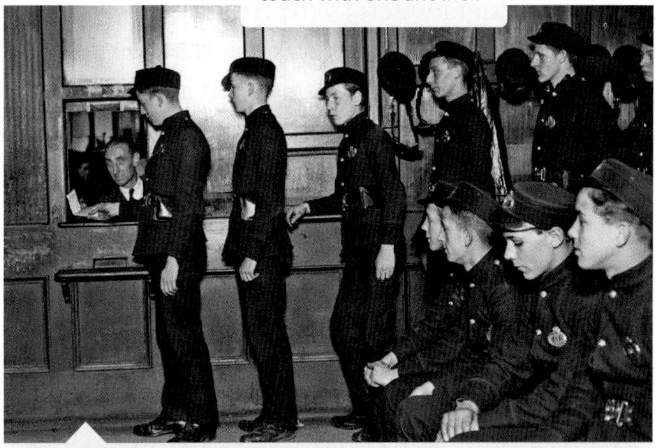

Telegraph boys waiting in line in a post office, ready to carry telegrams

Telephones

The telephone was invented by **Alexander Graham Bell** in 1876. By 1900, there were fifty-six exchanges in Ireland but most telephones were in offices. Only rich people had them in their homes.

To make a call, you told the **operator** what number you wanted. There were lots of stories told of operators listening in on calls! **Automatic exchanges** gradually replaced these **manual exchanges** but this was not done in some places until the 1980s.

From the 1960s, telephones became common in private houses. In the 1990s, **mobile phones** were invented. By 2000 one person in three had a mobile phone in Ireland. Now there are more mobile phones in Ireland than people.

Term

Operator
The person who connected telephone calls.

Manual exchange
Where telephone calls were connected by human operators.

An old 'candlestick' phone

A phone from the 1960s

A mobile phone from the 1990s

PART 3

Radio

Radio was invented by **Marconi.** In 1902 he set up a radio station in Clifden, Co. Galway to transmit signals across the Atlantic.

In Ireland, the first radio station began broadcasting in 1926. It was called **2RN**, and changed its name to **Radio Éireann** in 1937. It broadcast music, news, sports and talks. Radios were expensive and many families could not afford one.

Children listening to the radio

Television

The BBC began the first public television service in 1936. A lot of people along the east coast of Ireland could receive the signal, but it was not until December 1961 that an Irish TV station **Telefís Éireann** (later **RTÉ**) began. It was an instant success. By 1963 one third of houses had a television set, and by the 1980s that had risen to 90 per cent. Television changed the way people saw and understood the world.

Did you know?

In the early days a radio was called a 'wireless' because it sent its messages through the air rather than along wires like the telegraph.

Faxes and computers

In the 1990s, two new forms of communication became common. One was the **fax machine**, which sent images over the telephone line. The other was the **Internet.** Using it, people could access and exchange ideas from anywhere in the world.

Fax machines were used by many businesses in the 1990s to transmit information. Fax is short for facsimile

Conclusion

Better communications have brought people all over the world much closer together. We learn a lot more about other countries and cultures by watching them on TV and in films. The world is now often referred to as the **global village** because of these developments.

TIMELINE Communications in the twentieth century

1900–45	1945–2000
› People mostly communicated by **letter** › Post was fast and reliable › **Telegrams** were used in emergencies	› Letters and telegrams less popular › People **emailing** and **texting** from the 1990s rather than writing letters
› **Telephones** were rare and mainly in offices	› Phones became more common › Automatic phones replaced manual ones. Phones in most homes by the 1980s
› **Radio** was newly invented and used only to send direct messages › Radio broadcasting spread › 1926: 2RN opened, later called Radio Éireann	› 1939: **TV** invented › 1961: RTÉ began › 1970: Most homes had a black-and-white TV

Do you understand these key terms?

transport	**steamship**	**communications**	**manual exchange**
tram	**liner**	**telegram**	**wireless**
branch line	**flying boat**	**operator**	**fax machine**
Model T Ford			

QUESTIONS

1 Name three ways people could send messages to each other in 1900.
2 What were telegrams?
3 Who invented the first telephone?
4 How did the early telephones work?
5 What was the first Irish radio station called?
6 When did television come to Ireland? Was it popular?
7 List four new ways of communicating now.

EXAM QUESTIONS

1 Mention two consequences of the introduction of the Internet since the 1990s.
2 Write about five changes in transport in Ireland since 1945.

SOURCE QUESTION

› Look at the picture here and answer the questions that follow.

On which date was it taken?
(a) 1900
(b) 1930
(c) 1970
Write down four reasons why you chose this date.

This image is reproduced courtesy of the National Library of Ireland [H0408]

Chapter 5

Changes in Women's Lives 1900–2000

Key Learning Objectives

- **How did women's lives change in the twentieth century?**
  - **Education**
  - **Work**
  - **Social behaviour**
  - **Politics**

Education

Girls and boys have had equal access to free primary schools in Ireland since the 1830s. In the early 1900s most children left school at twelve years of age because they had to earn money to help their families. It was common for girls to be kept at home to look after younger brothers and sisters.

You had to pay a fee to go to secondary school, so few girls from poor families were able to go. Most schools were single sex. Many girls' schools did not teach science or higher maths, which made it difficult for girls to get work in these areas.

A girls' school in the 1960s. How does this classroom differ from a classroom today?
© RTÉ Stills Library

Few women attended **university** until the 1960s. Although Irish women could study and get a degree at the Royal University by the 1880s, they were not allowed to attend Trinity College Dublin until 1904. Even then most parents believed that their daughters would get married and have husbands to look after them, so they did not need to train for a career.

How did education change for women?

Since 1970, there have been many changes in education which have affected both boys and girls.

- In 1967 the government brought in free secondary education.
- The government set up schools in which boys and girls are taught together.
- Subjects such as science and metalwork are open to both boys and girls, though many girls still do not choose these subjects.
- Girls are now encouraged to go on to third-level education because having a career is seen as important.

Work

In the early 1900s, women from poorer families looked after children and did the cooking and cleaning without any of the labour-saving devices we have today. Up until the 1920s women often did extra work to earn money for the family.

- They did laundry and took in sewing in the towns.
- In the country they sold eggs, cheese and butter.
- They knitted Aran jumpers and made lace shawls.

A housewife washing clothes by hand during the 1950s

But with the development of new factories, creameries and farm machinery, these jobs were no longer necessary. Women became more dependent on what their husbands earned.

Some women did go to university. They became **doctors** or **teachers** or joined the **civil service.** But once they married most had to give up paid work. This was known as the **marriage bar.** The only exception was in teaching; from 1958 women were allowed to teach in primary schools because there was a shortage of male teachers.

Wages for 'women's work' were much lower than for men's work, even when the jobs were almost the same.

Term

Marriage bar
Laws that stated that women had to resign from well-paid jobs such as the civil service and banking when they got married.

How did work change for women?

In the 1970s women's work began to change. Here are some of the reasons.

- Labour-saving devices such as washing machines and vacuum cleaners gave women more time to seek paid work outside the home.
- Women became better educated and began to demand equal treatment.
- A new **women's liberation movement** won an end to the marriage bar and got laws passed ending discrimination in jobs on grounds of gender. The **Employment Equality Act** of 1977 meant that men and women doing the same job would get equal pay.

A washing machine from the 1960s

Although the law changed quickly, attitudes towards women working changed more slowly. It was not until the 1980s that it really became acceptable for married women to go out to work.

Social behaviour

Up until World War I (1914–18) it was not considered nice for a woman to smoke in public or to go into a public house. Some bars had special areas called 'snugs' where respectable women could get a drink.

It was also the norm for middle-class girls to have a **chaperone** if they were meeting a young man. There was no question of even kissing your boyfriend until you were engaged.

Term

Chaperone
A person, usually an older woman, who accompanied an unmarried girl when she went out.

How did social attitudes change?

Attitudes changed after World War II. Women gradually got more freedom. By the 1930s it was more acceptable for women to smoke and drink in public. The women's liberation movement demanded more sexual freedom for women. This became possible when **contraceptives** came on the market. Although a law passed in 1979 allowed contraceptives to be prescribed by doctors, it wasn't until 1985 that they could be openly sold.

Contraceptive train: the Women's Liberation Movement in Connolly Station, Dublin, after returning from purchasing contraceptives in Belfast, 22 May 1971

PART 3

How did women's fashion change?

In 1900 women's clothes were much more restrictive than today's fashions. All women wore long skirts. They kept their head covered with either a hat or a shawl when they were out. Many richer women wore corsets to keep their waist nipped in.

It was not until the 1960s and 1970s that women in Ireland began wearing trousers. By the end of the century all kinds of fashions, such as long or short skirts or trousers, were acceptable.

1900s

1990s

Women and politics

The right to vote

One of the big political debates in the early 1900s was whether women should have the right to vote for members of parliament. Some people believed that women would not be able to understand politics. Others thought that giving women the right to vote would lead to a lot of arguments in the home.

The **suffragette movement** fought for women to have the right to vote for and be elected to parliament. In Ireland the group that fought for women's right to vote was called the **Irish Women's Franchise League** (**IWFL**).

Term

Suffrage
The right to vote.

Franchise
The vote.

One of the founders of the IWFL was **Hanna Sheehy-Skeffington.** She had been to university. She and other women were angry that they were not allowed to vote, even though men who could neither read nor write were.

Hanna Sheehy Skeffington and her friends heckled politicians and threw bricks through windows. When they were arrested, they went on hunger strike. The Westminster Parliament finally gave the vote to women over thirty in 1918.

REBELLION THROUGH A MEGAPHONE: HOW A SUFFRAGETTE "MOUSE" WAS CHEERED IN HER PRISON CELL.

Hanna Sheehy-Skeffington talking to a crowd. This is a newspaper picture from 1 January 1914.
© RTÉ Stills Library

PART 3

Countess Markievicz was a Sinn Féin candidate who was elected to the first Dáil. When Sinn Féin set up an Irish government she was appointed **minister for labour**. She was the first woman elected to the British parliament, though she never took her seat. When the Free State was set up in 1922 women got the vote on the same terms as men.

Irish politician and nationalist Countess Constance Georgine Markiewicz (1868–1927), June 1922

Women and politics after 1922

Very few Irish women became involved in politics in the new Irish Free State. Between 1922 and 1970 there was an average of four female TDs in the Dáil out of a total of 166 members. There were no more female ministers until 1979, when Máire Geoghegan-Quinn was appointed. By 2000 only one in eight TDs was female.

However, in 1990 **Mary Robinson** became the first woman to be President of Ireland; in 1997 she was followed by **Mary McAleese**.

Mary Robinson

TIMELINE Women's lives in the twentieth century

	1900–45	1945–2000
Education	› 1900: Very few women went to university › Equal access to schools but parents were more interested in educating boys	› 1960s: Free secondary education from 1967 helped more girls to go to school and university › 1970s: Co-ed schools meant a wider range of subjects open to girls › 2000: More women than men graduating from university in many subjects
Work	› 1900: Many girls from middle-income families did not work before marriage › Poor women worked as servants or in farms and factories › The **marriage bar** kept most from reaching top of their professions	› 1973: Removal of marriage bar › 1977: **Employment Equality Act** gave equal pay for equal work and improved women's wages › 1980s: Most women work after marriage
Politics	› **Women's Franchise League** campaigned for the right to vote for parliament › 1918: Markievicz elected MP in the first Dáil and later made minister for labour › 1922: In the Irish Free State women had the same voting rights as men, but few were elected to Dáil Éireann	› 1970s: **women's liberation movement** encouraged women to seek election › 1979: Máire Geoghegan-Quinn appointed a minister › 1990: First woman President elected – Mary Robinson › 1997: Second woman President elected – Mary McAleese

Do you understand these key terms?

marriage bar
women's liberation movement
chaperone
suffrage
suffragette movement
Irish Women's Franchise League

QUESTIONS

1 Give two examples of how women's education has improved since 1900.
2 What was the 'marriage bar' and how did it affect women? When was it removed?
3 Give three reasons why women's place at work has improved since 1970.
4 Give two reasons why people were against the vote for women in 1900.
5 Who set up the Irish Women's Franchise League? Give two examples of what the IWFL did.
6 Which woman became a minister in the first Dáil?
7 Who was the first female President of Ireland?
8 In your opinion, why did so few women take part in politics up until the 1980s? Give a reason for your answer.

SOURCE QUESTION

› This is part of the report from the census taken in 1901. It lists the occupations of women at that time. Look at the figures and then answer the questions.

Women's work in the 1901 Census

1	Professional	32,675
2	Domestic servants	193,331
3	Commercial	5,026
4	Agricultural workers	85,587
5	Industrial workers	233,256
6	Indefinitive and non-productive*	1,708,861

* Women who worked in the home or as part of the family business. Most farms and family businesses were family run.

(a) What was the most popular type of work, apart from category 6?
(b) Why did so many work as domestic servants, do you think?
(c) What percentage were industrial workers? In what part of Ireland, do you think, did most of them live?
(d) Which was the biggest group? What do you think these women did?
(e) Which type of work would most women do today?
(f) Which type of work would not be done today?

People in History

Write about a woman born at the start of the twentieth century.

Talk about the **changes** in her life under the following headings: early life; education; working life; lifestyle.

Hint

Below is a sample answer, but use the information you might have about your own area.

Sample Answer

A woman born at the start of the twentieth century

Early life

My name is Mary Murphy. I was born in 1915 in Francis Street in Dublin. I lived in a tenement there with nine other families. My father was a carter and my mother would take in a bit of sewing.

There were eleven of us in the family and we all lived in one room. We had to go to the shed at the back of the house if we wanted to go to the toilet.

In 1932, the whole building collapsed and we were one of the first to get a new corporation house in Crumlin. There were three bedrooms and an indoor bathroom with running water. There was electricity so we had electric light and an electric cooker.

Education

I went to school in Baggot Street. I finished school at 12 years of age because I had to stay at home to help my mother and mind the younger ones. Later, when I was married with my own children, I made sure that the girls and the boys finished school. Now my grandchildren have all gone to secondary school since the free education started in 1967.

Working life

I started sewing at 12 years of age like my mother, but then I got a job in Jacob's factory and I worked there until I got married. Delia Larkin did a lot for women workers through the IWWU (Irish Women Workers Union). Our conditions improved at work. We were allowed breaks and got two weeks' holidays a year. But the pay was still very bad.

I gave up work when I got married. Very few women worked after they got married in those days. They stayed at home to rear their children. This changed in the 1970s with the Employment Equality Act and the ending of the marriage bar. They gave equal pay to women, and allowed more married women to work.

Lifestyle

We used to love the cinema and the dance halls in the 1930s and 1940s. I loved jazz and swing and I used to go to see all the big bands play. No alcohol was served, only lemonade. A respectable girl would not be seen drinking in public.

In the 1970s and 1980s people rarely went to the pictures, but it seems to be coming in again. People now spend a lot of their time on the computer playing games or using the Internet.

Exam Guide

Introduction

There are thirteen topics to prepare for the Junior Certificate history exam. Five topics are studied in First Year, five topics in Second Year and three topics in Third Year.

This guide will help you to prepare for the exam. It is divided into three sections:

1. Topics to prepare for the exam
2. The structure of the paper
3. How to tackle the exam in June

1 Topics to prepare for the exam

The chart contains the topics to prepare for Higher Level students. It is important to remember that topics can come up two years in a row!

First Year – Part 1: Sections 1–5

Section 1 **The Work of Historians and Archaeologists**	› Types of source › The work of an archaeologist, e.g. dating
Section 2 **Early Ireland**	› Different types of tombs from the Stone and Bronze Ages › The life of a farmer in Celtic Ireland, including housing, family life, work and burial customs › A monk's life in an early Irish monastery, especially the different types of building
Section 3 **Life in Ancient Rome**	› The sources historians use to find out about ancient civilisations › Everyday life under the following topics: housing, family life, work and burial customs › The influence of Ancient Rome
Section 4 **The Middle Ages**	› Life for a lord and lady and the main features of a castle › Training of a knight › The medieval manor and a serf › A craftsperson in a town, e.g. training › A monk in a medieval monastery
Section 5 **The Renaissance**	› Why it began in Italy › Advances in painting, sculpture and literature › The life of one Italian artist and one non-Italian artist › The invention of the moveable type printing press › Main developments in science and architecture

Second Year – Part 2: Sections 6–10

Section 6
The Age of Exploration

- Why the Age of Exploration began
- Instruments and ships used
- The contribution of Portugal
- **Special Study**: One voyage in detail
- Consequences for Europe and the native peoples

Section 7
The Reformation

- Problems in the Catholic Church
- **Special Study**: The career of one reformer
- Religious changes in England
- The consequences of the Reformation including the Counter-Reformation and religious wars

Section 8
Plantations

- Why the English started a policy of plantation
- **Special Study**: One plantation in detail
- The effects of the plantations on culture, political control and religion

Section 9
Revolutions

- The causes of the revolutions in America, France and Ireland
- **Special Study**: The life of one revolutionary leader
- The consequences of each revolution

Section 10
Industrial Britain and Rural Ireland

- Main changes during the Agricultural Revolution and its impact on life in Britain
- Textile and iron – the main inventions
- Changes in transport
- **Special Study**: Life in a factory town in England
- **Special Study**: Life in rural Ireland about 1850 – the Famine

Third Year – Part 3: Sections 11–13

Section 11
Political Developments in Twentieth-Century Ireland

Three main topics:

1. The struggle for independence 1900–23
2. Independent Ireland 1922–1985
3. Northern Ireland 1922–1985

Section 12
International Relations in the Twentieth Century

- The rise of fascism in Italy and Germany
- The drift to war 1933–39
- The main events during World War II in Europe
- You must also do one of the following options:

  Option 1: The Rise of the Superpowers:
  The Berlin Blockade; the Korean War; the Cuban Missile Crisis

  Option 2: Moves towards European Unity:
  Events up to the Treaty of Rome; the growth of the European Union; the Maastricht Treaty

  Option 3: African and Asian Nationalism
  Examine one country: the colonial background; the independence movement and developments since independence

Section 13
Social History in Twentieth-Century Ireland

The changes that have happened in Ireland in the following:

- The role of women
- Work and leisure
- Urban and rural life
- Transport (movement of goods and people)
- Communications (transfer of information)

For Ordinary Level students there are a few differences:

Second Year	Concentrate on the **Special Study for each topic**
Third Year	You must study **International Relations in the Twentieth Century** and one of the following: › Political Developments in Ireland 1900–2007, **or** › Social History For International Relations in the Twentieth Century only one topic needs to be studied from: › Peace and war in Europe › The rise of the superpowers › Moves towards European unity › African and Asian nationalism

How to study for history

Start by revising by topic

Follow the principle of **understanding** the Causes, Course and Consequences (the three Cs).

Use an active approach to studying

- **Preview** the text. Start with a quick skim of the chapter. Note section headings, key words, etc.
- **Look** for answers to the basic questions of Who? What? Where? Why? When?
- **Read** the chapter with these questions in mind. Make brief notes.
- **Test** yourself on the material that you have studied, e.g. do past questions from the sample papers.
- **Review** briefly the material on first a weekly and then a monthly basis.

Familiarise yourself with the paper

Practise as many different types of question as possible from the sample papers.

Make your notes useful

- Organise notes by year and then by topic.
- Notes should be summaries and not too detailed.
- Write up your notes in your own words and use examples where relevant.
- Use pictures and a highlighter pen to give your notes a memorable appearance.

2 The structure of the paper

The exam is made up of six questions at Higher Level and four questions at Ordinary Level. On both papers the questions total 180 marks.

Marks Needed for Different Grades (Higher and Ordinary)

A	B	C	D	E	F	NG
153–180	126–152	99–125	72–98	45–71	18–44	0–17

Questions 1, 2, 3 and 4 follow the same format for both levels. Questions 5 and 6 are asked **only** on the Higher Level paper.

	Question	Marks HL	Marks OL
1	Picture question	15	35
2	Two documents	15	35
3	Short questions	20	60
4	People in History	40	50
5	Source-based question	30	
6	Two attempted from Sections A, B, C and D	60	

Question 1: Pictures

- There will be three parts to this question – usually with one picture in each part.
- For each part, two questions will be asked on the picture while a further question will look for background information.
- **Key point:** Don't be put off by the fact that you may not have seen the image before.

Remember to answer all parts.

Popular Topics for Question 1 (Higher and Ordinary Levels)

Paintings from Renaissance artists
Tombs from ancient Ireland
Archaeologist at work
Crannógs
Round towers
Features of medieval castles
Maps
Propaganda posters
Political cartoons

Question 2: Documents

- There are two documents with about five short questions on each document.
- The documents are often from Irish history and the questions are usually very straightforward.
- Answers that you give should be brief – use the space allocated on the paper as a guide.
- **Key point:** For each document the last question can be tricky as it usually tests background knowledge on the subject matter of the document, e.g. for documents on WWII, a question asking you to name two Allied generals.

Question 3: Short answer questions

- You are expected to answer ten short questions from a total of twenty.
- Keep your answers brief and to the point – often only a word, name or phrase is required. Do not use more than the space allocated.
- Be careful to read the question carefully: if two reasons are required make sure that you give two reasons.
- **Key point:** Attempt as many questions as possible. As long as you get ten correct you will get full marks – no matter how many you get wrong!

Question 4: People in History

- You have to write two accounts – one from Section A and one from Section B.
- The person you write about may be a historical figure, e.g. **a revolutionary leader**, or a person who lived at the time, e.g. **a supporter of a revolutionary leader**.
- Be careful; the examiner is looking for historical facts, not a story.

- Don't write too much for this question – **remember your time allocation per question.**
- Commonly students give too much background detail on the life of a personality from history, e.g. for George Washington (revolutionary leader) the key detail is his leadership during the US War of Independence.
- For a person who was not a historical figure you don't have to personalise your answer, but you must write it from the perspective of the person chosen. For example, in answering 'A factory owner during the Industrial Revolution in Britain' you would lose marks if you wrote about a factory worker and did not mention the owner.
- Read questions closely – don't be discouraged by questions such as *a supporter of a reformer* **or** *a sailor on a voyage of exploration*. They are really asking you to write about Luther or Columbus.

An answer could start like this:

> A supporter of Luther would have been unhappy with the Catholic Church and the behaviour of the pope. He would have agreed with the views of Martin Luther. Martin Luther was born etc.

- Look closely at the dates in the question: Michael Collins is **not** relevant for 'An Irish political leader after 1945'.
- **Key point:** You should give about 10 points per answer. Remember: **quality** not **quantity**.

Question 5: Source-based question (HL)

- This question is based on one of the second year topics.
- It will consist of two or three sources – usually a combination of pictures and documents.
- There will be three parts: A and B will be questions on the sources, while part C requires students to write one or two accounts on the topic being examined.
- Part C tends to deal with the effects or consequences of the topic.
- **Key point:** This can be a difficult question, especially part C. Every year a high proportion of students do not attempt this part of the question or score very poorly.

Question 6: Topic-based question (HL)

- Question 6 is the most important on the paper as one-third of the marks are awarded for it. Some students do this question before questions 4 or 5 because of its importance. There are four sections – you should answer **two**.
- There are different question types in each section; short questions and paragraphs.
- The paragraph questions are usually marked out of 10, 12 or 14, so answers don't need to be as long as for question 4.
- As a guide, the examiner will give 2 marks for each valid point as with question 4 and question 5 (C).
- **Section A** is very difficult to predict.
  2013 – Ancient Civilisation outside Ireland
  2012 – The Middle Ages
  2011 – Our Roots in Ancient Civilisations
  2010 – The Renaissance
- **Section B** and **Section C**
  One of the above is usually Political Developments in Twentieth-Century Ireland and the other Social History in Twentieth-Century Ireland.
- **Section D** is based on International Relations in the Twentieth Century.

3 How to tackle the exam in June

How you deal with the paper on the day of the exam will contribute to a successful result in history. This is called exam technique. Here are some steps to follow:

1. Read the paper carefully before you start. Go through it positively! You will be surprised what material will come back to you.
2. Questions can be answered in any order that you wish. Questions 1, 2 and 3 are answered on the paper, questions 4, 5 and 6 in your answer book.
3. Plan your longer answers. A short plan, though – words or phrases only.
4. **Golden Rule Number 1**: Do not leave a question unanswered – you are throwing marks away!
5. **Golden Rule Number 2**: Follow a time allocation per question. The exam is 2.5 hours long. Not having enough time to finish your exam is an unforgivable error!

Suggested Time Allocation

Preview	Q1	Q2	Q3	Q4	Q5	Q6	Re-read
5 mins	10 mins	10 mins	15 mins	40 mins	25 mins	40 mins	5 mins

6. **Only** do extra questions if you have the time.
7. When there is a choice concentrate on doing one good option rather than two or three poor ones. Students who get a D or an E have often attempted three or four options in question 6.
8. If you change your mind just put a line through what you have written. Don't destroy it as it will be corrected. You may have been right the first time!
9. At the end of the exam make sure to re-read over your paper. Don't rush out of the exam – 5 minutes spent carefully here could be the difference between a high or low grade.

Here is an example of a plan for an answer in question 4: **A Factory Worker during the Industrial Revolution.**

Name of town – Manchester
Conditions – factory and housing
Machines used – power loom
Disease – e.g. cholera
Entertainment
Factory Acts

Good luck!

Index